BUSINESS MARKETING MANAGEMENT B2B

Europe, Middle East and Africa Edition

MICHAEL D. HUTT
ARIZONA STATE UNIVERSITY

THOMAS W. SPEH
MIAMI UNIVERSITY

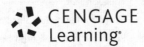

CENGAGE
Learning

an • Korea • Mexico • Singapore • Spain • United Kingdom • United States

Business Marketing Management B2B, Europe, Middle East and Africa Edition

Michael D. Hutt and Thomas W. Speh

Publishing Director: Linden Harris

Publisher: Emily Chandauka

Commissioning Editor: Annabel Ainscow

Senior Production Editor: Alison Burt

Senior Manufacturing Buyer: Eyvett Davis

Development Editor: Abigail Jones

Editorial Assistants: Ana Arêde and
   Jennifer Grene

Marketing Manager: Amanda Cheung

Typesetter: CENVEO Publisher Services

For product information and technology assistance,
contact **emea.info@cengage.com**.

For permission to use material from this text or product,
and for permission queries,
email **emea.permissions@cengage.com**.

This work is adapted from *Business Marketing Management B2B,* 11e by *Michael D. Hutt* & *Thomas W. Speh* published by South-Western, a division of Cengage Learning, Inc. © 2013.

British Library Cataloguing-in-Publication Data
A catalogue record for this book is available from the British Library.

ISBN: 978-1-4080-9371-9

Cengage Learning EMEA
Cheriton House, North Way, Andover, Hampshire, SP10 5BE United Kingdom

Cengage Learning products are represented in Canada by Nelson
Education Ltd.

For your lifelong learning solutions, visit **www.cengage.co.uk**

Purchase your next print book, e-book or e-chapter at **www.cengagebrain.com**

Printed in Croatia by Zrinski d.d.
1 2 3 4 5 6 7 8 9 10 – 16 15 14

To Rita and to Sara, and in memory of Michele

BRIEF CONTENTS

CONTENTS

PART IV FORMULATING BUSINESS MARKETING STRATEGY

PREFACE

Special challenges and opportunities confront the marketer who serves the needs of organisations rather than households. Business-to-business customers represent a lucrative and complex market worthy of separate analysis. A growing number of collegiate schools of business across the world have added industrial or business marketing to their curricula. In addition, a large and growing network of scholars across the world is actively engaged in research to advance theory and practice in the business marketing field. Both the breadth and quality of this research has increased markedly during the past decade.

The rising importance of the field can be demonstrated by several factors. First, because more than half of all business school graduates enter firms that compete in business markets, a comprehensive treatment of business marketing management appears to be particularly appropriate. The business marketing course provides an ideal platform to deepen a student's knowledge of the competitive realities of the global marketplace, customer relationship management, cross-functional decision-making processes, supply chain management, e-commerce, and related areas. Such core content areas strike a responsive chord with corporate recruiters and squarely address key educational priorities within this subject area.

Second, the business marketing course provides a perfect vehicle for examining the special features of high-technology markets and for isolating the unique challenges that confront the marketing strategist in this arena. High-tech markets represent a rapidly growing and dynamic sector of the world economy and a fiercely competitive global battleground but often receive only modest attention in the traditional marketing curriculum. Electronic (e) commerce also falls squarely into the domain of the business market. In fact, the opportunity for e-commerce in the business-to-business market is estimated to be several times larger than the opportunity that exists in the business-to-consumer market.

Third, the number of research studies centred on the business-to-business domain has significantly expanded in recent years, and specialised journals in the area attract a steady stream of submissions.

Three objectives guided the development of this edition:

1   To highlight the similarities between consumer-goods and business-to-business marketing and to explore in depth the points of departure. Particular attention is given to market analysis, organisational buying behaviour, customer relationship management, supply chain management, and the ensuing adjustments required in the marketing strategy elements used to reach organisational customers.

2   To present a managerial rather than a descriptive treatment of business marketing. Whereas some descriptive material is required to convey the dynamic nature of the business marketing environment, the relevance of the material is linked to marketing strategy decision making.

3   To integrate the growing body of literature into a strategic treatment of business marketing. In this text, relevant work is drawn from organisational buying behaviour, procurement, organisational behaviour, supply chain management, strategic management, and the behavioural sciences, as well as from specialised studies of business marketing strategy components.

The book is structured to provide a complete and timely treatment of business marketing while minimising the degree of overlap with other courses in the marketing curriculum. A basic marketing principles course (or relevant managerial experience) provides the needed background for this text.

NEW TO EUROPE, MIDDLE EAST AND AFRICA EDITION

Although the basic objectives, approach, and style of earlier editions have been maintained, several changes and additions have been made that reflect both the growing body of literature and the emerging trends in business marketing practice, together with a thorough focus on business 2 business within an international, EMEA-focussed context. Specifically, the following themes and distinctive features are incorporated into the eleventh edition:

- **Customer Relationship Strategies**: Expanded treatment of the drivers of relationship marketing effectiveness and the financial impact of marketing investments.

- **Sustainability**: A timely and richly illustrated discussion of the distinctive competitive advantages that can be secured by a focus on environmental priorities.

- **Global Marketing Strategies**: A fresh approach for developing strategies for a two-speed economy—low-growth developed markets and high-growth emerging economies.

- **Social Media**: A timely treatment of how the evolving social media landscape is impacting business-to-business communications.

- **Characteristics of High-Performing Salespeople**: A fresh treatment of the characteristics and processes that set top-performing salespersons apart from their peers, particularly in high-opportunity customer engagements.

- **Other New Topics of Interest**: The new edition includes expanded treatment of building strong B2B brands, sales force deployment, and marketing performance metrics.

- **Streamlined Coverage**: Content from two chapters—'Business Marketing Communications: Advertising and Sales Promotion' and 'Business Marketing Communications: Managing the Personal Selling Function'—has been streamlined and integrated into the discussion to provide a more engaging and actionable treatment in 14 compact chapters.

ORGANISATION OF THE EUROPE, MIDDLE EAST AND AFRICA EDITION

The needs and interests of the reader provided the focus in the development of this volume. The authors' goal is to present a clear, timely, and engaging examination of business marketing management. To this end, each chapter provides an overview, highlights key concepts, and includes several carefully chosen examples of contemporary business marketing practice, as well as a cogent summary and a set of provocative discussion questions. Contemporary business marketing strategies and challenges are illustrated with three types of vignettes: "B2B Top Performers," "Inside Business Marketing," and "Ethical Business Marketing."

The book is divided into five parts with a total of 14 chapters. Part I introduces the distinguishing features of the business marketing environment. Careful examination is given to each of the major types of customers, the nature of the procurement function, and key trends that are reshaping buyer–seller relationships. Relationship management establishes the theme of Part II, in which chapter-length attention is given to organisational buying behaviour and customer relationship management. By thoroughly updating and illustrating the core content, this section provides a timely and comprehensive treatment of customer profitability analysis and relationship management strategies for business markets. After this important background is established, Part III centres on the techniques that can be applied in assessing market opportunities: market segmentation and demand analysis, including sales forecasting.

Part IV centres on the planning process and on designing marketing strategy for business markets. Recent work drawn from the strategic management and strategic marketing areas provides the foundation for this section. This edition provides an expanded and integrated treatment of marketing strategy development using the balanced scorecard, enriched by strategy mapping. Special emphasis is given to defining characteristics of successful business-to-business firms and to the interfacing of marketing with other key functional areas such as manufacturing, research and development, and customer service. This functionally integrated planning perspective serves as a focal point in the analysis of the strategy development process. Here at the core of the volume, a separate chapter provides an integrated treatment of strategy formulation for the global market arena, giving particular attention to the new forms of competitive advantage that rapidly developing economies present (for example, China).

Next, each component of the marketing mix is examined from a business marketing perspective. The product chapter gives special attention to the brand-building process, to sustainability, and to the strategic importance of providing competitively superior value to customers. Adding further depth to this core section are the chapters on managing product innovation and managing services for business markets. In turn, special attention is given to supply chain strategies for business markets. Building on the treatment of customer relationship marketing provided in Part II, the personal selling chapter explores methods for organising the sales force and serving key accounts, the skills and characteristics of high-performing salespersons, and managerial tools to support sales force deployment decisions.

Marketing performance measurement provides the central focus for Part V. It provides a compact treatment of marketing control systems and uses the balanced scorecard as an organising framework for marketing profitability analysis. Special attention is given to identifying the drivers of marketing strategy performance and to the critical area of strategy implementation in the business marketing firm.

Chapter cases

A short case, isolating core concepts, is included for each chapter. Two-thirds of the chapter cases are new to this edition and uncover opportunities and challenges confronting firms such as: Nynas in Sweden; Tata in India; the Al-Muhaidib Group in Saudi Arabia; BMW in Germany; Virgin Money in the UK; and ISS in Europe. These cases provide a valuable tool for sparking lecture and seminar discussions and bringing strategy issues to life. The Chapter Cases can be found at the end of your textbook.

Instructor's manual

The Instructor's Manual for *Business Marketing Management: B2B* provides a variety of creative suggestions designed to help the instructor incorporate all the materials available to create a dynamic learning environment.

Testbank

The Testbank is also available on the companion web site in computerised format.

PowerPoint presentation slides

The PowerPoint presentation slides bring classroom lectures and discussions to life with the Microsoft PowerPoint presentation tool.

ACKNOWLEDGEMENTS

The authors would like to thank their students and colleagues for their invaluable input and feedback.

The content of this Europe, Middle East and Africa edition is predominantly adapted from the eleventh edition of Michael D. Hutt and Thomas W. Speh's *Business Marketing Management: B2B* but also includes some examples adapted from the following Cengage Learning EMEA textbooks:

Dibb, S.; Simkin, L.; Pride, W.M. & Ferrell, O.C., *Marketing Concepts and Strategies Sixth Edition* (2012)

Doole, I. & Lowe, R., *International Marketing Strategy: Analysis, Development and Implementation Sixth Edition* (2012)

Moutinho, L. & Southern, G., *Strategic Marketing Management* (2010)

Thompson, J. L. & Martin, F., *Strategic Management: Awareness and Change Sixth Edition* (2010)

van Weele, A.J., *Purchasing and Supply Chain Management Fifth Edition* (2010)

Verhage, B. *Marketing* (2014)

Full copyright details and acknowledgements will appear in the aforementioned publications.

Finally, but most importantly, our overriding debt is to our wives, Rita and Sara, whose encouragement, understanding, and direct support were vital to the completion of this edition. Their involvement and dedication are deeply appreciated.

Michael D. Hutt
Thomas W. Speh

ABOUT THE AUTHORS

Michael D. Hutt

Michael D. Hutt (PhD, Michigan State University) is the Ford Motor Company Distinguished Professor of Marketing at the W. P. Carey School of Business, Arizona State University. He has also held faculty positions at Miami University (Ohio) and the University of Vermont.

Dr. Hutt's teaching and research interests are concentrated in the areas of business-to-business marketing and strategic marketing. His current research centres on the marketing–finance interface, particularly the application of financial portfolio theory to customer management. Dr. Hutt's research has been published in the *Journal of Marketing, Journal of Marketing Research, MIT Sloan Management Review, Journal of Retailing, Journal of the Academy of Marketing Science*, and other scholarly journals. He is also the co-author of *Macro Marketing* (John Wiley & Sons) and contributing author of *Marketing: Best Practices* (South-Western).

Assuming a variety of leadership roles for American Marketing Association programmes, Dr. Hutt co-chaired the Faculty Consortium on Strategic Marketing Management. He is a member of the editorial review boards of the *Journal of Business-to-Business Marketing, Journal of Business and Industrial Marketing, Industrial Marketing Management, Journal of the Academy of Marketing Science*, and *Journal of Strategic Marketing*. For his 2000 contribution to *MIT Sloan Management Review*, he received the Richard Beckhard Prize and in 2007, he was named the Outstanding Professor for Doctoral Programmes by the W. P. Carey School of Business. Dr. Hutt has consulted on marketing strategy issues for firms such as IBM, Motorola, Honeywell, AT&T, Arvin Industries, ADT, and Black-Clawson, and for the food industry's Public Policy Subcommittee on the Universal Product Code.

Thomas W. Speh

Thomas W. Speh, PhD, is Professor of Marketing Emeritus and Associate Director of MBA Programmes at the Farmer School of Business, Miami University (Ohio). Dr. Speh earned his PhD from Michigan State University. Prior to his tenure at Miami, Dr. Speh taught at the University of Alabama.

Dr. Speh has been a regular participant in professional marketing and logistics meetings and has published articles in a number of academic and professional journals, including the *Journal of Marketing, Sloan Management Review, Harvard Business Review, Journal of the Academy of Marketing Sciences, Journal of Business Logistics, Journal of Retailing, Journal of Purchasing and Materials Management*, and *Industrial Marketing Management*. He was the recipient of the Beta Gamma Sigma Distinguished Faculty award for excellence in teaching at Miami University's School of Business and of the Miami University Alumni Association's Effective Educator award.

Dr. Speh has been active in both the Warehousing Education and Research Council (WERC) and the Council of Logistics Management (CLM). He has served as president of WERC and as president of the CLM. Dr. Speh has been a consultant on strategy issues to such organisations as Xerox, Procter & Gamble, Burlington Northern Railroad, Sara Lee, J. M. Smucker Co., and Millenium Petrochemicals, Inc.

PART I
THE
ENVIRONMENT
OF BUSINESS
MARKETING

1   A Business Marketing Perspective

CHAPTER 1
A BUSINESS
MARKETING
PERSPECTIVE

CHAPTER OBJECTIVES

The business market poses special challenges and significant opportunities for the marketing manager. This chapter introduces the complex forces that are unique to the business marketing environment. After reading this chapter, you will understand:

1   The dynamic nature of the business marketing environment and the basic similarities and differences between consumer-goods and business marketing

2   The types of customers in this important market

3   The underlying factors that influence the demand for industrial goods

4   The nature of buyer-seller relationships in a product's supply chain

5   The basic characteristics of industrial products and services

1.1 BUSINESS MARKETING

Business marketers serve the largest market of all: The euro volume of transactions in the industrial or business market significantly exceeds that of the ultimate consumer market. In the business market, a single customer can account for an enormous level of purchasing activity. For example, the corporate procurement department at IBM spends more than €30 billion annually on industrial products and services.* Indeed, all formal organisations—large or small, public or private, for-profit or not-for-profit—participate in the exchange of industrial products and services, thus constituting the business market.

Business markets are "markets for products and services, local to international, bought by businesses, government bodies, and institutions (such as hospitals) for incorporation (for example, ingredient materials or components), for consumption (for example, process materials, office supplies, consulting services), for use (for example, installations or equipment), or for resale.... The only markets not of direct interest are those dealing with products or services which are principally directed at personal use or consumption such as packaged grocery products, home appliances, or consumer banking."* The factors that distinguish business marketing from consumer marketing are the nature of the customer and how that customer uses the product. In business marketing, the customers are organisations (businesses, governments, and institutions).

Business firms buy industrial goods to form or facilitate the production process or use as components for other goods and services. Government agencies and private institutions buy industrial goods to maintain and deliver services to their own market: the public. Industrial or business marketing (the terms can be used interchangeably) accounts for more than half the economic activity in most nations. The heightened interest in high-technology markets—and the sheer size of the business market—has spawned an increased emphasis on business marketing management in universities and corporate executive training programmes.*

This book explores the business market's special opportunities and challenges and identifies the new requirements for managing the marketing function in this vital sector of the global economy. The following questions establish the theme of this first chapter: What are the similarities and differences between consumer-goods marketing and business marketing? What customers constitute the business market? How can the multitude of industrial goods be classified into manageable categories? What forces influence the behaviour of business market demand?

1.2 BUSINESS MARKET CUSTOMERS

Cisco Systems, Inc., provides the networking solutions that are the foundation of the Internet and of most corporate, education, and government networks on a global scale. Rather than serving individuals or household consumers, Cisco is a leading-edge business-to-business firm that markets its products and services to *organisations:* commercial enterprises (for example, corporations and telecommunications firms), governmental units, and institutions (for example, universities and health-care organisations). Marketing managers at Cisco give special attention to transforming complex technology products and services into concrete solutions to meet customer requirements. For example, when Heineken, one of the most recognised brewers in the world, wanted to expand into adjacent markets and provide consumers with a new way to interact with the brand, Cisco provided support and guidance.* Likewise, when the World Wildlife Fund wanted to find a more cost-effective option to conduct online meetings than their previous conferencing facilities, Cisco provided them with the Cisco WebEx Meeting Centre, which was installed across all of the WWF's network offices.*

Each of the four business market sectors—producers, sellers, public sector and government, plus institutions—has identifiable and unique characteristics that business marketers must understand if marketers wish to grow their client bases. A significant first step in creating successful marketing strategy is to isolate the unique dimensions of each major business market sector. How much market potential does each sector represent? Who makes the purchasing decisions? The answers provide a foundation on which managers can formulate marketing programmes that respond to the specific needs and characteristics of each business market sector.

1.2.1 Producer markets

Individuals and business organisations that purchase products to make a profit by using them to produce other products or by using them in their own operations are classified as producer markets. Producer markets include buyers of raw materials and semi-finished and finished items used to produce other products. For example, a manufacturer buys raw materials and component parts to use directly in the production of its products. Grocers and supermarkets are producer markets for numerous support products, such as paper and plastic bags, displays, scanners and floorcare products. Hotels are producer markets for food, cleaning equipment, laundry services and furniture. Producer markets cover a broad array of industries, ranging from agriculture, forestry, fisheries and mining, to construction, transport, communications and public utilities.

1.2.2 A concentration of customers

Manufacturers tend to be geographically concentrated in certain industries, particularly if dependent on certain locally available raw materials, grants and financial inducements or skills. This concentration occurs in Europe too, with heavy industry centred on the Ruhr valley in Germany, and on the Midlands and the north-west in the UK. Sometimes an industrial marketer may be able to serve customers more efficiently as a result. Within certain areas, production in just a few industries may account for a sizeable proportion of total industrial output.

In 2009, manufacturing was the third largest sector in the UK economy, after business services and the wholesale/retail sector in terms of share of UK Gross Domestic Product. It generated some £140bn in gross value added, representing just over 11 per cent of the UK economy. It also employed some 2.6 million people, representing over 8 per cent of total UK employment.*

As the rate of globalisation has accelerated, competition in domestic and international markets for manufactured goods has intensified. As well as competition from other leading manufacturing companies such as the United States, France, Germany and Italy, UK manufacturers are now facing increasing competition from emerging economies which are steadily moving up the value chain into higher value activities and industries.*

Based on sheer numbers, small businesses represent a dominant category of business market customers—but a market that is often difficult to serve.* Because the organisational buyer in smaller firms has different needs—and often a very different orientation—astute marketers adjust their marketing programmes to this market segment's particular needs. To illustrate, FedEx wanted to increase its share of the small shipper market but recognised that picking up packages at many small businesses is more expensive than picking them up at one larger location.* To cost-effectively reach these customers, FedEx encourages small shippers to bring their packages to conveniently located FedEx drop-off points. The strategy has been successful.

1.2.3 Government and public sector markets

National and local governments make up government markets and contribute to public sector markets. They spend huge amounts annually for a variety of goods and services to support their internal operations and to provide the public with education, utilities (in some countries), national defence, road systems and healthcare. In Europe, the amount spent by local governments varies from country to country, depending on the level and cost of services provided. The types and quantities of products bought by government markets reflect social demands on various government agencies. As the publics' needs for government services change, so do the government markets' demands for products.

Because government agencies spend public funds to buy the products they need to provide services, they are accountable to the public. This accountability is responsible for a relatively complex set of buying procedures. Some organisations, unwilling to deal with so much red tape, do not even try to sell to government buyers, while others have learned to deal efficiently with government procedures. For certain companies, such as BAE, and for certain products, such as defence-related items, the government may be one of only a few customers.

Governments usually make their purchases through bids or negotiated contracts. To make a sale under the bid system, a company must apply and receive approval to be placed on a list of qualified bidders. When a government unit wants to buy, it sends out a detailed description of the products to these qualified bidders. Organisations that wish to sell such products then submit bids. The government unit is usually required to accept the lowest bid. When buying non-standard or highly complex products, a government unit often uses a negotiated contract. Under this procedure, the government unit selects only a few companies, negotiates specifications and terms, and eventually awards the contract to one of the negotiating companies. Most large defence contracts held by such companies as BAE or Thales are reached through negotiated contracts.

Although government markets have complicated requirements, they can also be very lucrative. When government departments modernise obsolete computer systems, for example, successful bidders can make high sales with attractive margins during the life of a contract, which may last for five years or more. Some companies have established separate departments to facilitate marketing to government units, while others specialise entirely in this area. The buying behaviour of governments is complex, though. A business such as Fujitsu sells IT services to banks, retailers, manufacturers and utility companies. Fujitsu is a leading supplier of IT services to central and local government and the health service: it has specialist management teams and sales and marketing specialists who focus purely on these public-sector clients owing to the specialised nature of their buying.

1.2.4 Institutional markets

Organisations with charitable, educational, community or other non-business goals constitute institutional markets . Members of institutional markets include libraries, museums, universities, charitable organisations and some churches and hospitals. Some of these are also public-sector bodies, such as libraries and museums. Increasingly, government and institutional markets are being grouped together and referred to as public sector markets, although the term third sector has emerged to cover charities, the voluntary sector, not-for-profit organisations and NGOs.

Institutions purchase large amounts of products annually to provide goods, services and ideas to members, congregations, students and other stakeholder groups. For example, a library must buy new books for its readers; pay rent, fuel and water bills; fund the staffing and cleaning of its buildings; invest in IT facilities; and pay to produce publicity material about its services. Because such institutions often have different goals and fewer resources than other types of organisation, marketers may use special marketing activities to serve these markets. Public sector markets consist of government and institutional not-for-profit customers and stakeholder groups: public sector marketing is a significant growth area within the marketing discipline. Within some of these activities, notably government bodies promoting health and wellbeing for the population and the planet, there is a role for social marketing, which has further extended marketing's contribution in this domain.

1.2.5 Reseller markets

Reseller markets consist of intermediaries, such as wholesalers and retailers, who buy finished goods and resell them to make a profit. Other than making minor alterations, resellers do not change the physical characteristics of the products they handle. Tesco stocks and sells Heinz or Tilda products without altering the branding, content or packaging. With the exception of items that producers sell directly to consumers, all products sold to consumer markets are first sold to reseller markets.

Wholesalers or distributors purchase products for resale to retailers, other wholesalers and producers, governments and institutions. Although some highly technical products are sold directly to end users, many products are sold through wholesalers/intermediaries, who in turn sell products to other companies in the distribution system. Thus wholesalers are very important in helping to get a producer's product to customers. Wholesalers often carry many products, perhaps as many as 250 000 items. From the reseller's point of view, having access to such an array of products from a single source makes it much simpler to buy a variety of items. When inventories are vast, the reordering of products is normally automated and the wholesaler's initial purchase decisions are made by professional buyers and buying committees.

Retailers purchase products and resell them to final consumers. Some retailers carry a large number of items. Chemists, for example, may stock up to 12 000 items, and some supermarkets may handle in excess of 20 000 different products. In small, family-owned retail stores, the owner frequently makes purchasing decisions. Large department stores or supermarket retailers have one or more employees in each department who are responsible for buying products for that department. As for chain stores, a buyer or buying committee in the central office frequently decides whether a product will be made available for selection by store managers. For smaller businesses, local store managers make the actual buying decisions.

1.2.6 Factors considered by resellers

When making purchase decisions, resellers consider several factors. They evaluate the level of demand for a product to determine in what quantity and at what prices it can be resold. They assess the amount of space required to handle a product relative to its potential profit. Sometimes resellers will put a product on trial for a fixed period, allowing them to judge customers' reactions and to make better-informed decisions about shelf space and positions as a result. Retailers, for example, sometimes evaluate products on the basis of sales per square metre of selling area or contribution to overall gross margin. Since customers often depend on a reseller to have a product when they need it, a reseller typically evaluates a supplier's ability to provide adequate quantities when and where wanted. Resellers also take into account the ease of placing orders, and the availability of technical assistance and training programmes from the producer.

More broadly, when resellers consider buying a product not previously carried, they try to determine whether the product competes with or complements the products the company is currently handling. These types of concern distinguish reseller markets from other markets. Sometimes resellers will start stocking a new line of products in response to specific requests from customers. Marketers dealing with reseller markets must recognise these needs and be able to serve them.

1.3 BUSINESS MARKETING MANAGEMENT

Many large firms that produce goods such as steel, production equipment, or computer-memory chips cater exclusively to business market customers and never directly interact with their ultimate consumers. Other firms participate in both the consumer-goods and the business markets. The introduction of laser printers and personal computers brought Hewlett-Packard, historically a business-to-business marketer, into the consumer market. Conversely, the strength of Apple's brand extends to the business market where, for example, the iPad enjoyed immediate success and sparked demand for other Apple products, including Mac computers. To serve such corporate customers, some fundamental adjustments in marketing strategy are required.

Nectar Business

Many consumers have a purse or wallet full of loyalty cards, such as Tesco Clubcard, AirMiles or Nectar. How often when filling up with fuel at a BP service station are you asked whether you have a Nectar card? It is not only consumers who receive loyalty cards. Businesses also are persuaded to sign up, in B2B deals with the major loyalty schemes. Nectar Business was launched in 2005 and now has around 600 000 SMEs as corporate members.

Nectar Business customers can collect reward points when they hire Hertz vehicles, purchase from Dulux Decorator Centres, consume snacks from Brakes, buy business insurance from Premierline or stationery from Viking. 'It's easy to collect points on the things you already buy for your business everyday – from stationery and insurance to specialist trade equipment or even food supplies', explains Nectar Business. Perhaps for some surprises, too … 'Collect Nectar points when you purchase quality industrial and refrigerant gases, equipment and much more via BOC's nationwide network of retail stores or via the telephone'.

Just as for any consumer product, Nectar Business's marketers must work hard to reflect customer views, refresh the proposition and communicate effectively to both new account prospects and to the 600 000 business customers already signed up. In particular, the company wanted to increase redemption rates of its reward points so that more personnel in its 600 000 SME customers were actively using the service. A piece of marketing research found that many potential users were too 'time-poor' to spend their points on the items included in Nectar's official rewards portfolio.

As a result of the survey findings, the redemption process was re-thought and simplified. A group of highest value collectors was offered a one-to-one concierge service that identified, sourced, secured and shipped the items on which they wanted to spend their points. Certain call centre staff were dedicated to the Silver Service concierge proposition. In addition, the categorisation of rewards on offer was streamlined and made easier to navigate. Agency Crocodile developed a new campaign promoting the concierge service. Two mailings were developed, one for e-mail and one for direct mail. The e-mail response rate was 28 per cent with an 80 per cent increase in redemptions, while the direct mail approach enjoyed a response rate of 13 per cent and an uplift in people redeeming of 192 per cent. Further campaigns have since been run to support the Silver Service concept, resulting in good improvements in redemption rates and a growing number of active users.

Sources: http://www.nectar.com/business/NectarHomeForward. nectar, 22 March 2011; http://www.nectar.com/dynamic/business/about-nectar, 22 March 2011; http://www.boconline.co.uk/how_to_buy/nectar_business.asp, 22 March 2011; Meg Carter, 'Silver service', *The Marketer*, March 2011, pp. 20–22.

Products such as smart phones, office furniture, personal computers, and software are purchased in both the consumer and the business markets. What distinguishes business marketing from consumer-goods marketing is the *intended use of the product* and the *intended consumer*. Sometimes the products are identical, but a fundamentally different marketing approach is needed to reach the organisational buyer. Interestingly, some of the most valuable brands in the world belong to business marketers: Google, BlackBerry, Caterpillar, IBM, FedEx, Intel and Hewlett-Packard.[*]

1.3.1 Business markets versus consumer-goods markets

Although the marketing concept is equally applicable to business and consumer markets, there are several fundamental differences between the transactions that occur in each. Business buyers tend to order in much larger quantities than do individual consumers and often demand customised or tailored propositions. Suppliers must often sell their products in large quantities to make profits; consequently, they prefer not to sell to customers who place small orders.

Generally, business purchases are negotiated less frequently than consumer sales. Some purchases involve expensive items, such as machinery or office equipment, that are used for a number of years. Other products, such as raw materials and component items, are used continuously in production and may have to be supplied frequently. However, the contract regarding the terms of sale of these items is likely to be a long-term agreement, requiring periodic negotiations.

Negotiations in business sales may take much longer than those for consumer sales. Most consumers do not negotiate on prices paid, whereas many business customers never pay the list price. Purchasing decisions are often made by a committee; orders are frequently large, expensive and complex; and products may be custom built. There is a good chance that several people or departments in the purchasing organisation will be involved. One department might express a need for a product; a second department might develop its specifications; a third might stipulate the maximum amount to be spent; and a fourth might actually place the order. This approach allows individuals with relevant expertise to be incorporated into the process when required. Sales personnel play an important role in negotiations with customers. The quality of the relationship that develops has been shown to impact on the outcome of such negotiations.

One practice unique to business-to-business sales is reciprocity, an arrangement in which two organisations agree to buy from each other. In some countries, reciprocal agreements that threaten competition are illegal, and action may be taken to stop anti-competitive reciprocal practices. Nonetheless, a certain amount of reciprocal dealing occurs among small businesses and, to a lesser extent, among larger companies as well. Such companies often find that developing long-term relationships of this kind can be an effective competitive tool.[*] Reciprocity can create a problem because coercive measures may be used to enforce it or because reciprocity influences purchasing agents to deal only with certain suppliers.

1.3.2 What makes a marketing leader?[*]

Jeff Immelt, CEO at General Electric, recently issued a mandate that marketing must become a vital operating function across the firm and an engine for organic growth. In response, the firm doubled the size of the marketing function, from 2500 several years ago to more than 5000 managers today, and created chief marketing officer (CMO) positions at all GE businesses and at the corporate level. Likewise, the firm convened its best marketers to define the specific capabilities that a world-class business marketing function needed to master (for example, market knowledge, segmentation, and branding). Once the capabilities were defined, senior GE executives observed that some managers are better equipped at translating capabilities into actionable results, so they studied the characteristics of the firm's top-performing marketing managers. They have found that leaders transform marketing into a strategic function by performing four fundamental roles. They call them a marketer's DNA. These are:

- *The Instigator.* Marketing leaders need to capitalise on their close connection to customers, think strategically, and challenge the status quo in order to define opportunities that may not be apparent to others in the business. This role involves scanning the entire business landscape for marketing ideas as opposed to thinking exclusively about current products and markets.

- *The Innovator.* Marketing leaders need to take an active role in shaping the company's innovation agenda. In performing this role, the leader needs to expand beyond product features to consider new business models or fresh approaches to pricing, delivery, and customer engagement. To pursue a new strategic path, a leader must demonstrate courage and persistence, plus the political skills to overcome objections.

- *The Integrator.* The integrator builds bridges across multiple functions to unite organisational members on a clear strategy path. Marketing leaders are adept at making unique customer insights relevant and meaningful to those inside the organisation.

- *The Implementer*. To translate plans into actionable strategies, marketing executives must mobilise diverse organisational members across the firm, many of whom report to others. So marketing leaders are skilled at building coalitions and persuading others by using functional expertise, customer insights, and teamwork rather than by exercising authority.

1.4 CREATING THE CUSTOMER VALUE PROPOSITION*

Business marketing strategy must be based on an assessment of the company, the competitor, and the customer. A successful strategy focuses on identifying those opportunities in which the firm can deliver superior value to customers based on its distinctive competencies. From this perspective, marketing can be best understood as the process of defining, developing, and delivering value.

Market-driven firms attempt to match their resources, skills, and capabilities with particular customer needs that are not being adequately served. By understanding customer needs, marketing managers can define value from the customer's perspective and convert that information into requirements for creating satisfied customers. In turn, a firm's capabilities and skills determine the degree to which the company can meet these requirements and provide greater value than its competitors.

A business marketing firm's offering includes many technical, economic, service, or social benefits that provide value to customers—but so do the offerings of competitors. So, customers compare the value elements of a firm's offering with those offered by the next best alternative.*

A **customer value proposition** captures the particular set of benefits that a supplier offers to advance the performance of the customer organisation. Rather than merely attempting to list more benefits than competitors, "best practice suppliers base their value proposition on the few elements that matter most to target customers, demonstrate the value of this superior performance, and communicate it in a way that conveys a sophisticated understanding of the customer's business priorities."* The building blocks of a successful value proposition include:

- Points of parity—the value elements with essentially the same performance characteristics as the next best alternative.

- Points of difference—the value elements that render the supplier's offering either superior or inferior to the next best alternative.

Value proposition illustrated

Sonoco, a global packaging supplier headquartered in the US, approached a large European customer, a producer of consumer goods, about redesigning the packaging for one of its successful product lines. Although the redesigned packaging provided several favourable points of difference relative to the next best alternative, Sonoco executives decided to place special emphasis on one point of parity and two points of difference in the customer value proposition: The redesigned packaging will deliver significantly greater manufacturing efficiency in the customer's fill lines, through higher-speed closing, and provide a distinctive look that customers will find more appealing—all for the same price as the present packaging.

What matters most?

A point of parity was included in the value proposition because **key buying influentials** (those who have power in the buying process) within the customer organisation would not even consider a packaging redesign if the price increased. The first point of difference in the value proposition (increased efficiency) delivered cost savings, allowing the customer to dramatically streamline its production schedule. The second point of difference (more distinctive customer packaging) enhanced the firm's market position and appeal to its customers, allowing it to realise meaningful growth in its revenues and profit. While the other favourable points of difference were certainly mentioned in discussions with the customer organisation, Sonoco executives chose to emphasise those points that mattered most to the customer.

1.4.2 Characteristics of business markets

Products sold to business customers are called business products and, consequently, the demand for these products is called business demand. Unlike consumer demand, business demand – formerly known as industrial demand – is:

- derived
- inelastic
- joint, and
- more fluctuating.

Derived demand

As business customers, especially producers, buy products to be used directly or indirectly in the production of goods and services to satisfy consumers' needs, the demand for business products arises from the demand for consumer products; it is, therefore, called derived demand. In fact, all business demand can in some way be traced to consumer demand. This occurs at a number of levels, with business sellers being affected in various ways. For instance, consumers today are more concerned with good health and nutrition than ever before, and as a result are purchasing food products containing less cholesterol, saturated fat, sugar and salt. When some consumers stopped buying high-cholesterol cooking fats and margarine, the demand for equipment used in manufacturing these products also dropped. Thus factors influencing consumer buying of various food products have ultimately affected food processors, equipment manufacturers, suppliers of raw materials and even fast-food restaurants, which have had to switch to lower-cholesterol oils for frying. Changes in derived demand result from a chain reaction. When consumer demand for a product changes, a wave is set in motion that affects demand for all of the items involved in the production of that consumer product.

Inelastic demand

The demand for many business products at the industry level is inelastic demand – that is, a price increase or decrease will not significantly alter demand for the item. Because many business products contain a number of parts, price increases that affect only one or two parts of the product may yield only a slightly higher per-unit production cost. Of course, when a sizeable price increase for a component represents a large proportion of the total product's cost, demand may become more elastic, because the component price increase will cause the price at the consumer level to rise sharply. For example, if manufacturers of aircraft engines substantially increase the price of these engines, forcing Boeing in turn to raise the prices of its aircraft, the demand for aircraft may become more elastic as airlines reconsider whether they can afford them. An increase in the price of windscreens, however, is unlikely to affect greatly the price of the aircraft or the demand for them.

The characteristic of inelasticity applies only to industry demand for the business product, not to the demand curve faced by an individual company. For example, suppose that a car component company increases the price of rubber seals sold to car manufacturers, while its competitors retain their lower prices. The car component company would probably experience reduced unit sales because most of its customers would switch to the lower-priced brands. A specific organisation is vulnerable to elastic demand, even though industry demand for a particular product is inelastic.

Joint demand

The demand for certain business products, especially raw materials and components, is subject to joint demand. Joint demand occurs when two or more items are used in combination to produce a product. For example, a company that manufactures cork noticeboards for schools and colleges needs supplies of cork and wood to produce the item; these two products are demanded jointly. A shortage of cork will cause a drop in the production of wooden surrounds for noticeboards or a lack of chips will hinder computer manufacture.

Marketers selling many jointly demanded items must realise that when a customer begins purchasing one of the jointly demanded items, a good opportunity exists for selling related products. Similarly, when customers purchase a number of jointly demanded products, the producer must take care to avoid shortages of any one of them, because such shortages jeopardise sales of all the jointly demanded products. The susceptibility of producers to the shortage of a particular item is illustrated clearly when industrial action at companies producing microchips results in a halt in production at manufacturers of computers and related goods.

Fluctuating demand

Because the demand for business products fluctuates according to consumer demand, when particular consumer products are in high demand, their producers buy large quantities of raw materials and components to ensure that they can meet long-run production requirements. Such producers may also expand their production capacity, which entails the acquisition of new equipment and machinery, more workers, a greater need for business services, and more raw materials and component parts.

Conversely, a decline in the demand for certain consumer goods significantly reduces the demand for business products used to produce those goods. When consumer demand is low, business customers cut their purchases of raw materials and components, and stop buying equipment and machinery, even for replacement purposes. This trend is especially pronounced during periods of recession.

A marketer of business products may notice changes in demand when its customers change their inventory policies, perhaps because of expectations about future demand. For example, if several dishwasher manufacturers who buy timers from one producer increase their inventory of timers from a two-week to a one-month supply, the timer producer will experience a significant immediate increase in demand.

Sometimes price changes can lead to surprising temporary changes in demand. A price increase for a business item may initially cause business customers to buy more of the item because they expect the price to rise further. Similarly, demand for a business product may be significantly lower following a price cut as buyers wait for further price reductions. Such behaviour is often observed in companies purchasing information technology. Fluctuations in demand can be significant in industries in which price changes occur frequently.

1.5 BUSINESS AND CONSUMER MARKETING: A CONTRAST

Many consumer-goods companies with a strong reputation in the consumer market decide to capitalise on opportunities they perceive in the business market. The move is often prompted by a maturing product line, a desire to diversify operations, or the strategic opportunity to profitably apply R&D or production strength in a rapidly growing business market. P&G, departing from its packaged consumer-goods tradition, is using its expertise in oils, fats, and pulps to diversify into fast-growing industries.

Tate and Lyle operates successfully in both the consumer and the business markets. Tate and Lyle, drawing on its consumer product base (sugars and syrups), produces sweeteners and texturants to be used in hundreds of food and beverage products. Marketing sugar to ultimate consumers differs significantly from marketing a sweetener to, for example, a yoghurt manufacturer. Key differences are highlighted in the following illustration.

1.5.1 Tate and Lyle: A consumer and business marketer

Tate and Lyle reaches the consumer market with a line of products sold through retail outlets. New products are carefully developed, tested, targeted, priced, and promoted for particular market segments. To secure distribution, the firm employs food brokers who call on both whole-sale- and retail-buying units. The company's own sales force reaches selected larger accounts. Achieving a desired degree of market exposure and shelf space in key retail food outlets is essential to any marketer of consumer food products. Promotional plans for the line include media advertising, coupons, special offers, and incentives for retailers. Pricing decisions must reflect the nature of demand, costs, and the behaviour of competitors. In sum, the marketer must manage each component of the marketing mix: product, price, promotion, and distribution.

The marketing mix takes on a different form in the business market. Attention centres on manufacturers that potentially could use Tate and Lyle products to produce other goods; the Tate and Lyle product will lose its identity as it is blended into yoghurt, cakes, or biscuits. Once Tate and Lyle has listed all the potential users of its product (for example, large food processors, bakeries, yoghurt producers), the business marketing manager attempts to identify meaningful market segments that Tate and Lyle can profitably serve. A specific marketing strategy is developed for each market segment.

When a potential organisational consumer is identified, the company's sales force calls directly on the account. The salesperson may begin by contacting a company president but, at first, generally spends a great deal of time with the R&D director or the product-development group leader. The salesperson is thus challenged to identify the **key buying influentials**—those who have power in the buying process. Senior-level Tate and Lyle executives may also assist in the selling process.

Armed with product specifications (for example, desired taste, colour, calories), the salesperson returns to the Tate and Lyle R&D department to develop samples. Several months may pass before a mixture is finally approved. Next, attention turns to price, and the salesperson's contact point shifts to the purchasing department. Because large quantities are involved, a few cents per kilogram can be significant to both parties. Quality and service are also vitally important.

Once a transaction is culminated, the product is shipped directly from the Tate and Lyle warehouse to the manufacturer's plant. The salesperson follows up frequently with the purchasing agent, the plant manager, and other executives. Product movement and delivery information is openly shared, and close working relationships develop between managers at Tate and Lyle and key decision makers in the buying organisation. How much business can Tate and Lyle expect from this account? The performance of the new consumer product in the marketplace determines this: The demand for industrial goods is, as noted, derived from ultimate consumer demand. Note also the importance of: (1) developing a close and continuing working relationship with business market customers and (2) understanding the requirements of the total range of buying influentials in the target company.

1.5.2 Distinguishing characteristics

The Tate and Lyle illustration spotlights some of the features that differentiate business marketing strategy from consumer-goods marketing strategy. The business marketer emphasises personal selling rather than advertising (TV, newspaper) to reach potential buyers. Only a small portion of the business marketer's promotional budget is likely to be invested in advertising, most commonly through trade journals or direct mail. This advertising, however, often establishes the foundation for a successful sales call. The industrial salesperson must understand the technical aspects of the organisation's requirements and how those requirements can be satisfied, as well as know who influences the buying decision and why.

The business marketer's product also includes an important service component. The organisational consumer evaluates the quality of both the physical product and the attached services. Attention centres on the total package of benefits the consumer receives. Price negotiation is frequently an important part of the industrial buying/selling process. Products made to particular quality or design specifications must be individually priced. Business marketers generally find that direct distribution to larger customers strengthens relationships between buyer and seller. Smaller accounts can be profitably served through intermediaries—manufacturers' representatives or industrial distributors.

As the Tate and Lyle example illustrates, business marketing strategies differ from consumer-goods marketing strategies in the relative emphasis given to certain elements of the marketing mix. It is important to note that the example also highlights fundamental differences between the buyers in each market. In an organisation, a variety of individuals influence the purchase decision. Several major questions confront Tate and Lyle's business marketing manager: Who are the key participants in the purchasing process? What is their relative importance? What criteria does each participant apply to the decision? Thus, the business marketer must understand the process an organisation follows in purchasing a product and identify which organisational members have roles in this process. Depending on the complexity of the purchase, this process may span many weeks or months and may involve the participation of several organisation members. The business marketer who becomes involved in the purchase process early may have the greatest chance for success.

1.5.3 A relationship emphasis

Relationships in the business market are often close and enduring. Rather than constituting the end result, a sale signals the beginning of a relationship. By convincing a large food processor such as Danone to use its product, Tate and Lyle initiates a potential long-term business relationship. More than ringing up a sale, Tate and Lyle creates a customer! To maintain that relationship, the business marketer must develop an intimate knowledge of the customer's operations and contribute unique value to its business. **Relationship marketing** can be regarded as all of the activities and organisation uses to build, maintain and develop ongoing customer relations. The intention is to nurture a mutually beneficial sustainable relationship and to maximise the 'share of wallet' from the customer over a period of time. Figure 1.1 provides a recap of key characteristics of business market customers.

1.6 THE SUPPLY CHAIN

Figure 1.2 further illuminates the importance of a relationship perspective in business marketing by considering the chain of suppliers involved in the creation of an automobile. Consider PSA Peugeot Citroën. When designing the flexible roof system for the new Citroën C3 Pluriel, PSA selected Italdesign, an Italian company and Inalfa, a Dutch specialist supplier of roof systems to work out and manufacture the design. Italdesign in turn involved a German supplier, Saargummi for the sealing system. In all, communication took place in five different languages and the design consisted of 480 parts, of which, 80 per cent were new to Inalfa and to PSA Peugeot Citroën.

The relationships between the auto producers and their suppliers fall squarely into the business marketing domain. Similarly, business marketers such as TRW rely on a whole host of others farther back on the supply chain for raw materials, components, and other support. Each organisation in this chain is involved in the creation of a product, marketing processes (including delivery), and support and service after the sale. In performing these value-creating activities,

FIGURE 1.1 Characteristics of business market customers

Characteristic	Example
• Business market customers are comprised of commercial enterprises, institutions, and governments.	• Among Dell's customers are Boeing, Arizona State University, and numerous state and local government units.
• A single purchase by a business customer is far larger than that of an individual consumer.	• An individual may buy one unit of a software package upgrade from Microsoft while Citigroup purchases 10 000.
• The demand for industrial products is derived from the ultimate demand for consumer products.	• New home purchases stimulate the demand for carpeting, appliances, cabinets, timber, and a wealth of other products.
• Buyer-seller relationships tend to be close and enduring	• IBM's relationship with some key customers spans decades.
• Buying decisions by business customers often involve multiple buying influences, rather than a single decision maker.	• A cross-functional team at Procter & Gamble (P&G) evaluates alternative laptop personal computers and selects Hewlett-Packard.
• While serving different types of customers, business marketers and consumer-goods marketers share the same job titles.	• Job titles include marketing manager, product manager, sales manager, account manager.

© Cengage Learning 2013

FIGURE 1.2 The supply chain

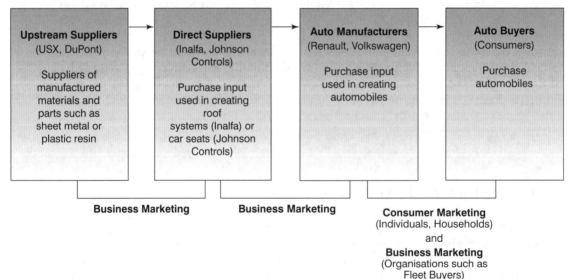

Upstream Suppliers (USX, DuPont)	**Direct Suppliers** (Inalfa, Johnson Controls)	**Auto Manufacturers** (Renault, Volkswagen)	**Auto Buyers** (Consumers)
Suppliers of manufactured materials and parts such as sheet metal or plastic resin	Purchase input used in creating roof systems (Inalfa) or car seats (Johnson Controls)	Purchase input used in creating automobiles	Purchase automobiles

Business Marketing   **Business Marketing**   **Consumer Marketing** (Individuals, Households) and **Business Marketing** (Organisations such as Fleet Buyers)

© Cengage Learning 2013

each also affects the quality level of the Citroën product. Michael Porter and Victor Millar observe that "to gain competitive advantage over its rivals, a company must either perform these activities at a lower cost or perform them in a way that leads to differentiation and a premium price (more value)."*

1.6.1 Supply chain management

Supply chain management is a technique for linking a manufacturer's operations with those of all of its strategic suppliers and its key intermediaries and customers to enhance efficiency and effectiveness. The Internet allows members of the supply chain all over the world to share timely information, exchange engineering drawings during new product development, and synchronise production and delivery schedules. The goal of supply chain strategy is to improve the speed, precision, and efficiency of manufacturing through strong supplier relationships. This goal is achieved through information sharing, joint planning, shared technology, and shared benefits. If the business marketer can become a valued partner in a customer's supply chain, the rewards are substantial: The focus shifts from price to value and from products to solutions.* To achieve these results, the business marketing firm must demonstrate the ability to meet the customer's precise quality, delivery, service, and information requirements.

1.6.2 Managing relationships in the supply chain

Customers in the business market place a premium on the business marketer's supply chain management capabilities. IBM spends 85 per cent of its purchasing euros with 50 suppliers.* Of particular importance to IBM is the quality of engineering support it receives from suppliers. IBM actively seeks supplier partners that will contribute fresh ideas, responsive service, and leading-edge technology to attract buyers of future IBM products.

To effectively initiate and sustain a profitable relationship with a customer like IBM, Volkswagen, or Unilever, the marketing manager must carefully coordinate the multiple linkages that define the relationships. Given these new marketing requirements, Frank V. Cespedes emphasises the importance of "concurrent marketing" among the groups that are most central to customer contact efforts: product, sales, and service units.* In his view, recent market developments place more emphasis on the firm's ability to:

- Generate timely market knowledge by segment and by individual account;
- Customise product service packages for diverse customer groups, and
- Capitalise on local field knowledge from sales and service units to inform product strategy in real time.

Developing and nurturing close, long-term relationships is an important goal for the business marketer. Built on trust and demonstrated performance, such strategic partnerships require open lines of communication between multiple layers of the buying and selling organisations. Given the rising importance of long-term, strategic relationships with both customers and suppliers, organisations are increasingly emphasising relationship management skills. Because these skills reside in people rather than in organisational structures, roles, or tasks, marketing personnel with these skills become valuable assets to the organisation.*

1.6.3 Commercial enterprises as consumers

Business market customers, as noted at the outset of the chapter, can be broadly classified into three categories: (1) commercial enterprises, (2) governmental organisations, and (3) institutions. However, the supply chain concept provides a solid foundation for classifying the commercial customers that constitute the business market. Commercial enterprises can be divided into three categories: (1) users, (2) original equipment manufacturers (OEMs), and (3) dealers and distributors.

Users

Users purchase industrial products or services to produce other goods or services that are, in turn, sold in the business or consumer markets. User customers purchase goods—such as computers, photocopiers, or automated manufacturing systems—to set up or support the manufacturing process. When purchasing machine tools, Volkswagen is a user. These machine tools do not become part of the automobile but instead help to produce it.

Original Equipment Manufacturers (OEMs)

The OEM purchases industrial goods to incorporate into other products it sells in the business or ultimate consumer market. For example, Intel Corporation produces the microprocessors that constitute the heart of Dell's personal computer. In purchasing these microprocessors, Dell is an OEM.

Dealers and distributors

Dealers and distributors include commercial enterprises that purchase industrial goods for resale (in basically the same form) to users and OEMs. The distributor accumulates, stores, and sells a large assortment of goods to industrial users, assuming title to the goods it purchases. Handling billions of euros worth of transactions each year, industrial distributors are growing in size and sophistication.

Overlap of categories

The three categories of commercial enterprises are not mutually exclusive. Their classification is based on the intended purpose the product serves for the customer. Volkswagen is a user when purchasing a machine tool for the manufacturing process, but the same company is an OEM when purchasing radios to be installed in the ultimate consumer product.

A marketer must have a good understanding of the diverse organisational consumers that make up the business market. Properly classifying commercial customers as users, OEMs, or dealers or distributors is an important first step to a sharpened understanding of the buying criteria that a particular commercial customer uses in evaluating an industrial product.

Understanding buying motivations

Consider the different types of commercial customers that purchase a particular industrial product such as electrical timing mechanisms. Each class of customer views the product differently because each purchases the product for a different reason.

A food-processing firm such as Baxters buys electrical timers for use in a high-speed canning system. For this customer, quality, reliability, and prompt and predictable delivery are critical. Beko, an OEM that incorporates the industrial product directly into consumer appliances, is concerned with the effect of the timers on the quality and dependability of the final consumer product. Because the timers are needed in large quantities, the appliance manufacturer is also concerned about the producer's production capacity and delivery reliability. Finally, an industrial distributor is most interested in matching the capability of the timing mechanisms to the needs of customers (users and OEMs) in a specific geographical market.

1.7 CLASSIFYING GOODS FOR THE BUSINESS MARKET[*]

Having classified business market customers, we must now ask what type of goods they require, and how each type is marketed. One useful method of classifying industrial goods is to ask the following questions: How does the industrial good or service enter the production process, and how does it enter the cost structure of the firm? The answer enables the marketer to identify those who are influential in the organisational buying process and to understand how to design an effective business marketing strategy. In general, industrial goods can be divided into three broad categories: entering goods, foundation goods, and facilitating goods (Figure 1.3).

FIGURE 1.3 Classifying goods for the business market

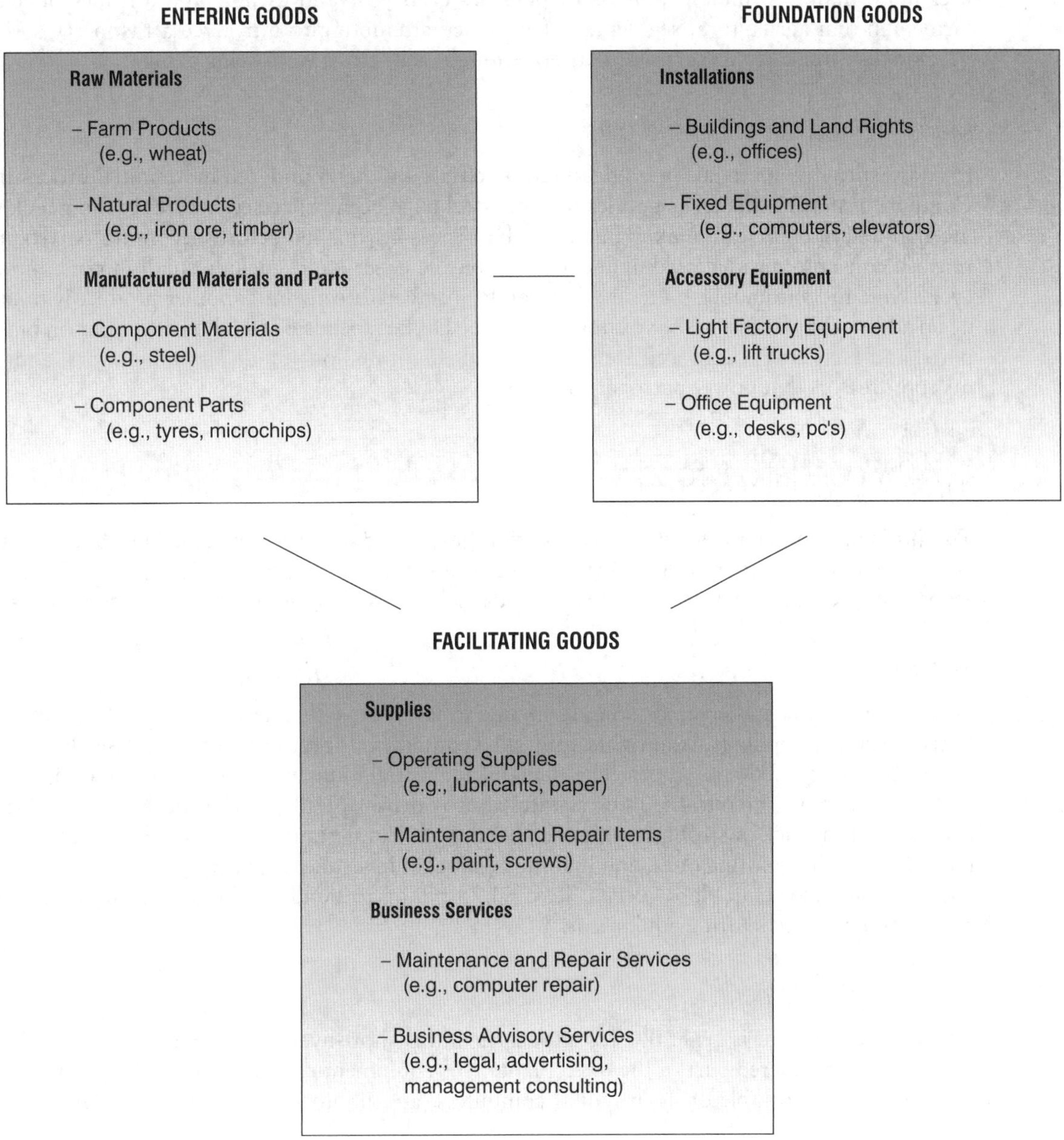

ENTERING GOODS

Raw Materials

– Farm Products
 (e.g., wheat)

– Natural Products
 (e.g., iron ore, timber)

Manufactured Materials and Parts

– Component Materials
 (e.g., steel)

– Component Parts
 (e.g., tyres, microchips)

FOUNDATION GOODS

Installations

– Buildings and Land Rights
 (e.g., offices)

– Fixed Equipment
 (e.g., computers, elevators)

Accessory Equipment

– Light Factory Equipment
 (e.g., lift trucks)

– Office Equipment
 (e.g., desks, pc's)

FACILITATING GOODS

Supplies

– Operating Supplies
 (e.g., lubricants, paper)

– Maintenance and Repair Items
 (e.g., paint, screws)

Business Services

– Maintenance and Repair Services
 (e.g., computer repair)

– Business Advisory Services
 (e.g., legal, advertising,
 management consulting)

Source: KOTLER, PHIL, *Marketing Management: Analysis, Planning & Control*, 4th Edition, © 1980, p. 172. Adapted by permission of Pearson Education, Inc., Upper Saddle River, NJ.

1.7.1 Entering goods

Entering goods become part of the finished product. This category of goods consists of raw materials and manufactured materials and parts. Their cost is an expense item assigned to the manufacturing process.

Raw materials

Observe in Figure 1.3 that **raw materials** include both farm products and natural products. Raw materials are processed only to the level required for economical handling and transport; they basically enter the buying organisation's production process in their natural state. McDonald's uses more than 700 million pounds of potatoes each year and dictates the fortunes of many farmers in that agricultural segment. In fact, when attempting to introduce a raspberry sorbet, McDonald's found, to its surprise, that not enough raspberries were being grown!*

Manufactured materials and parts

In contrast to raw materials, **manufactured materials and parts** undergo more initial processing. Component materials such as textiles or sheet steel have been processed before reaching a clothing manufacturer or automaker but must be processed further before becoming part of the finished consumer product. Component parts, on the other hand, include small motors, motorcycle tyres, and automobile batteries; they can be installed directly into another product with little or no additional processing. For example, Black & Decker spends €75 million each year on plastic parts, and Hewlett-Packard and Dell spend hundreds of millions on displays, monitors, and the microprocessors that power personal computers.

1.7.2 Foundation goods

The distinguishing characteristic of foundation goods is that they are capital items. As capital goods are used up or worn out, a portion of their original cost is assigned to the production process as a depreciation expense. Foundation goods include installations and accessory equipment.

Installations

Installations include the major long-term investment items that underlie the manufacturing process, such as buildings, land rights, and fixed equipment. Large computers and machine tools are examples of fixed equipment. The demand for installations is shaped by the economic climate (for example, favourable interest rates) but is driven by the market outlook for a firm's products. In the face of strong worldwide demand for its microprocessors, Intel is building new plants, expanding existing ones, and making significant investments in capital equipment. A typical semiconductor chip plant costs at least €3.75 billion to build, including the land, building, and installed manufacturing equipment.*

Accessory equipment

Accessory equipment is generally less expensive and is short-lived compared with installations, and it is not considered part of the fixed plant. This equipment can be found in the plant as well as in the office. Portable drills, personal computers, and photocopying machines illustrate this category.

1.7.3 Facilitating goods

Facilitating goods are the supplies and services (see Figure 1.3) that support organisational operations. Because these goods do not enter the production process or become part of the finished product, their costs are handled as expense items.

Supplies

Virtually every organisation requires operating supplies, such as printer cartridges, paper, or business forms, and maintenance and repair items, such as paint and cleaning materials. These items generally reach a broad cross section of industrial users. In fact, they are very similar to the kinds of supplies that consumers might purchase at a hardware or discount store.

For example, along with products specifically designed for commercial use, Procter & Gamble (P&G) sells adaptations of its well-known consumer products in its professional division.[*] Targeting the business market, customers here include hotels, fast-food restaurants, retailers, and health-care organisations.

Services

To capture the skills of specialised service firms and to direct attention to what they do best, many firms are shifting or "outsourcing" selected service functions to outside suppliers. This opens up opportunities for firms that provide such services as computer support, payroll processing, logistics, food operations, and equipment maintenance. These specialists possess a level of expertise or efficiency that organisations can profitably tap. Business services include **maintenance and repair support** (for example, machine repair) and **advisory support** (for example, management consulting or information management). Like supplies, services are considered expense items.

Moreover, the explosive growth of the Internet has increased the demand for a range of electronic commerce services, from Web site design to the complete hosting of an e-commerce site. The Internet also provides a powerful new channel for delivering technical support, customer training, and advertising. For example, Intel is shifting over half of its advertising budget to online media and is asking its partners in the "Intel Inside" cooperative ad campaign, like Sony, to increase spending on online media.[*] In turn, the Internet provides the opportunity to manage a particular activity or function from a remote, or even offshore, location. To illustrate, IBM manages the procurement functions for United Technologies Corporation via the Web.[*]

1.8 BUSINESS MARKETING STRATEGY

Marketing pattern differences reveal the significance of a goods classification system. A marketing strategy appropriate for one category of goods may be entirely unsuitable for another. Often, entirely different promotional, pricing, and distribution strategies are required. The physical nature of the industrial good and its intended use by the organisational customer dictate to an important degree the marketing programme's requirements. Some strategy highlights follow.

1.8.1 Illustration: Manufactured materials and parts

Recall that manufactured materials and parts enter the buying organisation's own product. Whether a part is standardised or customised often dictates the nature of marketing strategy. For custom-made parts, personal selling and customer relationship management activities assume an important role in marketing strategy. The value proposition centres on providing a product that advances the customer's competitive position. The business marketer must also demonstrate strong supply chain capabilities. Standardised parts are typically purchased in larger quantities on a contractual basis, and the marketing strategy centres on providing a competitive price, reliable delivery, and supporting services. Frequently, industrial distributors are used to provide responsive delivery service to smaller accounts.

For manufactured materials and parts, the marketer's challenge is to locate and accurately define the unique needs of diverse customers, uncover key buying influentials, and create solutions to serve these customers profitably.

1.8.2 Illustration: Installations

Installations such as fixed equipment were classified earlier as foundation goods because they are capital assets that affect the buyer's scale of operations. Here the product or technology itself, along with the service capabilities of the firm, are the central factors in marketing strategy, and direct manufacturer-to-user channels of distribution are the norm. Less costly, more standardised installations such as a drill press may be sold through marketing intermediaries.

Once again, personal selling or account management is the dominant promotional tool. The salesperson or account team works closely with prospective organisational buyers. Negotiations can span several months and involve the top executives in the buying organisation, especially for buildings or custom-made equipment. Customer buying motives centre on economic factors (such as the projected performance of the capital asset) and emotional factors (such as industry leadership). A buyer may be quite willing to select a higher-priced installation if the projected return on investment supports the decision. The focal points for the marketing of installations include a strong customer relationship management effort, effective engineering and product design support, and the ability to offer a product or technology solution that provides a higher return on investment than its competition. Initial price, distribution, and advertising play lesser roles.

1.8.3 Illustration: Supplies

The final illustration centres on a facilitating good: supplies. Again we find different marketing patterns. Most supply items reach a broad market of business customers from many different industries. Although some large users are serviced directly, a wide variety of channel partners are required to cover this broad and diverse market adequately.

The goal of the business marketer is to secure a place on the purchasing function's list of preferred or preapproved suppliers. Importantly, many firms are adopting e-procurement systems to dramatically streamline the process employees follow in buying supplies and other operating resources. From the desktop, an employee simply logs on to the system, selects the needed items from an electronic catalogue of suppliers the purchasing function has preapproved, and sends the order directly to the supplier.

For supplies, the marketer's promotional mix includes catalogue listings, advertising, and, to a lesser extent, personal selling. Advertising is directed to resellers (industrial distributors) and final users. Personal selling is less important for supplies than it is for other categories of goods with a high unit value, such as installations. Thus, personal selling efforts may be confined to resellers and large users of supplies. Price may be critical in the marketing strategy because many supply items are undifferentiated. However, customised service strategies might be designed to differentiate a firm's offerings from those of competitors. By providing the right product assortment, timely and reliable delivery, and customised services, the business marketer may be able to provide distinctive value to the customer and develop a long-term, profitable relationship.

1.9 A LOOK AHEAD

Figure 1.4 shows the chief components of the business marketing management process. Business marketing strategy is formulated within the boundaries established by the corporate mission and objectives. A corporation determining its mission must define its business and purpose, assess environmental trends, and evaluate its strengths and weaknesses. Building e-commerce capabilities and transforming these capabilities into offerings that provide superior customer value constitute vital corporate objectives at leading organisations like E-ON. Corporate objectives provide guidelines for forming specific marketing objectives. Business marketing planning must be coordinated and synchronised with corresponding planning efforts in R&D, procurement, finance, production, customer service, and other areas. Clearly, strategic plans emerge out of a bargaining process among functional areas. Managing conflict, promoting cooperation, and developing coordinated strategies are all fundamental to the business marketer's interdisciplinary role.

FIGURE 1.4 A framework for business marketing management

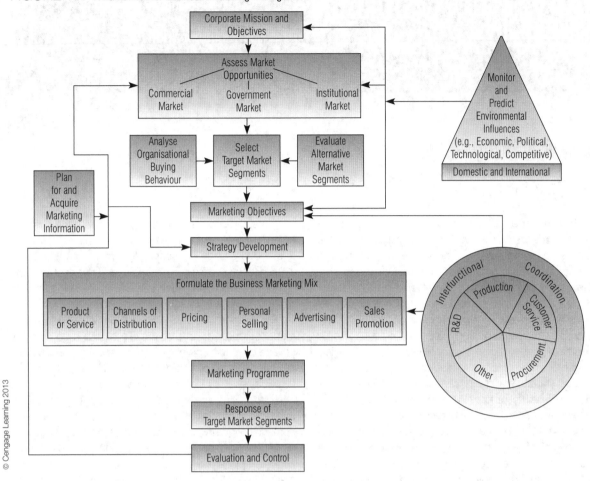

The business marketing management framework (see Figure 1.4) provides an overview of the five major parts of the text. This chapter introduced some of the features that distinguish industrial from consumer-goods marketing and explored the major types of customers that make up the business market: commercial enterprises, governmental units, and institutions. Each sector represents a sizable market opportunity, presents special characteristics and needs, and requires a unique marketing strategy response.

Part II examines the organisational buying process and the myriad forces that affect the organisational decision maker. Occupying a central position in Part II is customer relationship management—a managerial process that leading firms in business-to-business marketing have mastered. Here special attention is given to the specific strategies that business marketers can follow in developing profitable relationships with customers. Part III turns to the selection of target segments and specific techniques for measuring the response of these segments. Part IV centres on designing market-driven strategies. Each component of the marketing mix is treated from the business marketing perspective. Special attention is given to creating and managing offerings and managing connections, including treatment of supply chain strategies. Particular emphasis is also given to defining value from the customer's perspective and developing responsive pricing, advertising, and personal selling strategies to deliver that value proposition to target segments.

The processes of implementing, monitoring, and controlling the marketing programme are analysed in Part V. A central theme is how business marketing managers can enhance profitability by maximising the return on marketing strategy expenditures.

SUMMARY

The business market offers significant opportunities and special challenges for the marketing manager. Business markets consist of individuals or groups that purchase a specific kind of product for resale, for direct use in producing other products, or for use in their day-to-day operations. *Producer markets* include those individuals and business organisations that purchase products for the purpose of making a profit by using them either to produce other products or in their own operations. Classified as *reseller markets* are intermediaries, such as *wholesalers*, distributors and *retailers*, who buy finished products and resell them for the purpose of making a profit. *Government markets* consist of national and local governments, which spend huge amounts annually on goods and services to support their internal operations and provide citizens with needed services. Many businesses refer to government, local government and institutions collectively as the public sector, and the *public sector market* is a growing area of activity within the marketing discipline. Organisations that seek to achieve charitable, educational, community or other non-business goals constitute *institutional markets.* Aspects of government and much of institutional marketing today are described as the third sector, with social marketing addressing their customers.

Market-driven firms in the business market demonstrate superior skill for understanding and satisfying customers. They also possess strong market-sensing and customer-linking capabilities. To deliver strong financial performance, business-to-business firms must also demonstrate customer relationship management skills, which include all the skills required to identify, initiate, develop, and monitor profitable customer relationships. Best-practice marketing strategists base their value propositions on the points of difference that matter the most to target customers, responding clearly and directly to the customer's business priorities. Although a common body of knowledge and theory spans all of marketing, important differences exist between consumer and business marketing, among them the nature of markets, demand patterns, buyer behaviour, and buyer–seller relationships.

The dramatic worldwide rise in competition requires a global perspective on markets. To secure a competitive advantage in this challenging environment, business market customers are developing closer, more collaborative ties with fewer suppliers than they have used in the past. They are using the Internet to promote efficiency and real-time communication across the supply chain and demanding quality and speed from their suppliers to an unprecedented degree. These important trends in procurement place a premium on the supply chain management capabilities of the business marketer. Business marketing programmes increasingly involve a customised blend of tangible products, service support, and ongoing information services both before and after the sale. Customer relationship management constitutes the heart of business marketing.

Business demand differs from consumer demand along several dimensions. *Derived demand* is the demand for business products that arises from the demand for consumer products. At the industry level, *inelastic demand* is a demand that is not significantly affected by a price increase or decrease. If the price of an industrial item changes, demand for the product will not change proportionally. Some business products are subject to *joint demand*, which occurs when two or more items are used in combination to make a product. Finally, because business demand ultimately derives from consumer demand, the demand for business products can fluctuate widely.

DISCUSSION QUESTIONS

1 List several characteristics that differentiate business transactions from consumer ones.

2 Identify, describe and give examples of four major types of business market.

3 What are the underlying factors that influence the demand for industrial goods?

4 Why is it important to manage relationships in the supply chain? Do you agree that this should be the job of the marketing manager?

5 Describe the difference between entering goods, foundation goods and facilitation goods and give five examples of each.

INTERNET EXERCISES

http://www.made-in-china.com/

The attractiveness of the emerging Chinese market as a manufacturing base has grown to such an extent that many small firms now look towards China for suppliers.

Question:

1 As an SME considering using China as a source of supply, how useful is a site such as this in finding potential suppliers and what further actions do you think you would need to take before making a selection?

REFERENCES

Anderson, James C., Narus, James A., and van Rossum, Wouter, "Customer Value Propositions in Business Markets," *Harvard Business Review* 84 (March 2006): pp. 91–99.

Anderson, Narus, and van Rossum, "Customer Value Propositions," p. 93.

Bourde, Marc, Hawker, Charlie, and Theocharides, Theo, "Taking Center Stage: The 2005 Chief Procurement Officer Survey" (IBM Global Services, 2005), pp. 1–13, http://www.ibm.com, accessed July 15, 2005.

Byron, Ellen, "Aiming to Clean Up, P&G Courts Business Customers," *The Wall Street Journal*, January 26, 2007, pp. B1–B2.

Cannon, Joseph P., and Perreault Jr., William D., "Buyer–Seller Relationships in Business Markets," *Journal of Marketing Research* 36 (November 1999): pp. 439–460.

Carbone, James, "Reinventing Purchasing Wins Medal for Big Blue," *Purchasing* 129 (September 16, 1999): pp. 45–46.

Cespedes, Frank V., *Concurrent Marketing: Integrating Products, Sales, and Service* (Harvard Business School Press, 1995), chap. 2.

Cisco, "Heineken Expands Brand Equity with First 'Experience Store'," http://www.cisco.com, accessed August 19, 2013a.

Cisco, "Online Meetings Offer Eco-Charity Greener Way to Work," http://www.cisco.com, accessed August 21, 2013b.

Comstock, Beth, Gulati, Ranjay, and Liguori, Stephen, "Unleashing the Power of Marketing," *Harvard Business Review* 88 (October 2010): pp. 90–98.

Davenport, Thomas H., Harris, Jeanne G., and Kohli, Ajay K., "How Do They Know Their Customers So Well?", *MIT Sloan Management Review* 42 (Winter 2001): p. 65.

Department for Business Innovation and Skills, "Manufacturing in the UK: An economic analysis of the sector" (December 2010): p. v

Dibb, Sally, Simkin, Lyndon, Pride, Bill, and Ferrell, O.C., *Marketing Concepts & Strategies*, 6th ed. (Cengage, 2012).

Doole, Isobel, and Lowe, Robin, *International Marketing Strategy* 6th ed. (Cengage, 2012).

Elliot, Stuart "As Customers Flock to the Web, Intel Gives Chase with Its Ad Budget," *The New York Times*, October 10, 2007, p. C9.

Ferguson, Tim, "IBM Shifts Procurement HQ to China," ZDNet News: October 13, 2006, http://www.zdnet.com/news, accessed June 1, 2008.

Hutt, Michael D. and Speh, Thomas W., "Business Marketing Education: A Distinctive Role in the Undergraduate Curriculum," *Journal of Business-to-Business Marketing* 12 (1, 2, 1998): pp. 103–126.

IBM Corporation "United Technologies: Outsourcing Procurement Yields High Efficiency and Tight Spending Controls," IBM Corporation, June 5, 2005, http://www.ibm.com, accessed April 10, 2010.

Lichtenthal, J. David, "Business-to-Business Marketing in the 21st Century," *Journal of Business-to-Business Marketing* 12 (1, 2, 1998): pp. 1–5

Lichtenthal, J., "Advocating Business Marketing Education: Relevance and Rigor – Uttered as One," *Journal of Business-to-Business Marketing* 14 (1, 2007): pp. 1–12

Moutinho, Luiz, and Southern, Geoffrey, *Strategic Marketing Management: A process Based Approach* (Cengage, 2012).

Porter, Anne Millen and Murphy, Elena Epatko, "Hey Big Spender . . . The 100 Largest Industrial Buyers," *Purchasing* (November 9, 1995): pp. 31–42.

Porter, Anne Millen, "Containing Total Spend," *Purchasing* 132 (November 6, 2008): pp. 18–25.

Porter, Michael E., *Competitive Advantage* (The Free Press, 1985).

Porter, Michael E., and Millar, Victor E., "How Information Gives You Competitive Advantage," *Harvard Business Review* 63 (July–August 1985): pp. 149–160

Prospectus for the Institute for the Study of Business Markets, College of Business Administration, the Pennsylvania State University and Lichtenthal, J. David, Mummaleni, Venkatapparao, and Wilson, David T., "The Essence of Business Marketing Theory, Research, and Tactics: Contributions from the *Journal of Business-to-Business Marketing*," *Journal of Business-to-Business Marketing* 15 (2, 2008): pp. 91–123.

Quinn, James Brian, *Intelligent Enterprise: A Knowledge and Service Based Paradigm for Industry* (The Free Press, 1992), p. 20.

Randazzo, Ryan, Jensen, Edythe, and Pitzl, Mary Jo, "New $5B Intel Facility Planned for Chandler, *The Arizona Republic*, February 19, 2011, p. B-1.

Schwartz, Matthew, "B to B's Best: Brands," *B to B*, Special Issue (2007), http://www.btobonline.com, accessed May 15, 2008.

Sharma, Arun, Krishnan, R., and Grewal, Dhruv, "Value Creation in Business Markets," *Industrial Marketing Management* 30 (June 2001): pp. 391–402.

Tarasi, Crina O., Bolton, Ruth N., Hutt, Michael D., and Walker, Beth A., "Balancing Risk and Return in a Customer Portfolio," *Journal of Marketing* 75 (May 2011): pp. 1–17.

Ulaga, Wolfgang, and Eggert, Andreas, "Value-Based Differentiation in Business Relationships: Gaining and Sustaining Key Supplier Status," *Journal of Marketing* 70 (January 2006): pp. 119–136.

van Weele, Arjan, *Puchasing and Supply Chain Management: Analysis Strategy, Planning and Practice*, 5th ed. (Cengage, 2010).

Verhage, Bronis J., *Marketing: A Global Perspective* (Cengage, 2013).

Webster Jr., Frederick E., "The Changing Role of Marketing in the Corporation," *Journal of Marketing* 56 (October 1992): p. 14.

Webster Jr., Frederick E., and Keller, Kevin Lane, "A Roadmap for Branding in Industrial Markets," *Journal of Brand Management* 11 (May 2004): pp. 388–402

PART II
MANAGING RELATIONSHIPS IN BUSINESS MARKETING

CHAPTER 2
ORGANISATIONAL
BUYING BEHAVIOUR

CHAPTER OBJECTIVES

A wide array of forces inside and outside the organisation influence the organisational buyer. Knowledge of these forces provides the marketer with a foundation for responsive business marketing strategies. After reading this chapter, you will understand:

1   The decision process organisational buyers apply as they confront differing buying situations and the resulting strategy implications for the business marketer

2   The individual, group, organisational, and environmental variables that influence organisational buying decisions

3   A model of organisational buying behaviour that integrates these important influences

4   How a knowledge of organisational buying characteristics enables the marketer to make more informed decisions about product design, pricing, and promotion strategies

Want to win the support of buying influentials? *Enhance their customers' experience.* Market-driven business firms continuously sense and act on trends in their markets. Consider Johnson Controls, Inc., a diverse, multi-industry company that is a leading supplier of auto interiors (including seats, electronics, headliners, and instrument panels) to manufacturers.* The striking success of the firm rests on the close relationships that its sales reps and marketing managers have formed with design engineers and purchasing executives in the auto industry. To illustrate, some of Johnson Controls' salespersons work on-site with design teams at Ford, GM, or Honda. To provide added value to the new-product-design process, the firm emphasises environment-friendly materials and also invests annually in market research on the needs and preferences of auto buyers—the customer's customer! Moreover, to enhance the customer experience, technicians at Johnson Controls' research lab test seating and interior components for comfort, safety, ease-of-reach, usability, and function. Using a simulator that generates the bumps, dips, and turns of an open-road drive, scientists can record the passengers' experiences and capture valuable information for developing components that improve comfort and safety as well as customer satisfaction. By staying close to the needs of auto buyers, Johnson Controls became the preferred supplier to design engineers who are continually seeking innovative ways to make auto interiors more distinctive and inviting.

Understanding the dynamics of organisational buying behaviour is crucial for identifying profitable market segments, locating buying influences within these segments, and reaching organisational buyers efficiently and effectively with an offering that responds to their needs. Each decision the business marketer makes is based on organisational buyers' probable response. This chapter explores the key stages of the organisational buying process and isolates the salient characteristics of different purchasing situations. Next, attention turns to the myriad forces that influence organisational buying behaviour. Knowledge of how organisational buying decisions are made provides the business marketer with a solid foundation for building responsive marketing strategies.

2.1 THE ORGANISATIONAL BUYING PROCESS

Organisational buying behaviour is a process, not an isolated act or event. Tracing the history of a procurement decision uncovers critical decision points and evolving information requirements. In fact, organisational buying involves several stages, each of which yields a decision. Figure 2.1 lists the major stages in the organisational buying process.*

The purchasing process begins when someone in the organisation recognises a problem that can be solved or an opportunity that can be captured by acquiring a specific product. Problem recognition can be triggered by internal or external forces. Internally, a firm like Unilever may need new high-speed production equipment to support a new product launch. Or a purchasing manager may be unhappy with the price or service of an equipment supplier. Externally, a salesperson can precipitate the need for a product by demonstrating opportunities for improving the organisation's performance. Likewise, business marketers also use advertising to alert customers to problems and demonstrate how a particular product may solve them.

During the organisational buying process, many small or incremental decisions are made that ultimately translate into a supplier's final choice. To illustrate, a production manager might unknowingly establish specifications for a new production system that only one supplier can meet (Stages 2 and 3). This type of decision early in the buying process dramatically influences the favourable evaluation and ultimate selection of that supplier.

2.1.1 The search process

Once the organisation has defined the product that meets its requirements, attention turns to this question: Which of the many possible suppliers are promising candidates? The organisation invests more time and energy in the supplier search when the proposed product has a strong

FIGURE 2.1 Major stages of the organisational buying process

Stage	Description
1. Problem Recognition	Managers at P&G need new high-speed packaging equipment to support a new product launch.
2. General Description of Need	Production managers work with a purchasing manager to determine the characteristics needed in the new packaging system.
3. Product Specifications	An experienced production manager assists a purchasing manager in developing a detailed and precise description of the needed equipment.
4. Supplier Search	After conferring with production managers, a purchasing manager identifies a set of alternative suppliers that could satisfy P&G's requirements.
5. Acquisition and Analysis of Proposals	Alternative proposals are evaluated by a purchasing manager and a number of members of the production department.
6. Supplier Selection	Negotiations with the two finalists are conducted, and a supplier is chosen.
7. Selection of Order Routine	A delivery date is established for the production equipment.
8. Performance Review	After equipment is installed, purchasing and production managers evaluate the performance of the equipment and the service support provided by the supplier.

bearing on organisational performance. When the information needs of the buying organisation are low, Stages 4 and 5 occur simultaneously, especially for standardised items. In this case, a purchasing manager may merely check a catalogue or secure an updated price from the Internet. Stage 5 emerges as a distinct category only when the information needs of the organisation are high. Here, the process of acquiring and analysing proposals may involve purchasing managers, engineers, users, and other organisational members.

Supplier selection and performance review

After being selected as a chosen supplier (Stage 6) and agreeing to purchasing guidelines (Stage 7), such as required quantities and expected time of delivery, a marketer faces further tests. A performance review is the final stage in the purchasing process. The performance review may lead the purchasing manager to continue, modify, or cancel the agreement. A review critical of the chosen supplier and supportive of rejected alternatives can lead members of the decision-making unit to reexamine their position. If the product fails to meet the needs of the using department, decision makers may give further consideration to vendors screened earlier in the procurement process. To keep a new customer, the marketer must ensure that the buying organisation's needs have been completely satisfied. Failure to follow through at this critical stage leaves the marketer vulnerable.

The stages in this model of the procurement process may not progress sequentially and may vary with the complexity of the purchasing situation. For example, some of the stages are compressed or bypassed when organisations make routine buying decisions. However, the model provides important insights into the organisational buying process. Certain stages may be completed concurrently; the process may be discontinued by a change in the external environment or in upper-management thinking. The organisational buying process is shaped by a host of internal and external forces, such as changes in economic or competitive conditions or a basic shift in organisational priorities.

Organisations with significant experience in purchasing a particular product approach the decision quite differently from first-time buyers. Therefore, attention must centre on buying situations rather than on products. Three types of buying situations have been delineated: (1) new task, (2) modified rebuy, and (3) straight rebuy.[*]

2.1.2 New task

In a new task buying situation, the organisation is either a first-time buyer of a product or faces a unique purchase situation. Since there is considerable uncertainty and risk (especially in case of a large investment), the buying centre is often enlarged to include more participants who have a stake in the new purchase. Without any previous experience on which to base a decision, it takes considerable effort to collect and analyse information about qualified suppliers, as well as about the prices, quality and service levels they offer. The more suppliers are involved, the more complex the decision-making process will be.

In many ways, new task buying is similar to the extensive problem-solving orientation and buying behaviour of consumers shopping for a product that they have not bought before. Here, too, the Decision Making Unit (DMU) members do not have specific criteria yet to compare products or suppliers, nor do they have a preference for a particular solution or brand. Hence, making a decision is time-consuming.

Buying-decision approaches[*]

Two distinct buying-decision approaches are used: judgmental new task and strategic new task. The greatest level of uncertainty confronts firms in judgmental new-task situations because the product may be technically complex, evaluating alternatives is difficult, and dealing with a new supplier has unpredictable aspects. Consider purchasers of a special type of production equipment who are uncertain about the model or brand to choose, the suitable level of quality, and the appropriate price to pay. For such purchases, buying activities include a moderate amount of information search and a moderate use of formal tools in evaluating key aspects of the buying decision.

Even more effort is invested in **strategic new-task decisions.** These purchasing decisions are of extreme importance to the firm strategically and financially. If the buyer perceives that a rapid pace of technological change surrounds the decision, search effort is increased but concentrated in a shorter time period.[*] Long-range planning drives the decision process. To illustrate, a large health insurance company placed a €450 000 order for workstation furniture. The long-term effect on the work environment shaped the six-month decision process and involved the active participation of personnel from several departments.

Strategy guidelines

The business marketer confronting a new-task buying situation can gain a differential advantage by participating actively in the initial stages of the procurement process. The marketer should gather information on the problems facing the buying organisation, isolate specific requirements, and offer proposals to meet the requirements. Ideas that lead to new products often originate not with the marketer but with the customer.

Marketers who are presently supplying other items to the organisation ("in" suppliers) have an edge over other firms: They can see problems unfolding and are familiar with the "personality" and behaviour patterns of the organisation. The successful business marketer carefully monitors the changing needs of organisations and is prepared to assist new-task buyers.

2.1.3 Straight rebuy

This is the most common situation and entails the acquisition of a known product from a known supplier. Uncertainty regarding the outcome of the transaction is low because the terms and conditions of the contract are known and are periodically re-established in negotiations with the supplier. In the case of regularly recurring (repetitive) deliveries of identical goods, blanket orders or annual agreements are used that cover the main terms and conditions. Ordering takes place through call-off orders, often placed directly by the user department through advanced e-procurement solutions. This benefits both the speed and efficiency of the transaction (for buyer as well as supplier). Straight rebuy situations relate to all kinds of routine items and consumable items, such as office supplies, fixing materials, cleaning materials, catering products. These may also relate to bulk products, such as raw materials, that are negotiated once a year and then ordered weekly for production. After negotiations with the seller about the contract, orders should be placed directly by the users without interference from the purchasing department. Internet technology and especially e-commerce provide interesting solutions for efficient order handling in this area.

Buying decision approaches

Research suggests that organisational buyers employ two buying-decision approaches: causal and routine low priority. Causal purchases involve no information search or analysis, and the product or service is of minor importance. The focus is simply on transmitting the order. In contrast, routine low-priority decisions are somewhat more important to the firm and involve a moderate amount of analysis. Describing the purchase of €3750 worth of cable to be used as component material, a buyer aptly describes this decision-process approach:

> On repeat buys, we may look at other sources or alternate methods of manufacturing, etc., to make sure no new technical advancements are available in the marketplace. But, generally, a repeat buy is repurchased from the supplier originally selected, especially for low dollar items.

Strategy guidelines

The purchasing department handles straight rebuy situations by routinely selecting a supplier from a list of approved vendors and then placing an order. As organisations shift to e-procurement systems, purchasing managers retain control of the process for these routine purchases while allowing individual employees to directly buy online from approved suppliers.* Employees use a simple point-and-click interface to navigate through a customised catalogue detailing the offerings of approved suppliers, and then order required items. Individual employees like the self-service convenience, and purchasing managers can direct attention to more critical strategic issues. Marketing communications should be designed to reach not only purchasing managers but also individual employees who are now empowered to exercise their product preferences.

The marketing task appropriate for the straight rebuy situation depends on whether the marketer is an "in" supplier (on the list) or an "out" supplier (not among the chosen few). An "in" supplier must reinforce the buyer–seller relationship, meet the buying organisation's expectations, and be alert and responsive to the changing needs of the organisation.

The "out" supplier faces a number of obstacles and must convince the organisation that it can derive significant benefits from breaking the routine. This can be difficult because organisational buyers perceive risk in shifting from the known to the unknown. The organisational spotlight shines directly on them if an untested supplier falters. Buyers may view testing, evaluations, and approvals as costly, time consuming, and unnecessary.

The marketing effort of the "out" supplier rests on an understanding of the basic buying needs of the organisation: Information gathering is essential. The marketer must convince organisational buyers that their purchasing requirements have changed or that the requirements should be interpreted differently. The objective is to persuade decision makers to reexamine alternative solutions and revise the preferred list to include the new supplier.

2.1.4 Modified rebuy

This is when the organisation wants to purchase a new product from a known supplier, or an existing product from a new supplier, and usually occurs when there is some dissatisfaction about the current supplier, or when better alternatives for existing products have become available. This situation is more certain than the new-task situation because the relevant criteria on how to value the functionality of the product or service or how to select the supplier are more or less known.

Limited problem solving best describes the decision-making process for the modified rebuy. Decision makers have well-defined criteria but are uncertain about which suppliers can best fit their needs. In the consumer market, university students buying their second computer might follow a limited problem-solving approach.

Buying-decision approaches

Two buying-decision approaches typify this buying-class category. Both strongly emphasise the firm's strategic objectives and long-term needs. The simple modified rebuy involves a narrow set of choice alternatives and a moderate amount of both information search and analysis. Buyers concentrate on the long-term-relationship potential of suppliers.

The **complex modified rebuy** involves a large set of choice alternatives and poses little uncertainty. The range of choice enhances the buyer's negotiating strength. The importance of the decision motivates buyers to actively search for information, apply sophisticated analysis techniques, and carefully consider long-term needs. This decision situation is particularly well suited to a competitive bidding process.

Strategy guidelines

In a modified rebuy, the direction of the marketing effort depends on whether the marketer is an "in" or an "out" supplier. An "in" supplier should make every effort to understand and satisfy the procurement need and to move decision makers into a straight rebuy. The buying organisation perceives potential payoffs by reexamining alternatives. The "in" supplier should ask why and act immediately to remedy any customer problems. The marketer may be out of touch with the buying organisation's requirements.

The goal of the "out" supplier should be to hold the organisation in modified rebuy status long enough for the buyer to evaluate an alternative offering. Knowing the factors that led decision makers to reexamine alternatives could be pivotal. A particularly effective strategy for an "out" supplier is to offer performance guarantees as part of the proposal.[*] To illustrate, the following guarantee prompted International Circuit Technology, a manufacturer of printed circuit boards, to change to a new supplier for plating chemicals: "Your plating costs will be no more than x cents per square foot or we will make up the difference."[*] Given the nature of the production process, plating costs can be easily monitored by comparing the square footage of circuit boards moving down the plating line with the cost of plating chemicals for the period. Pleased with the performance, International Circuit Technology now routinely reorders from this new supplier.

The eight-stage model of the organisational buying process provides the foundation for exploring the myriad forces that influence a buying decision by an organisation. Observe in Figure 2.2 how organisational buying behaviour is influenced by environmental forces (for example, the growth rate of the economy); organisational forces (for example, the size of the buying organisation); group forces (for example, patterns of influence in buying decisions); and individual forces (for example, personal preferences).

FIGURE 2.2 Forces influencing organisational buying behaviour

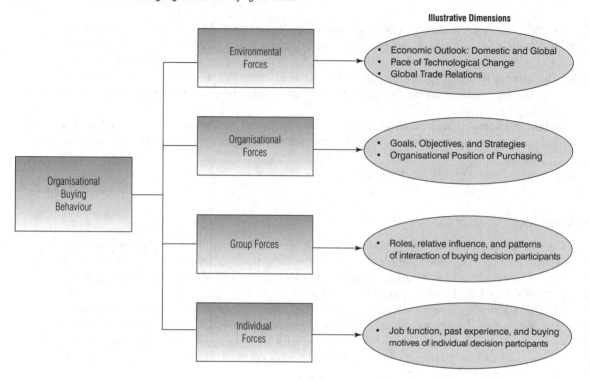

© Cengage Learning 2013

2.2 ENVIRONMENTAL FACTORS

Environmental factors are uncontrollable forces such as politics, laws, regulations and regulatory agencies, activities of interest groups, changes in the economy, competitors' actions and technological changes. These forces generate a considerable amount of uncertainty for an organisation, which can make individuals in the buying centre apprehensive about certain types of purchase. Changes in one or more environmental forces can create new purchasing opportunities. For example, changes in competition and technology can make buying decisions difficult in the case of products such as computers, a field in which competition is increasingly affected by new cooperative strategies between companies. Compaq Computers, for instance, grew into a billion-euro company by competing only against IBM and developing cooperative relationships with all other potential competitors, ultimately tying up with HP.*

2.3 ORGANISATIONAL FACTORS

Organisational factors influencing the buying decision process include the buyer's objectives, purchasing policies and resources, as well as the size and composition of its buying centre. An organisation may have certain buying policies to which buying centre participants must conform. For instance, a company's policies may require long-term contracts, perhaps longer than most sellers desire. The nature of an organisation's financial resources may require special credit arrangements. Any of these conditions could affect purchase decision processes.

2.3.1 Growing influence of purchasing

As a rule, the influence of procurement and supply chain management functions is growing. Why? Globalisation is upsetting traditional patterns of competition, and companies are feeling the squeeze from rising material costs and stiff customer resistance to price increases. Meanwhile, to enhance efficiency and effectiveness, many firms are outsourcing some functions that were traditionally performed within the organisation. As a result, at companies around the world, CEOs are counting on the procurement function to keep their businesses strongly positioned in today's intensively competitive marketplace.[*]

So the scope of a chief procurement officer's (CPO's) role has expanded beyond the traditional core values of cost savings, quality, and supply continuity to include more strategic responsibilities. CPOs remain responsible for delivering cost savings, improving asset utilisation, and preserving supplier viability but now must achieve these goals in a way that increases the attractiveness and competitiveness of the firm's end products and services.[*] CPOs are also responsible for procuring materials in a socially and environmentally responsible way that might even include monitoring the carbon footprints or labour practices of suppliers.

2.3.2 Strategic priorities in procurement

As the influence of purchasing grows, chief procurement officers feel the heat of the spotlight, so they are pursuing an ambitious set of strategic priorities (Figure 2.3). Here attention centres on corporate goals and how procurement can help their internal customers (that is, other business functions) achieve these goals. For example, Rick Hughes, CPO at Procter & Gamble, works closely with P&G's chief marketing officer (CMO) and has helped improve the return on the €5.63 billion in annual marketing and advertising investments that the firm makes.[*] As direct participants in the strategy process, procurement managers are also giving increased emphasis to suppliers' *capabilities*, exploring new areas where a strategic supplier can add value to the

FIGURE 2.3   Strategic priorities in procurement

Priority	Theme	Actions
Aligning Purchasing with Strategy	Not Just Buyers	Shift from an administrative role to a value-creating function that serves internal stakeholders and provides a competitive edge in the market.
Exploring New Value Frontiers	It's Not Just about Price	Focus on the capabilities of suppliers emphasising business outcomes, total cost of ownership, and the potential for long-term value creation.
Putting Suppliers Inside	The Best Value Chain Wins	Develop fewer and deeper relationships with strategic supplies and involve them in decision-making processes, ranging from new product development to cost-reduction initiatives.
Pursuing Best-Cost Sources	A World Worth Exploring	Overcome hurdles imposed by geographical differences and seek out cost-effective suppliers around the globe.

Source: Adapted from Marc Bourde, Charlie S. Hawker, and Theo Theocharides, "Taking Center Stage: The 2005 Chief Procurement Officer Survey," (IBM Global ServicesSomers, NY, May 2005), pp. 1–14. Accessed at http://www.ibm.com/bcs on July 1, 2005; and Chip W. Hardt, Nicholas Reinecke, and Peter Spiller, "Inventing the 21st Century Purchasing Organization," *The McKinsey Quarterly* 2007, No. 4, pp. 115–124.

firm's product or service offerings. Apple Inc.'s elite status as a premier product innovator is reinforced by its position as a recognised leader in supply chain management. In designing the iPad, Apple drew on some of the same skilled suppliers that it had used in developing the popular iPhone and iPod Touch.[*]

Leading-edge purchasing organisations have also learned that the "best value chain wins," so they are building closer relationships with a carefully chosen set of strategic suppliers and aligning the activities of the supply chain with customers' needs.[*] For example, Honda reduced the cost of the Accord's purchased content by setting cost targets for each component—engine, chassis, and so on.[*] Then, purchasing managers worked with global suppliers to understand the cost structure of each component, observe how it is manufactured, and identify ways to reduce costs, add value, or do both.

2.4 PROCUREMENT MANAGER'S TOOLKIT

Let's examine three tools that procurement managers use and the corresponding implications that each presents for business marketing strategy. Included here are the three approaches that procurement managers apply in: (1) calculating the total cost of ownership of an acquired good or service, (2) segmenting purchase categories to isolate those that have the greatest impact on firm performance, and (3) deploying e-procurement processes.

2.4.1 Total Cost of Ownership (TCO)

When purchasing a product or service, the procurement manager always considers a host of costs above and beyond the actual purchase price. **TCO** considers the full range of costs associated with the purchase and use of a product or service over its complete life cycle. For example, a firm can justify buying a higher-quality product and paying a premium price because the initial purchase cost will be offset by fewer manufacturing defects, lower inventory requirements, and lower administrative costs.

Observe in Table 2.1 that an organisational customer considers three different types of costs in a total cost-in-use calculation:

1 **Acquisition costs** include not only the selling price and transportation costs but also the administrative costs of evaluating suppliers, expediting orders, and correcting errors in shipments or delivery.

TABLE 2.1 Customers' Total Cost of Ownership

Acquisition Costs	+	Possession Costs	+	Usage Costs	=	Total Cost in Use
Price		Interest cost		Installation costs		
Paperwork cost		Storage cost		Training cost		
Transportation costs		Quality control		User labour cost		
Expediting cost		Taxes and insurance		Product longevity		
Cost of mistakes in order		Shrinkage and obsolescence		Replacement costs		
Prepurchase product evaluation costs		General internal handling costs		Disposal costs		

Source: Adapted from Frank V. Cespedes, "Industrial Marketing: Managing New Requirements," *Sloan Management Review* 35 (Spring 1994), p. 46.

2 **Possession costs** include financing, storage, inspection, taxes, insurance, and other internal handling costs.

3 **Usage costs** are those associated with ongoing use of the purchased product such as installation, employee training, user labour, and field repair, as well as product replacement and disposal costs.

2.4.2 Strategy response: Develop value-based sales tools

Astute business marketers can pursue value-based strategies that provide customers with a lower cost-in-use solution.[*] For example, the logistical expenses of health-care supplies typically account for 10 to 15 per cent of a hospital's operating costs. Medical products firms, like Becton, Dickinson and Company (BD), develop innovative product/service packages that respond to each component of the cost-in-use equation. Such firms can reduce a hospital's acquisition costs by offering an electronic ordering system, possession costs by emphasising just-in-time service, and usage costs by creating an efficient system for disposing of medical supplies after use. Sales teams at BD document those savings for their hospital customers and draw on those rich case histories to illustrate the lower total cost-in-use of their offerings in proposals to new customer prospects. Value-based strategies seek to move the selling proposition from one that centres on current prices and individual transactions to a longer-term relationship built on value and lower total cost-in-use.

2.4.3 Segmenting purchase categories[*]

Each firm purchases a unique portfolio of products and services. Leaders in procurement are giving increased attention to segmenting total purchases into distinct categories and sharpening their focus on those purchases that have the greatest effect on revenue generation or present the greatest risk to corporate performance. From Figure 2.4, observe that various categories of purchases are segmented on the basis of procurement complexity and the nature of the effect on corporate performance (that is, revenue impact/business risk).

Which purchases affect performance?

Procurement complexity considers factors such as the technical complexity, the scope of supply chain coordination required, and the degree to which life cycle costs are relevant. The revenue

FIGURE 2.4 **Segmenting the buy**

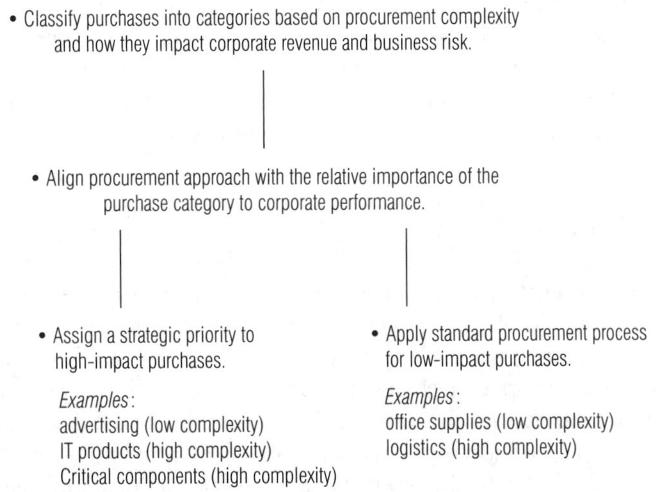

- Classify purchases into categories based on procurement complexity and how they impact corporate revenue and business risk.

- Align procurement approach with the relative importance of the purchase category to corporate performance.

- Assign a strategic priority to high-impact purchases.

  Examples:
  advertising (low complexity)
  IT products (high complexity)
  Critical components (high complexity)

- Apply standard procurement process for low-impact purchases.

  Examples:
  office supplies (low complexity)
  logistics (high complexity)

Source: Adapted with modifications from Matthew G. Anderson and Paul B. Katz, "Strategic Sourcing." *International Journal of Logistics Management 9* (1, 1998), p. 7.

impact/business risk dimension considers the degree to which a purchase category can influence customers' perceptions of value. For example, purchasing managers at Volkswagen decided that some components are important to brand identity, such as steering wheels, road wheels, and other highly visual parts.

Purchasing managers can use a segmentation approach to isolate those purchase categories that have the greatest effect on corporate revenues. For example, advertising services could have tremendous risk implications relative to customer perceptions of value, whereas office supplies remain a cost issue. Or, in the high-tech arena, the procurement of a new generation of semiconductor technology may essentially be a bet on the company's future.[*]

Strategy implications

Business marketers should assess where their offerings are positioned in the portfolio of purchases a particular organisation makes. This varies by firm and by industry. The revenue and profit potential for the business marketer is greatest in those purchasing organisations that view the purchase as strategic—high revenue impact and high customer-value impact. For example, in the auto industry, electronic braking systems, audio and navigation systems, as well as turbochargers, fit into this category and represent about one-quarter of a passenger vehicle's cost.[*] Here the marketer can contribute offerings directly tied to the customer organisation's strategy, enjoying an attractive profit margin. If the business marketer can become a central component of the customer's supply chain, the effect is even more significant: a valuable, long-term relationship in which the customer views the supplier as an extension of its organisation. For categories of goods that purchasing organisations view as less strategic (for example, office supplies), the appropriate marketing strategy centres on providing a complete product assortment, competitive pricing, timely service support, and simplified ordering. By understanding how customers segment their purchases, business marketers are better equipped to target profitable customer groups and develop customised strategies.

2.4.4 E-Procurement

Like consumers who are shopping at Amazon, purchasing managers use the Internet to find new suppliers, communicate with current suppliers, or place an order. Why are purchasing organisations embracing online purchasing technologies? Because they "deliver measurable benefits in the form of material cost savings, process efficiencies, and performance enhancements" according to Tim Minahan, a supply chain consultant at the Aberdeen Group.[*] Studying procurement processes at 60 companies, including American Express, Motorola, and Alcoa, Aberdeen found that e-procurement cut purchasing cycle time in half, reduced material costs by 14 per cent and purchasing administrative costs by 60 per cent, and enhanced the ability of procurement units to identify new suppliers on a global scale.

2.4.5 Reverse auctions

In this type of auction the buyer sets a starting price that the supplier needs to meet in order to get access to the auction. Visible in the auction is also the target price that the buyer wants to reach as a minimum. If this target price is not reached, the auction will not be awarded. During the auction suppliers can follow the price mechanism. How this information is presented towards the supplier can be decided by the buyer, who can decide to show the actual prices as they are offered by the suppliers, but can also decide to show them only their ranking. Next, the buyer may decide to show only the price difference between the actual supplier price and the best price. The supplier may perceive at any time the number of 'clicks' required to meet the best price proposal. Buyers can also each determine that suppliers need to come up with a proposal every five or ten minutes to assure sufficient activity during the auction and to prevent 'bird watching'. Suppliers that do not provide bids every ten minutes are to be eliminated from the auction.

Reverse auctions are best suited for commodity-type items such as purchasing materials, diesel fuel, metal parts, chemicals, and many raw materials. On the other hand, reverse auctions are generally *not* appropriate for strategic relationships, where suppliers have specialised capabilities and few suppliers can meet quality and performance standards. Rob Harlan, senior director of information technology for Motorola, aptly states: "We pride ourselves on strong supplier relationships. We are not going to jeopardise these for short-term gains with online auctions."[*]

A strategic approach to reverse auctions[*]

Pricing experts suggest that customers use reverse auctions for two purposes: (1) to purchase commodity products at the lowest possible price and (2) to tempt suppliers of differentiated products to sacrifice their profit margins in the heat of bidding. If a firm's offering is not highly differentiated from competition, participating in an auction may represent the only choice. However, to minimise the risk of winning an unprofitable bid, a careful estimate should be made of the true incremental cost of supplying the customer, including the costs associated with special terms and conditions as well as unique technical, marketing, and sales support. This analysis will provide the business marketing strategist with a "walk-away" price.

In contrast, if a firm's offering provides significant value to customers relative to competition, John Bloomer, Joe Zale, and John Hogan, consultants at the Strategic Pricing Group, recommend the following decisive tactics:

1   "Preempt the auction: convince the buyer not to go forward with the auction because you have a unique value proposition and are not inclined to participate.

2   Manage the process: influence bid specifications and vendor qualification criteria.

3   Walk away: simply refuse to participate. . ."[*]

A strategic approach to reverse auctions, then, defines success as winning only those bids that are profitable and that do not undermine pricing for other products or for other customers.

2.5 ORGANISATIONAL POSITIONING OF PURCHASING

As purchasing moves from a transaction-based support role and assumes a more prominent strategic spot at the executive level, many leading firms are centralising the procurement function. An organisation that centralises procurement decisions approaches purchasing differently than a company in which purchasing decisions are made at individual user locations. When purchasing is centralised, a separate organisational unit has authority for purchases at a regional, divisional, or headquarters level. For example, by centralising procurement, American Express realised nearly €450 million in purchasing savings in the first three years.[*] A marketer who is sensitive to organisational influences can more accurately map the decision-making process, isolate buying influentials, identify salient buying criteria, and target marketing strategy for centralised buyers.

2.5.1 Strategy response: Key account management

The organisation of the marketer's selling strategy should parallel the organisation of the purchasing function of key accounts. To avoid disjointed selling activities and internal conflict in the sales organisation, and to serve the special needs of important customers, many business marketers have developed key account management programmes to establish a close working relationship that, according to Benson Shapiro and Rowland Moriarty, "cuts across multiple levels, functions, and operating units in both the buying and selling organisations."[*]

> *Key account management can best be described as an enterprise-wide initiative (involving not just the sales force) to develop strategic relationships (not transactional relationships) with a limited number of customers in order to achieve long-term, sustained, significant, and measurable business value for both the customer and the provider.*[*]

For large, multinational organisations that have the structure, processes, and information systems to centrally coordinate purchases on a global scale, the customer might be considered for global account management status. A **global account management programme** treats a customer's worldwide operations as one integrated account, with coherent terms for pricing, service, and product specifications.[*] For example, Ricoh and Hewlett-Packard each have over 100 corporate clients who are given global account status.

2.6 GROUP FORCES

Multiple buying influences and group forces are critical in organisational buying decisions. The organisational buying process typically involves a complex set of smaller decisions made or influenced by several individuals. The group members' degree of involvement varies from

ETHICAL BUSINESS MARKETING

BAE Systems

BAE is Britain's largest defence contractor and the leading European arms manufacturer. It is an important foreign currency earner for the UK. In 2008 the company acknowledged that 'it had failed to pay sufficient attention to ethical standards'. This was the outcome of a company-funded investigation begun after BAE was caught up in accusations of alleged payments to an agent to help secure an arms deal with Saudi Arabia. The alleged recipient is a member of the Saudi Royal Family and so the situation was 'political dynamite'. Britain needs Saudi oil and was also negotiating further arms deals with the same country. Prime Minister Tony Blair had called off a formal investigation on security grounds.

BAE's response was to make a senior executive appointment to oversee the implementation of a new Code of Conduct.

The tale raises important issues about the problems faced by the industry worldwide.

The customers for defence products are governments, not private individuals. Some of these governments operate with a culture quite different from the accepted 'corporate responsibility of the West'. Bribery is not always frowned on; it may be expected, it

may even be essential, to win orders. One insightful comment made in the past is that there is no decision to make whether or not you offer payment; the real decision concerns who to pay. You have to find the right person, the one with influence!

It was in 2002 that 'sweeteners' of any kind were made illegal in the UK; previously the rules had been less stringent. And yet BAE and others were still anxious to win orders.

The stakes are huge. As well as foreign currency many thousands of jobs are at stake. Critical mass in the industry matters; it is important not to contract below a certain scale.

Many sales are being made to countries that are in the frontline of the fight against terrorism and drugs, two issues that both pose a major threat to the UK.

It is perhaps ironic that at the same time as the investigation into possible corruption in the arms industry there was a parallel Scotland Yard investigation into alleged corruption in professional football. Specifically whether leading clubs may have paid 'bungs' to players' agents to secure transfers. One might question how similar and how different these cases are.

routine rebuys, in which the purchasing agent simply takes into account the preferences of others, to complex new-task buying situations, in which a group plays an active role.

The industrial salesperson must address three questions.

- Which organisational members take part in the buying process?

- What is each member's relative influence in the decision?

- What criteria are important to each member in evaluating prospective suppliers?

The salesperson who can correctly answer these questions is ideally prepared to meet the needs of a buying organisation and has a high probability of becoming the chosen supplier.

2.6.1 The buying centre

Most business-to-business purchase decisions are made by more than one person. The group of people within an organisation who are involved in making business purchase decisions are usually referred to as the **buying centre**. These individuals include users, influencers, buyers, deciders and gatekeepers, although one person may perform several of these roles.* Participants in the buying process share the goals and risks associated with their decisions. Effective marketers strive to understand the constituents of risk, as perceived by their target customer personnel, so that they may tailor their messages and marketing propositions to reassure members of the buying centre. In this way, marketers hope to gain an advantage over those rivals that fail to understand these customer concerns and issues.

Isolating the buying situation

Defining the buying situation and determining whether the firm is in the early or later stages of the procurement decision-making process are important first steps in defining the buying centre. The buying centre for a new-task buying situation in the not-for-profit market is presented in Table 2.2. The product, intensive-care monitoring systems, is complex and costly. Buying centre members are drawn from five functional areas, each participating to varying degrees in the process. A marketer who concentrated exclusively on the purchasing function would be overlooking key buying influentials.

Erin Anderson and her colleagues queried a large sample of sales managers about the patterns of organisational buying behaviour their salespeople confront daily. Sales forces that frequently encounter new-task buying situations generally observe that:

TABLE 2.2 The Involvement of Buying Centre Participants at Different Stages of the Procurement Process

Stages of Procurement Process for a Medical Supplier				
Buying Centre Participants	Identification of Need	Establishment of Objectives	Identification and Evaluation of Buying Alternatives	Selection of Suppliers
Physicians	High	High	High	High
Nursing	Low	High	High	Low
Administration	Moderate	Moderate	Moderate	High
Engineering	Low	Moderate	Moderate	Low
Purchasing	Low	Low	Low	Moderate

Source: Adapted by permission. Reprinted from *Industrial Marketing Management, 8*(1), Gene R. Laczniak, "An Empirical Study of Hospital Buying," p. 61, copyright © 1979, with permission of Elsevier.

The buying centre is large, slow to decide, uncertain about its needs and the appropriateness of the possible solutions, more concerned about finding a good solution than getting a low price or assured supply, more willing to entertain proposals from "out" suppliers and less willing to favour "in" suppliers, more influenced by technical personnel, [and] less influenced by purchasing agents.

By contrast, Anderson and her colleagues found that sales forces facing more routine purchase situations (that is, straight and modified rebuys) frequently observe buying centres that are "small, quick to decide, confident in their appraisals of the problem and possible solutions, concerned about price and supply, satisfied with 'in' suppliers, and more influenced by purchasing agents."

Predicting composition

A marketer can also predict the composition of the buying centre by projecting the effect of the industrial product on various functional areas in the organisation. If the procurement decision will affect the marketability of a firm's product (for example, product design, price), the marketing department will be active in the process. Engineering will be influential in decisions about new capital equipment, materials, and components; setting specifications; defining product performance requirements; and qualifying potential vendors. Manufacturing executives will be included for procurement decisions that affect the production mechanism (for example, materials or parts used in production). When procurement decisions involve a substantial economic commitment or impinge on strategic or policy matters, top management will have considerable influence.

INSIDE BUSINESS MARKETING

LG innovating to the top

LG started as an original equipment manufacturer for well known companies before it started marketing 'cheap and cheerful' products under its own brand. When Kim Sang-su took over as chairman in 2003 LG's white goods business was losing money, but he instituted a broad-based innovation programme to transform the business and help LG to attack the global high end market.

It became Korea's biggest and now the third largest household appliance maker in the world after Whirlpool (US) and Electrolux (Sweden). It is the leader in home air conditioners, canister vacuum cleaners and microwave ovens and hopes to become number one in system air conditioners, frontloading washing machines and side by side refrigerators.

When CEO Yong Nam took over he realised that he needed to consolidate the improvements LG had made. LG jumped to number 7 in the most innovative companies list in 2010, but a key part of the success was the change he made to its procurement strategy, following the appointment of ex IBM purchasing manager Thomas Linton. Until then each procurement manager operated separately so the handset unit in Seoul did not know how much the flat screen TV unit in Mexico paid for the same chips from TSMC, the Taiwanese chip maker. Centralising purchasing saved €1.5 billion off the company's €22.5 billion shopping bill. Better forward forecasting enabled it to save another €0.75 billion on purchasing wafers, the silicon disks used to make chips. The lower cost base that resulted enabled LG to get through the global downturn, increase its global competitiveness and offer attractively priced innovative products to the global market.

The procurement strategy helped it price the LG Cookie 30 per cent lower than competitor products. LG spent €0.9 billion to market its latest electronic devices including the LG Cookie helping it to become the world's third largest handset maker.

References: Ihlwan, M. 'Innovation Close-up: LG Electronics', Business Week Magazine, 15 April 2010.

2.6.2 Buying centre influence

Members of the buying centre assume different roles throughout the procurement process. Frederick Webster Jr. and Yoram Wind have given the following labels to each of these roles: users, gatekeepers, influencers, deciders, and buyers.[*]

As the role name implies, **users** are the personnel who use the product in question. Users may have anywhere from inconsequential to extremely important influence on the purchase decision. In some cases, the users initiate the purchase action by requesting the product. They may even develop the product specifications.

Gatekeepers control information to be reviewed by other members of the buying centre. They may do so by disseminating printed information, such as advertisements, or by controlling which salesperson speaks to which individuals in the buying centre. To illustrate, the purchasing agent might perform this screening role by opening the gate to the buying centre for some sales personnel and closing it to others.

Influencers affect the purchasing decision by supplying information for the evaluation of alternatives or by setting buying specifications. Typically, those in technical departments, such as engineering, quality control, and R&D, have significant influence on the purchase decision. Sometimes, outside individuals can assume this role. For high-tech purchases, technical consultants often assume an influential role in the decision process and broaden the set of alternatives being considered.[*]

Deciders actually make the buying decision, whether or not they have the formal authority to do so. The identity of the decider is the most difficult role to determine: Buyers may have formal authority to buy, but the president of the firm may actually make the decision. A decider could be a design engineer who develops a set of specifications that only one vendor can meet.

The **buyer** has formal authority to select a supplier and implement all procedures connected with securing the product. More powerful members of the organisation often usurp the power of the buyer. The buyer's role is often assumed by the purchasing agent, who executes the administrative functions associated with a purchase order.

One person could assume all roles, or separate individuals could assume different buying roles. To illustrate, as users, personnel from marketing, accounting, purchasing, and production may all have a stake in which information technology system is selected. Thus, the buying centre can be a very complex organisational phenomenon.

Identifying patterns of influence

Key influencers are frequently located outside the purchasing department. To illustrate, the typical capital equipment purchase involves an average of four departments, three levels of the management hierarchy (for example, manager, regional manager, vice president), and seven different individuals.[*] In purchasing component parts, personnel from production and engineering are often most influential in the decision. It is interesting to note that a comparative study of organisational buying behaviour found striking similarities across four countries (the United States, the United Kingdom, Australia, and Canada) in the involvement of various departments in the procurement process.[*]

Past research provides some valuable clues for identifying powerful buying centre members (Table 2.3).[*] To illustrate, individuals who have an important personal stake in the decision possess, expert knowledge concerning the choice, and/or are central to the flow of decision-related information tend to assume an active and influential role in the buying centre. Purchasing managers assume a dominant role in repetitive buying situations.

Based on their buying centre research, Donald W. Jackson Jr. and his colleagues provide these strategy recommendations:

Marketing efforts will depend upon which individuals of the buying centre are more influential for a given decision. Because engineering and manufacturing are more influential in

TABLE 2.3 **Clues for Identifying Powerful Buying Centre Members**

- *Isolate the personal stakeholders.* Those individuals who have an important personal stake in the decision will exert more influence than other members of the buying centre. For example, the selection of production equipment for a new plant will spawn the active involvement of manufacturing executives.
- *Follow the information flow.* Influential members of the buying centre are central to the information flow that surrounds the buying decision. Other organisational members will direct information to them.
- *Identify the experts.* Expert power is an important determinant of influence in the buying centre. Those buying centre members who possess the most knowledge—and ask the most probing questions of the salesperson—are often influential.
- *Trace the connections to the top.* Powerful buying centre members often have direct access to the top-management team. This direct link to valuable information and resources enhances the status and influence of the buying centre members.
- *Understand purchasing's role.* Purchasing is dominant in repetitive buying situations by virtue of technical expertise, knowledge of the dynamics of the supplying industry, and close working relationships with individual suppliers.

Source: Adapted from John R. Ronchetto, Michael D. Hutt, and Peter H. Reingen, ''Embedded Influence Patterns in Organizational Buying Systems,'' Journal of Marketing 53 (October 1989): pp. 51–62.

product selection decisions, they may have to be sold on product characteristics. On the other hand, because purchasing is most influential in supplier selection decisions, they may have to be sold on company characteristics.[*]

2.7 INDIVIDUAL FACTORS

Individual factors are the personal characteristics of individuals in the buying centre, such as age, education, personality, position in the organisation and income level. For example, a 60-year-old manager who left school at 16 and has been with the organisation ever since may affect the decisions of the buying centre differently from a 30 year old with a two-year employment history, who left university with a business studies degree and an MBA. How influential these factors will be depends on the buying situation, the type of product being purchased and whether the purchase is new task, modified re-buy or straight re-buy. The negotiating styles of individuals will undoubtedly vary within an organisation and from one organisation to another. To be effective, a marketer needs to know customers well enough to be aware of these individual factors and the effects they may have on purchase decisions.

2.7.1 Differing evaluative criteria

Evaluative criteria are specifications that organisational buyers use to compare alternative industrial products and services; however, these criteria may conflict. Industrial product users generally value prompt delivery and efficient servicing; engineering values product quality, standardisation, and testing; and purchasing assigns the most importance to maximum price advantage and economy in shipping and forwarding.[*]

Product perceptions and evaluative criteria differ among organisational decision makers as a result of differences in their educational backgrounds, their exposure to different types of information from different sources, the way they interpret and retain relevant information (perceptual distortion), and their level of satisfaction with past purchases.* Engineers have an educational background different from that of plant managers or purchasing agents: They are exposed to different journals, attend different conferences, and possess different professional goals and values. A sales presentation that is effective with purchasing may be entirely off the mark with engineering.

Responsive marketing strategy

A marketer who is sensitive to differences in the product perceptions and evaluative criteria of individual buying centre members is well equipped to prepare a responsive marketing strategy. To illustrate, a research study examined the industrial adoption of solar air-conditioning systems and identified the criteria important to key decision makers.* Buying centre participants for this purchase typically include production engineers, heating and air-conditioning (HVAC) consultants, and top managers. The study revealed that marketing communications directed at production engineers should centre on operating costs and energy savings; HVAC consultants should be addressed concerning noise level and initial cost of the system; and top managers are most interested in whether the technology is state-of-the-art. Knowing the criteria of key buying centre participants has significant operational value to the marketer when designing new products and when developing and targeting advertising and personal selling presentations.

2.7.2 Information processing

Volumes of information flow into every organisation through direct-mail advertising, the Internet, journal advertising, trade news, word-of-mouth, and personal sales presentations. What an individual organisational buyer chooses to pay attention to, comprehend, and retain has an important bearing on procurement decisions.

Selective processes

Information processing is generally encompassed in the broader term cognition, which U. Neisser defines as "all the processes by which the sensory input is transformed, reduced, elaborated, stored, recovered, and used."* Important to an individual's cognitive structure are the processes of selective exposure, attention, perception, and retention.

1   *Selective exposure.* Individuals tend to accept communication messages consistent with their existing attitudes and beliefs. For this reason, a purchasing agent chooses to talk to some salespersons and not to others.

2   *Selective attention.* Individuals filter or screen incoming stimuli to admit only certain ones to cognition. Thus, an organisational buyer is more likely to notice a trade advertisement that is consistent with his or her needs and values.

3   *Selective perception.* Individuals tend to interpret stimuli in terms of their existing attitudes and beliefs. This explains why organisational buyers may modify or distort a salesperson's message in order to make it more consistent with their predispositions toward the company.

4   *Selective retention.* Individuals tend to recall only information pertinent to their own needs and dispositions. An organisational buyer may retain information concerning a particular brand because it matches his or her criteria.

Each of these selective processes influences the way an individual decision maker responds to marketing stimuli. Because the procurement process often spans several months and because the marketer's contact with the buying organisation is infrequent, marketing communications must be carefully designed and targeted.[*] Key decision makers "tune out" or immediately forget poorly conceived messages. They retain messages they deem important to achieving goals.

2.7.3 Risk-reduction strategies

Individuals are motivated by a strong desire to reduce risk in purchase decisions. Perceived risk includes two components: (1) uncertainty about the outcome of a decision and (2) the magnitude of consequences from making the wrong choice. Research highlights the importance of perceived risk and the purchase type in shaping the structure of the decision-making unit.[*] Individual decision making is likely to occur in organisational buying for straight rebuys and for modified rebuys when the perceived risk is low. In these situations, the purchasing agent may initiate action.[*] Modified rebuys of higher risk and new tasks seem to spawn a group structure.

In confronting "risky" purchase decisions, how do organisational buyers behave? As the risk associated with an organisational purchase decision increases, the following occur[*]:

- The buying centre becomes larger and comprises members with high levels of organisational status and authority.

- The information search is active and a wide variety of information sources are consulted. As the decision process unfolds, personal information sources (for example, discussions with managers at other organisations that have made similar purchases) become more important.

- Buying centre participants invest greater effort and deliberate more carefully throughout the purchase process.

- Sellers who have a proven track record with the firm are favoured—the choice of a familiar supplier helps reduce perceived risk.

Rather than price, product quality and after-sale service are typically most important to organisational buyers when they confront risky decisions. When introducing new products, entering new markets, or approaching new customers, the marketing strategist should evaluate the effect of alternative strategies on perceived risk.

SUMMARY

Knowledge of the process that organisational buyers follow in making purchasing decisions is fundamental to responsive marketing strategy. As a buying organisation moves from the problem-recognition phase, in which a procurement need is defined, to later phases, in which suppliers are screened and ultimately chosen, the marketer can play an active role. In fact, the astute marketer often triggers initial awareness of the problem and helps the organisation effectively solve that problem. Incremental decisions made throughout the buying process narrow the field of acceptable suppliers and dramatically influence the ultimate outcome.

The nature of the buying process depends on the organisation's level of experience with similar procurement problems. It is thus crucial to know how the organisation defines the buying situation: as a new task, a modified rebuy, or a straight rebuy. Each buying situation requires a unique problem-solving approach, involves unique buying influentials, and demands a unique marketing response.

Myriad forces—environmental, organisational, group, and individual—influence organisational buying behaviour. First, environmental forces define the boundaries within which industrial buyers and sellers interact, such as general business conditions or the rate of technological change. Second, organisational forces dictate the link between buying activities and the strategic priorities of the firm and the position that the purchasing function

occupies in the organisational structure. Rather than devoting exclusive attention to "buying for less," leading organisations tie procurement activities directly to corporate strategy and use online procurement tools to streamline processes and advance performance. Procurement managers emphasise the total cost of ownership in evaluating alternative offerings and adopt a segmentation approach to isolate those purchase categories that have the greatest impact on corporate performance.

Third, the relevant unit of analysis for the marketing strategist is the buying centre. The composition of this group evolves during the buying process, varies from firm to firm, and changes from one purchasing situation to another. Fourth, the marketer must ultimately concentrate attention on individual members of the buying centre. Each brings a particular set of experiences and a unique personal and organisational frame of reference to the buying decision. The marketer who is sensitive to individual differences is best equipped to develop responsive marketing communications that the organisational buyer will remember.

Unravelling the complex forces that encircle the organisational buying process is indeed difficult. This chapter offers a framework that enables the marketing manager to begin this task by asking the right questions. The answers provide the basis for effective and efficient business marketing strategy.

DISCUSSION QUESTIONS

1   Why should a marketing manager have an insight into what motivates a business customer to make purchase decisions?

2   What are the major components of a buying centre?

3   Identify the stages of the business buying decision process. How is this decision process used when making straight rebuys?

4   What is the value of e-procurement for a buyer? When would you go for a reverse auction? Provide arguments for and against.

5   What are the differences between the three main forces behind buying decisions? Which, if any, do you think is the most important?

INTERNET EXERCISES

Log on to Dell's website. Ignore the sections aimed at consumers. Instead, go to *Business* products. This section details Dell's business-to-business products, services and upcoming events such as trade shows. There are sections offering solutions for small business, public sector and large enterprises. Visit Dell's website at http://www1.euro.dell.com or http://www.dell.com

1   In what ways do Dell's web pages for business products reflect the requirements of business customers?

2   How have the messages been tailored to reflect the buying behaviour of Dell's business customers?

REFERENCES

Anderson, Erin, Chu, Wujin, and Weitz, Barton, "Industrial Purchasing: An Empirical Exploration of the Buyclass Framework," *Journal of Marketing* 51 (July 1987): pp. 71–86.

Anderson, Matthew G., and Katz, Paul B., "Strategic Sourcing," *International Journal of Logistics Management* 9 (1, 1998): pp. 1–13.

Avery, Susan, "American Express Changes Ahead," *Purchasing* 133 (November 4, 2004): pp. 34–38.

Banting, Peter, Ford, David, Gross, Andrew, and Holmes, George, "Similarities in Industrial Procurement across Four Countries," *Industrial Marketing Management* 14 (May 1985): pp. 133–144.

Bloomer, John, Zale, Joe, and Hogan, John E., "Battling Powerful Procurement Groups: How to Profitably Participate in Reverse Auctions," *SPG Insights* (Fall 2004): pp. 1–3, http://www.imakenews.com/strategicpricing, accessed August 1, 2008.

Booen, Brett, "The Best Chief Procurement Officers (CPOs) in the World," *Supply Chain Digital*, January 3, 2011, pp. 2–3, http://www.supplychaindigital.com, accessed April 10, 2011.

Bunn, Michele D., "Taxonomy of Buying Decision Approaches," *Journal of Marketing* 57 (January 1993): pp. 38–56.

Bunn, Michele D., Butaney, Gul T., and Huffman, Nicole P., "An Empirical Model of Professional Buyers' Search Effort," *Journal of Business-to-Business Marketing* 8 (4, 2001): pp. 55–81.

Cespedes, Frank V., "Industrial Marketing: Managing New Requirements," *Sloan Management Review* 35 (Spring 1994): pp. 45–60.

Choffray, Jean-Marie and Lilien, Gary L., "Assessing Response to Industrial Marketing Strategy," *Journal of Marketing* 42 (April 1978): pp. 20–31.

Clark, Don, "IPad Taps Familiar Apple Suppliers," *The Wall Street Journal*, April 5, 2010, p. 1, http://www.online.wsj.com, accessed April 10, 2011.

Dawes, Philip L., Lee, Don Y., and Midgley, David, "Organizational Learning in High-Technology Purchase Situations: The Antecedents and Consequences of the Participation of External IT Consultants," *Industrial Marketing Management* 36 (April 2007): pp. 285–299.

Dibb, Sally, Simkin, Lyndon, Pride, Bill, and Ferrell, O.C., *Marketing Concepts & Strategies*, 6th ed. (Cengage, 2012).

Doole, Isobel, and Lowe, Robin, *International Marketing Strategy* 6th ed. (Cengage, 2012).

Dowst, Somerby, "CEO Report: Wanted: Suppliers Adept at Turning Corners," *Purchasing* 101 (January 29, 1987): pp. 71–72.

Dozbaba, Mary Siegfried, "Critical Supplier Relationships: Converting Higher Performance," *Purchasing Today* (February 1999): pp. 22–29.

Farrell, Mark A., and Schroder, Bill, "Influence Strategies in Organizational Buying Decisions," *Industrial Marketing Management* 25 (July 1996): pp. 293–303.

Ghingold, Morry and Wilson, David T., "Buying Center Research and Business Marketing Practice: Meeting the Challenge of Dynamic Marketing," *Journal of Business and Industrial Marketing* 13 (2, 1998): pp. 96–108.

Ghingold, Morry, "Testing the 'Buygrid' Buying Process Model," *Journal of Purchasing and Materials Management* 22 (Winter 1986): pp. 30–36.

Gottfredson, Mark, Puryear, Rudy, and Phillips, Stephen, "Strategic Sourcing: From Periphery to the Core," *Harvard Business Review* 83 (February 2005): pp. 132–139.

Homburg, Christian and Kuester, Sabine, "Towards an Improved Understanding of Industrial Buying Behavior: Determinants of the Number of Suppliers," *Journal of Business-to-Business Marketing* 8 (2, 2001): pp. 5–29.

Inampudi, Srikant, Satpathy, Aurobind, and Singh, Anant, "Can North American Auto Suppliers Create Value?" *The McKinsey Quarterly*, June 2008, http://www.mckinsey.com, accessed June 8, 2008.

Jackson, Jr., Donald W., Keith, Janet E., and Burdick, Richard K., "Purchasing Agents' Perceptions of Industrial Buying Center Influence," *Journal of Marketing* 48 (Fall 1984): pp. 75–83.

Jarillo, J.C. and Stevenson, H.H. (1991) 'Cooperative strategies: the payoffs and the pitfalls', *Long Range Planning*, February, 64-70.

Johnson Controls, "Product Solutions: Smarter Seats," http://www.johnsoncontrols.com, accessed April 8, 2011.

Johnston and Lewin, "Organizational Buying Behavior: Toward an Integrative Framework," pp. 8–10.

Johnston, Wesley J. and Bonoma, Thomas V., "The Buying Center: Structure and Interaction Patterns," *Journal of Marketing* 45 (Summer 1981): pp. 143–156.

Katrichis, Jerome M., "Exploring Departmental Level Interaction Patterns in Organizational Purchasing Decisions," *Industrial Marketing Management* 27 (March 1998): pp. 135–146.

Kohli, Ajay, "Determinants of Influence in Organizational Buying: A Contingency Approach," *Journal of Marketing* 53 (July 1989): pp. 50–65.

LaPorta, John, "Assessing and Accelerating the Skills of Your Procurement Staff," *Supply and Demand Chain Executive*, January 12, 2011, pp. 1–4, http://www.sdcexec.com, accessed April 10, 2011.

Laseter, Timothy M., *Balanced Sourcing: Cooperation and Competition in Supplier Relationships* (San Francisco: Jossey-Bass, 1998), pp. 5–18.

Lewin, Jeffrey E., and Donthu, Naveen, "The Influence of Purchase Situations on Buying Center Structure and Investment: A Select Meta-Analysis of Organizational Buying Behavior Research," *Journal of Business Research* 58 (October 2005): pp. 1381–1390.

Lichtenthal, "Group Decision Making in Organizational Buying," pp. 119–157.

Lilien, Gary L., and Wong, M. Anthony, "An Exploratory Investigation of the Structure of the Buying Center in the Metalworking Industry," *Journal of Marketing Research* 21 (February 1984): pp. 1–11.

Lubkeman, Mark, and Taneja, Vikas, "Creating Value in Key Accounts," The Boston Consulting Group, Inc., 2011, p. 2, http://www.bcg.com, accessed April 13, 2011.

McQuiston, Daniel H., and Dickson, Peter R., "The Effect of Perceived Personal Consequences on Participation and Influence in Organizational Buying," *Journal of Business Research* 23 (September 1991): pp. 159–177.

Minahan, Tim A., "Best Practices in E-Sourcing: Optimizing and Sustaining Supply Savings," September 2004, p. 3, research report by Aberdeen Group, Inc., Boston, Massachusetts, http://www.ariba.com, accessed June 15, 2005.

Monczka, Robert M., "Value Focused Supply: Linking Supply to Competitive Business Strategies" (Tempe AZ: Institute for Supply Management and W. P. Carey School of Business at Arizona State University, 2010), pp. 2–22, http://www.capsresearch.org, accessed April 10, 2011.

Moutinho, Luiz, and Southern, Geoffrey, *Strategic Marketing Management: A process Based Approach* (Cengage, 2012).

Neisser, U., *Cognitive Psychology* (New York: Appleton, 1966), p. 4.

Osmonbekov, Talai, Bello, Daniel C., and Gillilard, David I., "Adoption of Electronic Commerce Tools in Business Procurement: Enhanced Buying Center Structure and Processes," *Journal of Business and Industrial Marketing* 17 (2/3, 2002): pp. 151–166.

Patterson, Paul G., and Dawes, Phillip L., "The Determinants of Choice Set Structure in High-Technology Markets," *Industrial Marketing Management* 28 (July 1999): pp. 395–411.

Patton III, W.E., Puto, Charles P., and King, Ronald H., "Which Buying Decisions Are Made by Individuals and Not by Groups?" *Industrial Marketing Management* 15 (May 1986): pp. 129–138.

Postma, P. (1998) *The New Marketing Era: Marketing to the Imagination of a Technology-Driven World*, New York,: McGraw-Hill.

Puto, Charles P., Patton III, W. E. and King, Ronald H., "Risk Handling Strategies in Industrial Vendor Selection Decisions," *Journal of Marketing* 49 (Winter 1985), pp. 89–98.

Robinson, Patrick J., Faris, Charles W., and Wind, Yoram, *Industrial Buying and Creative Marketing* (Boston: Allyn and Bacon, 1967), pp. 12–18.

Ronchetto, John R., Hutt, Michael D., and Reingen, Peter H., "Embedded Influence Patterns in Organizational Buying Systems," *Journal of Marketing* 53 (October 1989): pp. 51–62.

Shapiro, Benson P. and Moriarty, Rowland T., *National Account Management: Emerging Insights* (Cambridge, MA: Marketing Science Institute, 1982), p. 8.

Sheth, Jagdish N., "A Model of Industrial Buyer Behavior," *Journal of Marketing* 37 (October 1973): p. 51.

Sheth, Jagdish N., "Organizational Buying Behavior: Past Performance and Future Expectations," *Journal of Business & Industrial Marketing* 11 (3/4, 1996): pp. 7–24.

Thompson, J. L., and Martin, F., *Strategic Management: Awareness and Change Sixth Edition* (Cengage, 2010).

van Weele, Arjan, *Purchasing and Supply Chain Management: Analysis Strategy, Planning and Practice*, 5th ed. (Cengage, 2010).

Venkatesh, R., Kohli, Ajay K., and Zaltman, Gerald, "Influence Strategies in Buying Centers," *Journal of Marketing* 59 (October 1995): pp. 71–82.

Verhage, Bronis J., *Marketing: A Global Perspective* (Cengage, 2013).

Webster Jr., Frederick E. and Wind, Yoram, *Organizational Buying Behavior* (Englewood Cliffs, NJ: Prentice Hall, 1972), p. 77.

Weiss, Allen M., and Heide, Jan B., "The Nature of Organizational Search in High Technology Markets," *Journal of Marketing Research* 30 (May 1993): pp. 230–233.

Wilson, Elizabeth J., Lilien, Gary L., and Wilson, David T., "Developing and Testing a Contingency Paradigm of Group Choice in Organizational Buying," *Journal of Marketing Research* 28 (November 1991): pp. 452–466.

Woodside, Arch G., Liakko, Timo, and Vuori, Risto, "Organizational Buying of Capital Equipment Involving Persons across Several Authority Levels," *Journal of Business and Industrial Marketing* 14 (1, 1999): pp. 30–48.

Wren, Brent M. and Simpson, James T., "A Dyadic Model of Relationships in Organizational Buying: A Synthesis of Research Results," *Journal of Business and Industrial Marketing* 11 (3/4, 1996): pp. 68–79.

Yip, George S. , and Bink, Audrey J.M., "Managing Global Accounts," *Harvard Business Review* 85 (September 2007): pp. 103–111.

CHAPTER 3
CUSTOMER RELATIONSHIP MANAGEMENT STRATEGIES FOR BUSINESS MARKETS

CHAPTER OBJECTIVES

A well-developed ability to create and sustain successful working relationships with customers gives business marketing firms a significant competitive advantage. After reading this chapter, you will understand:

1   The patterns of buyer–seller relationships in the business market

2   The factors that influence the profitability of individual customers

3   A procedure for designing effective customer relationship management programmes

4   The critical determinants of relationship marketing effectiveness

Leading business marketing firms like Cisco and General Electric succeed by providing superior value to customers, by satisfying the special needs of even the most demanding customers, and by understanding the factors that influence individual customer profitability.[*] Compared with the consumer packaged-goods sector, customer profitability is particularly important in business markets because marketing managers allocate a greater proportion of their marketing resources at the individual customer level.[*] The ability of an organisation to create and maintain profitable relationships with these most valuable customers is a durable basis of competitive advantage. Building and maintaining lasting customer relationships requires paying careful attention to detail, meeting promises, and swiftly responding to new requirements.

The new era of business marketing is built upon effective relationship management.[*] Many business marketing firms create what might be called a **collaborative advantage** by demonstrating special skills in managing relationships with key customers or by jointly developing innovative strategies with alliance partners.[*] These firms have learned how to be good partners, and these superior relationship skills are a valuable asset. This chapter explores the types of relationships that characterise the business market. What market and situational factors are associated with different types of buyer–seller relationships? What factors influence customer profitability? What strategies can business marketers employ to build profitable relationships with customers? What are the critical drivers of relationship marketing effectiveness?

3.1 RELATIONSHIP MARKETING[*]

Relationship marketing centres on all activities directed toward establishing, developing, and maintaining successful exchanges with customers and other constituents.[*] Nurturing and managing customer relationships has emerged as an important strategic priority in most firms. Why? First, loyal customers are far more profitable than customers who are price sensitive and perceive few differences among alternative offerings. Second, a firm that is successful in developing strong relationships with customers secures important and durable advantages that are hard for competitors to understand, copy, or displace.

3.1.1 Types of relationships

A business marketer may begin a relationship with Rolls Royce as a supplier (one of many), move to a preferred supplier status (one of a few), and ultimately enter a collaborative relationship with Rolls Royce (sole source for particular items). Observe in Figure 3.1 that buyer–seller relationships are positioned on a continuum, with transactional exchange and collaborative exchange serving as the endpoints. Central to every relationship is an exchange process where each side gives something in return for a payoff of greater value. **Transactional exchange** centres on the timely exchange of basic products for highly competitive market prices. George Day notes that such exchanges

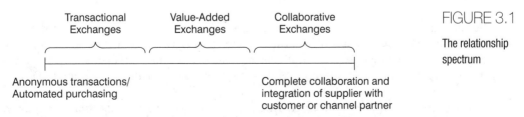

FIGURE 3.1

The relationship spectrum

Source: With kind permission from *Springer Science+Business Media: Journal of Academy of Marketing Science*, ''Managing Market Relationships,'' 28, 2000, p. 25, by George S. Day. Copyright © 2000.

include the kind of autonomous encounters a visitor to a city has with the taxi or bus from the airport, as well as a series of ongoing transactions in a business-to-business market where the customer and supplier focus only on the timely exchange of standard products at competitive prices.[*]

Moving across the continuum, relationships become closer or more collaborative. The open exchange of information is a characteristic of collaborative (close) versus transactional (distant) exchange. Likewise, **operational linkages** reflect how much the systems, procedures, and routines of the buying and selling firms have been connected to facilitate operations.[*] These relationship connectors are a feature of a collaborative relationship. **Collaborative exchange** features very close information, social, and operational linkages as well as mutual commitments made in expectation of long-run benefits. According to James Anderson and James Narus, collaborative exchange involves

a process where a customer and supplier firm form strong and extensive social, economic, service, and technical ties over time, with the intent of lowering total costs and/or increasing value, thereby achieving mutual benefit.[*]

3.1.2 Value-adding exchanges

Between the two extremes on the relationship continuum are value-adding exchanges, where the focus of the selling firm shifts from attracting customers to keeping customers. The marketer pursues this objective by developing a comprehensive understanding of a customer's needs and changing requirements, tailoring the firm's offerings to those needs, and providing continuing incentives for customers to concentrate most of their purchases with them.

3.1.3 Nature of relationships

Transactional exchange involves items like packaging materials or cleaning services where competitive bidding is often employed to secure the best terms. Such exchanges are purely contractual arrangements that involve little or no emotional commitment to sustaining the relationship in the future. By contrast, customised, high-technology products—like semiconductor test equipment—fit the collaborative exchange category. Whereas transactional exchange centres on negotiations and an arm's-length relationship, collaborative exchange emphasises joint problem solving and multiple linkages that integrate the processes of the two parties. Trust and commitment provide the foundation for collaborative exchange.[*] **Relationship commitment** is the extent to which both parties believe and feel the relationship is worth spending energy to maintain and promote. In turn, **trust** is the level of confidence that both parties have in each other and their willingness to open themselves to the other party. Recent research highlights the powerful role that contact personnel (for example, salespersons) assume in forging a long-term relationship. "Individuals who build trust in each other will transfer this bond to the firm level."[*]

3.1.4 Strategic choices

Business marketers have some latitude in choosing where to participate along the relationship continuum. However, limits are imposed by the characteristics of the market and by the significance of the purchase to the buyer. A central challenge for the marketer is to overcome the gravitational pull toward the transaction end of the exchange spectrum. According to Day,

Rivals are continually working to attract the best accounts away; customer requirements, expectations, and preferences keep changing, and the possibility of friction-free exploration of options in real time on the Web conspire to raise the rate of customer defections.[*]

FIGURE 3.2 The spectrum of buyer-seller relationships

	Transactional Exchange ←——→ Collaborative Exchange	
Availability of Alternatives	Many Alternatives	Few Alternatives
Supply Market Dynamism	Stable	Volatile
Importance of Purchase	Low	High
Complexity of Purchase	Low	High
Information Exchange	Low	High
Operational Linkages	Limited	Extensive

Source: Adapted from Joseph P. Cannon and William D. Perreault Jr., "Buyer-Seller Relationships in Business Markets," *Journal of Marketing Research* 36 (November 1999): pp. 439–460.

3.2 MANAGING BUYER–SELLER RELATIONSHIPS

Buyers and sellers craft different types of relationships in response to market conditions and the characteristics of the purchase situation. To develop specific relationship-marketing strategies for a particular customer, the business marketer must understand that some customers elect a collaborative relationship, whereas others prefer a more distant or transactional relationship. Figure 3.2 highlights the typical characteristics of relationships at the endpoints of the buyer–seller relationship spectrum.

3.2.1 Transactional exchange

Customers are more likely to prefer a **transactional relationship** when a competitive supply market features many alternatives, the purchase decision is not complex, and the supply market is stable. This profile fits some buyers of office supplies, commodity chemicals, and shipping services. In turn, customers emphasise a transactional orientation when they view the purchase as less important to the organisation's objectives. Such relationships are characterised by lower levels of information exchange and are less likely to involve operational linkages between the buying and selling firms.

3.2.2 Collaborative exchange

Buying firms prefer a more **collaborative relationship** when alternatives are few, the market is dynamic (for example, rapidly changing technology), and the complexity of the purchase is high. In particular, buyers seek close relationships with suppliers when they deem the purchase important and strategically significant. This behaviour fits some purchasers of manufacturing equipment, enterprise software, or critical component parts. Indeed, Cannon and Perreault state that "the closest partnerships ... arise both when the purchase is important and when there is a need—from the customer's perspective—to overcome procurement obstacles that result from fewer supply alternatives and more purchase uncertainty."[*]

Moreover, the relationships that arise for important purchases are more likely to involve operational linkages and high levels of information exchange. Switching costs are especially important to collaborative customers.

3.2.3 Switching costs

In considering possible changes from one selling firm to another, organisational buyers consider two **switching costs**: investments and risk of exposure. First, organisational buyers invest in their relationships with suppliers in many ways. As Barbara Bund Jackson states:

They invest money; they invest in people, as in training employees to run new equipment; they invest in *lasting assets*, such as equipment itself; and they invest in changing basic business *procedures* like inventory handling.[*]

Because of these past investments, buyers may hesitate to incur the disruptions and switching costs that result when they select new suppliers.

Risk of exposure provides a second major category of switching costs. Attention centres on the risks to buyers of making the wrong choice. Customers perceive more risk when they purchase products important to their operations, when they buy from less established suppliers, and when they buy technically complex products.

3.2.4 Strategy guidelines

The business marketer manages a portfolio of relationships with customers—some of these customers view the purchase as important and desire a close, tightly connected buyer–seller relationship; other customers assign a lower level of importance to the purchase and prefer a looser relationship. Given the differing needs and orientations of customers, the business marketer's first step is to determine which type of relationship matches the purchasing situation and supply-market conditions for a particular customer. Second, a strategy must be designed that is appropriate for each strategy type.

Collaborative customers

Relationship-building strategies, targeted on strong and lasting commitments, are especially appropriate for these customers. Business marketers can sensibly invest resources to secure commitments and directly assist customers with planning. Here sales and service personnel work not only with purchasing managers but also with a wide array of managers on strategy and coordination issues. Regular visits to the customer by executives and technical personnel can strengthen the relationship. Operational linkages and information-sharing mechanisms should be designed into the relationship to keep product and service offerings aligned with customer needs. Given the long time horizon and switching costs, customers are concerned both with the marketers' long-term capabilities and with their immediate performance. Because the customers perceive significant risk, they demand competence and commitment from sellers and are easily frightened by even a hint of supplier inadequacy.

Value drivers in collaborative relationships

A recent study examined this intriguing question: What avenues of differentiation can suppliers of routinely purchased products use to create value in business-to-business relationships, thereby winning key supplier status?[*] The results suggest that relationship benefits display a much stronger potential for differentiation in key supplier relationships than cost considerations. Importantly, service support and personal interaction were identified as the core differentiators, followed by a supplier's know-how and its ability to improve a customer's time to market. Product quality and delivery performance, along with cost savings associated with the acquisition process and from operations, display a moderate potential to help a firm gain key supplier status. Finally, price displayed the weakest potential for differentiation. The researchers, Wolfgang Ulaga and Andreas Eggert, conclude: "Whereas cost factors serve as key criteria to get a supplier on the short list of those vendors considered for a relationship, relationship benefits dominate when deciding which supplier" should be awarded key supplier status.[*]

Transaction customers

These customers display less loyalty or commitment to a particular supplier and can easily switch part or all of the purchases from one vendor to another. A business marketer who offers an immediate, attractive combination of product, price, technical support, and other benefits has a chance of winning business from a transactional customer. The salesperson centres primary attention on the purchasing staff and seldom has important ties to senior executives in the buying organisation. M. Bensaou argues that it is unwise for marketers to make specialised investments in transactional relationships:

> Firms that invest in building trust through frequent visits, guest engineers, and cross-company teams when the product and market context calls for simple, impersonal control and data exchange mechanisms are overdesigning the relationship. This path is not only costly but also risky, given the specialised investments involved, in particular, the intangible ones (for example, people, information, or knowledge).[*]

Rather than adopting the approach of "one design fits all," the astute marketer matches the strategy to the product and market conditions that surround a particular customer relationship and understands the factors that influence profitability.

3.3 MEASURING CUSTOMER PROFITABILITY[*]

To improve customer satisfaction and loyalty, many business-to-business firms have developed customised products and increased the specialised services they offer. Although customers embrace such actions, they often lead to declining profits, especially when the enhanced offerings are not accompanied by increases in prices or order volumes. For a differentiation strategy to succeed, "the value created by the differentiation—measured by higher margins and higher sales volumes—has to exceed the cost of creating and delivering customised features and services."[*] By understanding the drivers of customer profitability, the business marketing manager can more effectively allocate marketing resources and take action to convert unprofitable relationships into profitable ones.

3.3.1 Activity-based costing

Most studies of customer profitability yield a remarkable insight: "Only a minority of a typical company's customers is truly profitable."[*] Why? Many firms fail to examine how the costs of specialised products and services vary among individual customers. In other words, they focus on profitability at an aggregate level (for example, product or territory), fail to assign operating expenses to customers, and misjudge the profitability of individual customers. To capture customer-specific costs, many firms have adopted activity-based costing.

   Activity-based costing (ABC) illuminates exactly what activities are associated with serving a particular customer and how these activities are linked to revenues and the consumption of resources.[*] The ABC system and associated software link customer transaction data from customer relationship management (CRM) systems with financial information. The ABC system provides marketing managers with a clear and accurate picture of the gross margins and cost-to-serve components that yield individual customer profitability.

3.3.2 Unlocking customer profitability

Marketers sometimes say 'It is better to own a market than a factory.' By this they mean that demand for their products is more important in assuring the continuity of the company than the possession of a building and machinery. For if demand stagnates (and with it sales), the factory that takes care of the supply is superfluous.

We can take this line of reasoning a step further. In evaluating a business, it is not how many sales a product generates that is important but how much profit those sales contribute to the enterprise. Increased sales do not assure increased profits. If a firm cannot make a profit, the question of whether it is satisfying a customer or societal need is immaterial because the firm will not survive. In this sense, profit is not so much an objective as it is a constraint. Since profit contribution is a more important criterion than turnover, the firm may be forced to abandon a product that contributes to overall sales but not to profits. Hence, every company has to strive, for example by building brand equity, to make a profit in the long term.

3.3.3 The profitable few

Once a firm implements an ABC approach and plots cumulative profitability against customers, a striking portrait emerges that is often referred to as the *whale curve* (Figure 3.3). Robert S. Kaplan, who is codeveloper of activity-based costing, and his colleague, V. G. Narayanan, describe the pattern that many companies find:

> *Whereas cumulative sales usually follow the typical 20/80 rule (that is, 20 per cent of the customers provide 80 per cent of the sales), the whale curve for cumulative profitability usually reveals that the most profitable 20 per cent of customers generate between 150 per cent and 300 per cent of total profits. The middle 70 per cent of customers break even and the least profitable 10 per cent of customers lose from 50 to 200 per cent of total profits, leaving the company with its 100 per cent of total profits.* *

As a rule, large customers tend to be included among the most profitable (see left side of Figure 3.3) or the least profitable (see right side of Figure 3.3)—they are seldom in the middle. Interestingly, some of the firm's largest customers often turn out to be among the most

FIGURE 3.3   The Whale Curve illustration: 20% of customers generate 175% of cumulative profits

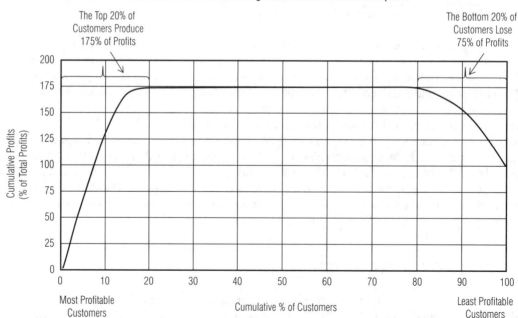

Source: Adapted with modifications from Robert S. Kaplan and V.G. Narayanan, "Measuring and Managing Customer Profitability," *Journal of Cost Management* 15 (September/October 2001): p. 8.

unprofitable. A firm does not generate enough sales volume with a small customer to incur large absolute losses. Only large buyers can be large-loss customers. In Figure 3.3, low-cost-to-serve customers appear on the profitable side of the whale curve and high-cost-to-serve customers end up on the unprofitable side unless they pay a premium price for the specialised support they require.

3.3.4 Managing high- and low-cost-to-serve customers

What causes some customers to be more expensive than others? Note from Table 3.1 that high-cost-to-serve customers, for example, desire customised products, frequently change orders, and require a significant amount of presales and post-sales support. By contrast, low-cost-to-serve customers purchase standard products, place orders and schedule deliveries on a predictable cycle, and require little or no presales or post-sales support.

Look inside first

After reviewing the profitability of individual customers, the business marketer can consider possible strategies to retain the most valuable customers and to transform unprofitable customers into profitable ones. However, managers should first examine their company's own internal processes to ensure that it can accommodate customer preferences for reduced order sizes or special services at the lowest cost. For example, a large publisher of business directories reduced the cost of serving its customer base by assigning key account managers to its largest customers (that is, the 4 per cent of customers who accounted for 45 per cent of its sales) and serving the smallest customers over the Internet and by a telephone sales force.* These actions not only cut costs dramatically but also gave each group of customers what they had wanted all along: Large customers wanted a central point of contact where they could secure services customised to their needs; small customers preferred minimal contact with a direct salesperson but wanted the assurance that they could receive advice and support if required.

A sharper profit lens

Business marketing managers can view their customers through the lens of a simple 2 × 2 diagram (Figure 3.4). The vertical axis shows the net margin earned from sales to a particular

TABLE 3.1   The characteristics of high- versus low-cost-to-serve customers

	High-Cost-to-Serve Customers	Low-Cost-to-Serve Customers
Presale Costs	Extensive presales support required (i.e., technical and sales resources)	Limited presales support (i.e., standard pricing and ordering)
Production Costs	Order custom products Small order quantities Unpredictable ordering pattern Manual processing	Order standard products Large order quantities Predictable ordering cycle Electronic processing
Delivery Costs	Fast delivery	Standard delivery
Post-sale Service Costs	Extensive post-sales support required (i.e., customer training, installation, technical support)	Limited post-sales support

Source: Adapted, with modifications, from Robert S. Kaplan and V. G. Narayanan, "Measuring and Managing Customer Profitability," *Journal of Cost Management* 15 (September/October 2001): p. 8 and Benson P. Shapiro, V. Kasturi Rangan, Rowland Moriarty, Jr., and Elliot B. Ross, "Manage Customers for Profits (Not Just Sales)," *Harvard Business Review* 65 (September–October 1987): pp. 101–108.

FIGURE 3.4

Customer profitability

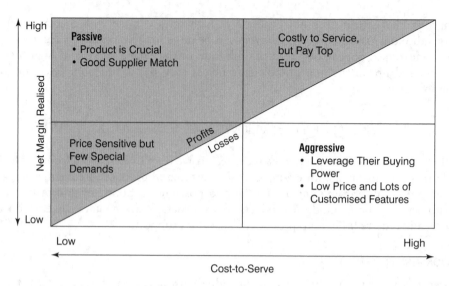

customer. The **net margin** equals the net price, after all discounts, minus manufacturing costs. The horizontal axis shows the **costs of serving the customer**, including order-related costs plus the customer-specific marketing, technical, and administrative expenses.

Identifying profitable customers

Observe from Figure 3.4 that profitable customers can take different forms. To illustrate, a customer like Honda would be at the lower left corner of the diagram: demanding low prices, so net margins are low, but also working with its suppliers to streamline activities so that the cost-to-serve is also low. High-cost-to-serve customers who occupy the upper right corner of Figure 3.4 can also be profitable if the net margins earned on sales to them more than compensate the company for the cost of the resources used in serving them.

A company is indeed fortunate if several of its customers occupy the upper left-hand quadrant of the diagram: high margins *and* low cost-to-serve. Because these customers represent a valuable asset, marketing managers should forge close relationships with them, anticipate their changing needs, and have protective measures (for example, special services) in place in case competitors attempt to win them away.

3.3.5 Managing unprofitable customers[*]

The most challenging set of customers for marketing managers is found in the lower right-hand corner of Figure 3.4: low margins and high cost-to-serve. First, the marketing manager should explore possible ways to reduce the cost of activities associated with serving these customers. For example, perhaps post-sales support could be shifted to the Internet. Second, the manager should direct attention to the customer actions that contribute to higher selling costs. To illustrate, the high cost-to-serve may be caused by the customer's unpredictable ordering patterns or by the large demands it places on technical and sales personnel. By detailing the costs of these activities and openly sharing this information with the customer, the business marketing manager can encourage the customer to work with the company more efficiently.

INSIDE BUSINESS MARKETING

The B2B Sales Experience

When it comes to building valuable relationships with customers in the business-to-business market, sales representatives are critical players on the front lines. But are they getting the basics right? Customers want to be contacted just enough, not bombarded. Sales representatives should know their products or services intimately and know how their offerings compare with those of their competitors. Customers need information on exactly how a product or service will make a difference to their businesses. And while they may say price is one of their biggest concerns, a satisfying sales experience is ultimately more important.

These were the key findings of a survey McKinsey conducted of more than 1 200 purchasing decision makers in small, medium and large companies throughout the United States and Western Europe who are responsible for buying high-tech products and services. The insights were consistent across simple to complex products and apply readily to most B2B industries, which also have complex, multi-touch point sales processes involving both end users and purchasing professionals.

The McKinsey study found a big difference between what customers said was important and what actually drove their behaviour. Customers insisted price and product aspects were the dominant factors that influenced their opinions of a supplier's performance and, as a result, their purchasing decisions. Yet, when the researchers examined what actually determined how customers rated a vendor's overall performance, the most important factors were product or service features and the overall sales experience. The upside of getting these two elements right is significant: a primary supplier seen as having a high-performing sales force can boost its share of a customer's business by an average of 12 percentage points.

That makes the next finding all the more important. Of the many habits that undermine the sales experience, two that are relatively easy to remedy accounted for 55 per cent of the behaviour customers described as 'most destructive' – failing to have adequate product knowledge and contacting customers too frequently. Only 3 per cent of the respondents said they weren't contacted enough, suggesting customers are open to fewer, more meaningful interactions.

Fortunately, both damaging habits can be fixed. Companies can address a lack of product knowledge by centralising content development to guarantee a uniform message and creation of compelling value propositions for customers. And to ensure deep understanding, sales representatives can receive experiential training and on-the-job coaching, preferably side by side with the content-development team. Finally, sales representatives don't need to know everything. When it comes to specifics, the study found that customers were more than happy to use online tools and selectively tap specialist support for the most complex situations.

Striking the right balance between contacting customers too much and too little requires understanding of their stated and actual needs. There should be a clear strategy for reaching out to customers based on needs and profit potential, with schedules dictating frequency. The best contact calendars centre on events that create value for customers, such as semi-annual business reviews, which provide an opportunity to assess customer needs and ensure satisfaction. The key is to recognise that customers are also looking to lower their interaction costs, so any contact with them must be meaningful.

In general, B2B customers say they care most about product and price, but what they really want is a great sales experience. For sales professionals, that means getting the basics right. Companies should examine exactly how they are performing by asking the following questions, 'What are the most influential drivers of the sales experience?' 'What things are your sellers doing that could damage relationships?' and 'How does the perception your customers have of your sales force compare to how they view your competitors?' It is only by knowing and understanding the answers to these questions that companies can begin to identify and pursue corrective action.*

3.3.6 Firing customers

By improving processes and refining pricing strategies, business marketing managers can transform many, but not all, customers from unprofitable to profitable. What should we do with those unprofitable customers that remain in the high-cost-to-serve quadrant of Figure 3.4? To answer this question, we have to dig deeper into the customer relationship and assess the other benefits that certain customers may provide. Some customers are new, and the initial investment to attract them will ultimately be repaid in higher sales volume and profitability. Other customers provide an opportunity for learning. For example, some firms that serve Toyota or Honda incurred initial losses in serving these demanding customers but secured insights into management processes and technology they could effectively apply to all their customers.

Suppose, however, that a customer is unprofitable, not new, and offers little or no opportunity for learning. Furthermore, suppose that the customer resists all attempts to convert the unprofitable relationship into a profitable one. Under these conditions, Robert S. Kaplan and Robin Cooper observe that we might consider firing them, but a more subtle approach will do: "We can, perhaps, let the customer fire itself by refusing to grant discounts and reducing or eliminating marketing and technical support."[*] Customer divestment is a viable strategic option, but one that must be exercised sparingly and only after other options have been thoroughly examined.[*]

3.4 CUSTOMER RELATIONSHIP MANAGEMENT

Customer retention has always been crucial to success in the business market, and it now provides the centrepiece of strategy discussions as firms embrace customer relationship management. **Customer relationship management (CRM)** aims to increase profitability by identifying the best customers within targeted segments, developing ongoing relationships and satisfying their needs in order to encourage these customers to remain loyal and keep returning.[*] The aim is to enhance the life time value to a company of a particular customer.[*] CRM provides the framework for achieving coordination between marketing, customer service and quality programmes.

To meet these challenging requirements, business marketing firms, large and small, are making substantial investments in CRM systems—enterprise software applications that integrate sales, marketing, and customer service information. To improve service and retain customers, CRM systems synthesise information from all of a company's contact points or "touch points"—including e-mail, call centres, sales and service representatives—to support later customer interactions and to inform market forecasts, product design, and supply chain management.[*] Salespersons, call centre personnel, Web managers, resellers, and customer service representatives all have the same real-time information on each customer.

For an investment in CRM software to yield positive returns, a firm needs a customer strategy. Strategy experts contend that many CRM initiatives fail because executives mistake CRM software for a marketing strategy. Darrell Rigby and his colleagues contend: "It isn't. CRM is the bundling of customer strategy and processes, supported by relevant software, for the purpose of improving customer loyalty and, eventually, corporate profitability."[*] CRM software can help, but only after a customer strategy has been designed and executed. To develop responsive and profitable customer strategies, special attention must be given to five areas: (1) acquiring the right customers, (2) crafting the right value proposition, (3) instituting the best processes, (4) motivating employees, and (5) learning to retain customers (Table 3.2). Observe how CRM technology from leading producers such as Oracle Corporation can be used to capture critical customer data, transform it into valuable information, and distribute it throughout the organisation to support the strategy process from customer acquisition to customer retention. Thus, a well-designed and executed customer strategy, supported by a CRM system, provides the financial payoff.

TABLE 3.2 Creating a customer relationship management strategy

CRM Priorities				
Acquiring the Right Customers	**Crafting the Right Value Proposition**	**Instituting the Best Processes**	**Motivating Employees**	**Learning to Retain Customers**
Critical Tasks				
• Identify your most valuable customers. • Calculate your share of their purchases (wallet) for your goods and services.	• Determine the products or services your customers need today and will need tomorrow. • Assess the products or services that your competitors offer today and tomorrow. • Identify new products or services that you should be offering.	• Research the best way to deliver your products or services to customers. • Determine the service capabilities that must be developed and the technology investments that are required to implement customer strategy.	• Identify the tools your employees need to foster customer relationships. • Earn employee loyalty by investing in training and development and constructing appropriate career paths for employees.	• Understand why customers defect and how to win them back. • Identify the strategies your competitors are using to win your high-value customers.
CRM Technology Can Help				
• Analyse customer revenue and cost data to identify current and future high-value customers. • Target marketing communications to high-value customers.	• Capture relevant product and service behaviour data from customer transactions. • Create new distribution channels. • Develop new pricing models.	• Process transactions faster. • Provide better information to customer contact employees. • Manage logistics and the supply chain more efficiently.	• Align employee incentives and performance measures. • Distribute customer knowledge to employees throughout the organisation.	• Track customer defection and retention levels. • Track customer service satisfaction levels.

Source: Adapted from Darrell K. Rigby, Frederick F. Reichheld, and Phil Schefter, ''Avoid the Four Perils of CRM,'' *Harvard Business Review* 80 (January–February 2002): p. 106.

3.4.1 Acquiring the right customers

Customer relationship management directs attention to two critical assets of the business-to-business firm: its stock of current and potential customer relationships and its collective knowledge of how to select, initiate, develop, and maintain profitable relationships with these customers.[*] Customer portfolio management, then, is the process of creating value across a firm's customer relationships—from transactional to collaborative—with an emphasis on balancing the customer's desired level of relationship against the profitability of doing so.[*]

Account selection requires a clear understanding of customer needs, a tight grasp on the costs of serving different groups of customers, and an accurate forecast of potential profit opportunities. The choice of potential accounts to target is facilitated by an understanding of how different customers define value. **Value**, as defined by James Anderson and James Narus, refers to "the economic, technical, service, and social benefits received by a customer firm in exchange for the price paid for a product offering."[*] By gauging the value of their offerings to different groups of customers, business marketers are better equipped to target accounts and to determine how to provide enhanced value to particular customers.

The account selection process should also consider profit potential. Because the product is critical to their operations, some customers place a high value on supporting services (for example, technical advice and training) and are willing to pay a premium price for them. Other customers are most costly to serve, do not value service support, and are extremely price sensitive. Because customers have different needs and represent different levels of current and potential opportunities, a marketer should divide its customers into groups. The marketer wishes to develop a broader and deeper relationship with the most profitable ones and assign a low priority to the least profitable ones.[*] Frank Cespedes asserts that "account selection, therefore, must be explicit about which demands the seller can meet and leverage in dealings with other customers. Otherwise, the seller risks overserving unprofitable accounts and wasting resources that might be allocated to other customer groups."[*]

3.4.2 Crafting the right value proposition

A **value proposition** represents the products, services, ideas, and solutions that a business marketer offers to advance the performance goals of the customer organisation. As noted previously, the customer value proposition must address this essential question: How do the value elements (benefits) in a supplier's offering compare to those of the next-best alternative? A value proposition may include points of parity (certain value elements are the same as the next-best option) and points of difference (the value elements that make the supplier's offering either superior or inferior to the next-best alternative). For example, a supplier may offer improved technology (positive) at a higher price (negative) and fail to convince customers that the new technology justifies the price increase: "Best-practice suppliers base their value proposition on the few elements that matter most to target customers, demonstrate the value of this superior performance, and communicate it in a way that conveys a sophisticated understanding of the customer's business priorities."[*]

The bandwidth of strategies

To develop customer-specific product offerings, the business marketer should next examine the nature of buyer–seller relationships in the industry. The strategies competing firms in an industry pursue fall into a range referred to as the industry bandwidth of working relationships.[*] Business marketers either attempt to span the bandwidth with a portfolio of relationship-marketing strategies or concentrate on a single strategy, thereby having a narrower range of relationships than the industry bandwidth.

Observe in Figure 3.5 how two different industries (medical equipment and hospital supplies) are positioned on the relationship continuum. Because the underlying technology is complex and dynamic, collaborative relations characterise the medical equipment industry. Here, a range of services—technical support, installation, professional training, and maintenance agreements— can augment the core product. By contrast, collaborative relations in hospital supply industry tend

FIGURE 3.5 Transactional and collaborative working relationships

(a) Industry Relationship Bandwidths

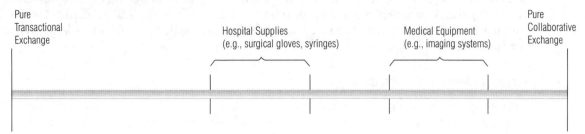

(b) "Flaring Out" from the Industry Bandwidth

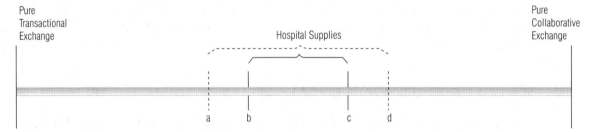

Source: Adapted from James C. Anderson and James A. Narus, "Partnering as a Focused Marketing Strategy," *California Management Review* 33 (Spring 1991): p. 97.

to be more focused and centre on helping health-care organisations meet their operational needs (for example, efficient ordering processes and timely delivery).

By diagnosing the spectrum of relationship strategies competitors in an industry follow, a business marketer can tailor strategies that more closely respond both to customers who desire a collaborative emphasis and to those who seek a transaction emphasis. The strategy involves *flaring out* from the industry bandwidth in the collaborative as well as in the transactional direction (see Figure 3.5b).

Flaring out by unbundling

An unbundling strategy can reach customers who desire a greater transaction emphasis. Here, related services are unbundled to yield the core product (**a** in Figure 3.5b), which meets a customer's basic price, quality, and availability requirements. For each service that is unbundled, the price is lowered. Augmented services, such as technical assistance, consulting, and just-in-time delivery, are each offered, but in a menu fashion, on an incremental price basis. Importantly, the price increments for the entire set of unbundled services should be greater than the price premium sought for the collaborative offering. This reflects the efficiencies of providing the complete bundle of services to a collaborative account. This pricing policy is market oriented in that it allows customer firms to choose the product and relationship offering that *they perceive* to provide the greatest value.

Flaring out with augmentation

At the other extreme, the collaborative offering (**d** in Figure 3.5b) becomes the augmented product enriched with features the customer values. Augmented features might include coordinated cost-reduction programmes, technical assistance, delivery schedule guarantees, and cooperative advertising. Because collaborative efforts are designed to add value or reduce the costs of exchange between partnering firms, a price premium should be received for the collaborative offering.

Allegiance Healthcare Corporation has developed ways to improve hospital supply ordering, delivery, and billing that provide enhanced value to the customer.* Instead of miscellaneous supplies arriving in boxes sorted at the convenience of Allegiance's needs, they arrive on "client-friendly" pallets customised to meet the distribution needs of the individual hospital. Moreover, hospitals can secure a structural connection to Allegiance through its ValueLink ordering system for added value and convenience.

Creating flexible service offerings

Business marketers can gain a competitive edge by creating a portfolio of service offerings and then drawing on this portfolio to provide customised solutions for groups of customers or even individual customers.* First, an offering should be created that includes the bare-bones-minimum number of services valued by all customers in a particular market segment. Microsoft refers to these offerings as "naked solutions." Second, optional services are created that add value by reducing costs or improving the performance of a customer's operations. To meet the needs of particular customers, optional services can then be "custom wrapped" with the core offering to create added value.

3.4.3 Instituting the best processes

The sales force assumes a central relationship–management role in the business market. Technical service and customer service personnel also assume implementation roles that are important and visible in buying organisations. Successful relationship strategies are shaped by an effective organisation and deployment of the personal selling effort and close coordination with supporting units, such as logistics and technical service. Some firms divide the sales organisation into units that each serve a distinct relationship category such as transactional accounts or partnership accounts. Through a careful screening process, promising transaction accounts are periodically upgraded to partnerships.

Best practices at IBM*

In serving a particular customer, a number of IBM employees come into contact with the customer organisation. To ensure consistent strategy execution, IBM identifies three customer-contact roles for each of its accounts, specifies desired measurable actions for each role, and monitors the customer's degree of satisfaction with each role (Table 3.3). The IBM client representative assigned to the customer is the *relationship owner*, but the account team may include other specialists who complete a project for the customer (*project owner*) or solve a particular customer problem (*problem resolution owner*). Any IBM employee who works on the account can secure timely information from the CRM system to identify recent actions or issues to be addressed. Moreover, for each role, there is an in-process measure and a customer feedback measure.

Consider an IBM technical manager assigned responsibility for installing CRM software for a large bank. As a project owner, this manager's goal is to determine the customer's conditions of satisfaction and then exceed those expectations. When the work is completed, members of the customer organisation are queried concerning their satisfaction and the project owner acts on the feedback to ensure that all promises have been kept. Clearly, a sound complaint management process is essential. Recent research found that if a complaint is ineffectively handled, the firm faces a high risk of losing *even* those customers who had previously been very satisfied.*

Research suggests that the performance attributes that influence the customer satisfaction of business buyers include:

- The responsiveness of the supplier in meeting the firm's needs
- Product quality

TABLE 3.3 Role-based strategy execution at IBM: Measured actions and results

Role	Strategy Goal	Measured Actions	Measured Results (Customer)
Relationship Owner	Improve Customer Relationships	Meet with customer twice per year to identify customer's expectations and set action plan	IBM Customer Satisfaction Survey Results
Project Owner	Exceed Customer Expectations for Each Transaction	Collect conditions of satisfaction, get customer feedback	IBM Transaction Survey Results
Problem Resolution	Fix Customer Problems	Solve in seven days or meet action plan	Customer Satisfaction with Problem Resolution

Source: Adapted from Larry Schiff, "How Customer Satisfaction Improvement Works to Fuel Business Recovery at IBM," *Journal of Organizational Excellence* (Spring 2001): pp. 12–14.

- A broad product line
- Delivery reliability
- Knowledgeable sales and service personnel[*]

3.4.4 Motivating employees

Dedicated employees are the cornerstone of a successful customer relationship strategy. As Frederick F. Reichheld notes:

> Leaders who are dedicated to treating people right drive themselves to deliver superior value, which allows them to attract and retain the best employees. That's partly because higher profits result from customer retention, but more important, it's because providing excellent service and value generates pride and a sense of purpose among employees.[*]

Employee loyalty is earned by investing heavily in training and development, providing challenging career paths to facilitate professional development, and aligning employee incentives to performance measures.[*]

Research clearly demonstrates the link between salespeople's job satisfaction and customer satisfaction in business markets. Christian Homburg and Ruth M. Stock report that the relationship between salespeople's job satisfaction is particularly strong when there is a high frequency of customer interaction, high intensity of customer integration into the value-creating process, and high product or service innovativeness.[*]

3.4.5 Learning to retain customers

Business marketers track customer loyalty and retention because the cost of serving a long-standing customer is often far less than the cost of acquiring a new customer.[*] Why? Established customers often buy more products and services from a trusted supplier, and, as they do, the cost of serving them declines. The firm learns how to serve them more efficiently and also spots opportunities for expanding the relationship. Thus, the profit from that customer tends to increase over the life of the relationship. To that end, a goal for IBM is to gain an increasing share of a customer's total information technology expenditures (that is, share of wallet). Rather than merely attempting to improve satisfaction ratings, IBM seeks to be recognised as providing superior value to its customers. Larry Schiff, an IBM strategist, notes: "If you delight your customers and are perceived to provide the best value in your market, you'll gain loyalty and market/wallet share."* Although loyal customers are likely to be satisfied, all satisfied customers do not remain loyal. Business marketers earn customer loyalty by providing superior value that ensures high satisfaction and by nurturing trust and mutual commitments.

Pursuing growth from existing customers

Business marketers should identify a well-defined set of existing customers who demonstrate growth potential and selectively pursue a greater share of their business. Based on the cost-to-serve and projected profit margins, the question becomes: Which of our existing customers represent the best growth prospects? In targeting individual customers, particular attention should be given to: (1) estimating the current share of wallet the firm has attained; (2) pursuing opportunities to increase that share; and (3) carefully projecting the enhanced customer profitability that will result.*

Evaluating relationships

Some relationship-building efforts fail because the expectations of the parties do not mesh—for example, when the business marketer follows a relationship approach and the customer responds in a transaction mode. By isolating customer needs and the costs of augmented service features, the marketer is better equipped to profitably match product offerings to the particular customer's needs.

The goal of a relationship is to enable the buyer and seller to maximise joint value. This points to the need for a formal evaluation of relationship outcomes. For example, sales executives at best-practice firms work closely with their partnership accounts to establish mutually defined goals. After an appropriate period, partnerships that do not meet these goals are downgraded and shifted from the strategic market sales force to the geographic sales force.

Business marketers should also continually update the value of their product and relationship offering. Attention here should centre on particular new services that might be incorporated as well as on existing services that might be unbundled or curtailed. Working relationships with customer firms are among the most important marketing assets of the firm. They deserve delicate care and continual nurturing!

3.5 RELATIONSHIP MARKETING SUCCESS*

Assuming a central role in implementing the customer relationship marketing (RM) strategy for the business-to-business firm is the salesperson. Firm-to-firm relationships in the business market involve multiple interactions among individuals, forming a network of relationships. To ensure that customers are as satisfied as possible, business marketers must effectively manage the complex web of influences that intersect in buyer–seller relationships.*

Figure 3.6 provides a model of interfirm relationship marketing. **Relationship marketing activities** represent dedicated relationship marketing programmes, developed and implemented to build strong relational bonds. These activities influence three important drivers of relationship marketing effectiveness—relationship quality, breadth, and composition—each capturing a different dimension of the relationship and exerting a positive influence on the seller's performance activity.

FIGURE 3.6 A model of interfirm relationship marketing

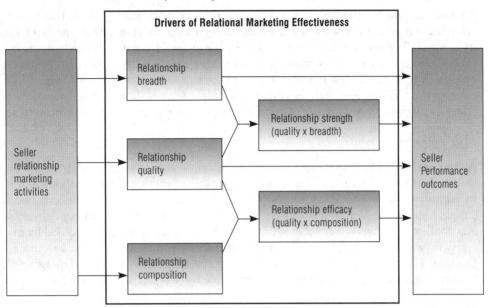

3.5.1 Drivers of relationship marketing effectiveness

Some customer relationships are characterised by extensive interactions and close bonds among members of the buying and selling organisations. By contrast, other relationships might be confined to a few relational ties that the salesperson has developed with members of the purchasing staff. Drawing on insights from social network theory, the following drivers of relational marketing effectiveness have been identified.

Relationship quality

Relationship quality represents a high-calibre relational bond with an exchange partner that captures a number of interaction characteristics such as commitment and trust. "Commitment represents a desire to maintain a valued relationship and, thus, an exchange partner's relationship motivation toward a partner. Trust involves the evaluation of a partner's reliability and integrity, which generates confidence in the partner's future actions that support cooperation."[*] Partners involved in high-quality, committed relationships are willing to disclose proprietary information, which enables sellers to identify the customer's unmet needs, cross-sell additional products more effectively, and price products properly, thereby enhancing profitability.

Relationship breadth

A key objective of the business marketer is to develop a keen understanding of a customer's needs in order to develop a value proposition that squarely addresses those needs. **Relationship breadth** represents the number of interpersonal ties that a firm has with an exchange partner. A seller that has forged more interpersonal ties with a customer can gain better access to information, identify profit-enhancing opportunities, and become more efficient in building and maintaining the relationship. Research indicates that multiple interfirm ties are particularly vital when serving customer organisations that have high employee turnover.[*]

Relationship composition

Relationship composition centres on the decision-making capability of relational contacts at the customer firm; a contact portfolio that includes high-level decision makers increases a seller's ability to effect change in customer organisations. For example, greater authority in the contact portfolio allows a salesperson to access information, adapt offerings, and reach influential decision makers. A competitor who has access only to contacts with less authority faces difficult odds in winning the account. Research suggests that building relationships with key decision makers generates the highest returns among customer organisations that are the most difficult to access.[*]

Relationship strength

A clear portrait of a buyer–seller relationship will consider both relationship quality and relationship breadth. (See Figure 3.6.) Therefore, **relationship strength** reflects the ability of a relationship to withstand stress and/or conflict, such that multiple, high-quality relational bonds result in strong, resilient relationships. A service failure, like equipment failure or poor delivery service, creates conflict in a buyer–seller relationship. A customer relationship characterised by many cursory contacts (greater breadth, low quality) will afford little protection to the seller during this period of stress. However, based on confidence (trust), multiple, high-quality relationship ties (greater breadth, high quality) will support the seller during the service recovery process.

Relationship efficacy

Representing the interaction between relationship quality and relationship composition, **relationship efficacy** captures the ability of an interfirm relationship to achieve desired objectives. High-quality relationships with members of the customer organisation, coupled with a well-structured and diverse contact portfolio, gives sellers the means to execute responsive strategy. Robert W. Palmatier observes that a "portfolio might encompass high-quality, broad relationships but it suffers if those contacts are restricted to one functional area with little decision-making (low composition) because the seller lacks access to divergent (nonredundant) information and cannot promote customer change."[*]

3.5.2 Relationship Marketing (RM) programmes

To strengthen relational ties with customers, three types of relationship marketing programmes are employed.

- **Social RM programmes** use social engagements (for example, meals and sporting events) or frequent, customised communication to personalise the relationship and highlight the customer's special status. The relational bonds that result from this specialised treatment are difficult for rivals to duplicate and may prompt customers to reciprocate in the form of repeat sales and positive recommendations of the seller to others.

- **Structural RM programmes** are designed to increase productivity and/or efficiency for customers through targeted investments that customers would not likely make themselves. For example, the seller might provide an electronic order-processing interface of customised packaging for the customer. By offering unique benefits and, in the case of electronic ordering, a structural bond, these programmes create competitive advantages and discourage customers from switching to competitors.

- **Financial RM programmes** provide economic benefits, such as special discounts, free shipping, or extended payment terms, to increase customer loyalty. Because competitors can readily match the economic incentives, the advantages tend to be unsustainable.

Such relationship marketing investments generate customer feelings of gratitude, which lead to gratitude-based reciprocal behaviours, resulting in enhanced seller performance.[*]

3.5.3 Financial impact of RM programmes[*]

Do RM programmes pay off? A recent study measured the incremental profits generated by RM programmes to isolate the return on investment (ROI).

Social

In evaluating the short-term financial returns of the different RM strategies, the study found that social RM investments have a direct and significant (approximately 180 per cent) impact on profit—far greater than the impact of structural or financial RM programmes. For the customer, social programmes create a feeling of interpersonal debt, stimulating a pressing need to reciprocate and thereby generating immediate returns. Yet, Robert Palmatier observes: "Social programmes may cause customers to think highly of the salesperson rather than the selling firm, which increases the risk that the selling firm loses the customer if the salesperson leaves. Therefore, the selling firm should keep other avenues open for direct communication with customers."[*]

Structural

The financial impact of structural RM programmes (for example, providing a value-enhancing linkage) depends on the frequency of interaction a firm has with customers. While break-even returns are achieved for customers with average interaction frequency, the return on structural RM investment is approximately 120 per cent for those customers who receive frequent contact from the seller. As a result, the business marketing strategist should target those customers for whom structural solutions offer the most value. Moreover, while merely breaking even in the short term, structural linkages like electronic order processing should increase long-term profits because customers are inclined to take advantage of the value provided.

Financial

Since economic incentives often attract "deal-prone" customers and are easy for rivals to match, financial RM programmes generally fail to generate positive economic returns. Of course, such programmes (for example, special discounts) may represent a necessary response to a competitive threat that is needed to protect existing customer relationships. By contrast, social and structural RM programmes are offensive weapons that provide greater financial returns and a more durable competitive advantage.

3.5.4 Targeting RM programmes[*]

Some customers are more receptive to relationship marketing initiatives than others. As purchasing managers emphasise cost-reducing and productivity-enhancing objectives, they carefully scrutinise the time and effort that can be invested in particular supplier relationships. **Relationship orientation** (RO) represents the customer's desire to engage in strong relationships with a current or potential supplier. "Customers tend to be more ... open to relationship building when they face some risk, uncertainty, or dependence in the exchange process or are very motivated about the product or service category. In these situations, customers find the expertise, added flexibility, and risk-reduction benefits of a relationship valuable and likely welcome the seller's relationship efforts."[*]

Allocating RM resources

Research demonstrates that the returns on RM investments improve if business marketers are able to target customers on the basis of their RO rather than size. For example, salespeople report higher returns for their RM efforts directed toward buyers with the highest self-reported RO than for those with the lowest RO. Importantly, the study reveals a separate strategy that can be used effectively for customers who demonstrate a *low* RO. These customers would shift 21 per cent of their business to another supplier of similar products if the transaction were completely automated (that is, if no salesperson was involved). This suggests that the business marketer could drastically lower costs and better serve some customers by accurately detecting those with a low RO and offering them the option of using an electronic ordering interface. By properly aligning RM resources to the needs of customers, the salesperson can direct attention to those customers who are most receptive to relationship-building efforts.

SUMMARY

Relationships, rather than simple transactions, provide the central focus in business marketing. By demonstrating superior skills in managing relationships with key customers as well as with alliance partners, business marketing firms can create a collaborative advantage.

To develop profitable relationships with customers, business marketers must first understand the different forms that exchange relationships can take. Transactional exchange centres on the timely exchange of basic products and services for highly competitive market prices. By contrast, collaborative exchange involves very close personal, informational, and operational connections the parties develop to achieve long-term mutual goals. Across the relationship spectrum, different types of relationships feature different relationship connectors. For example, collaborative relationships for important purchases emphasise operational linkages that integrate the operations of the buying and selling organisations and involve high levels of information exchange.

Activity-based costing provides a solid foundation for measuring and managing the profitability of individual customers. When the full costs of serving customers are known, many companies find that 15 to 20 per cent of the customers generate 100 per cent (or much more) of the profits, a large group of customers break even, and 5

to 10 per cent of the customers generate sizable losses. By measuring the cost-to-serve and the net profit from individual customers, business marketing managers can take actions to transform unprofitable relationships into profitable ones through process improvements, menu-based pricing, or relationship management.

Customer relationship management involves aligning customer strategy and business processes for the purpose of improving customer loyalty and, eventually, corporate profitability. To that end, a customer strategy encompasses: (1) acquiring the right customers, (2) crafting the right value proposition, (3) instituting the best processes, (4) motivating employees, and (5) learning to retain customers.

Relationship marketing (RM) activities represent dedicated relationship marketing programmes, developed and implemented to build strong relational bonds with customers. These activities influence the three important drivers of RM effectiveness—relationship quality, breadth, and composition. To strengthen relational ties with customers, three types of RM programmes are used: social, structural, and financial. Returns on RM investments improve when business marketers are able to target customers on the basis of their relationship orientation rather than size.

DISCUSSION QUESTIONS

1   Why is there a close relationship between marketing and CRM? What is involved in building the customer experience?

2   What are the problem areas for CRM? Critically defend CRM as a viable method despite the problems.

3   Make a short questionnaire (of approximately five questions) to measure the extent to which a company's relationship marketing efforts have been successful.

4   How can you measure customer profitability? If a customer is unprofitable, what can you do to make them profitable?

5   Why is it important to motivate employees and how can it affect relationships with customers?

INTERNET EXERCISES

Log on to BUPA's website. This provider of healthcare and health insurance targets both consumers and business clients. Look at the information BUPA provides for Individuals (consumers) and for Business (corporate clients).

http://www.bupa.co.uk

1 What are the key BUPA service products offered to private consumers and to business clients?

2 How are BUPA's messages about its products tailored to reflect the different needs and buying behaviour of its consumers and business clients?

REFERENCES

Anderson, James C., and Narus, James A. "Partnering as a Focused Market Strategy," *California Management Review* 33 (Spring 1991): p. 96.

Anderson, James C., and Narus, James A., "Capturing the Value of Supplementary Services," *Harvard Business Review* 73 (January–February 1995): pp. 75–83.

Anderson, James C., and Narus, James A., "Selectively Pursuing More of Your Customer's Business," *MIT Sloan Management Review* 44 (Spring 2003): pp. 42–49.

Anderson, James C., Narus, James A., and van Rossum, Wouter, "Customer Value Propositions in Business Markets," *Harvard Business Review* 84 (March 2006): p. 93.

Bensaou, M., "Portfolio of Buyer–Seller Relationships," *Sloan Management Review* 40 (Summer 1999): p. 43.

Beutin, Nikolas, "Understanding Customer Value in Business-to-Business Relationships," *Journal of Business-to-Business Marketing* 12 (2, 2005): pp. 1–33.

Bolton, Ruth N., Lemon, Katherine N., and Verhoof, Peter, "Expanding Business-to-Business Customer Relationships," *Journal of Marketing* 72 (January 2008): pp. 46–64.

Bowman, Douglas and Narayandas, Das, "Linking Customer Management Effort to Customer Profitability in Business Markets," *Journal of Marketing Research* 41 (November 2004): pp. 433–447.

Bund Jackson, Barbara, "Build Customer Relationships That Last," *Harvard Business Review* 63 (November–December 1985): p. 125.

Cannon, Joseph P., and Perreault Jr., William D., "Buyer-Seller Relationships in Business Markets," *Journal of Marketing Research* 36 (November 1999): pp. 439–460.

Cespedes, Frank V., *Concurrent Marketing: Integrating Product, Sales, and Service* (Boston: Harvard Business School Press, 1995), p. 193.

Comstock, Beth, Gulati, Ranjay, and Liguori, Stephen, "Unleashing the Power of Marketing," *Harvard Business Review* 88 (October 2010): pp. 1800–1808.

Day, George S., "Managing Market Relationships," *Journal of the Academy of Marketing Science* 28 (Winter 2000): pp. 24–30.

Day, George S., "Creating a Superior Customer-Relating Capability," *MIT Sloan Management Review* 44 (Spring 2003): pp. 77–82.

Dibb, Sally, Simkin, Lyndon, Pride, Bill, and Ferrell, O.C., *Marketing Concepts & Strategies*, 6th ed. (Cengage, 2012).

Doney, Patricia M., and Cannon, Joseph P. "An Examination of the Nature of Trust in Buyer-Seller Relationships," *Journal of Marketing* 61 (April 1997): pp. 35–51.

Doole, Isobel, and Lowe, Robin, *International Marketing Strategy* 6th ed. (Cengage, 2012).

Homburg, Christian, and Fürst, Andreas, "How Organizational Complaint Handling Drives Customer Loyalty: An Analysis of the Mechanistic and the Organic Approach," *Journal of Marketing* 69 (July 2005): pp. 95–114.

Homburg, Christian, and Stock, Ruth M., "The Link Between Salespeople's Job Satisfaction and Customer Satisfaction in a Business-to-Business Context: A Dyadic Analysis," *Journal of the Academy of Marketing Science* 32 (Spring 2004): pp. 144–158.

Homburg, Christian, and Stock, Ruth M., "Exploring the Conditions under Which Salesperson Work Satisfaction Can Lead to Customer Satisfaction," *Psychology and Marketing* 22 (5, 2005): pp. 393–420.

Homburg, Christian, Steiner, Viviana V., and Totzek, Dirk, "Managing Dynamics in a Customer Portfolio," *Journal of Marketing* 73 (September 2009): pp. 70–89.

Johnson, Michael D. and Selnes, Fred, "Diversifying Your Customer Portfolio," *MIT Sloan Management Review* 46 (Spring 2005): pp. 11–14.

Kanter, Rosabeth Moss, "Collaborative Advantage," *Harvard Business Review* 72 (July–August 1994): pp. 96–108.

Kaplan, Robert S., and Anderson, Steven R., "Time-Driven Activity-Based Costing," *Harvard Business Review* 82 (November 2004): pp. 131–138.

Kaplan, Robert S., "Add a Customer Profitability Metric to Your Balanced Scorecard," *Balanced Scorecard Report*, July–August 2005 (Boston: Harvard Business School Publishing Corporation): p. 3.

Kaplan, Robert S., and Cooper, Robin, *Cost and Effect: Using Integrated Cost Systems to Drive Profitability and Performance* (Boston: Harvard Business School Press, 1998), pp. 193–201.

Kaplan, Robert S., and Narayanan, V.G., "Measuring and Managing Customer Profitability," *Journal of Cost Management* 15 (5, September–October 2001): pp. 5–15.

Kaplan, Robert S., and Norton, David P., *The Execution Premium* (Boston: Harvard Business Press, 2008): pp. 255–261.

Mittal, Vikas, Sarkees, Matthew, and Murshed, Feisal, "The Right Way to Manage Unprofitable Customers," *Harvard Business Review* 86 (April 2008): pp. 95–102.

Morgan, Robert M. and Hunt, Shelby D., "The Commitment-Trust Theory of Relationship Marketing," *Journal of Marketing* 58 (July 1994): pp. 20–38.

Moutinho, Luiz, and Southern, Geoffrey, *Strategic Marketing Management: A process Based Approach* (Cengage, 2012).

Narayandas, Das, and Kasturi Rangan, V., "Building and Sustaining Buyer–Seller Relationships in Mature Industrial Markets," *Journal of Marketing* 68 (July 2004): p. 74.

Palmatier, Robert W., "Interfirm Relational Drivers of Customer Value," *Journal of Marketing* 72 (July 2008a): p. 77.

Palmatier, Robert W., *Relationship Marketing* (Boston: Marketing Science Institute, 2008b).

Palmatier, Robert W., Burke Jarvis, Cheryl, Bechkoff, Jennifer R., and Kardes, Frank R., "The Role of Customer Gratitude in Relationship Marketing," *Journal of Marketing* 73 (September 2009): pp. 1–18.

Palmatier, Robert W., Gopalakrishna, Srinath, and Houston, Mark B., "Returns on Business-to-Business Relationship Marketing Investments: Strategies for Leveraging Profits," *Marketing Science* 25 (September–October 2006): pp. 477–493.

Palmatier, Robert W., Scheer, Lisa K., and Steenkamp, Jan-Benedict E. M., "Customer Loyalty to Whom? Managing the Benefits and Risks of Salesperson-Owned Loyalty," *Journal of Marketing Research* 44 (May 2007): pp. 185–199.

Palmatier, Robert W., Scheer, Lisa K., Evans, Kenneth R., and Arnold, Todd J., "Achieving Relationship Marketing Effectiveness in Business-to-Business Exchanges," *Journal of the Academy of Marketing Science* 36 (June 2008): pp. 174–190.

Peppers, Don, Rogers, Martha, and Dorf, Bob, "Is Your Company Ready for One-to-One Marketing?" *Harvard Business Review* 77 (January–February 1999): pp. 151–160.

Reichheld, Frederick F., "Lead for Loyalty," *Harvard Business Review* 79 (July–August 2001): pp. 76–84.

Rickard, David, "The Joys of Bundling: Assessing the Benefits and Risks," The Boston Consulting Group, Inc., 2008, http://www.bcg.com, accessed May 15, 2008.

Rigby, Darrell K., Reichheld, Frederick F., and Schefter, Phil, "Avoid the Four Perils of CRM," *Harvard Business Review* 80 (January–February 2002): p. 102.

Rigby, Reichheld, and Schefter, "Avoid the Four Perils of CRM," p. 104.

Schiff, Larry, "How Customer Satisfaction Improvement Works to Fuel Full Business Recovery at IBM," *Journal of Organizational Excellence* 20 (Spring 2001): pp. 3–18.

Srivam, Ven, Krapfel, Robert, and Spekman, Robert, "Antecedents to Buyer–Seller Collaboration: An Analysis from the Buyer's Perspective," *Journal of Business Research* (December 1992): pp. 303–320.

Ulaga, Wolfgang, and Eggert, Andreas, "Value-Based Differentiation in Business Relationships: Gaining and Sustaining Key Supplier Status," *Journal of Marketing* 70 (January 2006): pp. 119–136.

van Weele, Arjan, *Puchasing and Supply Chain Management: Analysis Strategy, Planning and Practice*, 5th ed. (Cengage, 2010).

Verhage, Bronis J., *Marketing: A Global Perspective* (Cengage, 2013).

Yu, Larry, "Successful Customer-Relationship Management," *MIT Sloan Management Review* 42 (Summer 2001): p. 18.

Zeithaml, Valarie A., Rust, Roland T., and Lemon, Katherine N., "The Customer Pyramid: Creating and Serving Profitable Customers," *California Management Review* 43 (Summer 2001): p. 134.

PART III
ASSESSING
MARKET
OPPORTUNITIES

CHAPTER 4
SEGMENTING THE BUSINESS MARKET AND ESTIMATING SEGMENT DEMAND

CHAPTER OBJECTIVES

Marketing strategy revolves around the choice of which opportunities should be pursued and the specification of an appropriate target market strategy. Market segmentation is a fundamental part of marketing strategy, assisting organisations to deal with the fact that not all business customers share identical needs, buying behaviour or product requirements. Limited resources generally result in organisations being unable to serve all of the needs in the market, and marketers must make trade-off choices based on the relative merits of different market segments in determining which groups to prioritise. The business customers in those market segments deemed to be priorities for a company must be communicated with in a manner that emphasises their importance to the company: this is the positioning task. The market segmentation process, therefore, has a number of stages: segmenting, targeting and positioning. Many marketers believe these aspects of marketing are the most important decisions made by marketers. After reading this chapter, you will understand:

1   The benefits of and requirements for segmenting the business market

2   The potential bases for segmenting the business market

3   A procedure for evaluating and selecting market segments

4   The role of market segmentation in the development of business marketing strategy

5   A process for estimating demand in each market segment

6   Specific techniques to effectively develop a forecast of demand

A strategist at Hewlett-Packard notes:

> *Knowing customers' needs is not enough.... We need to know what new products, features, and services will surprise and delight them. We need to understand their world so well that we can bring new technology to problems that customers may not yet truly realise they have.*[*]

High-growth companies, large and small, succeed by:

- Selecting a well-defined group of potentially profitable customers

- Developing a distinctive value proposition (product and/or service offering) that meets these customers' needs better than their competitors

- Focusing marketing resources on acquiring, developing, and retaining profitable customers[*]

The business market consists of four broad sectors—producers, resellers, public sector and governments and institutions. Whether marketers elect to operate in one or all of these sectors, they encounter diverse organisations, purchasing structures, and decision-making styles. Each sector has many segments; each segment may have unique needs and require a unique marketing strategy. For example, some customers demonstrate attractive profit potential and are receptive to a relationship strategy, whereas others adopt a short-term, transaction focus, suggesting the need for a more streamlined strategy response.[*] The business marketer who recognises the needs of the various market segments is best equipped to isolate profitable market opportunities and respond with an effective marketing programme.

The goal of this chapter is to demonstrate how the manager can select and evaluate segments of the business market and then develop accurate estimates of demand. First, the chapter delineates the benefits of and the requirements for successful market segmentation. Second, it explores and evaluates specific bases for segmenting the business market. Third, the chapter provides a framework for evaluating and selecting market segments. Procedures for assessing the costs and benefits of entering alternative market segments and for implementing a segmentation strategy are emphasised. The final section of the chapter examines the demand forecasting process and explains the critical aspects of how business marketers create demand forecasts.

4.1 BUSINESS MARKET SEGMENTATION REQUIREMENTS AND BENEFITS

A **market segment** represents "a group of present or potential customers with some common characteristic which is relevant in explaining (and predicting) their response to a supplier's marketing stimuli."[*] Effective segmentation of markets is the first step in crafting a marketing strategy because the characteristics and needs of each segment will define the direction and focus of the marketing programme. Segmentation that is done well provides the necessary information for understanding what elements of the marketing mix are going to be critical in satisfying the target customers in those segments.

4.1.1 Requirements

Potential customers in a market segment have common characteristics that define what things are important to them and how they will respond to various marketing stimuli. The question for the business marketer is: "what are the key criteria for determining which characteristics best define a unique market segment?" A business marketer has four criteria for evaluating the desirability of potential market segments:

1   *Measurability*—The degree to which information on the particular buyer characteristics exists or can be obtained.

2   *Accessibility*—The degree to which the firm can effectively focus its marketing efforts on chosen segments.

3   *Substantiality*—The degree to which the segments are large or profitable enough to be worth considering for separate marketing cultivation.

4   *Responsiveness*—The degree to which segments respond differently to different marketing mix elements, such as pricing or product features.

In summary, the art of market segmentation involves identifying groups of customers that are large and unique enough to justify a separate marketing strategy. The ultimate goal is to have the greatest amount of difference *between* groups (segments) and high similarities *within* them.[*]

4.1.2 Benefits

If the requirements for effective segmentation are met, several benefits accrue to the firm. First, the mere attempt to segment the business market forces the marketer to become more attuned to the unique needs of customer segments. Second, knowing the needs of particular market segments helps the business marketer focus product-development efforts, develop profitable pricing

---

INSIDE BUSINESS MARKETING

Practitioners' Insights and Techniques

Raytheon

Marketing has played a major part in enabling our business to make fact-based decisions, which have seen a successful change in our strategy. Previously we were the type of business that spread itself 'too thinly', meaning we did not achieve the results we should in our real areas of expertise. By using tried and tested marketing tools, we have identified the attractive markets and equally those not so attractive, to enable us to focus on successfully moving towards the achievement of our vision. Currently we are achieving and forecasting major growth in turnover and profit, which is the result of implementing marketing processes in our business.

The global markets in which our business competes are increasingly competitive and the need for a marketing discipline in implementing marketing strategies is extremely important. Systematically analysing key developments in constantly changing markets and capturing customer needs is vital in providing us with a competitive advantage. Providing key decision-makers with the toolkit, and more importantly the information, to execute winning plans increases the effectiveness of the plans. The value and effectiveness of having the discipline is reflected in the continued success of this business.

Jim Trail, Chief Operating Officer Raytheon Systems Limited

Power & Control Systems is a business within Raytheon Systems Limited, a wholly owned subsidiary of Raytheon Company, and was established in Glenrothes, Fife, in 1960. Core capabilities of the company are the design, development and manufacture of power products for international aerospace, industrial and defence markets.

FIGURE 4.1 The Standard Industrial Classification (SIC) system for categorising industrial consumers

0	Agriculture, forestry and fishing
1	Energy and water supply industries
2	Extraction of minerals and ores other than fuels; manufacture of metals, mineral products and chemicals
3	Metal goods, engineering and vehicles
4	Other manufacturing industries
5	Construction
6	Distribution, hotels and catering; repairs
7	Transport and communication
8	Banking, finance, insurance, business services and leasing
9	Other services

strategies, select appropriate channels of distribution, develop and target advertising messages, and train and deploy the sales force. Thus, market segmentation provides the foundation for efficient and effective business marketing strategies.

Third, market segmentation provides the business marketer with valuable guidelines for allocating marketing resources. Business-to-business firms often serve multiple market segments and must continually monitor their relative attractiveness and performance. Research by Mercer Management Consulting indicates that, for many companies, nearly one-third of their market segments generate no profit and that 30 to 50 per cent of marketing and customer service costs are wasted on efforts to acquire and retain customers in these segments.[*] Ultimately, costs, revenues, and profits must be evaluated segment by segment—and even account by account.

Much information about business customers is based on the **Standard Industrial Classification (SIC) system**, which provides information on different industries and products, and was developed to classify selected economic characteristics of industrial, commercial, financial and service organisations. In the UK, this system is administered by the Office for National Statistics. Figure 4.1 shows how the SIC system can be used to categorise products.

The most recent SIC manual contains 10 broad divisions, each denoted by a single digit from 0 to 9. These are sub-divided into classes (each denoted by the addition of a second digit), the classes are divided into groups (three digits) and the groups into activity headings (four more digits). There are 10 divisions, 60 classes, 222 groups and 334 activity headings. For example, Division 4, 'Other manufacturing industries', has 8 classes, 50 groups and 91 activity headings. The numbering system follows that of NACE (Nomenclature Générale des Activités Économiques dans les Communautés Européennes) as far as possible.[*] To categorise manufacturers in more detail, the *Census of Distribution* further sub-divides manufacturers.

Data are available for each SIC category through various government publications and departments. Some data are available by town, county and metropolitan area. Business market data also appear in such non-government sources as Dun & Bradstreet's *Market Identifiers*.

The SIC system is a ready-made tool that allows business marketers to allocate industrial organisations to market segments based mainly on the type of product manufactured or handled. Although the SIC system is a vehicle for segmentation – identifying groupings of customers – it must be used in conjunction with other types of data to enable a business marketer to determine exactly which customers he or she can reach and how many of them can be targeted. The SIC system is a convenient grouping categorisation, but it does not negate the need to fully explore customer buying behavior, in order to properly consider target market priorities.

4.2 BASES FOR SEGMENTING BUSINESS MARKETS

Whereas the consumer-goods marketer is interested in securing meaningful profiles of individuals (demographics, lifestyle, benefits sought), the business marketer profiles organisations (size, end use) and organisational buyers (decision style, criteria). Thus, the business or organisational market can be segmented on several bases, broadly classified into two major categories: macro-segmentation and microsegmentation.

Macrosegmentation centres on the characteristics of the buying organisation and the buying situation and thus divides the market by such organisational characteristics as size, geographic location, the Standard Industrial Classification (SIC) system, and organisational structure. In contrast, **microsegmentation** requires a higher degree of market knowledge, focusing on the characteristics of decision-making units within each macrosegment—including buying decision criteria, perceived importance of the purchase, and attitudes toward vendors. Strategy experts recommend a two-stage approach to business market segmentation: (1) identify meaningful macrosegments, and then (2) divide the macrosegments into microsegments. [*]

In evaluating alternative bases for segmentation, the marketer is attempting to identify good predictors of differences in buyer behaviour. Once such differences are recognised, the marketer can approach target segments with an appropriate marketing strategy. Secondary sources of information, coupled with data in a firm's information system, can be used to divide the market into macrolevel segments. The concentration of the business market allows some marketers to monitor the purchasing patterns of each customer. For example, a firm that sells component parts to the automobile industry is dealing with a relatively small set of potential customers even on a global scale; an auto manufacturer selling to the end market is dealing with millions of potential customers. Such market concentration, coupled with rapidly advancing customer relationship management systems, makes it easier for business marketers to monitor the buying patterns of individual customer organisations.

4.2.1 Macrolevel bases

Table 4.1 presents selected macrolevel bases of segmentation. Recall that these are concerned with the general characteristics of the buying organisation, the nature of the product application, and the characteristics of the buying situation.

Macrolevel characteristics of buying organisations

A strategist may find it useful to partition the market by size of potential buying organisation. Large buying organisations may possess unique requirements and respond to marketing stimuli

TABLE 4.1 Selected macrolevel bases of segmentation

Variables	Illustrative Breakdowns
Characteristics of Buying Organisations	
Size (the scale of operations of the organisation)	Small, medium, large; based on sales or number of employees
Geographical location	Europe, Middle East, Africa, Asia Pacific and USA
Usage rate	Nonuser, light user, moderate user, heavy user
Structure of procurement	Centralised, decentralised
Product/Service Application	
SIC category	Varies by product or service
End market served	Varies by product or service
Value in use	High, low
Characteristics of Purchasing Situation	
Type of buying situation	New task, modified rebuy, straight rebuy
Stage in purchase decision process	Early stages, late stages

that are different from those responded to by smaller firms. The influence of presidents, vice presidents, and owners declines with an increase in corporate size; the influence of other participants, such as purchasing managers, increases.* Alternatively, the marketer may recognise regional variations and adopt geographical units as the basis for differentiating marketing strategies.

Usage rate constitutes another macrolevel variable. Buyers are classified on a continuum ranging from nonuser to heavy user. Heavy users may have needs different from moderate or light users. For example, heavy users may place more value on technical or delivery support services than their counterparts. Likewise, an opportunity may exist to convert moderate users into heavy users through adjustments in the product or service mix.

The structure of the procurement function constitutes a final macrolevel characteristic of buying organisations. Firms with a centralised purchasing function behave differently than do those with decentralised procurement. The structure of the purchasing function influences the degree of buyer specialisation, the criteria emphasised, and the composition of the buying centre. Centralised buyers place significant weight on long-term supply availability and the development of a healthy supplier complex. Decentralised buyers tend to emphasise short-term cost efficiency.* Thus the position of procurement in the organisational hierarchy provides a base for categorising organisations and for isolating specific needs and marketing requirements. Many business marketers develop a key account team to meet the special requirements of large, centralised procurement units.

Product/Service application

Because a specific industrial good is often used in different ways, the marketer can divide the market on the basis of specific end-use applications. The SIC system and related information sources are especially valuable for this purpose. To illustrate, the manufacturer of a component such as springs may reach industries incorporating the product into machine tools, bicycles, surgical devices, office equipment, telephones, and missile systems. Similarly, Intel's microchips are used in household appliances, retail terminals, toys, mobile phones, and aircraft as well as in computers. By isolating the specialised needs of each user group as identified by the SIC category, the firm is better equipped to differentiate customer requirements and to evaluate emerging opportunities.

At Apple's Web site, Mac customers are segmented into these categories: creative pro (e.g., publishers), science (e.g., research labs), business (e.g., small-business owners), and education (e.g., teachers or students). A tailored set of applications is available to meet the unique requirements of each segment.

Value in use

Strategic insights are also provided by exploring the value in use of various customer applications. **Value in use** is a product's economic value to the user relative to a specific alternative in a particular application. The economic value of an offering frequently varies by customer application. Milliken & Company, the textile manufacturer, has built one of its businesses by becoming a major supplier of towels to industrial laundries. These customers pay Milliken a 10 per cent premium over equivalent towels offered by competitors.* Why? Milliken provides added value, such as a computerised routing programme that improves the efficiency and effectiveness of the industrial laundries' pick-up and delivery function.

The segmentation strategy adopted by a manufacturer of precision motors further illuminates the value-in-use concept.* The firm found that its customers differed in the motor speed required in their applications and that a dominant competitor's new, low-priced machine wore out quickly in high- and medium-speed applications. The marketer concentrated on this vulnerable segment, demonstrating the superior life cycle cost advantages of the firm's products. The marketer also initiated a long-term programme to develop a competitively priced product and service offering for customers in the low-speed segment.

Purchasing situation

A final macrolevel base for segmenting the organisational market is the purchasing situation. First-time buyers have perceptions and information needs that differ from those of repeat buyers. Therefore, buying organisations are classified as being in the early or late stages of the procurement process, or, alternatively, as *new-task*, *straight rebuy*, or *modified rebuy* organisations. The position of the firm in the procurement decision process or its location on the buying situation continuum dictates marketing strategy.

These examples illustrate those macrolevel bases of segmentation that marketers can apply to the business market. Other macrolevel bases may more precisely fit a specific situation. A key benefit of segmentation is that it forces the manager to search for bases that explain similarities and differences among buying organisations.

4.2.2 Microlevel bases

Having identified macrosegments, the marketer often finds it useful to divide each macrosegment into smaller microsegments on the basis of the similarities and differences between decision-making units. Often, several microsegments—each with unique requirements and unique responses to marketing stimuli—are buried in macrosegments. To isolate them effectively, the marketer must move beyond secondary sources of information by soliciting input from the sales force or by conducting a special market segmentation study. Selected microbases of segmentation appear in Table 4.2.

Key criteria

For some business products, the marketer can divide the market according to which criteria are the most important in the purchase decision.[*] Criteria include product quality, prompt and reliable delivery, technical support, price, and supply continuity. The strategist also might divide the market based on supplier profiles that decision makers appear to prefer (for example, high quality, prompt delivery, premium price versus standard quality, less prompt delivery, low price).

Illustration: Price versus service[*]

Signode Corporation produces and markets a line of steel strapping used for packaging a range of products, including steel and many manufactured items. Facing stiff price competition and a

TABLE 4.2 Selected microlevel bases of segmentation

Variables	Illustrative Breakdowns
Key criteria	Quality, delivery, supplier reputation
Purchasing strategies	Single source . . . multiple sources
Structure of decision-making unit	Major decision participants (for example, purchasing manager and plant manager)
Importance of purchase	High importance . . . low importance
Organisational innovativeness	Innovator . . . follower
Personal characteristics	
Demographics	Age, educational background
Decision style	Normative, conservative, mixed mode
Risk	Risk taker, risk avoider
Confidence	High . . . low
Job responsibility	Purchasing, production, engineering

declining market share, management wanted to move beyond traditional macrolevel segmentation to understand how Signode's 174 national accounts viewed price versus service trade-offs. Four segments were uncovered:

1   **Programmed buyers** (sales = €4.95 million): Customers who were not particularly price or service sensitive and who made purchases in a routine fashion—product is not central to their operation.

2   **Relationship buyers** (sales = €23.25 million): Knowledgeable customers who valued partnership with Signode and did not push for price or service concessions—product is moderately important to the firm's operations.

3   **Transaction buyers** (sales = €18 million): Large and very knowledgeable customers who actively considered the price versus service trade-offs but often placed price over service—product is very important to their operations.

4   **Bargain hunters** (sales = €17.25 million): Large-volume buyers who were very sensitive to any changes in price or service—product is very important to their operations.

The study enabled Signode to sharpen its strategies in this mature business market and to understand more clearly the cost of serving the various segments. Particularly troubling to management was the bargain-hunter segment. These customers demanded the lowest prices and the highest levels of service and had the highest propensity to switch. Management decided to use price cuts only as a defence against competitors' cuts and directed attention instead at ways to add service value to this and other segments.

Value-based strategies

Many customers actively seek business marketing firms that can help them create new value to gain a competitive edge in their markets. Based on a comprehensive study of its customer base, Dow Corning identified three important customer segments and the value proposition that customers in each segment are seeking* :

innovation-focused customers who are committed to being first to the market with new technologies and who seek new-product-development expertise and innovative solutions that will attract new customers;

customers in fast-growing markets who are pressured by competitive battles over market growth and seek proven performance in technology, manufacturing, and supply chain management;

customers in highly competitive markets who produce mature products, centre on process efficiency and effectiveness in manufacturing, and seek cost-effective solutions that keep overall costs down.

The marketer can benefit by examining the criteria decision-making units in various sectors of the business market—commercial, governmental, and institutional—use. As organisations in each sector undergo restructuring efforts, the buying criteria that key decision makers use also change. For example, the cost pressures and reform efforts in the health-care industry are changing how hospitals buy medical equipment and pharmaceuticals. To reduce administrative costs and enhance bargaining power, hospitals are following the lead of commercial enterprises by streamlining their operations. Also, they are forming buying groups, centralising the purchasing function, and insisting on lower prices and better service. Reform efforts are likewise moving government buyers to search for more efficient purchasing procedures and for better value from vendors. Marketers that respond in this challenging environment are rewarded.

Purchasing strategies

Microsegments can be classified according to buying organisations' purchasing strategy. Some buyers seek to have several suppliers, giving each one a healthy share of their purchase volume;

others are more interested in assured supply and concentrate their purchases with one or perhaps two suppliers. Honda looks for suppliers who are able to make suggestions for improving its business operations. Honda has realised that many of the innovations it has developed in its processes have come from its suppliers' suggestions. So a key strategy for Honda is to identify suppliers who are creative and invest in new technology for possibly improving Honda's business.

Structure of the decision-making unit

The structure of the decision-making unit, or buying centre, likewise provides a way to divide the business market into subsets of customers by isolating the patterns of involvement in the purchasing process of particular decision participants (for example, engineering versus top management). For the medical equipment market, DuPont initiated a formal positioning study among hospital administrators, radiology department administrators, and technical managers to identify the firm's relative standing and the specific needs (criteria) for each level of buying influence within each segment.[*] The growing importance of buying groups, multihospital chains, and nonhospital health-care delivery systems pointed to the need for a more refined segmentation approach.

The study indicates that the medical equipment market can be segmented on the basis of the type of institution and the responsibilities of the decision makers and decision influencers in those institutions. The structure of the decision-making unit and the decision criteria used vary across the following three segments:

- Groups that select a single supplier that all member hospitals must use, such as investor-owned hospital chains;

- Groups that select a small set of suppliers from which individual hospitals may select needed products;

- Private group practices and the nonhospital segment.

Based on the study, DuPont's salespersons can tailor their presentations to the decision-making dynamics of each segment. In turn, advertising messages can be more precisely targeted. Such an analysis enables the marketer to identify meaningful microsegments and respond with finely tuned marketing communications.

Importance of purchase

Classifying organisational customers on the basis of the perceived importance of a product is especially appropriate when various customers apply the product in various ways. Buyer perceptions differ according to the effect of the product on the total mission of the firm. A large commercial enterprise may consider the purchase of consulting services routine; the same purchase for a small manufacturing concern is "an event."

Organisational innovativeness

Some organisations are more innovative and willing to purchase new industrial products than others. A study of the adoption of new medical equipment among hospitals found that psychographic variables can improve a marketer's ability to predict the adoption of new products.[*] These include such factors as an organisation's level of change resistance or desire to excel. When psychographic variables are combined with organisational demographic variables (for example, size), accuracy in predicting organisational innovativeness increases.

Because products diffuse more rapidly in some segments than in others, microsegmentation based on organisational innovativeness enables the marketer to identify segments that should be targeted first when it introduces new products. The accuracy of new-product forecasting also improves when diffusion patterns are estimated segment by segment.[*]

Personal characteristics

Some microsegmentation possibilities deal with the personal characteristics of decision makers: demographics (age, education), personality, decision style, risk preference or risk avoidance, confidence, job responsibilities, and so forth. Although some interesting studies have shown the usefulness of segmentation based on individual characteristics, further research is needed to explore its potential as a firm base for microsegmentation.

4.3 THE SEGMENTATION PROCESS

Macrosegmentation centres on characteristics of buying *organisations* (for example, size), *product application* (for example, end market served), and the *purchasing situation* (for example, stage in the purchase decision process). Microsegmentation concentrates on characteristics of organisational decision-making units—for instance, choice criteria assigned the most importance in the purchase decision.

4.3.1 Choosing market segments

Business marketers begin the segmentation process at the macrolevel. If they find that the information about the macrosegments is sufficient to develop an effective marketing strategy, then it may not be necessary to go on to any further microsegmentation. However, if they cannot develop a distinct strategy based on the macrosegment, then it may be necessary to undertake research on microsegmentation variables within each macrosegment. A marketing research study is often needed to identify characteristics of decision-making units. At this level, chosen macrosegments are divided into microsegments on the basis of similarities and differences between the decision-making units to identify small groups of buying organisations that each exhibit a distinct response to the firm's marketing strategy. As firms develop more segments with special requirements, it then becomes necessary to assess whether the cost of developing a unique strategy for a specific segment is worth the profit to be generated from that segment. The marketer must evaluate the potential profitability of alternative segments before investing in separate marketing strategies. As firms develop a clearer picture of the revenue and costs of serving particular segments and customers, they often find that a small group of customers subsidises a large group of marginal and, in some cases, unprofitable customers.[*]

Innovate through segmentation!

In some cases it may be more effective to examine existing customers in a new light. As A. G. Lafley and Lam Charam note, "segmentation itself can be an innovative act, if we identify a corner of our market that is rarely treated as a segment. Can we look at buyers through some other lens than typical tried and true variables such as company size and industry? Identifying an overlooked segment is less expensive than inventing a new technology and may sprout even more opportunities."[*]

Account-based marketing

The rise of account-based marketing (ABM) represents the ultimate expression of the trend toward smaller and more precisely targeted marketing strategies. ABM is an approach that treats an individual account as a market in its own right. Done right, it ensures that marketing and sales are fully focused on a target client's most important business issues and that they work collaboratively to create value propositions that specifically address those issues. Far beyond the basics of personalised messaging and segmented offers, true ABM has the potential to deepen relationships with existing clients and build profitability by shortening the sales cycle and increasing win rates and sole-sourced contracts.[*]

ABM is the ultimate in segmentation, as one company is viewed as a separate segment. This approach may become more prevalent in the future as industry consolidation continues to grow. One could see the commercial aircraft industry as a good example of this ultimate level of segmentation—only two companies now produce large, commercial airliners: Boeing and Airbus S.A.S.

4.3.2 Isolating market segment profitability

To improve on traditional market segmentation, many business marketing firms categorise customers into tiers that differ in current and/or future profitability to the firm. "By knowing the characteristics of profitable customers, companies can direct their marketing efforts to specific segments that are most likely to yield profitable customers."[*] This requires a process of evaluation that makes explicit the near-term potential and the longer-term resource commitments necessary to effectively serve customers in a segment. In particular, special attention is given to the individual drivers of customer profitability, namely, the cost to serve a particular group of customers and the revenues that result.

FedEx Corporation, for example, categorises its business customers (for internal purposes) as the good, the bad, and the ugly—based on their profitability.[*] Rather than using the same strategy for all customers, the company assigns a priority to the good, tries to convert the bad to good, and discourages the ugly. Like many other firms, FedEx discovered that many customers are too costly to serve and demonstrate little potential to become profitable, even in the long term. By understanding the needs of customers at different tiers of profitability, service can be tailored to achieve even higher levels of profitability. For example, FedEx encourages small shippers to bring their packages to conveniently located drop-off points and offers a rapid-response pick-up service for large shippers. Once profitability tiers are identified, "highly profitable customers can be pampered appropriately, customers of average profitability can be cultivated to yield higher profitability, and unprofitable customers can be either made more profitable or weeded out."[*]

4.4 IMPLEMENTING A SEGMENTATION STRATEGY

A well-developed segmentation plan will fail without careful attention to implementing the plan. Successful implementation requires attention to the following issues:

- How should the sales force be organised?
- What special technical or customer service requirements will organisations in the new segment have?
- Who will provide these services?
- Which media outlets can be used to target advertising at the new segment?
- Has a comprehensive online strategy been developed to provide continuous service support to customers in this segment?
- What adaptations will be needed to serve selected international market segments?

The astute business marketing strategist must plan, coordinate, and monitor implementation details. Frank Cespedes points out that "as a firm's offering becomes a product-service-information mix that must be customised for diverse segments, organisational interdependencies increase"[*] and marketing managers, in particular, are involved in more cross-functional tasks. Managing the critical points of contact with the customer is fundamental to the marketing manager's role.

4.5 ESTIMATING SEGMENT DEMAND

Looking back at the Internet boom, executives at telecommunications firms like Alcatel-Lucent and others now openly acknowledge that they did not see the steep drop in demand coming. Indeed, spending by phone companies on telecommunications gear nearly doubled from 1996 to 2000, to €35.63 billion; all forecasts indicated that this attractive growth path would continue.[*] During this period, telecom equipment makers were dramatically expanding production capacity and aggressively recruiting thousands of new employees. However, in 2001, the demand failed to materialise and the major telecom equipment makers reported significant financial losses. In turn, firms across the industry announced a series of massive job cuts. What happened? "Lousy" sales forecasts played an important role, according to Gregory Duncan, a telecom consultant at National Economic Research Associates.[*]

4.5.1 The role of the demand estimation

Estimating demand within selected market segments is vital to marketing management. The forecast of demand reflects management's estimate of the probable level of company sales, taking into account both the potential opportunity and the level and type of marketing effort demanded. Virtually every decision made by the marketer is based on a forecast, formal or informal.

Laying the foundation

Consider a company that wishes to introduce new telecommunications services to businesses. How large is the market opportunity? An estimate of demand provides the foundation for the planning process. Three broad groups of stakeholders require demand forecasts: engineering design and implementation teams; marketing and commercial development teams; and external entities, such as potential investors, government regulators, equipment and application suppliers, and distribution partners. In the marketing area, strategic questions that must be answered before launch of service and that depend on the estimate of demand include: Where should sales outlets be located? How many are required to cover the target market? What sales levels should be expected from each outlet? What performance targets should be established for each? Demand forecasts are needed to project the company's revenues, profits, and cash flow to assess business viability; to determine cash, equity, and borrowing requirements; and to set up appropriate pricing structures and levels.[*] In short, without knowledge of market demand, marketing executives cannot develop sound strategy and make effective decisions about the allocation of resources.

Setting the course

A primary application of the estimate of demand is clearly in the planning and control of marketing strategy by market segment. Once demand is estimated for each segment, the manager can allocate expenditures on the basis of potential sales volume. Spending huge sums of money on advertising and personal selling has little benefit in segments where the market opportunity is low. Of course, expenditures would have to be based on both expected demand and the level of competition. Actual sales in each segment can also be compared with forecasted sales, taking into account the level of competition, in order to evaluate the effectiveness of the marketing programme.

Consider the experience of a South African manufacturer of quick-connective couplings for power transmission systems. For more than 20 years, one of its large distributors had been increasing its sales volume. In fact, this distributor was considered one of the firm's top producers. The manufacturer then analysed the estimates of demand for each of its 31 distributors. The large distributor ranked thirty-first in terms of volume relative to potential business, achieving only 15.4 per cent of estimated demand. A later evaluation revealed that the distributor's sales personnel did not know the most effective way to sell couplings to its large-customer accounts.

Estimates of probable demand should be developed *after* the firm has made decisions about its marketing strategy for a particular segment. Only after the marketing strategy is developed can expected sales be forecasted. Many firms are tempted to use the forecast as a tool for deciding the level of marketing expenditures. One study (which sampled 900 firms) found that slightly more than 25 per cent of the respondent firms set their advertising budgets after the forecast of demand was developed.[*] Small companies whose budgeting and forecasting decisions were fragmented made up the majority of the firms in this group. Clearly, marketing strategy is a determinant of the level of sales and not vice versa.

Supply chain links

Sales forecasts are critical to the smooth operation of the entire supply chain. When timely sales forecast information is readily available to all firms in the supply chain, plans can be tightly coordinated and all parties share in the benefits.[*] Sales forecast data is used to distribute inventory in the supply chain, manage stock levels at each link, and schedule resources for all the members of a supply chain that provide materials, components, and services to a manufacturer. Accurate forecasts go hand-in-hand with effective management practices in directing the entire supply chain process. Specific tools are available to develop accurate estimates of market potential; the business marketer must understand the purpose of each alternative technique as well as its strengths and limitations.

4.6 METHODS OF FORECASTING DEMAND

Estimating demand may be highly mathematical or informally based on sales force estimates. Two primary approaches to demand forecasting are recognised: (1) qualitative and (2) quantitative, which includes time series and causal analysis.

4.6.1 Qualitative techniques

Qualitative techniques, which are also referred to as **management judgment** or **subjective techniques,** rely on informed judgment and rating schemes. The sales force, top-level executives, or distributors may be called on to use their knowledge of the economy, the market, and the customers to create qualitative demand estimates. Techniques for qualitative analysis include the executive judgment method, the sales force composite method, and the Delphi method.

The effectiveness of qualitative approaches depends on the close relationships between customers and suppliers that are typical in the business-to-business market. Qualitative techniques work well for such items as heavy capital equipment or when the nature of the forecast does not lend itself to mathematical analysis. These techniques are also suitable for new-product or new-technology forecasts when historical data are scarce or nonexistent.[*] An important advantage of qualitative approaches is that it brings users of the forecast into the forecasting process. The effect is usually an increased understanding of the procedure and a higher level of commitment to the resultant forecast.

Executive judgment

According to a large sample of business firms, the **executive judgment method** enjoys a high level of usage.[*] The judgment method, which combines and averages top executives' estimates of future sales, is popular because it is easy to apply and to understand. Typically, executives from various departments, such as sales, marketing, production, finance, and procurement, are brought together to apply their collective expertise, experience, and opinions to the forecast.

The primary limitation of the approach is that it does not systematically analyse cause-and-effect relationships. Further, because there is no established formula for deriving estimates, new executives may have difficulty making reasonable forecasts. The resulting forecasts are only as good as the executives' opinions. The accuracy of the executive judgment approach is also difficult to assess in a way that allows meaningful comparison with alternative techniques.[*]

The executives' "ballpark" estimates for the intermediate and the long-run time frames are often used in conjunction with forecasts developed quantitatively. However, when historical data are limited or unavailable, the executive judgment approach may be the only alternative. Mark Moriarty and Arthur Adams suggest that executive judgment methods produce accurate forecasts when: (1) forecasts are made frequently and repetitively, (2) the environment is stable, and (3) the linkage between decision, action, and feedback is short.[*] Business marketers should examine their forecasting situation in light of these factors in order to assess the usefulness of the executive judgment technique.

Sales force composite

The rationale behind the **sales force composite** approach is that salespeople can effectively estimate future sales volume because they know the customers, the market, and the competition. In addition, participating in the forecasting process helps sales personnel understand how forecasts are derived and boosts their incentive to achieve the desired level of sales. The composite forecast is developed by combining the sales estimates from all salespeople. By providing the salesperson with a wealth of customer information that can be conveniently accessed and reviewed, customer relationship management (CRM) systems enhance the efficiency and effectiveness of the sales force composite.[*] CRM systems also allow a salesperson to track progress in winning new business at key accounts.

Few companies rely solely on sales force estimates; rather, they usually adjust or combine the estimates with forecasts developed either by top management or by quantitative methods. The advantage of the sales force composite method is the ability to draw on sales force knowledge about markets and customers. This advantage is particularly important for a market in which buyer–seller relationships are close and enduring. The salesperson is often the best source of information about customer purchasing plans and inventory levels. The method can also be executed with relative ease at minimal cost. Research suggests that salespeople who: (a) are properly trained to gather and incorporate customer data into the forecast, (b) receive appropriate levels of feedback in the form of forecast accuracy measures on the effectiveness of their efforts, and (c) understand the impact of the forecast on resource allocations throughout the organisation are more active contributors to the sales forecasting process.[*]

The problems with sales force composites are similar to those of the executive judgment approach: They do not involve systematic analysis of cause and effect, and they rely on informed judgment and opinions. Some sales personnel may overestimate sales in order to look good or underestimate them in order to generate a lower quota. Management must carefully review all estimates. As a rule, sales force estimates are relatively accurate for short-run projections but less effective for long-term forecasts.

Delphi method

In the **Delphi approach to forecasting**, the opinions of a panel of experts on future sales are converted into an informed consensus through a highly structured feedback mechanism.[*] As in the executive judgment technique, management officials are used as the panel, but each estimator remains anonymous. On the first round, written opinions about the likelihood of some future event are sought (for example, sales volume, competitive reaction, or technological breakthroughs). The responses to this first questionnaire are used to produce a second. The objective is to provide feedback to the group so that first-round estimates and information available to some of the experts are made available to the entire group.

After each round of questioning, the analyst who administers the process assembles, clarifies, and consolidates information for dissemination in the succeeding round. Throughout the process, panel members are asked to reevaluate their estimates based on the new information from the group. Opinions are kept anonymous, eliminating both "me-too" estimates and the need to defend a position. After continued reevaluation, the goal is to achieve a consensus. The number of experts varies from six to hundreds, depending on how the process is organised and its purpose. The number of rounds of questionnaires depends on how rapidly the group reaches consensus.

Generally, the Delphi technique is applied to long-term forecasting of demand, particularly for new products or situations not suited to quantitative analysis. This approach can provide some good ballpark estimates of demand when the products are new or unique and when there is no other data available. Like all qualitative approaches to estimating demand, it is difficult to measure the accuracy of the estimates.

Qualitative forecasting approaches are important in the process of assessing future product demand, and they are most valuable in situations where little data exists and where a broad estimate of demand is acceptable. New or unique products do not lend themselves to more quantitative approaches to forecasting, so the qualitative methods play a very important role in estimating demand for these items.

4.6.2 Quantitative techniques

Quantitative demand forecasting, also referred to as systematic or objective forecasting, offers two primary methodologies: (1) time series and (2) regression or causal. **Time-series** techniques use historical data ordered chronologically to project the trend and growth rate of sales. The rationale behind time-series analysis is that the past pattern of sales will apply to the future. However, to discover the underlying pattern of sales, the analyst must first understand all of the possible patterns that may affect the sales series. Thus, a time series of sales may include trend, seasonal, cyclical, and irregular patterns. Once the effect of each has been isolated, the analyst can then project the expected future of each pattern. Time-series methods are well suited to short-range forecasting because the assumption that the future will be like the past is more reasonable over the short run than over the long run.[*]

Regression or **causal** analysis, on the other hand, uses an opposite approach, identifying factors that have affected past sales and implementing them in a mathematical model.[*] Demand is expressed mathematically as a function of the items that affect it. A forecast is derived by projecting values for each of the factors in the model, inserting these values into the regression equation, and solving for expected sales. Typically, causal models are more reliable for intermediate than for long-range forecasts because the magnitude of each factor affecting sales must first be estimated for some future time, which becomes difficult when estimating farther into the future.

The specifics of the quantitative approaches to estimating demand are beyond the scope of this chapter. However, the key aspects of these approaches for the business-to-business manager to keep in mind are as follows:

1   To develop an estimate of demand with time-series analysis, the analyst must determine each pattern (the trend, cycle, seasonal pattern) and then extrapolate them into the future. This requires a significant amount of historical sales information. Once a forecast of each pattern is developed, the demand forecast is assembled by combining the estimates for each pattern.

2   A critical aspect of regression analysis is to identify the economic variable(s) to which past sales are related. For forecasting purposes, the *Survey of Current Business* (see http://www.bea.gov/scb) is particularly helpful because it contains monthly, quarterly, and annual figures for hundreds of economic variables. The forecaster can test an array of economic variables from the *Survey* to find the variable(s) with the best relationship to past sales. Similar surveys are published by the European Union and by the Bureau for Economic Research in South Africa.

3   Although causal methods have measurable levels of accuracy, there are some important caveats and limitations. The fact that demand and some causal variables (independent variables) are

correlated (associated) does not mean that the independent variable "caused" sales. The independent variable should be logically related to demand.

4   Regression methods require considerable historical data for equations to be valid and reliable, but the data may not be available. Caution must always be used in extrapolating relationships into the future. The equation relates what has happened; economic and industry factors may change in the future, making past relationships invalid.

5   A valuable study on forecasting methods suggests choosing a methodology based on the underlying behaviour of the market rather than the time horizon of the forecast.[*] This research indicates that when markets are sensitive to changes in market and environmental variables, causal methods work best, whether the forecast is short or long range; time-series approaches are more effective when the market exhibits no sensitivity to market and/or environmental changes.

4.6.3 CPFR: A new collaborative approach to estimating demand

CPFR, or Collaborative Planning Forecasting and Replenishment, is a unique approach to forecasting demand that involves the combined efforts of many functions within the firm as well as with partners in the supply chain. In this approach, one individual in the firm is given the responsibility for coordinating the forecasting process with functional managers across the firm. So sales, marketing, production, logistics, and procurement personnel will be called upon to jointly discuss their plans for the upcoming period. In this way, all the parties who may influence sales performance will participate directly in the demand estimation process.

Once the firm has a good grasp internally of each function's forthcoming strategies and plans, the "demand planner" from the firm will then reach out to customers, distributors, and manufacturers' representatives to assess what their marketing, promotion, and sales plans are for the product in question.

These plans are then shared with the company's functional managers, and demand estimates are adjusted accordingly. The demand planner then develops a final demand estimate for the coming period based on this wide array of input. As one might expect, the CPFR approach to estimating demand often results in a very accurate forecast of demand due to the intensive sharing of information among the firm's functional managers and key supply chain and channel partners.

The most practical approach for application of CPFR is for the trading parties to map their partners' forecasts into their own terms, understand where their partners' plans deviate significantly from their own, and then collaborate on the assumptions that may be leading to different estimates. Through this iterative process, intermediaries and manufacturers use collaborative feedback to synchronise their supply chains, while keeping their enterprise planning processes intact.[*]

4.6.4 Combining several forecasting techniques

Recent research on forecasting techniques indicates that forecasting accuracy can be improved by combining the results of several forecasting methods.[*] The results of combined forecasts greatly surpass most individual projections, techniques, and analyses by experts. Mark Moriarty and Arthur Adams suggest that managers should use a composite forecasting model that includes both systematic (quantitative) and judgmental (qualitative) factors.[*] In fact, they suggest that a composite forecast be created to provide a standard of comparison in evaluating the results provided by any single forecasting approach. Each forecasting approach relies on varying data to derive sales estimates. By considering a broader range of factors that affect sales, the combined approach provides a more accurate forecast. Rather than searching for the single "best" forecasting technique, business marketers should direct increased attention to the composite forecasting approach.

SUMMARY

The business market contains a complex mix of customers with diverse needs and objectives. The marketing strategist who analyses the aggregate market and identifies neglected or inadequately served groups of buyers (segments) is ideally prepared for a market assault. Specific marketing strategy adjustments can be made to fit the unique needs of each target segment. Of course, such differentiated marketing strategies are feasible only when the target segments are measurable, accessible, responsive, and large enough to justify separate attention.

Procedurally, business market segmentation involves categorising actual or potential buying organisations into mutually exclusive clusters (segments), each of which exhibits a relatively homogeneous response to marketing strategy variables. To accomplish this task, the business marketer can draw upon two types of segmentation bases: macrolevel and microlevel. Macrodimensions are the key characteristics of buying organisations and of the purchasing situation. The SIC together with other secondary sources of information are valuable in macrolevel segmentation. Microlevel bases of segmentation centre on key characteristics of the decision-making unit and require a higher level of market knowledge.

This chapter outlined a systematic approach for the business marketer to apply when identifying and selecting target segments. Before a final decision is made, the marketer must weigh the costs and benefits of a segmented marketing strategy. In developing a market segmentation plan, the business marketing manager isolates the costs and revenues associated with serving particular market segments. By directing its resources to its most profitable customers and segments, the business marketer is less vulnerable to focused competitors that may seek to "cherry-pick" the firm's most valuable customers.

The forecasting techniques available to the business marketer are: (1) qualitative and (2) quantitative. Qualitative techniques rely on informed judgments of future sales and include executive judgment, the sales force composite, and the Delphi methods. By contrast, quantitative techniques have more complex data requirements and include time-series and causal approaches. The time-series method uses chronological historical data to project the future trend and growth rate of sales. Causal methods, on the other hand, seek to identify factors that have affected past sales and to incorporate them into a mathematical model. The essence of sound demand forecasting is to combine effectively the forecasts provided by various methods.

DISCUSSION QUESTIONS

1 Describe the basic conditions required for effective segmentation.

2 What are the potential benefits to a firm if they have effectively segmented their market?

3 A young, recently graduated entrepreneur argues in an interview that they are more interested in studying the behaviour of people who do not buy their products than the behaviour of their current customers. Do you agree with them?

4 What role can market segmentation play in developing the business marketing strategy?

5 What techniques could you use to effectively develop a forecast of demand?

INTERNET EXERCISES

Carlson Wagonlit Travel is an Internet company that offers a variety of travel products. Learn more about its goods, services and travel advice through its website at: www.carlsonwagonlit.co.uk

1 Based on the information provided at the website, what are some of Carlson Wagonlit Travel's basic products?

2 What market segments does Carlson Wagonlit Travel appear to be targeting with its website?

3 What segmentation variables is the company using to segment these markets?

REFERENCES

Armstrong, J. Scott, "The Forecasting Canon: Nine Generalizations to Improve Forecast Accuracy," *FORESIGHT: The International Journal of Applied Forecasting* 1 (1, June 2005): pp. 29–35.

Balinski, Eric W., Allen, Philip, and DeBonis, J. Nicholas, *Value-Based Marketing for Bottom-Line Success* (New York: McGraw-Hill and the American Marketing Association, 2003), pp. 147–152.

Bellizzi, Joseph A., "Organizational Size and Buying Influences," *Industrial Marketing Management* 10 (February 1981): pp. 17–21.

Berman, Dennis K., "'Lousy Sales Forecasts Helped Fuel the Telecom Mess," *The Wall Street Journal*, July 7, 2001, p. B1.

Boejgaard, John, and Ellegaard, Chris, "Unfolding Implementation in Industrial Market Segmentation," *Industrial Marketing Management* 39 (November 2010): pp. 1291–1299.

Brooks, R., "Alienating Customers Isn't Always a Bad Idea, Many Firms Discover," *The Wall Street Journal*, January 7, 1999, pp. A1 and A12.

Cespedes, Frank V., *Concurrent Marketing: Integrating Product, Sales, and Service* (Boston: Harvard Business School Press, 1995), p. 271.

Coles, Gary L., and Culley, James D., "Not All Prospects Are Created Equal," *Business Marketing* 71 (May 1986): pp. 52–57.

Dibb, Sally, Simkin, Lyndon, Pride, Bill, and Ferrell, O.C., *Marketing Concepts & Strategies*, 6th ed. (Cengage, 2012).

Doole, Isobel, and Lowe, Robin, *International Marketing Strategy* 6th ed. (Cengage, 2012).

Doyle, Peter, and Saunders, John "Market Segmentation and Positioning in Specialized Industrial Markets," *Journal of Marketing* 49 (Spring 1985): pp. 24–32.

Garda, Robert A., "How to Carve Niches for Growth in Industrial Markets," *Management Review* 70 (August 1981): pp. 15–22.

Gertz, Dwight L., and Baptista, João P.A., *Grow to Be Great: Breaking the Downsizing Cycle* (New York: The Free Press, 1995), p. 54.

Jackson Jr., Donald W., Burdick, Richard K., and Keith, Janet E., "Purchasing Agents' Perceived Importance of Marketing Mix Components in Different Industrial Purchase Situations," *Journal of Business Research* 13 (August 1985): pp. 361–373.

Kaplan, Robert S., and Narayanan, V.G., "Measuring and Managing Customer Profitability," *Journal of Cost Management* 15 (September–October 2001): p. 13.

Kasturi Rangan, V., Moriarty, Rowland T., and Swartz, Gordon S., "Segmenting Customers in Mature Industrial Markets," *Journal of Marketing* 56 (October 1992): pp. 72–82.

Kotler, Philip, "Marketing's New Paradigm: What's Really Happening Out There," *Planning Review* 20 (September–October 1992): pp. 50–52.

Lafley, A.G., and Charan, Ram, "Making Inspiration Routine," *Inc* 30 (6, June 2008): pp. 98–101.

Laseter, Timothy M., *Balanced Sourcing: Cooperation and Competition in Supplier Relationships* (San Francisco: Jossey-Bass, 1998), pp. 59–86.

Lehmann, Donald R., and O'Shaughnessy, John, "Decision Criteria Used in Buying Different Categories of Products," *Journal of Purchasing and Materials Management* 18 (Spring 1982): pp. 9–14.

Makridakis, Spyros, "A Survey of Time Series," *International Statistics Review* 44 (1, 1976): p. 63.

Mast, Kenneth E., and Hawes, Jon M., "Perceptual Differences between Buyers and Engineers," *Journal of Purchasing and Materials Management* 22 (Spring 1986): pp. 2–6.

McBurney, Peter, Parsons, Simon, and Green, Jeremy, "Forecasting Market Demand for New Telecommunications Services: An Introduction," *Telematics and Information* 19 (2002): p. 233.

McCarthy Byrne, Teresa M., Moon, Mark A., Mentzer, John T., "Motivating the Industrial Sales Forecasting Process," *Industrial Marketing Management* 40 (January 2011): pp. 128–138.

Mentzer, John T., and Moon, Mark A., "Understanding Demand," *Supply Chain Management Review* 8 (May–June 2004): p. 45.

Mirani, Robert, Moore, Deanne, and Weber, John A., "Emerging Technologies for Enhancing Supplier-Reseller Partnerships," *Industrial Marketing Management* 30 (February 2001): pp. 101–114

Mitchell, Vincent-Wayne and Wilson, Dominic F., "Balancing Theory and Practice: A Reappraisal of Business-to-Business Segmentation," *Industrial Marketing Management* 27 (September 1998): pp. 429–455.

Moriarty and Adams, "Management Judgment Forecasts," p. 248.

Moutinho, Luiz, and Southern, Geoffrey, *Strategic Marketing Management: A process Based Approach* (Cengage, 2012).

Oracle, "Taking It One Step at a Time: Tapping into the Benefits of Collaborative Planning, Forecasting, and Replenishment (CPFR)," *An Oracle White Paper* (August 2005), http://www.oracle.com/applications/retail/library/white-papers/taking-itone-step.pdf.

Robertson, Thomas S., and Gatignon, Hubert, "Competitive Effects on Technology Diffusion," *Journal of Marketing* 50 (July 1986): pp. 1–12.

Robertson, Thomas S., and Wind, Yoram, "Organizational Psychographics and Innovativeness," *Journal of Consumer Research* 7 (June 1980): pp. 24–31.

Sanders, Nada, "Forecasting Practices in U.S. Corporations: Survey Results," *Interfaces* 24 (March–April 1994): pp. 92–100.

Sands, Jeff, "Account-Based Marketing," *B to B*, 91 (6, May 8, 2006): p. 11.

Schnedler, David E., "Use Strategic Market Models to Predict Customer Behavior," *Sloan Management Review* 37 (Spring 1996): p. 92.

Segalo, A. Michael, *The IBM/PC Guide to Sales Forecasting* (Wayne, PA: Banbury, 1985), p. 21.

Sharma, Arun, Krishnan, R., and Grewal, Dhruv, "Value Creation in Markets: A Critical Area of Focus for Business-to-Business Markets," *Industrial Marketing Management* 30 (June 2001): pp. 391–402.

Thomas, Robert J., "Method and Situational Factors in Sales Forecast Accuracy," *Journal of Forecasting* 12 (January 1993): p. 75.

Tsai, Jessica, "The Smallest Slice," *CRM Magazine* 12 (2, February 2008): p. 37.

Vagn Freytog, Per and Clarke, Ann Højbjerg, "Business to Business Market Segmentation," *Industrial Marketing Management* 30 (August 2001): pp. 473–486.

van Weele, Arjan, *Puchasing and Supply Chain Management: Analysis Strategy, Planning and Practice*, 5th ed. (Cengage, 2010).

Verhage, Bronis J., *Marketing: A Global Perspective* (Cengage, 2013).

von Hippel, Eric, Thomke, Stefan, and Sonnack, Mary, "Creating Breakthroughs at 3M," *Harvard Business Review* 77 (September–October 1999): pp. 47–57.

West, Douglas C., "Advertising Budgeting and Sales Forecasting: The Timing Relationship," *International Journal of Advertising* 14 (1, 1995): pp. 65–77.

Willis, Raymond E., *A Guide to Forecasting for Planners and Managers* (Englewood Cliffs, NJ: Prentice Hall, 1987), p. 343.

Wind, Yoram, and Cardozo, Richard N., "Industrial Market Segmentation," *Industrial Marketing Management* 3 (March 1974): p. 155.

Wind, Yoram, Robertson, Thomas S., and Fraser, Cynthia, "Industrial Product Diffusion by Market Segment," *Industrial Marketing Management* 11 (February 1982): pp. 1–8.

Woodside, Arch G., Liukko, Timo, and Vuori, Risto, "Organizational Buying of Capital Equipment Involving Persons across Several Authority Levels," *Journal of Business and Industrial Marketing* 14 (1, 1999): pp. 30–48.

Zeithaml, Valarie A., Rust, Roland, T., and Lemon, Katherine, N., "The Customer Pyramid: Creating and Serving Profitable Customers," *California Management Review* 43 (Summer 2001): p. 118.

PART IV
FORMULATING BUSINESS MARKETING STRATEGY

CHAPTER 5
BUSINESS
MARKETING
PLANNING:
STRATEGIC
PERSPECTIVES

CHAPTER OBJECTIVES

To this point, you have developed an understanding of organisational buying behaviour, customer relationship management, market segmentation, and a host of other tools managers use. All of this provides a fundamentally important perspective to the business marketing strategist. After reading this chapter, you will understand:

1   Marketing's strategic role in corporate strategy development

2   The multifunctional nature of business marketing decision making

3   The components of a business model that can be converted into superior positions of advantage in the business market

4   A valuable framework for detailing the processes and systems that drive strategy success

Consider GE's bold new initiative to recognise and reward marketing leaders who demonstrate special promise:

> *We identify our top 50 up-and-coming marketers as rock stars and make their development a company priority. They receive additional coaching and career counseling, and GE includes them in planning the marketing function's future.*[*]

To meet the challenges brought on by growing domestic and global competition, business-to-business firms are increasingly recognising the vital role of the marketing function in developing and implementing successful business strategies. Effective business strategies share many common characteristics, but at a minimum they are responsive to market needs, they exploit the special competencies of the organisation, and they use valid assumptions about environmental trends and competitive behaviour. Above all, they must offer a realistic basis for securing and sustaining a competitive advantage.[*] This chapter examines the nature and critical importance of strategy development in the business marketing firm.

First, the chapter highlights the special role of the marketing function in corporate strategy development, with a functionally integrated perspective of business marketing planning. Next, it identifies the sources of competitive advantage by exploring the key components of a business model and how they can be managed to secure distinctive strategic positioning. Finally, a framework is offered for converting strategy goals into a tightly integrated customer strategy. This discussion provides a foundation for exploring business marketing strategy on a global scale.

5.1 MARKETING'S STRATEGIC ROLE

Market-driven firms are centred on customers—they take an outside-in view of strategy and demonstrate an ability to sense market trends ahead of their competitors.[*] Many firms—like Unilever, 3M, and AkzoNobel—have numerous divisions, product lines, products, and brands. Policies established at the corporate level provide the framework for strategy development in each business division to ensure survival and growth of the entire enterprise. In turn, corporate and divisional policies establish the boundaries within which individual product or market managers develop strategy.

5.1.1 The hierarchy of strategies

Three major levels of strategy dominate most large multiproduct organisations: (1) corporate strategy, (2) business-level strategy, and (3) functional strategy.[*]

Corporate strategy defines the businesses in which a company competes, preferably in a manner that uses resources to convert distinctive competence into competitive advantage. Essential questions at this level include: What are our core competencies? What businesses are we in? What businesses should we be in? How should we allocate resources across these businesses to achieve our overall organisational goals and objectives? At this level of strategy, the role of marketing is to: (1) assess market attractiveness and the competitive effectiveness of the firm, (2) promote a customer orientation to the various constituencies in management decision making, and (3) formulate the firm's overall value proposition (as a reflection of its distinctive competencies, in terms reflecting customer needs), articulating it to the market and to the organisation at large. According to Frederick Webster Jr., "At the corporate level, marketing managers have a critical role to play as advocates, for the customer and for a set of values and beliefs that put the customer first in the firm's decision making."[*]

Business-level strategy centres on how a firm competes in a given industry and positions itself against its competitors. The focus of competition is not between corporations; rather, it is between their individual business units. A **strategic business unit** (SBU) is a single business or collection of businesses that has a distinct mission, a responsible manager, and its own competitors and that is relatively independent of other business units. Each SBU develops a plan describing how it will manage its mix of products to secure a competitive advantage consistent with the level of investment and risk that management is willing to accept. An SBU could be one or more divisions of the industrial firm, a product line within one division, or, on occasion, a single product. Strategic business units may share resources such as a sales force with other business units to achieve economies of scale. An SBU may serve one or many product-market units.

For each business unit in the corporate portfolio, the following essential questions must be answered: How can we compete most effectively for the product market the business unit serves? What distinctive skills can give the business unit a competitive advantage? Similarly, the former CEO at GE, Jack Welch, would ask his operating executives to crisply answer the following questions[*]:

- Describe the global competitive environment in which you operate.

- In the last two years, what have your competitors done?

- In the same period, what have you done to them in the marketplace?

- How might they attack you in the future?

- What are your plans to leapfrog them?

The marketing function contributes to the planning process at this level by providing a detailed and complete analysis of customers and competitors and the firm's distinctive skills and resources for competing in particular market segments.

Functional strategy centres on how resources allocated to the various functional areas can be used most efficiently and effectively to support the business-level strategy. The primary focus of marketing strategy at this level is to allocate and coordinate marketing resources and activities to achieve the firm's objective within a specific product market.

5.1.2 Strategy formulation and the hierarchy[*]

The interplay among the three levels of the strategy hierarchy can be illustrated by examining the collective action perspective of strategy formulation. This approach applies to strategic decisions that: (1) cut across functional areas, (2) involve issues related to the organisation's long-term objectives, or (3) involve allocating resources across business units or product markets. Included here are decisions about the direction of corporate strategy, the application of a core technology, or the choice of an alliance partner.

Observe in Figure 5.1 that strategic decision processes often involve the active participation of several functional interest groups that hold markedly different beliefs about the appropriateness of particular strategies or corporate goals. Strategic decisions represent the outcome of a bargaining process among functional interest groups (including marketing), each of which may interpret the proposed strategy in an entirely different light.

Turf issues and thought-world views

Two forces contribute to the conflict that often divides participants in the strategy formulation process. First, different meanings assigned to a proposed strategy are often motivated by deeper differences in what might be called "organisational subcultures." Subcultures exist when one subunit shares different values, beliefs, and goals than another subunit, resulting in different **thought-worlds**.[*] For example, marketing managers are concerned with market opportunities and competitors, whereas R&D managers value technical sophistication and innovation.

FIGURE 5.1 A collective action perspective of the strategy formulation process

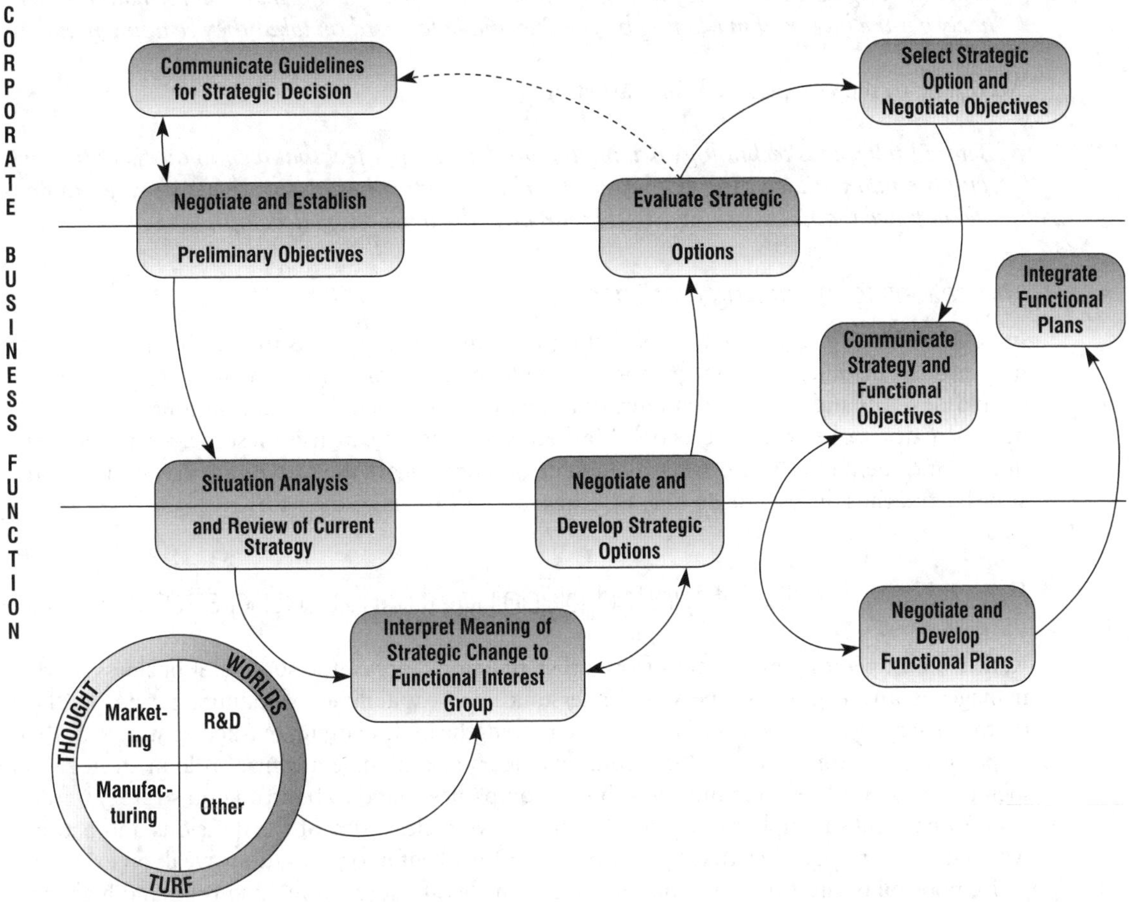

Source: Gary L. Frankwick, James C. Ward, Michael D. Hutt, and Peter H. Reingen, "Evolving Patterns of Organizational Beliefs in the Formation of Strategy," *Journal of Marketing* 58 (April 1994): p. 98. Reprinted with permission by the American Marketing Association.

Second, functional managers are likely to resist strategic changes that threaten their turf. To the extent that the subunit defines the individual's identity and connotes prestige and power, the organisational member may be reluctant to see it altered by a strategic decision.

Negotiated outcomes

Collective decisions emerge from negotiation and compromise among partisan participants. The differences in goals, thought-worlds, and self-interests across participants lead to conflicts about actions that should be taken. Choices must be negotiated with each interest group attempting to achieve its own ends. The ultimate outcomes of collective decisions tend to unfold incrementally and depend more on the partisan values and influence of the various interest groups than on rational analysis. A study of a highly contested strategic decision in a *Fortune* 500 company illustrates the tension that may exist between marketing and R&D.

Two marketing executives describe how the decision was ultimately resolved.* According to the marketing manager:

> [Marketing] did an extremely effective job of stepping right in the middle of it and stran-
> gling it... . What has happened is by laying out the market unit concerns and again, refo-
> cusing on the fact that we are market-based, basically what Marketing did was force the

R&D team into submission where they no longer have the autonomy they once had to go about making decisions—they now get input. And whether it's formal or informal, they definitely get the buy-in of marketing before they move forward on what they're doing now.

According to the vice president of marketing:

Before I felt it was technology driving the process. Now I feel that technology is partnering with the marketplace. And the reason I feel that way is because we have [marketing people] in place that are working closely with how the technology develops.

Implications for marketing managers

In advocating a strategic course, marketing managers must be sensitive to the likely response it may arouse in other interest groups. To build pockets of commitment and trust, managers should develop and use a communication network that includes organisational members who have a major stake in the decision. Marketing managers can use these personal networks to understand the interests of other stakeholders, communicate their own interests clearly and sensitively, and thus diffuse the anxiety of others about threats to their turf.

5.1.3 Functionally integrated planning: the marketing strategy centre[*]

Rather than operating in isolation from other functional areas, the successful business marketing manager is an integrator—one who understands the capabilities of manufacturing, R&D, and customer service and who capitalises on their strengths in developing marketing strategies that are responsive to customer needs. Marketing managers also assume a central role in strategy implementation.[*] Recent research indicates that in companies found to be strong on strategy execution, over 70 per cent of employees affirm that they have a clear idea of the decisions and actions for which they are responsible; that figure drops to 32 per cent in organisations weak on execution.[*]

Responsibility charting is an approach that can classify decision-making roles and highlight the multifunctional nature of business marketing decision making. The decision areas (rows) in the matrix might, for example, relate to a planned product-line expansion. The various functional areas that may assume particular roles in this decision process head the matrix columns. The following list defines the alternative roles that participants can assume in the decision-making process.[*]

1   *Responsible* (R): The manager takes the initiative for analysing the situation, developing alternatives, and assuring consultation with others and then makes the initial recommendation. Upon approval of the decision, the role ends.

2   *Approve* (A): The manager accepts or vetoes a decision before it is implemented or chooses from alternatives developed by the participants assuming a ''responsible'' role.

3   *Consult* (C): The manager is consulted or asked for substantive input before the decision is approved but does not possess veto power.

4   *Implement* (M): The manager is accountable for implementing the decision, including notifying other relevant participants about the decision.

5   *Inform* (I): Although the manager is not necessarily consulted before the decision is approved, he or she is informed of the decision once it is made.

Representatives of a particular functional area may, of course, assume more than one role in the decision-making process. The technical service manager may be consulted during the new-product-development process and may also be held accountable for implementing service-support strategy. Likewise, the marketing manager may be responsible for and approve many of the

INSIDE BUSINESS MARKETING

Working Without a Strategic Plan

In most companies there are countless ideas and plans for the future floating around. Unfortunately, many of these ideas are never converted into activities, and many plans never become anything more than plans. Research shows that small and medium-sized companies often do not even go through the trouble of trying to put a *strategic plan* down on paper!

Too many managers simply allow the future to run its course. They are stuck in their old ways of thinking and tend to concentrate on internal *operational problems* or side issues. Acting more like supervisors who are always putting out fires, they lose sight of their primary role as strategically thinking executives. Also, because they lack much needed insight into markets, technologies and competitors, their work may be based on inaccurate assumptions. Given this mindset, strategic alternatives (such as entering a new market or adopting more innovative ways of approaching the current market) are rarely considered. Without a sound strategy, managers fail to detect or respond to the opportunities and threats that their company faces.

Why do managers make decisions without a sound business plan? There are six major reasons for a lack of strategic planning:

1 *Inability to stand back*
Some managers never view the market and their company with any degree of abstraction. As a result, a deliberate choice of target markets and a critical analysis of the products offered never get off the ground. Even the company's mission and business definition may not be clear.

2 *Too operationally oriented*
Day-to-day operations come first. Everything revolves around sales, even at the expense of developing and implementing a long-term strategy.

3 *Lack of self-criticism*
Because some managers do not allow themselves to be critical and open-minded, they rarely exchange views or ideas. Comments about the company's weaknesses are taken personally.

4 *No vision*
Since management lacks a clear vision of the future, the company responds to every trend in the market – under the guise of 'flexibility'. This kind of drifting benefits neither growth nor profitability.

5 *Reluctance to make choices*
A common question is: 'How can we implement a strategy when the market keeps changing?' Yet, particularly in turbulent times, it is crucial to develop a long-term plan to determine which developments are most relevant for the firm. Unfortunately, some managers lack the confidence, courage and decisiveness to make strategic choices.

6 *Insufficient time*
If a company does not allocate time to make a strategic plan, it probably does not consider strategy development as a top priority. Or, perhaps its management does not *know how* to develop and implement strategy.

Research among executives in Europe, Asia and the US shows that market leaders consistently do three things better than their competition: they *focus*, they *simplify* and they *adapt*. Top performing companies, for example, typically try to increase speed-to-market, simplify communications between the boardroom and the 'front lines' and constantly adapt their business model. 'The findings show a fundamental shift in the nature of strategy and competitive advantage,' concluded James Allen of global consultancy Bain & Company. 'Most executives say that strategy is now more about their ability to *sense and adapt*, and they expect to deal with different key *competitors* within five years. They also spend more time with key *customers* to understand their emerging needs and wants. Today's speed of change and need for immediate responsive actions is remarkable.'*

decisions related to the product-line expansion. For other actions, several decision makers may participate. To illustrate, the business unit manager, after consulting R&D, may approve (or veto) a decision for which the marketing manager is responsible.

The members of the organisation involved in the business marketing decision-making process constitute the **marketing strategy centre**. The composition or functional area representation of the strategy centre evolves during the marketing strategy development process, varies from firm to firm, and varies from one situation to another. Likewise, the composition of the marketing strategy centre is not strictly prescribed by the organisational chart. The needs of a particular strategy situation, especially the information requirements, significantly influence the composition of the strategy centre. Thus, the marketing strategy centre shares certain parallels with the buying centre.

Managing strategic interdependencies

A central challenge for the business marketer in the strategy centre is to minimise interdepartmental conflict while fostering shared appreciation of the interdependencies with other functional units. Individual strategy centre participants are motivated by both personal and organisational goals. They interpret company objectives in relation to their level in the hierarchy and the department they represent. Various functional units operate under unique reward systems and reflect unique orientations or thought-worlds. For example, marketing managers are evaluated on the basis of sales, profits, or market share, whereas production managers are assessed on the basis of manufacturing efficiency and cost-effectiveness. In turn, R&D managers may be oriented toward long-term objectives; customer service managers may emphasise more immediate ones. Strategic plans emerge out of a bargaining process among functional areas. Managing conflict, promoting cooperation, and developing coordinated strategies are all fundamental to the business marketer's interdisciplinary role. By understanding the concerns and orientations of personnel from other functional areas, the business marketing manager is better equipped to forge effective cross-unit working relationships.

5.2 THE COMPONENTS OF A BUSINESS MODEL*

For a strategy to succeed, individuals must understand and share a common definition of a firm's existing business concept. For example, ask any employee at Dell and they will tell you about the "Dell model" that sets them apart from competitors. A **business concept** or model consists of four major components (Figure 5.2):

FIGURE 5.2 Components of a business model

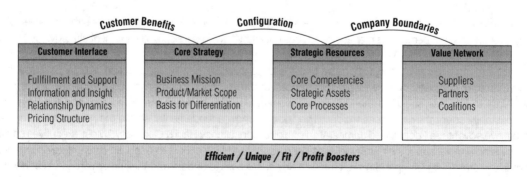

- Customer Interface
- Core Strategy
- Strategic Resources
- Value Network

The major components of the business concept are tied together by three important "bridge" elements: customer benefits, configuration, and company boundaries.

5.2.1 Customer interface

Customer benefits provide the bridge between the core strategy and the customer interface. Customer benefits link the core strategy directly to the needs of customers. The customer interface includes four elements:

1 **Fulfilment and support** refers to the channels a business marketing firm uses to reach customers and the level of service support it provides.

2 **Information and insight** refers to the knowledge captured from customers and the degree to which this information is used to provide enhanced value to the customer.

3 **Relationship dynamics** refers to the nature of the interaction between the firm and its customers (for example, the proportion of relational versus transactional customers. Key question: What steps can be taken to raise the hurdle for competitors by exceeding customer expectations or strengthening the customer's sense of affiliation with the firm?

4 **Pricing structure.** A business concept may offer several pricing choices. For example, a firm can bundle products and services or price them on a menu basis. For example, when airlines buy an Airbus A350, which is equipped with jet engines produced by Rolls Royce, they pay Rolls Royce a fee for each flight hour in line with a fixed-priced maintenance agreement. So, rather than products, Rolls Royce is selling "power by the hour."

5.2.2 Core strategy

The **core strategy** determines how the firm chooses to compete. From Figure 5.2, observe that three elements are involved in setting a core strategy:

1 The **business mission** describes the overall objectives of the strategy, sets a course and direction, and defines a set of performance criteria that are used to measure progress. The business mission must be broad enough to allow for business concept innovation, and it should be distinguished from the mission of competitors in the industry. For example, by focusing its mission on copiers and copying, Xerox allowed Hewlett-Packard to build a dominant lead in the printer business.

2 **Product/market scope** defines *where* the firm competes. The product markets that constitute the domain of a business can be defined by customer benefits, technologies, customer segments, and channels of distribution.* Strategists might consider this question: Are particular customer segments being overlooked by competitors or customers who might welcome a new product-service solution?

3 **Basis for differentiation** captures the essence of how a firm competes differently than its rivals. George Day and Robin Wensley explain:
   A business is differentiated when some value-adding activities are performed in a way that leads to perceived superiority along dimensions that are valued by customers. For these activities to be

B2B TOP PERFORMERS

Fujitsu

Marketing lies at the heart of business decision-making in driving profitable growth. There are three primary elements to this – go-to-market strategy, innovation and brand:

- Go-to-market strategy: we help our business units prioritise who to talk to, about what and when; we provide them with the customer and competitor intelligence to engage with priority target customers in the most compelling manner; and we help them to powerfully position our business with this customer.

- Innovation: we lead cross-functional teams from every part of our business in developing distinctive new-thinking that challenges the accepted norms; we package and communicate the new value propositions that emerge from this work; and we ensure that our sales and account teams understand and connect with it, so they can actively use these propositions to better engage with their customers.

- Brand: we define our brand positioning, and how this positioning will develop over time; we make this positioning manifest in our internal and external communications; and we work with others across the business to ensure that the positioning translates into a coherent employee and customer experience.

Marketing strategy is critical to our business. Without it we are left behaving in an utterly responsive manner to the latest new business opportunity, whether or not it is well suited to our goals, talents and current market positioning. With it we can maximise the return from our marketing, sales and account management effort through targeting only those customers whose business we really want – and that we can realistically expect to win. Understanding the external trading environment is very important because this helps us to determine the nature and the scale of our resourcing requirements, and how we can best deploy these resources to generate the maximum business value.

George Miller, Group Marketing Director
Fujitsu Services

Fujitsu is the world's third largest IT services group and works closely with large government and commercial organisations to help them seize the possibilities of effective, innovative IT.

profitable, the customer must be willing to pay a premium for the benefits and the premium must exceed the added costs of superior performance.[*]

There are many ways for a firm to differentiate products and services:

- Provide superior service or technical assistance competence through speed, responsiveness to complex orders, or ability to solve special customer problems.

- Provide superior quality that reduces customer costs or improves their performance.

- Offer innovative product features that use new technologies.

5.2.3 Strategic resources

A business marketing firm gains a competitive advantage through its superior skills and resources. The firm's strategic resources include core competencies, strategic assets, and core processes.

1 **Core competencies** are the set of skills, systems, and technologies a company uses to create uniquely high value for customers.* Concerning core competencies, the guiding questions for the strategist are: What important benefits do our competencies provide to customers? What do we know or do especially well that is valuable to customers and is transferable to new market opportunities?

2 **Strategic assets** are the more tangible requirements for advantage that enable a firm to exercise its capabilities. Included are brands, customer data, distribution coverage, patents, and other resources that are both rare and valuable. Attention centres on this question: Can we use these strategic assets in a different way to provide new levels of value to existing or prospective customers?

3 **Core processes** are the methodologies and routines companies use to transform competencies, assets, and other inputs into value for customers. For example, drug discovery is a core process at Merck, and delivery fulfilment is a core process at DHL. Here the strategist considers these questions: Which processes are most competitively unique and create the most customer value? Could we use our process expertise effectively to enter other markets?

From Figure 5.2, note that a configuration component links strategic resources to the core strategy. "Configuration refers to the unique way in which competencies, assets, and processes are interrelated in support of a particular strategy."* For example, Volkswagen manages key activities in the new-product-development process differently than its rivals.

5.2.4 The value network

The final component of a business concept is the **value network** that complements and further enriches the firm's research base. Included here are suppliers, strategic alliance partners, and coalitions. To illustrate, nimble competitors such as Fujitsu IT services and Apple demonstrate special skills in forging relationships with suppliers and alliance partners. Concerning the value network, the guiding question for the strategist is: What market opportunities might become available to us "if we could 'borrow' the assets and competencies of other companies and marry them with our own?"*

5.2.5 Strategic positioning*

Competitive strategy, at the core, is about being different, choosing to compete in a distinctive way. A business model should reveal the way in which a firm is deliberately emphasising a different set of activities in order to deliver a unique mix of customer value. Michael Porter asserts that six fundamental principles provide a company with the foundation for establishing and maintaining a distinctive strategic positioning (see Figure 5.3).

- Centre on the *right goal*—superior long-term return on investment rather than performance goals defined in terms of sales volume or market share leadership.

- Deliver a *customer value proposition*, or set of benefits, that differs from those of rivals. (For example, easyJet delivers low-cost, convenient service to customers—particular benefits that full-service rivals cannot match.)

- Create a *distinctive value chain* by performing different activities than rivals or performing similar activities in different ways. (For example, by streamlining the passenger boarding process, easyJet achieves faster turnaround at the gate and can provide more frequent departures with fewer planes.)

- Accept *trade-offs* and recognise that a company must forgo some product features or services to remain truly distinctive in others. (For example, British Airways introduced Go Fly to compete directly

FIGURE 5.3 The principles of strategic positioning

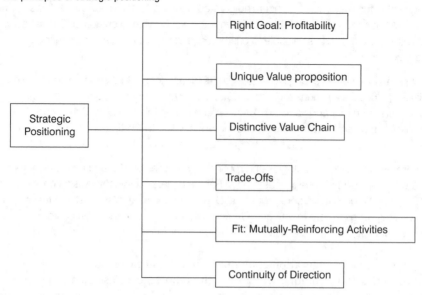

Source: Adapted from Michael E. Porter, "What Is Strategy?" *Harvard Business Review* 74 (November–December 1996): pp. 61–78.

against easyJet. However, there were concerns that Go Fly was attracting customers away from British Airways and it was subsequently sold to easyJet.)

● Emphasise the way in which all the elements of the strategy *fit* and reinforce one another. (For example, from its standardised fleet of Airbus A320 aircraft to its well-trained ground crews that speed flight turnaround, and its strict limits on the type and length of routes, easyJet's activities complement and reinforce one another, creating a whole system of competing that locks out imitators.)

● Build strong customer relationships and develop unique skills by defining a distinctive value proposition that provides *continuity of direction*. (For example, easyJet continues to pursue its disciplined strategic agenda.)

Michael Porter observes:

> *Having a strategy is a matter of discipline. It requires a strong focus on profitability rather than just growth, an ability to define a unique value proposition, and a willingness to make tough trade-offs in choosing what not to do…. It involves the configuration of a tailored value chain—the series of activities required to produce and deliver a product or service—that enables a company to offer unique value.* [*]

Let's examine how a business-to-business firm has used these principles to establish a business model and maintain a distinctive strategic positioning.

5.2.6 Strategic positioning illustrated[*]

Paccar operates in the fiercely competitive heavy-duty lorry industry, designing and manufacturing lorries under the Kenworth and Peterbilt brand names. The firm, headquartered in Bellevue, Washington, commands 20 per cent of the North American heavy lorry market and derives approximately half of its revenues and profits from outside the United States.

A unique focus

Rather than centring on large-fleet buyers or large leasing companies, Paccar has chosen to focus on one group of customers—drivers who own their own lorries and contract directly with shippers or serve as contractors to larger trucking companies. Paccar provides an array of specialised services that specifically address the needs of owner-operators: luxurious sleeper cabins, noise-insulated cabins, and sleek interior and exterior options (numbering in the thousands) that prospective buyers can select to put their personal signatures on their trucks. Paccar delivers its products and services to customers through an extensive dealer network of nearly 1800 locations worldwide.

Distinctive value proposition

Built to order, these customised trucks are delivered to customers in six to eight weeks and incorporate features and value-added services that are embraced by owner-operators. Paccar's trucks feature an aerodynamic design that reduces fuel consumption, and they maintain resale value better than the trucks offered by rivals. To reduce out-of-service time, Paccar offers a comprehensive roadside assistance programme and an information-technology-supported system for expediting and delivering spare parts. According to Michael Porter, "Customers pay Paccar a 10 per cent premium, and its Kenworth and Peterbilt brands are considered status symbols at transport cafe."[*] Moreover, Paccar has received recognition for consistently leading the heavy-duty truck market in quality, innovation, and customer satisfaction.[*]

By configuring its activities on new-product development, manufacturing, and service support differently from rivals, and by tailoring these activities to its customer value proposition, Paccar has achieved an enviable record of financial performance: 68 straight years of profitability, averaging a long-run return on equity above 20 per cent.

5.3 BUILDING THE STRATEGY PLAN

By finding an intricate match between strategy and operations, strategic positioning depends on doing many things well—not just a few. But yet, the underperformance of most companies is caused by breakdowns between strategy and operations. Robert S. Kaplan and David P. Norton contend that execution of successful strategy involves two basic rules: "understand the management cycle that links strategy and operations, and know what tools to apply at each stage of the cycle."[*] To that end, they propose that companies develop a management system to plan, coordinate, and monitor the links between strategy and operations. This **management system** represents "the integrated set of processes and tools that a company uses to develop its strategy, translate it into operational actions, and monitor and improve the effectiveness of both."[*] (See Figure 5.4.)

Observe that the management system involves five stages, beginning with strategy development (Stage 1) and then moving on to the crucial stage of translating the strategy (Stage 2) into objectives and measures that can be clearly communicated to all functional areas and employees. We will give special attention to two tools: (1) the **balanced scorecard** that provides managers with a comprehensive system for converting a company's vision and strategy into a tightly connected set of performance measures; and (2) the **strategy map**—a tool for visualising a firm's strategy as a chain of cause-and-effect relationships among strategic objectives. These tools and processes assume a central role in designing key processes (Stage 3), monitoring performance (Stage 4), and adapting the strategy (Stage 5).

5.3.1 The balanced scorecard[*]

Measurement is a central element in the strategy process. The balanced scorecard combines financial measures of past performance with measures of the drivers of performance. Observe in

FIGURE 5.4 The management system: Linking strategy and operations

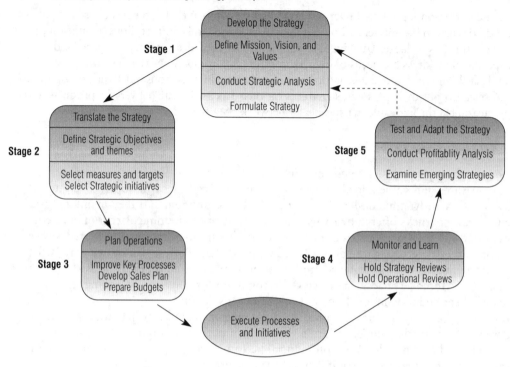

Source: Adapted with modifications from Robert S. Kaplan and David P. Norton, "Mastering the Management System," *Harvard Business Review* 86 (January 2008): p. 65.

Figure 5.5 that the scorecard examines the performance of a business unit from four perspectives: (1) financial, (2) customer, (3) internal business processes, and (4) learning and growth.

The architects of the approach, Robert Kaplan and David Norton, emphasise that "the scorecard should tell the story of the strategy, starting with the long-run financial objectives, and then linking them to the sequence of actions that must be taken with financial processes, customers, and finally employees and systems to deliver the desired long-run economic performance."[*]

5.3.2 Financial perspective

Financial performance measures allow business marketing managers to monitor the degree to which the firm's strategy, implementation, and execution are increasing profits. Measures such as return on investment, revenue growth, shareholder value, profitability, and cost per unit are among the performance measures that show whether the firm's strategy is succeeding or failing. Companies emphasise two basic levers in developing a financial strategy: revenue growth and productivity.[*] The revenue-growth strategy centres on securing sales from new markets and new products or strengthening and expanding relationships with existing customers. The productivity strategy can also take two forms: improve the company's cost structure by reducing expenses and/or use assets more efficiently by decreasing the working and fixed capital needed to support a given level of output.

Recent research confirms the wisdom of a balanced approach to strategy by isolating the strategy that winning firms follow to survive a recession and thrive when it ends.[*] These firms cut costs mainly by improving operational efficiency rather than by slashing the number of employees more than peers. However, the offensive moves of winning firms are comprehensive. "They develop new business opportunities by making significantly greater investments than their rivals do in R&D and marketing, and they invest in assets, such as plants and machinery."[*]

FIGURE 5.5 The balanced scorecard: A framework to translate a strategy into operational terms

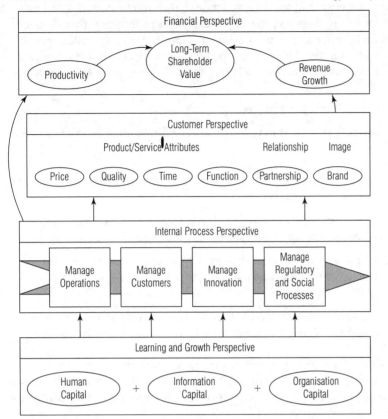

Cause-and-Effect Relationships

Defines the chain of logic by which intangible assets will be transformed to tangible value.

Customer Value Proposition

Clarifies the conditions that will create value for the customer.

Value-Creating Processes

Defines the processes that will transform intangible assets into customer and financial outcomes.

Clustering of Assets and Activities

Defines the intangible assets that must be aligned and integrated to create the value.

Source: Reprinted by permission of *Harvard Business Review*. From "Balanced Scorecard Framework" by Robert S. Kaplan in *Strategy Maps*, p. 31. Copyright © 2004 by the Harvard Business School Publishing Corporation; all rights reserved.

The balanced scorecard seeks to match financial objectives to a business unit's growth and life cycle stages. Three stages of a business are isolated and linked to appropriate financial objectives:

1   **Growth:** Business units that have products and services with significant growth potential and that must commit considerable resources (for example, production facilities and distribution networks) to capitalise on the market opportunity.
     Financial Objectives: Sales growth rate by segment; percentage of revenue from new product, services, and customers.

2   **Sustain:** Business units, likely representing the majority of businesses within a firm, that expect to maintain or to perhaps moderately increase market share from year to year.
     Financial Objectives: Share of target customers and accounts; customer and product-line profitability.

3   **Harvest:** Mature business units that warrant only enough investment to maintain production equipment and capabilities.
     Financial Objectives: Payback; customer and product-line profitability.

5.3.3 Customer perspective

In the customer component of the balanced scorecard, the business unit identifies the market segments it will target. Those segments supply the revenue stream that support critical financial objectives. Marketing managers must also identify the value proposition—how the firm proposes to deliver competitively superior and sustainable value to the target customers and market segments. The central element of any business strategy is the value proposition that describes a company's unique product and service attributes, customer relationship management practises, and corporate reputation. Importantly, the value proposition should clearly communicate to targeted customers what the company expects to do better and differently than its competitors.

Key value propositions and customer strategies

Business-to-business firms typically choose among four forms of differentiation in developing a value proposition[*]:

- **Low total cost**—customers are offered attractive prices, excellent and consistent quality, ease of purchase, and responsive service (for example, Dell, Inc.).

- **Product innovation and leadership**—customers receive products that expand existing performance boundaries through new features and functions (for example, Intel and Sony).

- **Complete customer solutions**—customers feel that the company understands them and can provide customised products and services tailored to their unique requirements (for example, IBM).

- **Lock-in**—customers purchase a widely used proprietary product or service from the firm and incur high switching costs (for example, Microsoft's operating system or Google's search engine).

For the chosen strategy, Table 5.1 presents the core customer outcome measures used to monitor performance in each target segment. The customer perspective complements traditional market share analysis by tracking customer acquisition, customer retention, customer satisfaction, and customer profitability.

5.3.4 Internal business process perspective

To develop the value proposition that will reach and satisfy targeted customer segments and to achieve the desired financial objectives, critical internal business processes must be developed and continually enriched. Internal business processes support two crucial elements of a company's strategy: (1) they create and deliver the value proposition for customers and (2) they

TABLE 5.1   The customer perspective—core measures

Market Share	Represents the proportion of business in a given market (in terms of number of customers, euros spent, or unit volume sold) that a business unit sells.
Customer Acquisition	Tracks, in absolute or relative terms, the rate at which a business unit attracts or wins new customers or business.
Customer Retention	Tracks, in absolute or relative terms, the rate at which a business unit retains customers.
Customer Satisfaction	Matches the satisfaction level of customers on specific performance criteria such as quality, service, or on-time delivery reliability.
Customer Profitability	Assesses the net profit of a customer, or segment, after deducting the unique expenses required to support that customer or segment.

Source: Adapted from Robert S. Kaplan and David P. Norton, *The Balanced Scorecard: Translating Strategy into Action* (Boston: Harvard Business School Press, 1996): p. 68.

improve processes and reduce costs, enriching the productivity component in the financial perspective. Among the processes vital to the creation of customer value are:

1 Operations Management Processes,

2 Customer Management Processes,

3 Innovation Management Processes.

Strategic alignment

Robert S. Kaplan and David P. Norton emphasise that "value is created through internal business processes."[*] Table 5.2 shows how key internal processes can be aligned to support the firm's customer strategy or differentiating-value proposition. First, observe that the relative emphasis (see shaded areas) given to a particular process varies by strategy. For example, a firm that actively pursues a product-leadership strategy highlights innovation-management processes, whereas a company adopting a low-total-cost strategy assigns priority to operations-management processes. Second, although the level of emphasis might vary, note how the various processes work together to reinforce the value proposition. For example, a low-total-cost strategy can be reinforced by an innovation-management process that uncovers process improvements and a customer relationship management process that delivers superb post-sales support.

From our discussion of strategic positioning, recall that it is much harder for a rival to match a set of interlocked processes than it is to replicate a single process. Michael Porter observes:

Strategic fit among many activities is fundamental not only to competitive advantage but also to the sustainability of that advantage… . Positions built on systems of activities are far more sustainable than those built on individual activities.[*]

TABLE 5.2 Aligning internal business processes to the customer strategy

Customer Strategy	The Focus of Internal Business Processes		
	Operations Management	Customer Relationship Management	Innovation Management
Low-Total-Cost Strategy	Highly Efficient Operating Processes; Efficient, Timely Distribution	Ease of Access for Customers; Superb Post-sales Service	Seek Process Innovations Gain Scale Economies
Product Leadership Strategy	Flexible Manufacturing Processes; Rapid Introduction of New Products	Capture Customer Ideas for New Offering; Educate Customers about Complex New Products/Services	Disciplined, High-Performance Product Development; First-to-Market
Complete Customer Solutions Strategy	Deliver Broad Product/Service Line; Create Network of Suppliers for Extended Product/Service Capabilities	Create Customised Solutions for Customers; Build Strong Customer Relationships; Develop Customer Knowledge	Identify New Opportunities to Serve Customers; Anticipate Future Customer Needs
Lock-in Strategies	Provide Capacity for Proprietary Product/Service; Reliable Access and Ease of Use	Create Awareness; Influence Switching Costs of Existing and Potential Customers	Develop and Enhance Proprietary Product; Increase Breadth/Applications of Standard

Source: Adapted from Robert S. Kaplan and David P. Norton, *Strategy Maps: Converting Intangible Assets into Tangible Outcomes* (Boston: Harvard Business School Publishing Corporation, 2004), pp. 322–344.

Learning and growth

The fourth component of the balanced scorecard, **learning and growth,** highlights how the firm's intangible assets must be aligned to its strategy to achieve long-term goals. **Intangible assets** represent "the capabilities of the company's employees to satisfy customer needs."[*] The three principal drivers of organisational learning and growth are:

1 *Human capital*—the availability of employees who have the skills, talent, and know-how to perform activities required by the strategy;

2 *Information capital*—the availability of information systems, applications, and information-technology infrastructure to support the strategy;

3 *Organisation capital*—the culture (for example, values), leadership, employee incentives, and teamwork to mobilise the organisation and execute the strategy.

Strategic alignment

To create value and advance performance, the intangible assets of the firm must be aligned with the strategy. For example, consider a company that plans to invest in staff training and has two choices—a training programme on total quality management (TQM) or a training initiative on customer relationship management (CRM). A company like Dell, which pursues a low-total-cost strategy, might derive higher value from TQM training, whereas IBM's consulting unit, which pursues a total customer solution strategy, would benefit more from CRM training. Unfortunately, research suggests that two-thirds of organisations fail to create a strong alignment between their strategies and their human resources and information technology programmes.[*]

Measuring strategic readiness

Senior management must ensure that the firm's human resources and information technology systems are aligned with the chosen strategy. To achieve desired performance goals in the other areas of the scorecard, key objectives must be achieved on measures of employee satisfaction, retention, and productivity. Likewise, front-line employees, such as sales or technical service representatives, must have ready access to timely and accurate information. However, skilled employees who are supported by a carefully designed information system will not contribute to organisational goals if they are not motivated or empowered to do so. Many firms, such as DHL and Virgin, have demonstrated the vital role of motivated and empowered employees in securing a strong customer franchise.

Now that each of the components of the balanced scorecard has been defined, let's explore a clever tool that can be used to communicate the desired strategy path to all employees while detailing the processes that will be used to implement the strategy.

5.3.5 Strategy map

To provide a visual representation of the cause-and-effect relationships among the components of the balanced scorecard, Kaplan and Norton developed what they call a strategy map. They say that a strategy must provide a clear portrait that reveals how a firm will achieve its desired goals and deliver on its promises to employees, customers, and shareholders. "A strategy map enables an organisation to describe and illustrate, in clear and general language, its objectives, initiatives, and targets; the measures used to assess performance (such as market share and customer surveys); and the linkages that are the foundation for strategic direction."[*]

Key strategy principles

Figure 5.6 shows the strategy map template for a firm pursuing a product-leadership strategy. We can use this illustration to review and reinforce the key principles that underlie a strategy map:

FIGURE 5.6 **Strategy map template: Product leadership**

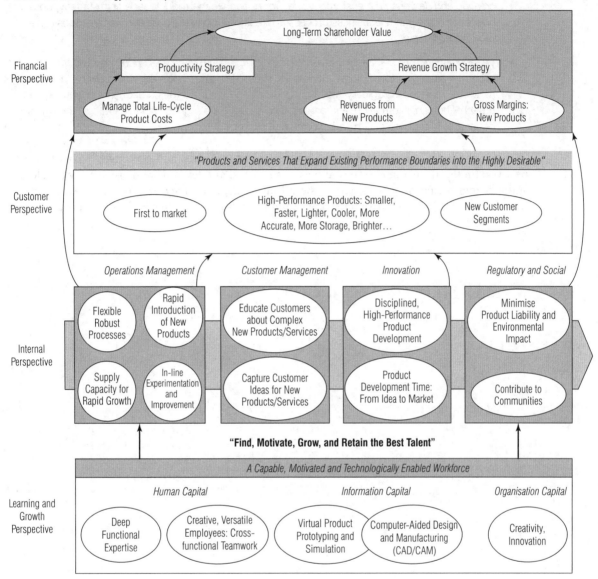

- *Companies emphasise two performance levels in developing a financial strategy—a productivity strategy and a revenue-growth strategy.*

- *Strategy involves choosing and developing a differentiated customer value proposition*. Note the value proposition for product leadership: ''Products and services that expand existing performance boundaries into the highly desirable.'' Recall that the other value propositions and customer strategies include low total cost, complete customer solutions, and system lock-in.

- *Value is created through internal business processes*. The financial and customer perspectives in the balanced scorecard and strategy map describe the performance outcomes the firm seeks, such as increases in shareholder value through revenue growth and productivity improvements, as well as enhanced performance outcomes from customer acquisition, retention, loyalty, and growth.

● *Strategy involves identifying and aligning the critical few processes that are most important for creating and delivering the customer value proposition.* For a product-leadership strategy, observe how each of the internal business processes directly supports the customer value proposition — product leadership.

● *Value is enhanced when intangible assets (for example, human capital) are aligned with the customer strategy.* From Figure 5.6, note the strategic theme for learning and growth: ''a capable, motivated, and technologically enabled workforce.'' When the three components of learning and growth — human, information, and organisation capital — are aligned with the strategy, the firm is better able to mobilise action and execute that strategy.

To recap, the balanced scorecard provides a series of measures and objectives across four perspectives: financial, customer, internal business process, and learning and growth. By developing mutually reinforcing objectives across these four areas, a strategy map can be used to tell the story of a business unit's customer strategy and to highlight the internal business processes that drive performance.

SUMMARY

Guided by a deep understanding of the needs of customers and the capabilities of competitors, market-driven organisations are committed to a set of processes, beliefs, and values that promote the achievement of superior performance by satisfying customers better than competitors do. Because many business-to-business firms have numerous divisions, product lines, and brands, three major levels of strategy exist in most large organisations: (1) corporate, (2) business level, and (3) functional. Moving down the strategy hierarchy, the focus shifts from strategy formulation to strategy implementation. Marketing is best viewed as the functional area that manages critical connections between the organisation and customers. Business marketing planning must be coordinated and synchronised with corresponding planning efforts in other functional areas. Strategic plans emerge out of a bargaining process among functional areas. Managing conflict, promoting cooperation, and developing coordinated strategies are all fundamental to the business marketer's role.

A business model or concept consists of four major components: (1) a core strategy, (2) strategic resources, (3) the customer interface, and (4) the value network. The core strategy is the essence of how the firm competes, whereas strategic resources capture what the firm knows (core competencies), what the firm owns (strategic assets), and what employees actually do (core processes). Specifying the benefits to customers is a critical decision when designing a core strategy. The customer interface component refers to how customer relationship management strategies are designed and managed, whereas the value network component considers how partners and supply chain members can complement and strengthen the resource base of the firm. To establish and maintain a distinctive strategic positioning, a company should focus on profitability, rather than just revenue growth, deliver a unique value proposition, and configure activities—like new-product development or customer relationship management—differently from rivals and in a manner that supports its value proposition.

Successful execution involves linking strategy to operations, using tools and processes such as the balanced scorecard and strategy map. The balanced scorecard converts a strategy goal into concrete objectives, and measures are organised into four different perspectives: financial, customer, internal business process, and learning and growth. The approach involves identifying target customer segments, defining the differentiating customer value proposition, aligning the critical internal processes that deliver value to customers in these segments, and selecting the organisational capabilities necessary to achieve customer and financial objectives. Business marketers primarily emphasise one of the following value propositions or customer strategies: low total cost, product leadership, complete customer solutions, or system lock-in. A strategy map provides a visual representation of a firm's critical objectives and the cause-and-effect relationships among them that drive superior organisational performance.

DISCUSSION QUESTIONS

1 Identify the major components of strategic market planning and explain how they are interrelated.

2 In what ways should implementation of a marketing strategy be managed and facilitated?

3 Can a company be successful without a strategic marketing plan? Give reasons for your answer.

4 If you were the marketing manager of a company that markets sophisticated audio equipment, how would you respond with your strategy to demographic developments and major trends in the marketing environment?

5 It has been suggested that in a service organisation, particularly in a public service organisation such as the BBC, that the customer scorecard should be at the top and the finance scorecard should be at the bottom. What are the arguments for and against this proposal, and how would the decision be related to the organisation's strategic mission?

INTERNET EXERCISES

http://www.zeroz.cz/

Zeroz is a Czech company involved in the manufacture of labels. They are a relatively small operation situated towards the Czech / Slovak border and, because of their relatively remote location they need to maximise routes to market. For them, the World Wide Web offers a very attractive platform.

Questions:

1 How effectively do you feel they have used their website as a sales platform?

2 Have they made appropriate provisions for attracting a wider, international market?

REFERENCES

Casadesus-Masanell, Ramon, and Ricart, Joan E., "How to Design a Winning Business Model," *Harvard Business Review* 89 (January–February 2011): pp. 100–107.

Comstock, Beth, Gulati, Ranjay, and Liquori, Stephen, "Unleashing the Power of Marketing," *Harvard Business Review* 88 (October 2010): p. 98.

Day, George S., *Strategic Market Planning: The Pursuit of Competitive Advantage* (St. Paul, MN: West Publishing, 1984).

Day, George S., and Wensley, Robin, "Assessing Advantage: A Framework for Diagnosing Competitive Superiority," *Journal of Marketing* 52 (April 1988): pp. 3–4.

Dibb, Sally, Simkin, Lyndon, Pride, Bill, and Ferrell, O.C., *Marketing Concepts & Strategies*, 6th ed. (Cengage, 2012).

Doole, Isobel, and Lowe, Robin, *International Marketing Strategy* 6th ed. (Cengage, 2012).

Frankwick, Gary L., Ward, James C., Hutt, Michael. D., and Reingen, Peter H., "Evolving Patterns of Organizational Beliefs in the Formation of Marketing Strategy," *Journal of Marketing* 58 (April 1994): pp. 96–110.

Gulati, Ranjay, Nohria, Nitin, and Wohlgezogen, Franz, "Roaring Out of Recession," *Harvard Business Review* 88 (March 2010): pp. 62–69.

Hamel, Gary, *Leading the Revolution* (Boston: Harvard Business School Press, 2000), pp. 70–94.

Homburg, Christian, and Jensen, Ore, "The Thought Worlds of Marketing and Sales: Which Differences Make a Difference?" *Journal of Marketing* 71 (July 2007): pp. 124–141.

Homburg, Christian, Jensen, Ore, and Krohmer, Harley, "Configurations of Marketing and Sales," *Journal of Marketing* 72 (March 2008): pp. 123–154.

Hutt, Michael D., and Speh, Thomas W., "The Marketing Strategy Center: Diagnosing the Industrial Marketer's Interdisciplinary Role," *Journal of Marketing* 48 (Fall 1984): pp. 53–61.

Hutt, Michael D., Walker, Beth A., and Frankwick, Gary L., "Hurdle the Cross-Functional Barriers to Strategic Change," *Sloan Management Review* 36 (Spring 1995): pp. 22–30.

Kaplan, Robert S., and Norton, David P., "Having Trouble with Your Strategy? Then Map It," *Harvard Business Review* 78 (September–October 2000): pp. 167–176.

Kaplan, Robert S., and Norton, David P., "Mastering the Management System," *Harvard Business Review* 86 (January 2008): p. 63.

Kaplan, Robert S., and Norton, David P., *The Balanced Scorecard: Translating Strategy into Action* (Boston: Harvard Business School Press, 1996), chaps. 1–3.

Kaplan, Robert S., and Norton, David P., *Strategy Maps: Converting Intangible Assets into Tangible Outcomes* (Boston: Harvard Business School Publishing Corporation, 2004).

Kirca, Ahmet H., Jayachandran, Satish, and Bearden, William O., "Market Orientation: A Meta Analytic Review of Its Antecedents and Impact on Performance," *Journal of Marketing* 69 (April 2005): pp. 24–41.

Lim, Jeen-Su, and Reid, David A., "Vital Cross-Functional Linkages with Marketing," *Industrial Marketing Management* 22 (February 1993): pp. 159–165.

McCann, Joseph E., and Gilmore, Thomas N., "Diagnosing Organizational Decision Making through Responsibility Charting," *Sloan Management Review* 25 (Winter 1983): pp. 3–15.

Moutinho, Luiz, and Southern, Geoffrey, *Strategic Marketing Management: A process Based Approach* (Cengage, 2012).

Neilson, Gary L., Martin, Karla L., and Powers, Elizabeth, "The Secrets to Successful Strategy Execution," *Harvard Business Review* 86 (June 2008): p. 63.

Noble, Charles H., and Mokwa, Michael P., "Implementing Marketing Strategies: Developing and Testing a Managerial Theory," *Journal of Marketing* 63 (October 1999): pp. 57–73.

Paccar, "Kenworth Wins J.D. Power Awards," August 27, 2007, http://www.paccar.com/company/jdpower, accessed July 11, 2008.

Porter, Michael E., "What Is Strategy?" *Harvard Business Review* 74 (November–December 1996): pp. 61–78.

Porter, Michael E., "Strategy and the Internet," *Harvard Business Review* 79 (March 2001): p. 72.

Porter, "Michael E., The Five Competitive Forces that Shape Strategy," *Harvard Business Review* 86 (January 2008): p. 89.

Quinn, James Brian, "Strategic Outsourcing: Leveraging Knowledge Capabilities," *Sloan Management Review* 40 (Summer 1999): pp. 9–21.

Rust, Roland T., Moorman, Christine, and Bhalla, Gaurav, "Rethinking Marketing," *Harvard Business Review* 88 (January–February 2010): pp. 94–101.

Stewart, Thomas A., *Intellectual Capital: The New Wealth of Organizations* (New York: Doubleday, 1998), p. 67.

Tichy, Noel M., and Sherman, Stratford, *Control Your Destiny or Someone Else Will* (New York: Doubleday, 1993), p. 26.

van Weele, Arjan, *Puchasing and Supply Chain Management: Analysis Strategy, Planning and Practice*, 5th ed. (Cengage, 2010).

Varadarajan, Rajan, "Strategic Marketing and Marketing Strategy: Domain, Definition, Fundamental Issues and Foundational Promises," *Journal of the Academy of Marketing Science* 38 (January 2010): pp. 119–140.

Verhage, Bronis J., *Marketing: A Global Perspective* (Cengage, 2013).

Verhoef, Peter, and Leeflang, Peter S.H., "Understanding the Marketing Department's Influence within the Firm," *Journal of Marketing* 73 (March 2009): pp. 14–37.

Vorhies, Douglas W., and Morgan, Neil A., "Benchmarking Marketing Capabilities for Sustainable Competitive Advantage," *Journal of Marketing* 69 (January 2005): pp. 80–94.

Webster Jr., Frederick E., "The Changing Role of Marketing in the Corporation," *Journal of Marketing* 56 (October 1992): pp. 1–17.

Welch, Jack, and Byrne, John A., *Jack: Straight from the Gut* (New York: Warner Books, 2001).

CHAPTER 6
BUSINESS
MARKETING
STRATEGIES FOR
GLOBAL MARKETS

CHAPTER OBJECTIVES

Business marketing firms that restrict their attention to the domestic market are overlooking enormous international market opportunities and a challenging field of competitors. After reading this chapter, you will understand:

1   The nature of international involvement in rapidly developing economies

2   Alternative market entry strategies for becoming involved in international marketing activities

3   The different focuses of integrated strategies

4   The importance of adapting and localising business models to the regional market

A recent *Business Week* article focused on the significant increase in global competition that large US industrial corporations are facing. Huge but relatively unknown firms from emerging markets are challenging Western firms in almost every global setting.

> *From India's Infosys Technologies (IT services) to Brazil's Embraer (light jets), and from Taiwan's Acer (computers) to Mexico's Cemex (building materials), a new class of formidable competitors is rising. There are 25 world-class emerging multinationals today, and within 15 years, there will be at least 100 of them. The biggest challenge posed by these up-and-coming rivals will not be in Western markets, but within developing nations. That's the arena of fastest global growth—and home to 80 per cent of the world's 6 billion consumers, hundreds of millions of whom have moved into the middle class. The rise of these new multinationals will force American business marketers to rethink strategies for Third World product development, marketing, and links with local companies.* [*]

Truly, business-to-business marketing is worldwide in scope, and the very existence of many business marketing firms will hinge on their ability to act decisively, compete aggressively, and seize market opportunities in rapidly expanding global economies. Numerous business marketing firms—such as GE, IBM, Intel, Airbus, and JCB—currently derive much of their profit from global markets. They have realigned operations and developed a host of new strategies to strengthen market positions and compete effectively against the new breed of strong global rivals.

This chapter will examine the need for, and the formulation of, global business marketing strategies. The discussion is divided into four parts. First, attention centres on rapidly developing economies, like China, and the sources of global advantage they can represent for business marketing firms. Second, international market-entry options are isolated and described. Third, "multi-domestic" and "global" strategies are compared, and prescriptions are provided for where they are most effectively applied. Fourth, the critical requirements for a successful global strategy are explored.

6.1 CAPTURING GLOBAL ADVANTAGE[*]

Global companies face a radically altered business landscape following the recent financial crisis, most notably a slowdown in world economic growth. Moreover, a two-speed world economy is emerging, sharply defined by slower growth in the developed economies of the United States, Europe, and Japan and much faster growth in Southeast Asia and the BRIC countries (Brazil, Russia, India, and China). For example, rapidly developing economies (RDEs) such as China, India, and Brazil enjoy high growth but low average household income. For these countries, the growth of the gross domestic product (GDP) ranges from 8 to 12 per cent. By contrast, low-growth countries like the United States and western Europe experience annual GDP growth of 2 to 4 per cent, but their households have higher salaries and more disposable income.

Competing successfully in this challenging business environment requires business-to-business companies to meet the needs of both low-growth and high-growth markets while differentiating their offerings from foreign and local competitors. Many formidable rivals from RDEs are capitalising on their low-cost position in these fast-growing markets and assuming a leading role in some global markets from natural gas and iron ore to automotive forgings, micromotors, and regional jets. "These global trends—the shifting centre of gravity from the West to the East, the rise of new global challengers from RDEs, and the growing volatility and complexity of the business environment ... call for new competitive models to win." [*]

In the past, the underlying philosophy guiding globalisation strategies was "oneness"—replicating the home country business model and its key processes across markets. However, Arindam Bhattacharya and his colleagues at the Boston Consulting Group (BCG) assert that the new global reality requires a philosophy of "manyness"—many products and services drawing on many skills, ideas, and systems to compete in many markets. To that end, they offer the BCG

FIGURE 6.1

The BCG global advantage
diamond

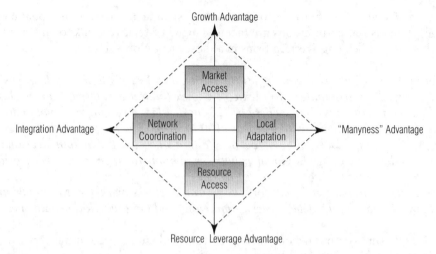

Source: BCG analysis. Figure located in "Competing for Advantage: How to Succeed in the New Global Reality," January 2010, by Arindam Bhattacharya, Jim Hemerling, and Bernd Waltermann, The Boston Consulting Group. (http://www.bcg.com/documents/file37656.pdf).

Global Advantage Diamond to portray the key elements that must be developed and integrated to secure a strong position in global markets (see Figure 6.1).

Successful companies are able to adapt their business models to new groups of target customers in RDEs and develop new ways to integrate these different business models to achieve synergies and share best practices within the firm. To achieve global leadership, integrated strategies should incorporate the following elements:

- *Market access*: driving sales growth by reaching new markets and targeting new market segments;

- *Resource access*: leveraging valuable resources (for example, talent, assets, raw materials, and knowledge) in RDEs to achieve competitive advantage;

- *Local adaptation*: developing and adapting products and services to satisfy the unique needs of RDE customers;

- *Network coordination*: integrating operations to capitalise on the strength of the company's global network.

6.1.1 Market access

Companies can expand market access in RDEs by: (1) increasing the number of countries served and/or (2) penetrating more deeply into new customer segments and new product categories in existing markets. Deeper market penetration often poses more difficult challenges for Western companies because their business models have traditionally targeted premium products for customers located on the top of the income pyramid. Based on cost advantages, this allows local competitors in RDEs to offer lower priced, simpler products and services to customers below the premium segment.

To capture the next wave of growth, multinational companies must go beyond the premium segments. "That means addressing the so-called midmarket, which has grown the fastest in many emerging markets and product categories, as well as the next *billion* consumers, who sit above the poorest of the poor in the income pyramid, often in difficult to reach locations."* While routinely ignored by multinational companies, the next billion purchase more than €0.75 trillion in goods and services per year. These consumers spend more than one-third of their household income on nonessentials. Products created for the developed world, however, do not meet their requirements or budgets.

Reverse innovation at GE[*]

Rising to this challenge, General Electric has delivered on its promise to create health-care innovations that would substantially lower costs, increase access, and improve quality. Two products issuing from this strategic initiative include: (1) a portable, PC-based ultrasound machine that sells for as little as €11 250 compared to the €75 000 to €225 000 price range for conventional ultrasound equipment; and (2) a €750 handheld electrocardiogram (ECG) device. Importantly, these products were originally developed for markets in RDEs (the ECG device for rural India and the ultrasound machine for rural China) and are now being widely adopted in the United States. This approach stands in sharp contrast to the typical innovation model in which products are developed for the home market and then adapted to local conditions in the RDE if possible. GE refers to this process as *reverse innovation.*

The portable ultrasound is being used by rural clinics in China that serve more than 90 per cent of the population but lack the funds for sophisticated imaging equipment. Of course, the performance of the portable model does not match that of high-end ultrasound machines, but it fits the requirements and budgets of rural clinics where doctors use it for simple applications. In the United States, customers for the portable ultrasound include ambulance squads and casualty. Portable ultrasounds now represent a rapidly growing global product line for GE and generate more than €206 million in revenue. GE's handheld ECG device not only enjoys success in emerging economies but is now being widely adopted by general practitioners in the United States.

6.1.2 Resource access

Many leading-edge companies have shifted their focus from low-cost-country sourcing to "best-cost-country sourcing," an approach that considers a full range of factors beyond labour costs. Companies must weigh the trade-offs among factor costs, supply chain restraints, transportation costs, and relative strengths and weaknesses of RDEs. Longer lead times in a global supply chain add cost risk and variability to delivery schedules. Jesús de Juan, the lead author of a recent Boston Consulting Group study on sourcing, observes: "The days of reducing costs simply from sourcing from China are probably over. In the future, companies will rely on a more diversified base of low-cost suppliers across multiple regions."[*]

Expanding resource access can allow companies to create a diversified portfolio of supply sources in different regions and develop "best-cost" supply chains that provide competitive advantage in RDEs and on a global scale. Many companies like GE, Microsoft, and Apple are transferring steps in their value chain—like R&D or manufacturing—in order to attract talented personnel and to enhance design and manufacturing capabilities. Apart from enhancing global competitiveness, companies are leveraging their sourcing efforts in RDEs to secure access and penetration in local markets.

A twofold strategy

As major industrial sectors relocate manufacturing operations to RDEs, business-to-business firms that supply these sectors must take decisive action. Jim Hemerling and his associates at the Boston Consulting Group provide this advice:

> *Most companies need to develop a twofold strategic plan: to fill market gaps at home, and to follow selected customers to their new locations. In our experience, it is rarely feasible to pursue only one or the other.*[*]

For example, gaps can be filled at home by pursuing new lines of business or new product or service opportunities where the home country advantage can be defended. In turn, when moving to a RDE, suppliers must adjust their operating models to fully capture the cost advantages.

TABLE 6.1 Determining which products to outsource to Rapidly Developing Economies (RDEs) and which to keep at home

Selected Criteria	Maintain Home-Based Manufacturing	Relocate to RDEs
Labour Contract	Low	High
Growth of Demand in Home Market	Low	High
Size of RDE Market	Low	High
Degree of Standardisation	Low	High
Intellectual Property Content	High	Low
Logistical Requirements	High	Low

Source: Adapted from Arindam Bhattacharya et al., "Capturing Global Advantage: How Leading Industrial Companies Are Transforming Their Industries by Sourcing and Selling in China, India, and Other Low-Cost Countries," *The Boston Consulting Group, Inc.*, April 2004, pp. 26–30, accessed at http://www.bcg.com.

The outsourcing decision[*]

The decision to relocate manufacturing, R&D, or customer service to RDEs is a strategic decision involving a host of economic, competitive, and environmental considerations. Clearly, some products and services are better candidates for outsourcing than others.

What should go?

The criteria that favour relocation to RDEs include products or services with high labour content, high growth potential, large RDE markets, and standardised manufacturing or service delivery processes (Table 6.1). These criteria reflect each of the sources of global advantage we have explored. For services, the processes most easily relocated are those that have well-defined process maps or those that are rule-based (for example, the established protocol that a customer service call centre uses).

What should not go?

Products and services that should remain at home include "those for which protection of intellectual property is critical, those with extreme logistical requirements, those with very high technology content or performance requirements, and those for which customers are highly sensitive to the location of production" (for example, certain military contracts).[*] Concerns about intellectual property (IP) theft is a major issue in most RDEs, particularly in China. Experts suggest that some multinational companies in China are losing the battle to protect their IP, largely because they emphasise legal tactics rather than including IP directly into their strategic and operational decisions. By carefully analysing and selecting which products and technologies to sell in China, the best companies reduce the chance that competitors will steal their IP.

6.1.3 Local adaptation

Reaching new customers in RDEs requires a different business model from the one used to reach a firm's high-priced, premium market segments. So, a differentiated approach that responds to local demands in RDEs is needed if market success is to be achieved. Established priorities and organisational rigidities in the global business present formidable barriers to change. To unlock the potential, GE created a local growth team (LGT) model to create new offerings for customers in RDEs, such as China and India, and empowered them to develop their own strategies, organisations, and products.[*] The LGT model is based on five critical principles:

- Shift power to where the growth is.

- Build new offerings from the ground up.

INSIDE BUSINESS MARKETING

The changing geography of global outsourcing

The A.T. Kearney 2009 Global Services Locator Index (GSLI) suggests outsourcing is still expected to grow, as shortages are experienced in the talent pool in the home country and firms gain confidence in outsourcing higher added value functions. However, the geography of outsourcing is changing dramatically with some regions suffering falls, for example, in central European countries, such as Poland Czech Republic and Hungary, while countries in South East Asia and the Middle East are gaining. The reasons for this can be cost advantages but also improved labour quality in the outsourcing countries. Governments around the world are investing in the skills necessary to attract outsourcing business.

While India is the top destination, China has identified business process outsourcing and IT services as future key growth sectors. Different countries offer different advantages, for example, the prevalence of English or multilingual speakers, small time differences, for example South Africa has no more than two hours' difference with Europe, Egypt and Jordan have low cost, highly skilled workers that have worked as migrants in other Gulf states for years. Northern Ireland is close to the UK, but costs there are estimated by IBM to be 32 per cent cheaper than the rest of the UK.

Newer countries are emerging as outsourcing destinations including Vietnam and smaller islands, too, such as Jamaica and Mauritius.

Kearney observed that while offshoring slowed following the recession, the percentage of companies' staff offshore were likely to increase as companies sought to maintain service but reduce costs. Newer offshore facilities tended to be more efficient because onshore facilities tended to be older and more inefficient resulting from years of bad practices and legacy systems.

References: Twentyman, J. (2010) 'Where in the World', Raconteur Media, 10 August; and Kearney, A.T. (2009) *Global Services Locator Index* (GSLI).

- Build LGTs from the ground up, just like forming a new company.

- Customise objectives, targets, and metrics for the RDE environment.

- Provide senior executive support to the LGT, including a direct reporting link to senior management.

LGTs empower local executives to meet customer needs in RDEs. For example, maternal and infant care represents a large potential market in India with its infant mortality rate of 55 children for every 1000 born. GE's baby warmer, developed and built in India, is aimed at this market.[*] Eighty per cent of Indian hospitals use baby warmers, which provide direct heat in open cradles. The appeal of GE's offering is its low price (€2250), simple design, and user-friendly display board. Ravi Kaushik, GE Marketing Director for Maternal Care, observes: "We're targeting the bottom of the pyramid ... I have the technology, and I need to get it to the lowest market."[*] The product is now sold in 62 countries, including Brazil, Russia, Egypt, and Italy.

6.1.4 Network coordination

Even while adapting to local conditions, the best managed global firms leverage their global networks by sharing best practices, knowledge, technology, and systems. Economies of scale and scope can be advanced through process standardisation, adoption of common technology, and rapid information sharing. For example, resource advantages developed in different markets can be shared and diffused to other operating units around the world. Likewise, network advantage is promoted by sharing successes around the world—taking innovations developed in RDEs back to developed markets (like the GE examples presented earlier).

While capturing a network advantage seems to clash with the concept of local adaptation, successful companies have been able to exploit "a diverse and distributed global network in order to simultaneously foster and leverage this diversity, rather than streamlining it."* For example, a global device manufacturer uses a highly standardised approach to assess a market, then uses it to generate differentiated strategies for each of its markets. A strong network of production bases around the world and a highly efficient global supply chain provide a strong platform to support these differentiated strategies.

INSIDE BUSINESS MARKETING

The Dangers of Outsourcing

The telecom market in many European countries has been a playing field of fierce competition over the past decade. Traditional, state owned telecom companies have been privatised and new players have entered the field. The period of unprecedented growth for mobile phones in many European markets has come to an end; as new technologies and applications have become more mature, value propositions have become more alike among the different providers, enabling consumers and businesses to shop around for the most attractive prices and rates. This is facilitated by the Internet, where consumers have better access to benchmark information, enabling them to go for the best rates and deals. This has put significant pressure on the fat margins of the providers, who as a result are desperately seeking for opportunities to slash costs.

Against this background a major telecom player in Europe looked for drastic measures to both reduce its operational cost dramatically and improve its cash position. After a careful selection of projects it decided to outsource all of its IT-activities and call centres. The outsourcing deal for IT, which was closed some years ago with one of the large IT-providers encompassed the sale and lease back of all hardware, peripherals and other IT-infrastructure and all software. The IT-provider, which was selected after a competitive tender, also had to take over most of the company's IT-staff. The future relationship was based upon a thorough long-term, service-level agreement, which consisted of a detailed description of the activities to be performed by the IT-provider, and the costs and rates that could be incurred. Of course the agreement described the impressive sum of money to be paid to the Telecom company. It was agreed that rates and fees would be paid to the IT-provider based upon a limited number of critical key performance indicators, which would be monitored and discussed on a monthly basis between the parties involved. For this an impressive communication structure was built up at both organisations, involving several working groups, technical committees and steering platforms.

After two years it became clear to the telecom Account Team that things had not worked out as intended. First of all, the IT-provider was dissatisfied about the sums that were paid; in hindsight, since prices of hardware and software had gone down significantly, the IT provider thought it had paid far too much when buying the hardware and software. In order to secure its margin and recoup part of the investment it started to cut costs in its services to the telecom company. By putting inexperienced, lower paid staff on crucial service functions (such as help desks) the service level to the telecom's internal staff developed to a surprisingly low level, leading to all kinds of disruptions in simple, but crucial operational processes. Next, although the contract stipulated the use of leading edge technology and although investment schedules were agreed upon, the IT-provider postponed investments in new solutions. Furthermore, there was a constant debate about extra allowances, rates and fees to be incurred by the IT provider. The final development was that the IT provider warned that if bills were not paid by the telecom provider in time, this would lead to disruptions or even temporary stoppage of services. This all led to a situation where internal staff constantly started to challenge the outsourcing decision that was made. Most of the staff felt that the ITprovider was not up to its tasks and wanted to insource most of the IT-activities again.

6.2 GLOBAL MARKET ENTRY OPTIONS*

To develop an effective global marketing strategy, managers must evaluate the alternative ways that a firm can participate in international markets. The particular mode of entry should consider the level of a firm's experience overseas and the stage in the evolution of its international involvement. Figure 6.2 illustrates a spectrum of options for participating in global markets. They range from low-commitment choices, such as exporting, to highly complex levels of participation, such as global strategies. Each is examined in this section.

6.2.1 Exporting

A company's first encounter with an overseas market usually involves **exporting** because it requires the least commitment and risk. Goods are produced at one or two home plants, and sales are made through distributors or importing agencies in each country. Exporting is a workable entry strategy when the firm lacks the resources to make a significant commitment to the market, wants to minimise political and economic risk, or is unfamiliar with the country's market requirements and cultural norms. Exporting is the most popular global market entry option among small and medium-sized firms.*

Many companies begin export activities haphazardly, without carefully screening markets or options for market entry. These companies may or may not have a measure of success, and they might overlook better export opportunities. If early export efforts are unsuccessful because of poor planning, the company may be misled into abandoning exporting altogether. Formulating an export strategy based on good information and proper assessment increases the chances that the best options will be chosen, that resources will be used effectively, and that efforts will consequently be carried through to success.

Although it preserves flexibility and reduces risk, exporting may limit the future prospects for growth in the country. First, exporting involves giving up direct control of the marketing programme, which makes it difficult to coordinate activities, implement strategies, and resolve conflicts with customers and channel members. George Day explains why customers may sense a lack of exporter commitment:

> In many global markets customers are loath to form long-run relationships with a company through its agents because they are unsure whether the business will continue to service the market, or will withdraw at the first sign of adversity. This problem has bedevilled US firms in many countries, and only now are they living down a reputation for opportunistically participating in many countries and then withdrawing abruptly to protect short-run profits.*

6.2.2 Contracting

A somewhat more involved and complex form of international market entry is **contracting**. Included among contractual entry modes are: (1) licencing and (2) management contracts.

FIGURE 6.2 Spectrum of involvement in global marketing

Low Commitment					High Commitment
Exporting	Contracting	Strategic Alliance	Joint Venture	Multi-domestic Strategy	Global Strategy
Low Complexity					High Complexity

Licensing

Under a **licencing** agreement, one firm permits another to use its intellectual property in exchange for royalties or some other form of payment. The property might include trademarks, patents, technology, know-how, or company name. In short, licensing involves exporting intangible assets.

As an entry strategy, licensing requires neither capital investment nor marketing strength in foreign markets. This lets a firm test foreign markets without a major commitment of management time or capital. Because the licensee is typically a local company that can serve as a buffer against government action, licensing also reduces the risk of exposure to such action. With increasing host-country regulation, licensing may enable the business marketer to enter a foreign market that is closed to either imports or direct foreign investment.

Licencing agreements do pose some limitations. First, some companies are hesitant to enter into licence agreements because the licensee may become an important competitor in the future. Second, licencing agreements typically include a time limit. Although terms may be extended once after the initial agreement, many foreign governments do not readily permit additional extensions. Third, a firm has less control over a licensee than over its own exporting or manufacturing abroad.

Management contracts

To expand their overseas operations, many firms have turned to management contracts. In a **management contract** the industrial firm assembles a package of skills that provide an integrated service to the client. When equity participation, either full ownership or a joint venture, is not feasible or is not permitted by a foreign government, a management contract provides a way to participate in a venture. Management contracts have been used effectively in the service sector in such areas as computer services, hotel management, and food services. Michael Czinkota and Ilka Ronkainen point out that management contracts can "provide organisational skills not available locally, expertise that is immediately available rather than built up, and management assistance in the form of support services that would be difficult and costly to replicate locally."[*]

One specialised form of a management contract is a turnkey operation. This arrangement permits a client to acquire a complete operational system, together with the skills needed to maintain and operate the system without assistance. Once the package agreement is online, the client owns, controls, and operates the system. Management contracts allow firms to commercialise their superior skills (know-how) by participating in the international market.

Other contractual modes of entry have grown in prominence in recent years. **Contract manufacturing** involves sourcing a product from a producer located in a foreign country for sale there or in other countries. Here assistance might be required to ensure that the product meets the desired quality standards. Contract manufacturing is most appropriate when the local market lacks sufficient potential to justify a direct investment, export entry is blocked, and a quality licensee is not available.

6.2.3 Strategic Global Alliances (SGA)

A **strategic global alliance** (SGA) is a business relationship established by two or more companies to cooperate out of mutual need and to share risk in achieving a common objective. This strategy works well for market entry or to shore up existing weaknesses and increase competitive strengths. A South African firm with a reliable supply base might partner with a Japanese importer that has the established distribution channels and customer base in Japan to form a strong entry into the Japanese market. Alliances offer a number of benefits, such as access to markets or technology, economies of scale in manufacturing and marketing, and the sharing of risk among partners.

Although global strategic alliances offer potential, they pose a special management challenge. Among the stumbling blocks are these:[*]

- Partners are organised quite differently for making marketing and product-design decisions, creating *problems in coordination and trust*.

- Partners that combine the best set of skills in one country may be poorly equipped to support each other in other countries, leading to *problems in implementing alliances on a global scale*.

- The quick pace of technological change often guarantees that the most attractive partner today may not be the most attractive partner tomorrow, leading to *problems in maintaining alliances over time*.

Building a dedicated alliance function

Although many firms generate positive results from strategic alliances, an elite group of firms has demonstrated the capability to generate superior alliance value as measured by the extent to which the alliance met its stated objectives, the degree to which the alliance enhanced the company's competitive position, stock market gains from alliance announcements, and related performance dimensions. Included among the top performers are firms such as Hewlett-Packard, Siemens, and Volkswagen. How did they do it? By creating a dedicated strategic alliance function—headed by a vice president or director of strategic alliances with his or her own staff and budget, says Jeffrey H. Dyer and his research team.[*] The dedicated function coordinates all alliance-related activity within the organisation and is charged with institutionalising processes and systems to teach, share, and leverage prior alliance management experience and know-how throughout the company.[*]

Integrating points of contact

Firms that are adept at managing strategic alliances use a flexible approach, letting their alliances evolve in form as conditions change over time. They invest adequate resources and management attention in these relationships, and they integrate the organisations so that the appropriate points of contact and communication are managed. Successful alliances achieve five levels of integration:[*]

1 *Strategic integration*, which entails continuing contact among senior executives to define broad goals or discuss changes in each company;

2 *Tactical integration*, which brings middle managers together to plan joint activities, to transfer knowledge, or to isolate organisational or system changes that will improve interfirm connections;

3 *Operational integration*, which provides the information, resources, or personnel that managers require to carry out the day-to-day work of the alliance;

4 *Interpersonal integration*, which builds a necessary foundation for personnel in both organisations to know one another personally, learn together, and create new value; and

5 *Cultural integration*, which requires managers involved in the alliance to have the communication skills and cultural awareness to bridge the differences.

6.2.4 Joint ventures

In pursuing international entry options, a corporation confronts a wide variety of ownership choices, ranging from 100 per cent ownership to a minority interest. Frequently, full ownership may be a desirable, but not essential, prerequisite for success. Thus a joint venture becomes feasible. The **joint venture** involves a joint-ownership arrangement (between, for example, a UK firm and one in the host country) to produce and/or market goods in a foreign market. In contrast to a strategic alliance, a joint venture creates a new firm. Some joint ventures are structured so that each partner holds an equal share; in others, one partner has a majority stake. The contributions of partners can also vary widely and may include financial resources, technology, sales organisations, know-how, or plant and equipment. An example of this type of relationship is the 50-50 joint venture between Daimler AG and Bosch GmbH for the development of a new electric motor.

Advantages

Joint ventures offer a number of advantages. First, they may open up market opportunities that neither partner could pursue alone. Kenichi Ohmae explains the logic:

> If you run a pharmaceutical company with a good drug to distribute in Japan but have no sales force to do it, find someone in Japan who also has a good product but no sales force in your country. You get double the profit by putting two strong drugs through your fixed cost sales network, and so does your new ally. Why duplicate such high expenses all down the line? … Why not join forces to maximise contribution to each other's fixed costs?[*]

Second, joint ventures may provide for better relationships with local organisations (for example, local authorities) and with customers. By being attuned to the host country's culture and environment, the local partner may enable the joint venture to respond to changing market needs, be more aware of cultural sensitivities, and be less vulnerable to political risk.

The downside

Problems can arise in maintaining joint-venture relationships. A study suggests that perhaps more than 50 per cent of joint ventures are disbanded or fall short of expectations.[*] The reasons involve problems with disclosing sensitive information, disagreements over how profits are to be shared, clashes over management style, and differing perceptions on strategy. Mihir Desai, Fritz Foley, and James Hines studied more than 3000 American global companies and report that joint ventures appear to be falling out of favour.[*] Why? Increasing forces of globalisation such as fragmented production processes make the decision to not collaborate payoff. If a firm is considering a joint venture, Desai, Foley, and Hines suggest that they first isolate the reasons for considering a joint venture and make sure that "they can't buy the required services or that knowledge through an arms-length contract that doesn't require sharing ownership.... Second, explicitly lay out expectations for the partners in legal and informal documents prior to the creation of the entity so that it's clear what each party is providing. Third, try out partners without setting up a joint venture by conducting business with them in some way.... Finally, specify simple exit provisions at the onset and then don't be afraid to walk and go it alone."

6.2.5 Choosing a mode of entry

For an initial move into the global market, the full range of entry modes, presented earlier, may be considered—from exporting, licencing, and contract manufacturing to joint ventures and wholly owned subsidiaries. In high-risk markets, firms can reduce their equity exposure by adopting low-commitment modes such as licencing, contract manufacturing, or joint ventures with a minority share. Although non-equity modes of entry—such as licencing or contract manufacturing—involve minimal risk and commitment, they may not provide the desired level of control or financial performance. Joint ventures and wholly owned subsidiaries provide a greater degree of control over operations and greater potential returns.

Once operations are established in a number of foreign markets, the focus often shifts away from foreign opportunity assessment to local market development in each country. This shift might be prompted by the need to respond to local competitors or the desire to more effectively penetrate the local market. Planning and strategy assume a country-by-country focus.

6.2.6 Multi-domestic versus global strategies

Business marketing executives are under increasing pressure to develop globally integrated strategies to achieve efficiency and rationalisation across their geographically dispersed subsidiaries. As such, the challenge of internationalising the firm is not in providing a homogeneous offering across markets, but rather in finding the best balance between local adaptation (a multi-domestic strategy) and global optimisation, where one integrated strategy is applied globally.* Multinational firms have traditionally managed operations outside their home country with **multi-domestic strategies** that permit individual subsidiaries to compete independently in their home-country markets. The multinational headquarters coordinates marketing policies and financial controls and may centralise R&D and some support activities. Each subsidiary, however, resembles a strategic business unit that is expected to contribute earnings and growth to the organisation. The firm can manage its international activities like a portfolio. Examples of multi-domestic industries include most types of retailing, construction, metal fabrication, and many services.

In contrast, a **global strategy** seeks competitive advantage with strategic choices that are highly integrated across countries. For example, features of a global strategy might include a standardised core product that requires minimal local adaptation and that targets foreign-country markets chosen on the basis of their contribution to globalisation benefits. Prominent examples of global industries are automobiles, commercial aircraft, consumer electronics, and many categories of industrial machinery. Major volume and market share advantages might be sought by directing attention to the United States, Europe, and Japan, as well as to the rapidly developing economies of China and India.

6.2.7 Source of advantage: Multi-domestic versus global

When downstream activities (those tied directly to the buyer, such as sales and customer service) are important to competitive advantage, a multi-domestic pattern of international competition is common. In **multi-domestic industries**, firms pursue separate strategies in each of their foreign markets—competition in each country is essentially independent of competition in other countries (for example, Elbit Systems in the defence electronics industry, Honeywell in the controls industry).

Global competition is more common in industries in which upstream and support activities (such as technology development and operations) are vital to competitive advantage. A **global industry** is one in which a firm's competitive position in one country is significantly influenced by its position in other countries (for example, Intel in the semiconductor industry, Airbus in the commercial aircraft industry).

In his book, *Redefining Global Strategy: Crossing Borders in a World Where Differences Still Matter*, Pankaj Ghemawat suggests that most types of economic activity that can be conducted either within or across borders are still quite localised.* He argues that firms must be very careful in deciding between a multi-domestic or global strategy because the "internationalisation of numerous key economic activities, including fixed capital investment, telephone and Internet traffic, tourism, patents, stock investments, etc., remains at around only 10 per cent." In his view, national borders are still significant, and effective international strategies need to take into account both cross-border similarities and critical differences.* In the current global business environment where security is a major issue, intellectual property rights are in question, there are increased threats of economic protectionism, and a number of countries are reasserting national sovereignty, the decision to follow a purely global strategy must be carefully scrutinised.

Coordination and configuration

Further insights into international strategy can be gained by examining two dimensions of competition in the global market: configuration and coordination. **Configuration** centres on where each activity is performed, including the number of locations. Options range from concentrated (for example, one production plant serving the world) to dispersed (for example, a plant in each country—each with a complete value chain from operations to marketing, sales, and customer service). By concentrating an activity such as production in a central location, firms can gain economies of scale or speed learning. Alternatively, dispersing activities to a number of locations may minimise transportation and storage costs, tailor activities to local market differences, or facilitate learning about market conditions in a country.

Coordination refers to how similar activities performed in various countries are coordinated or coupled with each other. If, for example, a firm has three plants—one in the United States, one in England, and one in China—how do the activities in these plants relate to one another? Numerous coordination options exist because of the many possible levels of coordination and the many ways an activity can be performed. For example, a firm operating three plants could, at one extreme, allow each plant to operate autonomously (unique production processes, unique products). At the other extreme, the three plants could be closely coordinated, utilising a common information system and producing products with identical features. AkzoNobel, for example, uses an enterprise software system that allows it to shift purchasing, manufacturing, and distribution functions worldwide in response to changing patterns of supply and demand.

6.2.8 Types of international strategy

Figure 6.3 portrays some of the possible variations in international strategy. Observe that the purest global strategy concentrates as many activities as possible in one country, serves the world

FIGURE 6.3 **Types of international strategy**

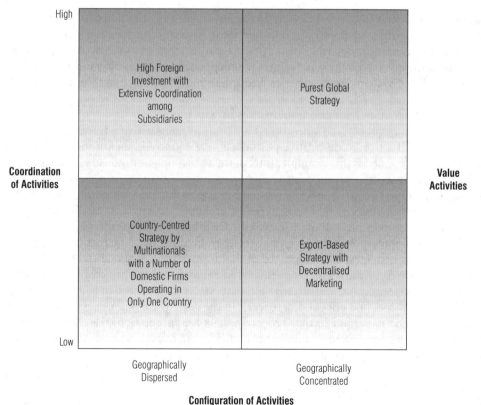

Source: Figure: "Types of International Strategy," from Michael E. Porter, "Changing Patterns of International Competition," in California Management Review vol. 28, no. 2 (Winter 1986), pp. 9–40. © 1986 by the Regents of the University of California. Reprinted by permission of University of California Press.

market from this home base, and closely coordinates activities that must be performed near the buyer (for example, service). Caterpillar, for example, views its battle with the formidable Japanese competitor Komatsu in global terms. As well as using advanced manufacturing systems that allow it to fully exploit the economies of scale from its worldwide sales volume, Caterpillar also carefully coordinates activities in its global dealer network. This integrated global strategy gives Caterpillar a competitive advantage in cost and effectiveness.[*] By serving the world market from its home base in France and by closely coordinating sales and service with customers around the world, Airbus—the European aerospace consortium—also aptly illustrates a pure global strategy. Airbus competes aggressively with Boeing for orders at airlines around the world.[*]

A global battle for the PC market

Other interesting global face-offs involve Dell, Inc., versus Lenovo Group, Inc. Dell is now pursuing an integrated global strategy and challenging Lenovo, China's largest producer in its home market.[*] Meanwhile, Lenovo gained worldwide reach when it purchased IBM's PC division. In turn, Hewlett-Packard remains a formidable rival for both.

Other paths

Figure 6.3 illustrates other international strategy patterns. Canon, for example, concentrates manufacturing and support activities in Japan but gives local marketing subsidiaries significant latitude in each region of the world. Thus, Canon pursues an export-based strategy. In contrast, Xerox concentrates some activities and disperses others. Coordination, however, is extremely high: The Xerox brand, marketing approach, and servicing strategy are standardised worldwide. Michael Porter notes:

> Global strategy has often been characterised as a choice between worldwide standardisation and local tailoring, or as the tension between the economic imperative (large-scale efficient facilities) and the political imperative (local content, local production).... A firm's choice of international strategy involves a search for competitive advantage from configuration/coordination throughout the value chain.[*]

6.2.9 A strategic framework

Recall that companies may pursue multi-domestic strategies or global strategies. The need for a global strategy is determined by the nature of international competition in a particular industry. On the one hand, many industries are multi-domestic, and competition takes place on a country-by-country basis with few linkages across operating units (for example, construction and many service offerings). Multi-domestic industries do not need a global strategy because the focus should be on developing a series of distinct domestic strategies.

Multi-domestic strategy[*]

Pankaj Ghemawat provocatively argues that the world is not flat but semi-globalised, and that borders still exist and they matter when it comes to designing strategy. However, instead of focusing exclusively on the physical boundaries, he suggests that managers look at differences between countries and regions in terms of a framework that includes the following dimensions:

1 Cultural

2 Administrative/Political

3 Geographic

4 Economic

By analysing these dimensions, a strategist can illuminate country-to-country differences, understand the liability of "foreignness," identify and evaluate foreign competitors, and discount market sizes by distance. Following this assessment, the business-to-business manager is better equipped to develop a responsive strategy for each country.

Global strategy

For truly global industries, a firm's position in one country significantly affects its position elsewhere, so it needs a global strategy. Competing across countries through an integrated global strategy requires a series of choices that are described below.

6.3 GLOBAL STRATEGY[*]

6.3.1 Build on a unique competitive position

A business marketing firm should globalise first in those business and product lines where it has unique advantages. To achieve international competitive success, a firm must enjoy a meaningful advantage on either cost or differentiation. To this end, the firm must be able to perform activities at a lower cost than its rivals or perform activities in a unique way that creates customer value and supports a premium price. For example, Denmark's Novo-Nordisk Group (Novo) is the world's leading exporter of insulin and industrial enzymes. By pioneering high-purity insulins and advancing insulin delivery technology, Novo achieved a level of differentiation that gave it a strong competitive position in the health-care market in the United States, Europe, and Japan.

6.3.2 Emphasise a consistent positioning strategy

Rather than modifying the firm's product and service offerings from country to country, "a global strategy requires a patient, long-term campaign to enter every significant foreign market while maintaining and leveraging the company's unique strategic positioning."[*] One of the greatest barriers to the success of firms in smaller countries is the perceived need to serve all customer segments and to offer an expanded product assortment to capture the limited market potential. However, by maintaining a consistent position, a firm reinforces its distinctive strategy and keeps its strategic attention focused on the much larger international opportunity.

6.3.3 Establish a clear home base for each distinct business

Although the location of corporate headquarters is less important and may reflect historical factors, a firm must develop a clear home base for competing in each of its strategically distinct businesses. "The **home base** for a business is the location where strategy is set, core product and process technology is created and maintained, and a critical mass of sophisticated production and service activities reside."[*] For example, Japan, Honda's home base for both motorcycles and automobiles, is where 95 per cent of its R&D employees are located and all of its core engine research is conducted. For Hewlett-Packard (H-P), the United States hosts 77 per cent of the physical space dedicated to manufacturing, R&D, and administration but only 43 per cent of H-P's physical space dedicated to marketing. At H-P's home base, R&D managers with specialised expertise are designated worldwide experts; they transfer their knowledge either electronically or through periodic visits to subsidiaries around the world. Regional subsidiaries take responsibility for some process-oriented R&D activities and for local marketing.

The home base should be located in a country or region with the most favourable access to required resources (inputs) and supporting industries (for example, specialised suppliers). Such a location provides the best environment for capturing productivity and innovation benefits.

Honda as well as H-P benefit from a strong supplier network that supports each of its principal businesses. The home base should also serve as the central integrating point for activities and have clear worldwide responsibility for the business unit.

6.3.4 Leverage product-line home bases at different locations

As a firm's product line broadens and diversifies, different countries may best provide the home bases for some product lines. Responsibility for leading a particular product line should be assigned to the country with the best locational advantages. Each subsidiary, then, specialises in products for which it has the most favourable advantages (for example, specialised suppliers) and serves customers worldwide. For example, H-P locates many product-line home bases outside the United States, such as its line of compact ink-jet printers, which is based in Singapore. In turn, Honda has begun to create a product-line home base for Accord estate car in the United States. The model was conceived, designed, and developed through the joint efforts of Honda's California and Ohio R&D facilities.

6.3.5 Disperse activities to extend home-base advantages

Alth... the home base is where core activities are concentrated, other activities can be dispersed to ext... ...ive position. Potential opportunities should be examined in three areas:

...s that are not central to the innovation ...mponent parts, must be purchased from the

...ected activities near the market, a firm ...sponds to actual or threatened government ...erings to local preferences. For example, Honda ...e United States. Likewise, a host of firms, like ...ents in China and India.

...*er locations*. To improve capabilities in important ...s can locate selected activities in centres of ...supplement, but not replace, the home base. To ...styling expertise and Germany's high-performance ...pany-financed design centres that transfer

...spersed activities

...d locations raises formidable challenges, among ...es and of aligning the reward systems for individ-...of the global enterprise as a whole. However, suc-...tion by:

...s understood by organisational members across countries;

...systems that are consistent on a worldwide basis, thereby

...d the transfer of learning among subsidiary managers across

...ve systems that weigh the overall contribution to the entire ...erformance.

SUMMARY

Rapidly developing economies (RDEs) such as China and India present a host of opportunities and a special set of challenges for business-to-business firms. Companies that decisively and intelligently pursue integrated strategies can secure a sustainable advantage. Such strategies should centre on: (1) expanding *market access* to reach new segments like the mid-market and consumers that reside at lower levels on the income pyramid; (2) leveraging *resource access* to create "best-cost" supply chains; (3) pursuing *local adaptation initiatives* to tailor products to the unique requirements and budgets of RDE consumers; and (4) emphasising *network coordination* to capture the benefits of the company's global reach, including economies of scale and best-practices sharing. Top-performing companies are those that are able to adapt and localise their business models to target new market segments in RDEs. In turn, they are also adept at finding innovative ways to integrate these different business models into their mainstream operations to achieve synergies and share winning strategies across the global business.

Once a business marketing firm decides to sell its products in a particular country, it must select an entry strategy. The range of options includes exporting, contractual entry modes (for example, licencing), strategic alliances, and joint ventures. A more elaborate form of participation is represented by multinational firms that use multi-domestic strategies. Here a separate strategy might be pursued in each country served. The most advanced level of participation in international markets is provided by firms that use a global strategy. Such firms seek competitive advantage by pursuing strategies that are highly interdependent across countries. Global competition tends to be more common in industries in which primary activities, like R&D and manufacturing, are vital to competitive advantage.

A global strategy must begin with a unique competitive position that offers a clear competitive advantage. Providing the best odds of global competitive success are businesses and product lines where companies have the most unique advantages. The home base for a business is the location where strategy is set, and the home base for some product lines may be best positioned in other countries. Although core activities are located at the home base, other activities can be dispersed to strengthen the company's competitive position. Successful global competitors demonstrate special capabilities in coordinating and integrating dispersed activities. Coordination ensures clear positioning and a well-understood concept of global strategy among subsidiary managers across countries. Successful global marketers understand the key risks associated with operating in the global environment, and they take steps to mitigate these risks through their strategic approach to different global markets. To create effective global strategies and capture important market opportunities, business-to-business firms must develop a deep understanding of local markets and the special competitive and environmental forces that will drive performance.

DISCUSSION QUESTIONS

1   Which essential elements need to be considered when implementing an integrated strategy?

2   What are the factors that a multinational firm should consider when deciding to use a joint venture as a market entry strategy for a developing country?

What are the potential benefits and risks in taking this course of action?

3   Why do many companies prefer joint ventures to direct investment for entering foreign markets?

4 What are the pros and cons of licencing as a possible entry strategy?

5 What are the main factors which might influence a company's decision to adopt a multi-domestic strategy over a global one? Discuss.

INTERNET EXERCISES

1 Siemens sells over €6.35 billion worth of goods and services to Chinese customers in the business market. Go to http://www.siemens.com and first identify the various Siemens divisions, like

Healthcare, that contribute to sales volume and then identify a few products from each division that likely address important needs or priorities in China.

REFERENCES

Bahree, Megha, "GE Remodels Business in India," *The Wall Street Journal*, April 26, 2011, p. B8.

Bhattacharya, Arindam, Bradtke, Thomas, Hemerling, Jim, Lebreton, Jean, Mosquet, Xavier, Rupf, Immo, Sirkin, Harold L., and Young, Dave, "Capturing Global Advantage: How Leading Industrial Companies Are Transforming Their Industries by Sourcing and Selling in China, India, and Other Low-Cost Countries," The Boston Consulting Group, Inc., April 2004, http://www.bcg.com.

Bhattacharya, Arindam, Hemerling, Jim, and Waltermann, Bernd, "Competing for Advantage: How to Succeed in the New Global Reality," The Boston Consulting Group, Inc., January 2010, pp. 1–13, http://www.bcg.com.

Czinkota, Michael R. and Ronkainen, Ilka A., *International Marketing*, 2nd ed. (Hinsdale, IL: Dryden Press, 1990).

Day, George S., *Market Driven Strategy: Processes for Creating Value* (New York: The Free Press, 1990), p. 272.

de Juan, Jesús, Du, Victor, Lee, David, Nandgaonkar, Sachin, and Waddell, Kevin, "Global Sourcing in the Postdownturn Era," The Boston Consulting Group, Inc., September 2010, pp. 1–10, http://www.bcg.com.

Desai, Mihir A., Foley, C. Fritz, and Hines, James, "The Costs of Shared Ownership: Evidence From International Joint Ventures," *Journal of Financial Economics* 73 (2004): pp. 323–374.

Dibb, Sally, Simkin, Lyndon, Pride, Bill, and Ferrell, O.C., *Marketing Concepts & Strategies*, 6th ed. (Cengage, 2012).

Doole, Isobel, and Lowe, Robin, *International Marketing Strategy* 6th ed. (Cengage, 2012).

Dyer, Jeffrey, Kale, Prashant, and Singh, Harbir, "How to Make Strategic Alliances Work," *MIT Sloan Management Review* 42 (2001): pp. 37–43.

Fites, Donald V., "Make Your Dealers Your Partners," *Harvard Business Review* 74 (March–April 1996): pp. 84–95.

Garten, Jeffrey E., "A New Threat to America, Inc.," *Business Week*, July 25, 2005, p. 114.

Ghemawat, Pankaj, *Redefining Global Strategy: Crossing Borders in a World Where Differences Still Matter* (Boston: Harvard Business School Press, 2007), pp. 9–32.

Hayes, Simon, "Getting Strategic Alliances Right," *Synnovation* 3 (May 2008), p. 72, www.eds.com/synnovation, accessed July 5, 2008.

Hemerling, Jim, Young, Dave, and Bradtke, Thomas, "Navigating the Five Currents of Globalization: How Leading Companies Are Capturing Global Advantage" *BCG Focus* (April 2005), pp. 9–10, The Boston Consulting Group, Inc., http://www.bcg.com.

Hult, G. Tomas M., Cavusgil, S. Tamer, Deligonul, Seyda, Kiyak, Tunga, and Lagerström, Katarina, "What Drives Performance in Globally Focused Marketing Organizations? A Three-Country Study," *Journal of International Marketing* 15 (2007): pp. 58–85.

Immelt, Jeffrey R., Govindarajan, Vijay, and Trimble, Chris, "How GE Is Disrupting Itself," *Harvard Business Review* 87 (October 2009): pp. 56–65.

Kanter, Rosabeth Moss, "Collaborative Advantage," *Harvard Business Review* 72 (July–August 1994): pp. 96–108.

Kosnik, Thomas J., "Stumbling Blocks to Global Strategic Alliances," *Systems Integration Age,* October 1988, pp. 31–39.

Moutinho, Luiz, and Southern, Geoffrey, *Strategic Marketing Management: A process Based Approach* (Cengage, 2012).

Ohmae, Kenichi, "The Global Logic of Strategic Alliances," *Harvard Business Review* 67 (March–April 1989): p. 147.

Parkhe, Arvind, "Building Trust in International Alliances," *Journal of World Business* 33 (Winter 1998): pp. 417–437.

Porter, Michael E., "Changing Patterns of International Competition," *California Management Review* 28 (Winter 1986): p. 25.

Porter, Michael E., "Competing across Locations: Enhancing Competitive Advantage through a Global Strategy," in Michael E. Porter, ed., *On Competition* (Boston: Harvard Business School Press, 1998), pp. 309–350.

Ramstad, Evan, and McWilliams, Gary, "For Dell, Success in China Tells Tale of Maturing Market," *The Wall Street Journal*, July 5, 2005, pp. A1, A8.

Root, Franklin R., *Entry Strategy for International Markets* (Lexington, MA: D. C. Heath, 1987).

Rule, Eric and Keon, Shawn, "Competencies of High-Performing Strategic Alliances," *Strategy and Leadership*, 27 (September–October 1998): pp. 36–37.

Sirkin, Harold L., Hemerling, James W., and Bhattacharya, Arindam K., *Globality: Competing with Everyone from Everywhere for Everything* (New York: Business Plus, 2008).

Taylor III, Alex, "Blue Skies for Airbus," *Fortune*, August 2, 1999, pp. 102–108.

van Weele, Arjan, *Puchasing and Supply Chain Management: Analysis Strategy, Planning and Practice*, 5th ed. (Cengage, 2010).

Verhage, Bronis J., *Marketing: A Global Perspective* (Cengage, 2013).

Whitelock, Jery and Jobber, Damd, "An Evaluation of External Factors in the Decision of UK Industrial Firms to Enter a New Non-Domestic Market: An Exploratory Study," *European Journal of Marketing* 38 (11/12, 2004): p. 1440.

Zou, Shaoming, and Cavusgil, S. Tamer, "The GMS: A Broad Conceptualization of Global Marketing Strategy and Its Effect on Firm Performance," *Journal of Marketing* 66 (October 2002): pp. 40–56.

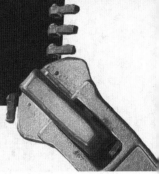

CHAPTER 7
MANAGING
PRODUCTS FOR
BUSINESS MARKETS

CHAPTER OBJECTIVES

By providing a solution for customers, the product is the central force of business marketing strategy. The firm's ability to put together a line of products and services that provide superior value to customers is the heart of business marketing management. After reading this chapter, you will understand:

1   The different components of a strong business to business brand

2   The way in which mega-trends impact the competitive landscape

3   The importance of the different aspects of customer value

4   The product positioning process according to the different types of industrial product lines and markets

5   How to manage discontinuous innovations across the stages of the technology adoption life cycle

A business marketer's marketplace identity is established through its brand and through the products and services it offers. Because brands constitute one of the most valuable intangible assets that firms possess, branding has emerged as a priority to marketing executives, CEOs, and the financial community.[*] Product management is directly linked to market analysis and market selection. Products are developed to fit the needs of the market and are modified as those needs change. Drawing on such tools of demand analysis as business market segmentation and market potential forecasting, the marketer evaluates opportunities and selects profitable market segments, thus determining the direction of product policy. Product policy cannot be separated from market selection decisions. In evaluating potential product/market fits, a firm must evaluate new market opportunities, determine the number and aggressiveness of competitors, and gauge its own strengths and weaknesses. The marketing function assumes a lead role in transforming an organisation's distinctive skills and resources into products and services that enjoy positional advantages in the market.[*]

This chapter first explores the nature of the brand-building process and the way in which a strong brand can sharpen the focus and energise the performance of the firm. Second, it examines product quality, sustainability, and value from the customer's perspective and directly links them to business marketing strategy. Award-winning branding campaigns by leading business-to-business firms are profiled. Third, because industrial products can assume several forms, the chapter describes industrial product-line options, while offering an approach for positioning and managing products in high-technology markets.

7.1 BUILDING A STRONG B2B BRAND

Although consumer packaged-goods companies like Procter & Gamble (P&G), Coca-Cola, and Nestle have excelled by developing a wealth of enduring and highly profitable brands, some of the most valuable and powerful brands belong to business-to-business firms: IBM, Microsoft, General Electric, Intel, Epson, Fujitsu IT Services, Google, Oracle, Canon, Siemens, JCB, and a host of others. For most business marketers, the company name is the brand, so the key questions become: "What do you want your company name to stand for? What do you want it to mean in the mind of the customer?"[*]

David Aaker says, "**Brand equity** is a set of brand assets and liabilities linked to a brand, its name, and symbol that add to or subtract from the value provided by a product or service and/or to that firm's customers."[*] As we will explore, the assets and liabilities that impact brand equity include brand loyalty, name awareness, perceived quality and other brand associations, and proprietary brand assets (for example, patents). A **brand**, then, is a name, sign, symbol, or logo that identifies the products and services of one firm and differentiates them from competitors.

Providing a rich and incisive perspective, Kevin Lane Keller defines **customer-based brand equity** (CBBE) as the differential effect that customers' brand knowledge has on their response to marketing activities and programmes for that brand.[*] The basic premise of his CBBE model is that the power of a brand lies in "what consumers have learned, felt, seen, and heard about the brand over time."[*] So, the power of a brand is represented by all the thoughts, feelings, perceptions, images, and experiences that become linked to the brand in the minds of customers.

7.1.1 Brand-building steps[*]

The CBBE model lays out a series of four steps for building a strong brand (see Figure 7.1, right side): (1) develop deep brand awareness or a brand identity; (2) establish the meaning of the brand through unique brand associations (that is, points of difference); (3) elicit a positive brand response from customers through marketing programmes; and (4) build brand relationships with customers, characterised by intense loyalty. Providing the foundation for successful brand

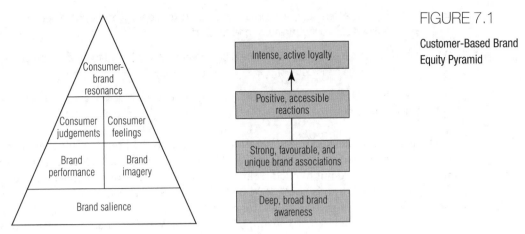

FIGURE 7.1

Customer-Based Brand
Equity Pyramid

Source: Reprinted with permission from Marketing Management, "Building Customer-Based Brand Equity," published by American
Marketing Association, Kevin Lane Keller, Volume 10 (July/August 2001): p. 19.

management is the set of brand-building blocks (see Figure 7.1, left side) aligned with the branding ladder—salience, performance, imagery, judgements, feelings, and resonance.

Brand identity

To achieve the right identity for a brand, the business marketer must create brand salience with
customers. **Brand salience** is tied directly to brand awareness: How often is the brand evoked in
different situations? What type of cues or reminders does a customer need to recognise a brand?
Brand awareness refers to the customer's ability to recall or recognise a brand under different
conditions. The goal here is to ensure that customers understand the particular product or service category where the brand competes by creating clear connections to the specific products or
services that are solely under the brand name.

Brand meaning

Brand positioning involves establishing unique brand associations in the minds of customers to
differentiate the brand and establish competitive superiority.* Although a multitude of different
types of brand associations are possible, brand meaning can be captured by examining two
broad categories: (1) **brand performance**—the way in which the product or service meets customers' more functional needs (for example, quality, price, styling, and service effectiveness)
and (2) **brand imagery**—the ways in which the brand attempts to meet customers' more abstract
psychological or social needs.

Brand positioning should incorporate both points of parity and points of difference in the customer value proposition. "Points of difference are strong, favourable, unique brand associations
that drive customers' behaviour; points of parity are those associations where the brand 'breaks
even' with competitors and negates their intended points of difference."* Strong business-to-
business brands such as Fujitsu IT Services, IBM, Google, and Siemens have clearly established
strong, favourable (that is, valuable to customers), and unique brand associations with customers.

Brand response

As a branding strategy is implemented, special attention should be directed to how customers
react to the brand and the associated marketing activities. Four types of **customer judgements**
are particularly vital to the creation of a strong brand (in ascending order of importance):

1   *Quality*—the customers' attitudes toward a brand's perceived quality as well as their perceptions of
    value and satisfaction;

2   *Credibility*—the extent to which the brand as a whole is perceived by customers as credible in terms of expertise, trustworthiness, and likeability;

3   *Consideration set*—the degree to which customers find the brand to be an appropriate option worthy of serious consideration;

4   *Superiority*—the extent to which customers believe that the brand offers unique advantages over competitors' brands.

Feelings relate to the customers' emotional reaction to the brand and include numerous types that have been tied to brand building, including warmth, fun, excitement, and security. For example, Apple's brand might elicit feelings of **excitement** (customers are energised by the brand and believe that the brand is cool); IBM or FedEx may evoke feelings of **security** (the brand produces a feeling of comfort or self-assurance); and Cisco's branding campaign, "Welcome to the Human Network," might elicit **warmth** (the brand makes customers feel peaceful). Cisco's vice president–corporate marketing, Marilyn Mersereau, says, "Instead of being a product player with the 'Powered by Cisco' campaign, we're trying to position Cisco to be a platform for your life experience," educating customers about the ways Cisco makes it easier for people to connect with one another via the Web.[*]

Forging brand relationships

An examination of the level of personal identification and the nature of the relationship a customer has formed with the brand is the final step in the brand-building process. **Brand resonance** represents the strength of the psychological bond that a customer has with a brand and the degree to which this connection translates into loyalty, attachment, and active engagement with the brand. Keller observes, "Brand resonance reflects a completely harmonious relationship between customers and the brand.... The strongest brands will be the ones to which those consumers become so attached that they, in effect, become evangelists and actively seek means to interact with the brand and share their experiences with others."[*]

7.1.2 Brand strategy guidelines

In building a strong brand, Kevin Lane Keller identifies some key guidelines that are particularly crucial in the business-to-business setting.[*] First, employees at all levels of the organisation must understand the meaning and vision for the brand. A **brand mantra**—a short three- to five-word summary of the essence of the brand—can be powerful in communicating the core values of the brand to employees (e.g., Accenture—"High performance. Delivered."; DHL—"Always First"; or DuPont—"The miracle of science"). Second, larger and more complex companies should develop a coherent branding strategy and then build on the reputation of that brand. This provides the opportunity to develop sub-brands with descriptive product modifiers that capitalise on the highly credible corporate brand name (e.g., Fujitsu Laboratories, Fujitsu Technology Solutions).

Third, a firm with a strong brand can command a price premium for its products or services. However, to sustain that premium, important points of differentiation must be clearly communicated to target customer segments in order to ensure that customers appreciate the unique value that the brand provides. An often overlooked means of differentiation is to link the brand to relevant non-product-related brand associations such as the company's customer list of leading-edge companies. Fourth, successful branding requires a well-conceived market segmentation plan. Since business customers are primarily interested in a solution to a problem, not just a product, different market segments value different sets of benefits. Likewise, within the same buying organisation, senior executives employ different choice criteria and often seek different solutions (e.g., drive business performance) than those sought by middle managers (e.g., meet technical requirements). By recognising such differences, a more sharply focused brand communication strategy can be developed.

7.1.3 Profiling a strong brand: IBM

The powerful differentiating benefits that a strong brand can convey are revealed in IBM's brand strategy. The company launched its "Smarter Planet" business strategy to build a clear perception concerning what IBM is all about. Rather than a hardware or mainframe computer manufacturer, IBM is the world's largest professional service organisation based on its depth of industry knowledge and number of consultants. John Kennedy, VP of Integrated Communications at IBM, asserts:

> *We're a company that builds smarter traffic systems ... makes utility grids smarter ... makes financial systems smarter ... makes healthcare systems smarter. And of course, we can help midsize companies tackle their biggest problems and become smarter, as well.*[*]

To that end, IBM launched a communication programme involving all marketing channels, promoting the way in which the firm's knowledge and capabilities are uniquely positioned to help corporations, government, transportation, energy, education, health care, and cities work smarter, contributing to a smarter planet. Such smarter-planet style projects require a collaborative partner that can tackle the integrating challenges involving computer hardware, sensor networks, specialised software, and hands-on work by industry experts. And IBM persuasively argues that it is best equipped to serve "as the digital general contractor on big projects."[*]

In a major speech to the Council on Foreign Relations, Samuel J. Palmisanno, IBM's CEO, provided a vision of how smart technology could improve the way in which the world works and described how IBM is devoting significant resources to make smarter systems a reality in every part of the world. The smarter-planet campaign appears to be resonating with senior-level decision makers and government officials, allowing IBM to: (1) stake out a leadership position on issues vital to business and government; (2) establish thought leadership in new areas such as smart grids and transportation systems in cities; and (3) position the company as a collaborative partner in driving new solutions.[*]

The smarter-planet strategy has also significantly expanded IBM's market potential. During the first year, the goal set by IBM's CEO was to create 300 smarter solutions in partnership with clients. Over 1200 solutions were developed across industry sectors, from smart supply chains to smart traffic congestion management systems. And the list continues to grow.[*] Based on creativity and demonstrated business performance against competing brands on multiple continents, the smarter-planet campaign has received numerous awards, including the Gold Global Effie in recognition of marketplace success.[*]

How financial markets react

A host of business-to-business companies have launched brand-building initiatives, but do such investments generate positive returns? Some recent research on the brand attitude of buyers in evaluating computer-related firms provides some answers.[*] Brand attitude is a component and indicator of brand equity. **Brand attitude** is defined as the percentage of organisational buyers who have a positive image of a company minus those with a negative opinion. This study found that changes in brand attitude are associated with stock market performance and tend to lead accounting financial performance (that is, an increase in brand attitude will be reflected in improved financial performance three to six months later). In short, the research demonstrates that investments in building brand attitude for high-technology firms do indeed pay off and increase the firm's value.

In another intriguing study, Thomas J. Madden, Frank Fehle, and Susan Fournier provide empirical evidence of the link between branding and shareholder value creation.[*] They found that a portfolio of brands identified as strong by the Interbrand/*Business Week* valuation method displays significant performance advantages compared to the overall market. "Firms that have developed strong brands create value for their shareholders by yielding returns that are greater in magnitude than a relevant market benchmark, and perhaps more important, do so with less risk."[*]

7.2 PRODUCT QUALITY AND CUSTOMER VALUE

Rising customer expectations make product quality and customer value important strategic priorities. On a global scale, many international companies insist that suppliers, as a prerequisite for negotiations, meet quality standards set out by the Geneva-based International Standards Organization (ISO). These quality requirements, referred to as **ISO-9000 standards**, were developed for the European Community but have gained a global following.[*] Certification requires a supplier to thoroughly document its quality-assurance programme. The certification programme is becoming a seal of approval to compete for business not only overseas but also in the United States. For instance, the Department of Defense employs ISO standards in its contract guidelines. Although Japanese firms continue to set the pace in the application of sophisticated quality-control procedures in manufacturing, companies such as Kodak, Vodafone, Ricoh, Volkswagen, Epson, Intel, GE, and others have made significant strides.

The quest for improved product quality touches the entire supply chain as these and other companies demand improved product quality from their suppliers, large and small. For example, GE has an organisation-wide goal of achieving Six Sigma quality, meaning that a product would have a defect level of no more than 3.4 parts per million. Using the Six Sigma approach, GE measures every process, identifies the variables that lead to defects, and takes steps to eliminate them. GE also works directly to assist suppliers in using the approach. Overall, GE reports that Six Sigma has produced striking results—cost savings in the billions and fundamental improvements in product and service quality. Recently, GE has centred its Six Sigma efforts on functions that "teach customers," such as marketing and sales.[*]

7.2.1 Meaning of quality

The quality movement has passed through several stages.[*] *Stage one* centred on conformance to standards or success in meeting specifications. But conformance quality or zero defects do not satisfy a customer if the product embodies the wrong features. *Stage two* emphasised that quality was more than a technical specialty and that pursuing it should drive the core processes of the entire business. Particular emphasis was given to total quality management and measuring customer satisfaction. However, customers choose a particular product over competing offerings because they perceive it as providing superior *value*—the product's price, performance, and service render it the most attractive alternative. *Stage three*, then, examines a firm's quality performance relative to that of competitors and examines customer perceptions of the value of competing products. The focus here is on market-perceived quality and value versus that of competitors. Moreover, attention shifts from zero defects in products to zero defections of customers (that is, *customer loyalty*). Merely satisfying customers who have the freedom to make choices is not enough to keep them loyal.[*]

7.2.2 Sustainability: Strategic imperative

Mega-trends, like the quality movement, force companies to adapt or innovate, or be left behind. Sustainability is an emerging mega-trend that is transforming the competitive landscape, forcing companies to change the way they think about products, processes, and business models.* Fueling this mega-trend is the intensified global competition for natural resources (particularly oil) coupled with escalating public and governmental concern about climate change, industrial pollution, food safety, and natural resource depletion. Broadly defined, **sustainability** involves the integration of economic, environmental, and societal considerations into business decision making. For experienced business strategists, sustainability is an integral part of value creation.*

Rather than damaging the bottom line, research shows that, when properly conceived, "sustainability is a mother lode of organisational and technological innovations that yield both bottom-line and top-line returns. Becoming environmentally friendly lowers costs because companies end up reducing the inputs they use. In addition, the process generates additional revenue from better products ..." or from new businesses.*

Enthusiasm for sustainability is growing across industries, particularly in commodity, chemical, consumer product, industrial goods, machinery, and retail companies. A recent comprehensive global survey of firms across industries reveals that executives are virtually united in the view that sustainability will have a powerful impact on their processes and competitive strategies.* Some firms, however, are adopting sustainability practices faster than their peers. Two distinct segments emerge: cautious adopters and embracers. Cautious adopters view sustainability as a vehicle for cost cutting, resource efficiency, and risk management (e.g., complying with regulatory mandates). By contrast, embracer companies recognise that sustainability strategies provide a means for gaining competitive advantage through innovation, process improvements, brand building, and access to new markets. And, as it turned out in the study, embracers represent the highest-performing businesses in the study. In short, these firms view sustainability investments as an important driver of value creation for the firm, providing opportunities for enhanced profitability from margin improvement and revenue growth (see Figure 7.2). In addition to these tangible benefits, observe that sustainability efforts also confer intangible benefits such as an improved brand reputation and the enhanced ability to attract and retain talented employees.

Capturing opportunities

Companies that excel in sustainability do "old things in new ways" such as outperforming competition on regulatory compliance and environment-related cost management.* Leading performers also do "new things in new ways" such as redesigning products, processes, and whole systems to optimise natural resource efficiencies across their value chains.* As the vision expands for these top-performing companies, sustainability innovations transform core businesses and even lead to the creation of new businesses and new sources of differentiation.

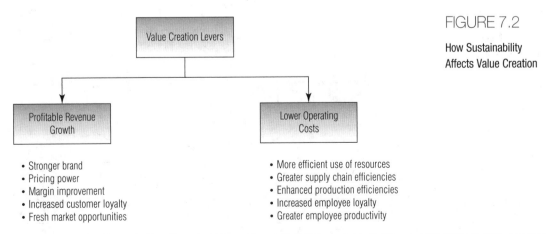

FIGURE 7.2

How Sustainability Affects Value Creation

Source: Adapted from Maurice Berns, Andrew Townend, Zayna Khayat, Balu Balagopal, Martin Reeves, Michael S. Hopkins, and Nina Kruschwitz, "Sustainability and Competitive Advantage," *MIT Sloan Management Review* 51 (Fall 2009): pp. 19–26.

In developing a sustainability initiative, a firm must select an area where customer and company interests intersect. These areas present an opportunity to create shared value—a meaningful benefit for customers and for society that is also valuable to the business. Companies that make the right strategy choices and build focused and integrated sustainability initiatives in concert with their core capabilities will increasingly distance themselves from competitors. Michael E. Porter and Mark R. Kramer aptly observe: "When a well-run business applies its vast resources, expertise, and management talent to problems that it understands and in which it has a stake, it can have a greater impact on social good than any other institution or philanthropic organisation."[*]

7.2.3 Meaning of customer value

Delivering customer value is the heart of business marketing strategy. Strategy experts Dwight Gertz and João Baptista suggest that "a company's product or service is competitively superior if, at price equality with competing products, target segments always choose it. Thus, value is defined in terms of consumer choice in a competitive context."[*] In turn, the value equation includes a vital service component. For the service component, business marketing strategists must "recognise that specifications aren't just set by a manufacturer who tells the customer what to expect; instead, consumers also may participate in setting specifications." Frontline sales and service personnel add value to the product offering and the consumption experience by meeting or, indeed, exceeding the customer's service expectations.[*] **Customer value,** then, represents a "business customer's overall assessment of a relationship with a supplier based on perceptions of benefits received and sacrifices made."[*]

Benefits

Customer benefits take two forms (Figure 7.3):

1   *Core benefits*—the core requirements (for example, specified product quality) for a relationship that suppliers must fully meet to be included in the customer's consideration set;

2   *Add-on benefits*—attributes that differentiate suppliers, go beyond the basic denominator provided by all qualified vendors, and create added value in a buyer–seller relationship (for example, value-added customer service).

FIGURE 7.3

What Value Means to Business Customers

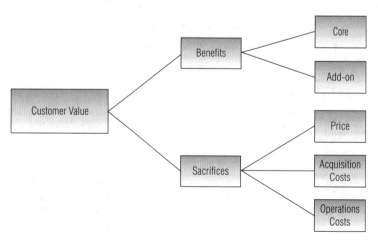

Source: Adapted from Ajay Menon, Christian Homburg, and Nikolas Beutin, "Understanding Customer Value," *Journal of Business-to-Business Marketing* 12 (2, 2005): pp. 4–7.

Sacrifices

Consistent with the total cost perspective that business customers emphasise, sacrifices include: (1) the purchase price, (2) acquisition costs (for example, ordering and delivery costs), and (3) operations costs (for example, defect-free incoming shipments of component parts reduces operations costs).

What matters most?

Based on a large study of nearly 1000 purchasing managers across a wide variety of product categories in the United States and Germany, Ajay Menon, Christian Homburg, and Nikolas Beutin uncovered some rich insights into customer value in business-to-business relationships.*

Add-on Benefits   First, the research demonstrates that add-on benefits more strongly influence customer value than do core benefits. Why? All qualified suppliers perform well on core benefits, so add-on benefits tend to be the differentiator for customer value as customers choose among competing offerings. Therefore, business marketers can use value-added services or joint working relationships that influence add-on benefits to strengthen customer relationships. For example, a leading manufacturer of tyres for earth-moving equipment offers free consulting services that help customers design maintenance procedures that yield significant cost savings.*

Trust   Second, the study reinforces the vital role of trust in a business relationship, demonstrating, in fact, that trust has a stronger impact on core benefits than product characteristics.

Reducing Customer's Costs   Third, the results highlight the importance of marketing strategies that are designed to assist the customer in reducing operations costs. The research team observes:

> *Ensuring on-time delivery of components and raw materials, getting involved in the customer firm's manufacturing and R&D strategy-making processes, and deploying resources needed to ensure a smooth relationship with the customer will help reduce the customer's operations costs.**

By pursuing such initiatives, the business marketer does not have to rely solely on price to demonstrate and deliver value to the customer.

7.2.4 Product support strategy: the service connection

The marketing function must ensure that every part of the organisation focuses on delivering superior value to customers. Business marketing programmes involve a number of critical components that customers carefully evaluate: tangible products, service support, and ongoing information services both before and after the sale. To provide value and to successfully implement these programmes, the business marketing firm must carefully coordinate activities among personnel in product management, sales, and service.* For example, to customise a product and delivery schedule for an important customer requires close coordination among product, logistics, and sales personnel. Moreover, some customer accounts might require special field-engineering, installation, or equipment support, thereby increasing the required coordination between sales and service units.

Post-purchase service is especially important to buyers in many industrial product categories ranging from computers and machine tools to custom-designed component parts. Responsibility for service support, however, is often diffused throughout various departments, such as applications engineering, customer relations, or service administration. Significant benefits accrue to the business marketer who carefully manages and coordinates product, sales, and service connections to maximise customer value.

7.3 PRODUCT POLICY

Product policy involves the set of all decisions concerning the products and services that the company offers. Through product policy, a business marketing firm attempts to satisfy customer needs and to build a sustainable competitive advantage by capitalising on its core competencies. This section explores the types of industrial product lines and the importance of anchoring product-management decisions on an accurate definition of the product market. A framework is also provided for assessing product opportunities on a global scale.

7.3.1 Types of product lines defined

Because product lines of industrial firms differ from those of consumer-packaged-goods firms, classification is useful. Industrial product lines can be categorised into four types[*] :

1   **Proprietary or catalogue products.** These items are offered only in certain configurations and produced in anticipation of orders. Product-line decisions concern adding, deleting, or repositioning products in the line.

2   **Custom-built products.** These items are offered as a set of basic units, with numerous accessories and options. The basic workstation can be expanded to connect to scanners, cheque readers, electronic payment devices, and other accessories to meet a business's particular needs. The firm's wide array of products provides retailers with an end-to-end solution, from data warehousing to the point-of-service workstation at checkout. The marketer offers the organisational buyer a set of building blocks. Product-line decisions centre on offering the proper mix of options and accessories.

3   **Custom-designed products.** These items are created to meet the needs of one or a small group of customers. Sometimes the product is a unique unit, such as a power plant or a specific machine tool. In addition, some items produced in relatively large quantities, such as an aircraft model, may fall into this category. The product line is described in terms of the company's capability, and the customer buys that capability. Ultimately, this capability is transformed into a finished good.

4   **Industrial services.** Rather than an actual product, the buyer is purchasing a company's capability in an area such as maintenance, technical service, or management consulting.

All types of business marketing firms confront product policy decisions, whether they offer physical products, pure services (no physical product), or a product-service combination. Each product situation presents unique problems and opportunities for the business marketer; each draws on a unique capability. Product strategy rests on the intelligent use of the firm's distinctive capabilities.

7.3.2 Defining the product market

Accurately defining the product market is fundamental to sound product-policy decisions.[*] Careful attention must be given to the alternative ways to satisfy customer needs. For example, many different products could provide competition for personal computers. Application-specific products, such as enhanced pocket pagers and smart phones that send e-mail and connect to the Web, are potential competitors. A wide array of information appliances that provide easy access to the Internet also pose a threat. In such an environment, Regis McKenna maintains, managers "must look for opportunities in—and expect competition from—every possible direction. A company with a narrow product concept will move through the market with blinders on, and it is sure to run into trouble."[*] By excluding products and technology that compete for the same end-user needs, the product strategist can quickly become out of touch with the market. Both customer needs and the ways of satisfying those needs change.

Product market

A **product market** establishes the distinct arena in which the business marketer competes. Four dimensions of a market definition are strategically relevant:

1 *Customer function dimension*. This involves the benefits that are provided to satisfy the needs of organisational buyers (for example, mobile messaging).

2 *Technological dimension*. There are alternative ways a particular function can be performed (for example, mobile phone, pager, notebook computer).

3 *Customer segment dimension*. Customer groups have distinct needs that must be served (for example, sales representatives, physicians, international travellers).

4 *Value-added system dimension*. Competitors serving the market can operate along a sequence of stages.* The value-added system for smart phones includes equipment providers, such as Siemens and Nokia, and service providers, like T-Mobile and Vodafone. Analysis of the value-added system may indicate potential opportunities or threats from changes in the system (for example, potential alliances between equipment and service providers).

Planning for today and tomorrow

Competition to satisfy the customer's need exists at the technology level as well as at the supplier or brand level. By establishing accurate product-market boundaries, the product strategist is better equipped to identify customer needs, the benefits sought by the market segment, and

B2B TOP PERFORMERS

BASF: Using Services to Build a Strong Brand

BASF AG, headquartered in Germany, is the world's largest chemical company, with global sales of over €24.75 billion. Consistently ranked as one of Fortune's most admired global companies, the firm competes in what many would describe as a commodity business. Rather than pursue a low-total-cost strategy and compete on price, BASF decided to transform itself into an innovative service-oriented company. Services, like R&D support or on-site field services, are hard for rivals to duplicate and when well executed, provide the ultimate differentiation strategy. To communicate its value proposition to customers, the firm launched its advertising campaign with the familiar tag line:

"We don't make a lot of products you buy. We make a lot of the products you buy better."

A senior executive at BASF's ad agency, Tony Graetzer, describes the rationale for this campaign, which has been recognised with numerous awards: "Companies are frequently viewed as tied on the quality of their products, but they are never viewed as tied on the quality of their services." Winning companies provide superior service. By emphasising how it helps make its customers' products better and delivering on its promises, the BASF brand has become synonymous with customer partnerships and technology leadership.

Source: Bob Lamons, *The Case for B2B Branding* (Mason, Ohio: Thomson, 2005), pp. 91–94.

the turbulent nature of competition at both the technology and supplier or brand levels. Derek Abell offers these valuable strategy insights:

● Planning for today requires a clear, precise *definition* of the business—a delineation of target customer segments, customer functions, and the business approach to be taken; planning for tomorrow is concerned with how the business should be *redefined* for the future.

● Planning for today focuses on *shaping up* the business to meet the needs of today's customers with excellence. It involves identifying factors that are critical to success and smothering them with attention; planning for tomorrow can entail *reshaping* the business to compete more effectively in the future.[*]

Seeing what is next

Strategy experts also argue provocatively that many firms are overlooking three important customer groups that may present the greatest opportunity for explosive growth[*]:

● *Nonconsumers* who may lack the specialised skills, training, or resources to purchase the product or service;

● *Undershot customers* for whom existing products are not good enough;

● *Overshot customers* for whom existing products provide more performance than they can use.

7.4 PLANNING INDUSTRIAL PRODUCT STRATEGY

Formulating a strategic marketing plan for an existing product line is the most vital part of a company's marketing planning efforts. Having identified a product market, attention now turns to planning product strategy. Product-positioning analysis provides a useful tool for charting the strategy course.

7.4.1 Product positioning

Once the product market is defined, a strong competitive position for the product must be secured. **Product positioning** represents the place that a product occupies in a particular market; it is found by measuring organisational buyers' perceptions and preferences for a product in relation to its competitors. Because organisational buyers perceive products as bundles of attributes (for example, quality, service), the product strategist should examine the attributes that assume a central role in buying decisions.

7.4.2 The process[*]

Observe from Figure 7.4 that the positioning process begins by identifying the relevant set of competing products (Step 1) and defining those attributes that are **determinant** (Step 2)— attributes that customers use to differentiate among the alternatives and that are important to them in determining which brand they prefer. In short, then, determinant attributes are choice criteria that are both important and differentiating. Of course, some attributes are important to organisational buyers, but they may not be differentiating. For example, safety might be an important attribute in the heavy-duty truck market, but business market customers may consider the competing products offered by Daimler AG, Volvo, and Leyland Trucks as quite comparable on this dimension. Durability, reliability, and fuel economy might constitute the determinant attributes.

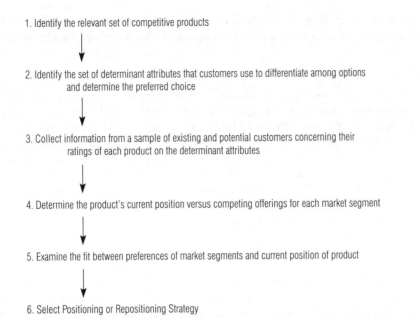

FIGURE 7.4

Steps in the Product-
Positioning Process

1. Identify the relevant set of competitive products

2. Identify the set of determinant attributes that customers use to differentiate among options
   and determine the preferred choice

3. Collect information from a sample of existing and potential customers concerning their
   ratings of each product on the determinant attributes

4. Determine the product's current position versus competing offerings for each market segment

5. Examine the fit between preferences of market segments and current position of product

6. Select Positioning or Repositioning Strategy

Source: Adapted with modifications from Harper W. Boyd Jr., Orville C. Walker Jr., and Jean-Claude Larréché, *Marketing Management: A Strategic Approach with a Global Orientation* (Chicago: Irwin/McGraw-Hill, 1998), p. 197.

Step 3 involves collecting information from a sample of existing and potential customers concerning how they perceive the various options on each of the determinant attributes. The sample should include buyers (particularly buying influentials) from organisations that represent the full array of market segments the product strategist wishes to serve. After examining the product's current position versus competing offerings (Step 4), the analyst can isolate: (1) the competitive strength of the product in different segments and (2) the opportunities for securing a differentiated position in a particular target segment (Step 5).

7.4.3 Isolating strategy opportunities

Step 6 involves the selection of the positioning or repositioning strategy. Here the product manager can evaluate particular strategy options. First, for some attributes, the product manager may wish to: (1) pursue a strategy to increase the importance of an attribute to customers and (2) increase the difference between the competition's and the firm's products. For example, the importance of an attribute such as customer training might be elevated through marketing communications emphasising how the potential buyer can increase its efficiency and employee performance through the firm's training. If successful, such efforts might move customer training from an important attribute to a determinant attribute in the eyes of customers. Second, if the firm's performance on a determinant product attribute is truly higher than that of competitors—but the market perceives that other alternatives enjoy an edge—marketing communications can be developed to bring perceptions in line with reality. Third, the competitive standing of a product can be advanced by improving the firm's level of performance on determinant attributes that organisational buyers emphasise.

7.4.4 Product positioning illustrated[*]

This product-positioning approach was successfully applied to a capital equipment product at a major corporation. The product that provided the focus of the analysis is sold in three sizes to two market segments: end users and consulting engineers. Marketing research identified 15 attributes, including reliability, service support, company reputation, and ease of maintenance.

A new strategy

The research found that the firm's brand enjoyed an outstanding rating on product reliability and service support. Both attributes were generally determinant for the company against most competitors. To reinforce the importance of both attributes, management decided to offer an enhanced warranty programme. Both end users and consulting engineers view warranties as important but not a point of differentiation across competing brands. Management surmised, however, that by establishing a new warranty standard for the industry, the attribute could become determinant, adding to the brand's leverage over competitors. In addition, management felt that the new warranty programme might also benefit the brand's reputation on other attributes such as reliability and company reputation.

Better targeting

The study also provided some surprises. Price was not nearly as important to organisational buyers as management had initially believed. This suggested that there were opportunities to increase revenue through product differentiation and service support. Likewise, the research found that the firm's brand dominated all competitors in the large- and medium-sized products, but not in the small-sized products. This particular product had an especially weak competitive position in the consulting engineer segment. Special service support strategies were developed to strengthen the product's standing in this segment. Clearly, product positioning provides a valuable tool for designing creative strategies for business markets.

7.5 THE TECHNOLOGY ADOPTION LIFE CYCLE

After decades of being content with letters, telegrams, and telephones, consumers have embraced voice-mail, e-mail, Internet browsers, and a range of information appliances. In each case, the conversion of the market came slowly. Once a particular threshold of consumer acceptance was achieved, there was a stampede. Geoffrey Moore defines **discontinuous innovations** as "new products or services that require the end-user and the marketplace to dramatically change their past behaviour, with the promise of gaining equally dramatic new benefits."[*] During the past quarter century, discontinuous innovations have been common in the computer-electronics industry, creating massive new spending, fierce competition, and a whole host of firms that are redrawing the boundaries of the high-technology marketplace.

A popular tool employed by strategists at high-technology firms is the technology adoption life cycle—a framework developed by Geoffrey Moore, a leading consultant to Hewlett-Packard and a host of other Silicon Valley firms.

7.5.1 Types of technology customers

Fundamental to Moore's framework are five classes of customers who constitute the potential market for a discontinuous innovation (Table 7.1). Business marketers can benefit by putting innovative products in the hands of **technology enthusiasts**. They serve as gatekeepers to the rest of the technology life cycle, and their endorsement is needed for an innovation to get a fair hearing in the organisation. Whereas technology enthusiasts possess influence, they do not have ready access to the resources needed to move an organisation toward a large-scale commitment to the new technology. By contrast, **visionaries** have resource control and can often be influential in publicising an innovation's benefits and giving it a boost during the early stages of market development. However, visionaries are difficult for a marketer to serve because each demands special and unique product modifications. Their demands can quickly tax a technology firm's R&D resources and stall the market penetration of the innovation.

The chasm

Truly innovative products often enjoy a warm welcome from early technology enthusiasts and visionaries, but then sales falter and often even plummet. Frequently, a chasm develops between visionaries who are intuitive and support revolution and **pragmatists** who are analytical, support evolution, and provide the pathway to the mainstream market. The business marketer that can successfully guide a product across the chasm creates an opportunity to gain acceptance with the mainstream market of pragmatists and conservatives. As Table 7.1 relates, pragmatists make most technology purchases in organisations, and conservatives include a sizable group of customers who are hesitant to buy high-tech products but do so to avoid being left behind.

7.5.2 Strategies for the technology adoption life cycle

The fundamental strategy for crossing the chasm and moving from the early market to the mainstream market is to provide pragmatists with a 100 per cent solution to their problems. Many high-technology firms err by attempting to provide something for everyone while never meeting the complete requirements of any particular market segment. Pragmatists seek the whole product—the minimum set of products and services that provide them with a compelling reason to buy. Geoffrey Moore notes that "the key to a winning strategy is to identify a simple beachhead of pragmatist customers in a mainstream market segment and to accelerate the formation of 100 per cent of their whole product. The goal is to win a niche foothold in the mainstream as quickly as possible—that is what is meant by *crossing the chasm*."[*]

TABLE 7.1 The Technology Adoption Life Cycle: Classes of Customers

Customer	Profile
Technology enthusiasts (*innovators*)	Interested in exploring the latest innovation, these consumers possess significant influence over how products are perceived by others in the organisation but lack control over resource commitments.
Visionaries (*early adopters*)	Desiring to exploit the innovation for a competitive advantage, these consumers are the true revolutionaries in business and government who have access to organisational resources but frequently demand special modifications to the product that are difficult for the innovator to provide.
Pragmatists (*early majority*)	Making the bulk of technology purchases in organisations, these individuals believe in technology evolution, not revolution, and seek products from a market leader with a proven track record of providing useful productivity improvements.
Conservatives (*late majority*)	Pessimistic about their ability to derive any value from technology investments, these individuals represent a sizable group of customers who are price sensitive and reluctantly purchase high-tech products to avoid being left behind.
Sceptics (*laggards*)	Rather than potential customers, these individuals are ever-present critics of the hype surrounding high-technology products.

Source: Adapted from Geoffrey A. Moore, *Inside the Tornado: Marketing Strategies from Silicon Valley's Cutting Edge* (New York: HarperCollins, 1995), pp. 14–18.

INSIDE BUSINESS MARKETING

The Gorilla Advantage in High-Tech Markets

High-tech companies that can get their products designed into the very standards of the market have enormous influence over the future direction of that market. For example, all PC-based software has to be Microsoft- and Intel-compatible. All networking solutions must be compatible with Cisco Systems' standards; all printers must be Hewlett-Packard–compatible. This is the essence of gorilla power in high-tech markets that firms such as Microsoft, Intel, Cisco, and Hewlett-Packard enjoy. The gorilla advantage allows these market leaders to

- *Attract more customers* by enjoying better press coverage and shorter sales cycles just because information technology managers expect it to be the winner;

- *Keep more customers* because the cost of switching is high for customers and the cost of entry is high for competitors;

- *Drive costs down* by shifting some costly enhancements that customers demand to suppliers while retaining control of the critical components of value creation;

- *Keep profits up* because business partners place a priority on developing complementary products and applications that make the *whole product* of the market leader worth more to customers than competing products are worth (e.g., Apple's iPad).

The Internet presents an explosive area of growth in many sectors of the high-tech market as firms square off to gain a leadership position in mobile computing, wireless technologies, supply chain integration, and Web-focused security. The gorilla games are just beginning!

Source: Geoffrey A. Moore, Paul Johnson, and Tom Kippola, *The Gorilla Game: An Investor's Guide to Picking Winners in High-Technology* (New York: HarperBusiness, 1998), pp. 43–70.

7.5.3 The bowling alley

In technology markets, each market segment is like a bowling pin, and the momentum from hitting one segment successfully carries over into surrounding segments. The bowling alley represents a stage in the adoption life cycle where a product gains acceptance from mainstream market segments but has yet to be adopted widely.

Consider the evolution of strategy for IBM Notes.[*] When first introduced, Notes was offered as a new paradigm for corporate-wide communication. To cross into the mainstream market, the IBM team shifted the product's focus from an enterprise-wide vision of corporate communication to specific solutions for particular business functions. The first niche served was the global account-management function of worldwide accounting and consulting firms. The solution was enhanced account activity coordination for highly visible products. This led to a second niche—global account management for sales teams, where enhanced coordination and information sharing spur productivity.

A focused strategy

A logical next step for IBM was movement into the customer service function, where openly sharing information can support creative solutions to customer problems. Successful penetration of these segments created another opportunity—incorporating the customer into the Notes loop.

Note the key lesson here: A customer-based, application-focused strategy provides leverage so that a victory in one market segment cascades into victories in adjacent market segments.

7.5.4 The tornado

Although economic buyers who seek particular solutions are the key to success in the bowling alley, technical or infrastructure buyers in organisations can spawn a tornado. Information-technology (IT) managers are responsible for providing efficient and reliable infrastructures—the systems organisational members use to communicate and perform their jobs. They are pragmatists, and they prefer to buy from an established market leader.

IT professionals interact freely across company and industry boundaries and discuss the ramifications of the latest technology. IT managers watch each other closely—they do not want to be too early or too late. Often, they move together and create a tornado. Because a massive number of new customers are entering the market at the same time and because they all want the same product, demand dramatically outstrips supply and a large backlog of customers can appear overnight. At a critical stage, such market forces have surrounded Hewlett-Packard's laser and inkjet printers, Microsoft's Windows products, Intel's Pentium microprocessors, and Apple's iPhones and iPads.

Tornado strategy

The central success factors for the tornado phase of the adoption life cycle differ from those that are appropriate for the bowling alley. Rather than emphasising market segmentation, the central goal is to gear up production to capitalise on the opportunity the broad market presents. In its printer business, Hewlett-Packard demonstrated the three critical priorities during a tornado[*]:

1 "Just ship."
2 Extend distribution channels.
3 Drive to the next lower price point.

First, Hewlett-Packard's quality improvement process allowed it to significantly increase production—first with laser printers, and later with ink-jet printers—with few interruptions. Second, to extend market coverage, H-P began to sell its laser printers through PC dealer channels and extended its distribution channels for ink-jet printers to computer superstores, office superstores, mail order, and, more recently, to price clubs and other consumer outlets. Third, H-P drove down the price points for its printers—moving ink-jet printers below €750, then below €375, and then well below that. As this example demonstrates, tornado strategy emphasises product leadership and operational excellence in manufacturing and distribution.

7.5.5 Main street

This stage of the technology adoption life cycle represents a period of aftermarket development. The frantic waves of mass-market adoption of the product begin to subside. Competitors in the industry have increased production, and supply now exceeds demand. Moore points out that "the defining characteristic of Main Street is that continued profitable market growth can no longer come from selling the basic commodity to new customers and must come instead from developing niche-specific extensions to the basic platform for existing customers."[*]

Main street strategy

The goal here is to develop value-based strategies targeted to particular end-user segments. H-P, for example, matches its printers to the special needs of different segments of home-office users by offering:

- A compact portable printer for those users who are space-constrained;
- The OfficeJet printer-fax for those who do not yet own a fax;
- A high-performance colour printer for those who create commercial flyers.

Main Street strategy emphasises operational excellence in production and distribution as well as finely tuned market segmentation strategies. What signals the end of the technology adoption life cycle? A discontinuous innovation appears that incorporates breakthrough technology and promises new solutions for customers.

SUMMARY

Some of the most valuable and enduring global brands belong to business-to-business firms. The power of a brand resides in the minds of customers through what they have experienced, seen, and heard about the brand over time. The customer-based brand equity model consists of four steps: establishing the right brand identity, defining the meaning of the brand through unique brand associations, developing responsive marketing programmes to elicit a positive brand response from customers, and building brand relationships with customers, marked by loyalty and active engagement. Research vividly demonstrates that investments in building a strong brand yield a positive payoff in the financial performance of the firm.

Conceptualising a product must go beyond mere physical description to include all the benefits and services that provide value to customers. The unifying goal for the business marketer is: *Provide superior market-perceived quality and value versus competitors*. To a business customer, value involves a trade-off between benefits and sacrifices. Business marketers can strengthen customer relationships by providing value-added services and helping customers reduce operations costs. A carefully coordinated product strategy recognises the role of various functional areas in providing value

to business customers. Special attention should be given to synchronising the activities among the product-management, sales, and service units.

Industrial product lines can be broadly classified into: (1) proprietary or catalogue items, (2) custom-built items, (3) custom-designed items, and (4) industrial services. Product management can best be described as the management of capability. In monitoring product performance and in formulating marketing strategy, the business marketer can profitably use product-positioning analysis. By isolating a product's competitive standing in a market, positioning analysis provides strategy insights to the planner. A product attribute is determinant if it is both important and differentiating.

Rapidly changing high-technology markets present special opportunities and challenges for the product strategist. The technology adoption life cycle includes five categories of customers: technology enthusiasts, visionaries, pragmatists, conservatives, and sceptics. New products gain acceptance from niches within the mainstream market, progress from segment to segment like one bowling pin knocking over another, and, if successful, experience the tornado of general, widespread adoption by pragmatists. Importantly, the technology adoption life cycle calls for different marketing strategies at different stages.

DISCUSSION QUESTIONS

1　Draft a proposal for an effective brand, following the four steps of brand building.

2　What impact can Mega-trends have on companies? Choose a company and analyse the way it has adapted to a specific Mega-trend (eg. Quality Movement, Sustainability etc.)

3　Name the main ways in which you can add customer value to your product.

4　Define the four dimensions of the product market and explain their relevance.

5　How do the five types of customers impact the choice of a strategy for the technology adoption life cycle?

INTERNET EXERCISE

1   TAT Technologies provides a broad range of
environmental control products and services for
the commercial and military aviation industries.

Go to http://www.tat-technologies.com/ and identify
TAT's major businesses (product lines).

REFERENCES

Aaker, David, *Managing Brand Equity* (New York: The Free
Press, 1991), p. 15.

Aaker, David A. and Jacobson, Robert, "The Value Relevance of
Brand Attitude in High-Technology Markets," *Journal of
Marketing Research* 38 (November 2001): pp. 485–493.

Abell, Derek F., "Competing Today While Preparing for
Tomorrow," *Sloan Management Review* 40 (Spring 1999):
p. 74.

B to B "B to B's Best Brands: Cisco," B to B's Best, 2007,
http://www.btobonline.com accessed July 15, 2008.

Berns, Maurice, Townend, Andrew, Khayat, Zayna, Balagopal,
Balu, Reeves, Martin, Hopkins, Michael S., and, Kruschwitz,
Nina, "Sustainability and Competitive Advantage," *MIT Sloan
Management Review* 51 (Fall 2009): pp. 19–26.

Boyd Jr., Harper W., Walker Jr., Orville C., and Larréché, Jean-
Claude, *Marketing Management: A Strategic Approach with a
Global Orientation* (Chicago: Irwin/McGraw-Hill, 1998),
pp. 190–200.

Cespedes, Frank V., *Concurrent Marketing: Integrating Product,
Sales, and Service* (Boston: Harvard Business School Press,
1995), pp. 58–85.

Christensen, Clayton M., and Raynor, Michael E., *The
Innovator's Solution: Creating and Sustaining Successful
Growth* (Boston: Harvard Business School Press, 2003),
pp. 73–95.

Christensen, Clayton M., Anthony, Scott D., and Roth, Erik A.,
Seeing What's Next (Boston: Harvard Business School
Press, 2004), p. 5.

Day, George S., *Strategic Market Planning: The Pursuit of
Competitive Advantage* (St. Paul, MN: West, 1984), p. 73.

Dibb, Sally, Simkin, Lyndon, Pride, Bill, and Ferrell, O.C.,
Marketing Concepts & Strategies, 6th ed. (Cengage, 2012).

Doole, Isobel, and Lowe, Robin, *International Marketing Strategy*
6th ed. (Cengage, 2012).

Ferguson, Wade, "Impact of ISO 9000 Series Standards on
Industrial Marketing," *Industrial Marketing Management* 25
(July 1996): pp. 325–310.

Gale, Bradley T., *Managing Customer Value: Creating Quality
and Service That Customers Can See* (New York: The Free
Press, 1994), pp. 25–30.

Gertz, Dwight L., and Baptista, João P.A., *Grow to Be Great:
Breaking the Downsizing Cycle* (New York: The Free Press,
1995), p. 128.

Glynn, Mark S., "Primer in B2B Brand-building Strategies with a
Reader Practicum," *Journal of Business Research* (2011),
Vol 56 No.5 666-675.

Haanaes, Knut, Balagopal, Balu, Kong, Ming Tech, Velken,
Ingrid, Arthur, David, Hopkins, Michael S. and Kruschwitz,
Nina, "New Sustainability Study: The 'Embracers' Seize
Advantage," *MIT Sloan Management Review* 52 (Spring
2011): pp. 23–35.

Hansotia, Behram J., Shaikh, Muzaffar A., and Sheth, Jagdish
N., "The Strategic Determinacy Approach to Brand
Management," *Business Marketing* 70 (Fall 1985):
pp. 66–69.

Homburg, Christian, Klarmann, Martin, and Schmitt, Jens,
"Brand Awareness in Business Markets," *International
Journal of Research in Marketing* 27 (3, 2010):
pp. 201–212.

Jones, Thomas O., and Sasser, W. Earl, "Why Satisfied
Customers Defect," *Harvard Business Review* 73
(November–December 1995): pp. 88–99.

Keller, Kevin Lane, "Building a Strong Business-to-Business
Brand," in Mark S. Glynn and Arch G. Woodside (eds.),
*Business-to-Business Brand Management: Theory,
Research and Executive Case Study Exercises* [Advances in
Business Marketing and Purchasing, Volume 15], Bingley,
UK: Emerald Group Publishing, 2009, pp. 11–31.

Keller, Kevin Lane, "Building Customer-Based Brand Equity,"
Marketing Management 10 (July/August 2001): pp. 15–19.

Keller, Kevin Lane, *Strategic Brand Management* (3rd ed., Upper
Saddle River, NJ: Prentice Hall, 2007).

Keller, Kevin Lane, Sternthal, Brian, and Tybout, Alice, "Three
Questions You Need to Ask about Your Brand," *Harvard
Business Review* 80 (September 2002): pp. 80–89.

Lohr, Steve, "Big Blue's Smarter Marketing Playbook," January
12, 2010, p. 1, http://bits.blogs.nytimes.com accessed June
2, 2011.

Lubin, David A., and Esty, "Daniel C., The Sustainability
Imperative," *Harvard Business Review* 88 (May 2010):
42–50.

Madden, Thomas J., Fehle, Frank, and Fournier, Susan, "Brands
Matter: An Empirical Demonstration of the Creation of
Shareholder Value through Branding," *Journal of the
Academy of Marketing Science* 34 (2, 2006): pp. 224–235.

Makower, Joel, "A Closer Look at IBM's 'Smarter Planet'
Campaign," GreenBiz.com, January 4, 2009, p. 6, http://
www.greenbiz.com, accessed June 4, 2011.

Martin, Dick, *Secrets of the Marketing Masters* (New York:
AMACOM, 2009), pp. 196–200.

McKenna, Regis, *Relationship Marketing* (Reading MA: Addison-
Wesley, 1991), p. 184.

Menon, Ajay, Homburg, Christian, and Beutin, Nikolas, "Understanding Customer Value in Business-to-Business Relationships," *Journal of Business-to-Business Marketing* 12 (2, 2005): p. 5.

Moore, Geoffrey A., *Inside the Tornado: Marketing Strategies from Silicon Valley's Cutting Edge* (New York: HarperCollins, 1995), p. 13.

Moutinho, Luiz, and Southern, Geoffrey, *Strategic Marketing Management: A process Based Approach* (Cengage, 2012).

Narayandas, Das, "Building Loyalty in Business Markets," *Harvard Business Review* 83 (September–October 2005): p. 134.

Nidumolu, Ram, Prahalad, C.K., and Rangaswami, M. R., "Why Sustainability Is Now the Driver of Innovation," *Harvard Business Review* 87 (September 2009): pp. 56–64.

Ogilvy, "IBM Smarter Planet Campaign from Ogilvy & Mather Wins Golden Effie," June 9, 2010, p. 1, http://www.ogilvy.com, accessed June 2, 2011.

Oliver, Richard L., "Whence Customer Loyalty," *Journal of Marketing* 63 (Special Issue 1999): pp. 33–44.

Palmisano, Samuel J., Chief Executive Officer, IBM, Speech "A Smarter Planet," January 12, 2010, p. 2, London, http://www.ibm.com, accessed June 2, 2011.

Porter, Michael E., and Kramer, Mark R., "Strategy & Society: The Link between Competitive Advantage and Corporate Social Responsibility," *Harvard Business Review* 84 (December 2006): p. 92.

Prahalad, C.K., and Krishnan, M.S., "The New Meaning of Quality in the Information Age," *Harvard Business Review* 77 (September–October 1999): pp. 109–112.

Prahalad, C.K., and Ramaswamy, Venkat, *The Future of Competition: Co-Creating Unique Value with Customers* (Boston: Harvard Business School Press, 2004).

PRSA, "IBM: Smarter Branding for a Smarter Planet," Public Relations Society of America, January 1, 2010, pp. 1–3, http://www.prsa.org, accessed June 4, 2011.

Shapiro, Benson P., *Industrial Product Policy: Managing the Existing Product Line* (Cambridge, MA: Marketing Science Institute, 1977), pp. 37–39.

Ulaga, Wolfgang, and Eggert, Andreas, "Value-Based Differentiation in Business Relationships: Gaining and Sustaining Key Supplier Status," *Journal of Marketing* 70 (January 2006): pp. 119–136.

van Weele, Arjan, *Puchasing and Supply Chain Management: Analysis Strategy, Planning and Practice*, 5th ed. (Cengage, 2010).

Varadarajan, Rajan, and Jayachandran, Satish, "Marketing Strategy: An Assessment of the State of the Field and Outlook," *Journal of the Academy of Marketing Science* 27 (Spring 1999): pp. 120–143.

Verhage, Bronis J., *Marketing: A Global Perspective* (Cengage, 2013).

Walker, Beth A., Kapelianis, Dimitri, and Hutt, Michael D., "Competitive Cognition," *MIT Sloan Management Review* 46 (Summer 2005): pp. 10–12.

Webster Jr., Frederick E., and Keller, Kevin Lane, "A Roadmap for Branding in Industrial Markets," *Journal of Brand Management* 12 (May 2004): p. 389.

White, Erin, "Rethinking the Quality-Improvement Program," *The Wall Street Journal*, September 19, 2005, p. B3.

Yoder, Stephen Kreider, "Shaving Back: How H-P Used Tactics of the Japanese to Beat Them at Their Game," *The Wall Street Journal*, September 8, 1994, pp. A1, A6.

CHAPTER 8 MANAGING SERVICES FOR BUSINESS MARKETS

CHAPTER OBJECTIVES

The important and growing market for business services poses special challenges and meaningful opportunities for the marketing manager. This chapter explores the unique aspects of business services and the special role they play in the business market environment. After reading this chapter, you will understand:

1   The importance of the different stages in the customer experience life cycle.

2   The nature and characteristics of services

3   The crucial concepts of service quality, costumer satisfaction and loyalty

4   How to explore the concept of hybrid offerings.

FedEx Corporation, the global package delivery service, mobilises for trouble before it occurs: Each night, five empty FedEx jets roam over the United States.* Why? So the firm can respond on a moment's notice to unexpected events such as overbooking of packages in Atlanta or an equipment failure in Denver. FedEx excels by making promises to its customers and keeping them. The first major service organisation to win the Malcolm Baldrige National Quality Award, FedEx makes specific promises about the timeliness and reliability of package delivery in its advertising and marketing communications. More importantly, FedEx aligns its personnel, facilities, information technology, and equipment to meet those promises. Says Scot Struminger, vice president of information technology at FedEx, "We know that customer loyalty comes from treating customers like you want to be treated."*

As this example demonstrates, *services* play a critical role in the marketing programmes of many business-to-business firms, whether their primary focus is on a service (FedEx) or whether services provide a promising new path for growth. Indeed, high-tech brands, like IBM or Oracle, are built on a promise of value to customers, and service excellence is part of the value package customers demand. In fact, over 65 per cent of IBM's massive revenue base now comes from services—not products. Clearly, many product manufacturers are now using integrated product and service solutions as a core marketing strategy for creating new growth opportunities. Moreover, a vast array of "pure service" firms exist to supply organisations with everything from office cleaning to management consulting and just-in-time delivery to key customers.*

This chapter examines the nature of business services, the role that services assume in customer solutions, the major strategic elements related to services marketing, and creative strategies for combining goods and services into hybrid offerings.

8.1 UNDERSTANDING THE FULL CUSTOMER EXPERIENCE

The traditional product-centric mindset rests on the assumption that companies win by creating superior products and continually enhancing the performance of existing products. But services are fundamental to the customer experience that every business-to-business firm provides. Customer experience encompasses every dimension of a company's offering—product and service features, advertising, ease of use, reliability, the process of becoming a customer, or the way problems are resolved—not to mention the ongoing sales relationship.*

8.1.1 The customer experience life cycle

Recent research highlights the importance of examining the customer's experience. A survey of the customers of 362 firms by Bain & Company revealed that only 8 per cent described their experience as "superior," yet 80 per cent of the companies surveyed believed that the experience that they were delivering was indeed superior.* By focusing narrowly only on core-related product elements and overlooking the full customer experience, companies "can end up losing customers without understanding why. Moreover, such companies are missing out on some powerful opportunities to create value and cement their customers' loyalty," says David Rickard.*

Customer experience represents the internal and subjective response a business customer has to any direct or indirect contact with a company. We will devote special attention to **touchpoints**—those instances in which the customer has direct contact with either the product or service itself or with representatives of it by a third party, such as a channel partner. A customer experience map provides a valuable tool for diagnosing key touchpoints or interactions between the company and the customer from the moment contact is made with a potential customer through the maintenance of an ongoing relationship (see Figure 8.1). Developed from interviews with customers, the map provides a foundation for defining what is most important in your customers' experience.

FIGURE 8.1 The first step in understanding a customer's experience is to develop a life cycle map

A representative set of customer-company interactions

Relationship initiation	Provider evaluation	Account setup	Order placement	Product reception and use	Problem resolution	Payment	Account maintenance
The company exposes the customer to its marketing message	The customer gets initial price and lead-time quotes	The customer obtains materials for account setup	The customer selects the product	The customer tracks order status	The customer files a claim and obtains resolution	The customer receives and validates the invoice	The customer maintains profile information
The customer seeks relevant information	The customer puts out an RFP	The customer provides account profile information	The customer places the order (fills out the order form)	The company and the customer arrange the final delivery terms	The customer notifies the company of a problem and obtains resolution	The customer makes the payment	The customer maintains supplies
	The customer evaluates providers and negotiates terms and pricing	The company confirms setup and activation	The customer prepares specialty documents when required (for example, for rush delivery)	The customer receives the product-shipped notice	The customer seeks an invoice adjustment and obtains resolution		The company provides general support (not related to problems)
	The customer selects the provider	The company performs courtesy follow-up	The company and the customer arrange initial delivery terms	The customer receives and inspects the product			The customer obtains ongoing price quotes
		The customer requests product information		The customer refuses or accepts the product			

Source: David Rickard, "Winning by Understanding the Full Customer Experience," *The Boston Consulting Group, Inc.*, 2006, p. 6. Accessed on July 26, 2008 at http://www.bcg.com.

8.1.2 Applying the customer experience map

The map was developed by the Boston Consulting Group for a large industrial-goods company that faced this dilemma: Traditional measures of product quality continued to indicate superb performance, but customer satisfaction remained stagnant and the company was losing market share.* Once the customer experience map is developed, the next step is to meet with customers and pare down the list to a smaller set of the most critical interactions and product and service characteristics. The ultimate goal of the analysis is to identify: (1) the value that customers place on different levels of performance (for example, high, average, low) for each element of their experience, (2) the customers' minimal expectations for each element, and (3) the customers' perception of the firm's performance versus that of key competitors.

Based on the analysis, strategists at the industrial-goods company were surprised to learn that only 40 per cent of customers' most critical experiences were tied to the core product, whereas 60 per cent were related to softer considerations (for example, the ease of making invoice corrections and resolving problems). This revelation proved crucial to understanding why the company was losing market share even though its customers' ratings of product quality were improving.

8.1.3 Customer experience management

As previously explained, customer relationship management captures what a company knows about a particular customer. Christopher Meyer and Andre Schwager persuasively argue that there is a corresponding need for well-developed **customer experience management** processes that capture customers' subjective thoughts about a particular company.* Such an approach requires surveys and targeted studies at points of customer interaction that identify gaps between customer expectations and their actual experience. "Because a great many customer experiences aren't the direct consequence of the brand's message or the company's actual offerings ... the customers themselves ... must be monitored and probed."*

8.1.4 A solution-centred perspective*

As global competition intensifies and product differentiation quickly fades, strategists at leading firms are giving increased attention to services, particularly a solution-centric mindset. Rather than starting with the product, a solution-centred approach begins with an analysis of a customer problem and ends by identifying the products and services required to solve the problem. Rather than transaction based, the focus of the exchange process is interaction based, and value is co-created by the firm in concert with the customer (Table 8.1). So, customer offerings represent an "integrated combination of products and services designed to provide customised experiences for specific customer segments."* Services, as a critical feature of the solution, become a valuable basis for competitive advantage and an important driver of profitability.

Determine unique capabilities

In developing solutions, business marketing firms must define their unique capabilities and determine how to use them to help customers reduce costs, increase responsiveness, or improve quality. In some cases, this may involve taking in some of the work or activities that customers now perform. To illustrate, DuPont first sold paint to Ford but now runs Ford's paint shops. "DuPont, which is paid on the basis of the number of painted vehicles, actually sells less paint than before because it has an incentive to paint cars with the least amount of waste. But the company makes more money as a result of the improved efficiency."* The DuPont example demonstrates a central point about solutions marketing: *Products provide the platform for the delivery of services.**

8.2 DELIVERING EFFECTIVE CUSTOMER SOLUTIONS

A recent research study suggests that companies can deliver more effective solutions at profitable prices if they adopt a stronger relationship focus.* The authors suggest that business marketers

TABLE 8.1 From a product to a solutions perspective

	Product Perspective	Solutions Perspective
Value Proposition	Win by creating innovative products and enriching features of existing products	Win by creating and delivering superior customer solutions
Value Creation	Value is created by the firm	Value is co-created by the customer and the firm
Designing Offerings	Start with the product or service, and then target customer segments	Start with the customer problem, and then assemble required products and services to solve the problem
Company-Customer Relationship	Transaction-based	Interaction-based and centred on the co-creation of solutions
Focus on Quality	Quality of internal processes and company offerings	Quality of customer–firm interactions

Source: Adapted from Mohanbir Sawhney, "Going Beyond the Product: Defining, Designing, and Delivering Customer Solutions," Working Paper, Kellogg School of Management, Northwestern University, December 2004; and C. K. Prahalad and Venkat Ramaswamy, *The Future of Competition: Co-Creating Unique Value with Customers* (Boston: Harvard Business School Press, 2004).

FIGURE 8.2 Relational processes comprising a customer solution

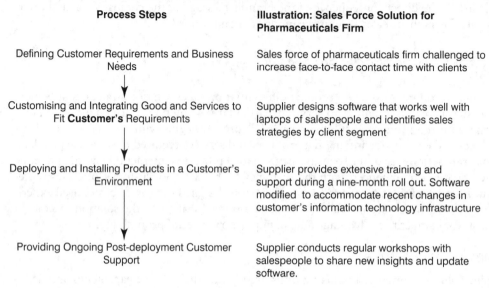

Process Steps	Illustration: Sales Force Solution for Pharmaceuticals Firm
Defining Customer Requirements and Business Needs	Sales force of pharmaceuticals firm challenged to increase face-to-face contact time with clients
Customising and Integrating Good and Services to Fit **Customer's** Requirements	Supplier designs software that works well with laptops of salespeople and identifies sales strategies by client segment
Deploying and Installing Products in a Customer's Environment	Supplier provides extensive training and support during a nine-month roll out. Software modified to accommodate recent changes in customer's information technology infrastructure
Providing Ongoing Post-deployment Customer Support	Supplier conducts regular workshops with salespeople to share new insights and update software.

Source: Adapted, with modifications, from Kapil R. Tuli, Ajay K. Kohli and Sundar G. Bharadwaj, "Rethinking Customer Solutions: From Product Bundles to Relational Processes," *Journal of Marketing* 71 (July 2007), pp. 5–8.

mistakenly view a solution as a customised and integrated combination of products and services for meeting a customer's business needs. In sharp contrast, customers view a solution as a set of customer–company relational processes that involve: "(1) customer requirements definition, (2) customisation and integration of goods and/or services and (3) their deployment, and (4) postdeployment customer support, all of which are aimed at meeting customers' business needs."[*]

From Figure 8.2, observe how these relational processes took shape as a business marketing firm developed a software solution for the sales unit of a large pharmaceuticals customer.

8.2.1 The supplier's role[*]

Detailing the four relational processes that comprise a solution brings into sharp focus the challenging coordination issues that a solution strategy presents for the business marketing strategist. Indeed, success hinges on developing appropriate mechanisms for coordinating the activities of different organisational units that contribute to particular stages of the customer solution development process.

First, the sales function typically performs requirements definition, whereas the customer service function provides postdeployment support. In fact, some solutions may require contributions from different business units. To deliver effective solutions, these different functional groups and business units have to be "on the same page." Solutions require employees to develop two types of skills that go beyond product-oriented selling: **multi-domain skills** (the ability to incorporate multiple products and services) and **boundary-spanning skills** (the ability to forge connections across internal units).[*]

Second, cross-unit coordination of a customer solution is promoted if employee incentives of the sales, development, operations, and support staff complement one another. For example, if the compensation of salespeople, beyond an initial commission, also depends on the customer's satisfaction with the solution, better postdeployment support is likely to result. For example, Lloyds TSB uses a Web-based survey to determine the pre- and post-sale satisfaction of customers.

Third, solution effectiveness can be enhanced by documenting the history of effective and ineffective customer solution engagements.[*] **Document emphasis** refers to the extent to which employees of the business marketing firm are required to document the key milestones in the creation and deployment of a solution, including work performed, key functions involved, and outcomes. Documentation emphasis provides a tool for managing the complexity involved in creating solutions and for synchronising work and sharing information across units.

Fourth, solution effectiveness can be facilitated by laying out a blueprint or process to guide employees in developing a specific solution. **Process articulation** refers to the extent to which a supplier firm clarifies the roles and responsibilities of organisational units and provides guidelines for sharing customer and product information in developing a solution.

8.2.2 The customer's role

Research also clearly reveals that solution effectiveness hinges on particular customer behaviours as well. First, a supplier can do a more effective job if the customer is willing to adapt to the supplier's needs or to unforeseen contingencies as they arise. **Customer adaptiveness** refers to the degree to which a customer is willing to adjust its routines and processes to accommodate a supplier's products.

Second, solution effectiveness is enhanced if the customer provides information and guidelines concerning the priorities and sensitivities of various stakeholders in the customer firm. **Political counselling** refers to the degree to which a customer provides a supplier with information regarding the political landscape in the customer organisation. For example, the lack of political counselling created blunders for a supplier of an information-technology solution. While the sales team continued to centre on the chief technology officer who had defined solution requirements, attention should have been directed to user groups in the customer organisation who had been given total control of implementation.

Finally, solution effectiveness can be enhanced if the customer provides counselling to a supplier concerning the unique elements of its operations. **Operational counselling** refers to information provided to suppliers concerning the relevant technical systems, business processes, and company policies in the customer organisation. Based on their research on solution selling, Kapil Tuli and his research colleagues observe:

> *A supplier may want to avoid conducting business with a customer that is not adaptive or is unlikely to "educate" the supplier about its internal politics and operations. The solution that a supplier implements for such a customer is likely to be ineffective.*[*]

8.2.3 Choose customers wisely

Some customers are better candidates for a solution offering than others. To illustrate, GE Healthcare developed a solution focus built around consulting services and a menu of products to address customer needs in a comprehensive fashion.[*] GE originally targeted solutions at large national accounts that turned out to be poor candidates for the solution offering because of their focus on price. The company then refined its target customer profile by centring on multihospital systems that: (1) generated at least €375 million in annual revenue and (2) demonstrated a willingness to provide GE with access to senior executives. Using this screening process, GE isolated 150 of the roughly 400 multihospital systems in the United States, directing particular attention to the 50 customer accounts that expressed a willingness to work with GE. The solutions group at GE secured over €375 million in new contracts.

8.2.4 Benefits of solution marketing

By shifting from a product to a solutions strategy, business-to-business firms gain two important benefits, namely, new avenues for growth and differentiation.

B2B TOP PERFORMERS

Customer Service Enhanced by E-commerce for Yellow Freight

Shipping costs are a major expense in the physical distribution process, and companies around the world are always looking for the most efficient, reliable and convenient means of moving supplies and products in order to satisfy their own customers. To help marketers fulfil these objectives, Yellow Freight, a global transportation company and market leader in North America, has introduced new high-tech services, including electronic data interchange, E-Tools, Yellow Live/Voice, and Yellow Freight's E-Channels.

Electronic data interchange (EDI) allows Yellow Freight and its customers to share documents over the Internet. This service can be useful for transferring invoices, bills of loading, shipment tracking and other data files. The use of EDI almost eliminates the need for paper communications, and establishes a new medium for communication between Yellow Freight and its customers. Most logistics companies now use EDI for communicating with regular clients. However, a look at www.myyellow.com reveals the extent to which Yellow Freight has harnessed technology in its dealings with clients.

My Yellow E-Tools is a system designed to simplify business interactions by allowing customers to use the Internet to create bills of loading, schedule collections, track shipments, view account information and invoices, and, if necessary, dispute invoices. Through E-Tools, customers can obtain instant quotes, and then complete bills of loading and schedule collections if the quoted rates are satisfactory. Registered customers of Yellow Freight's E-Tools can also grant designated partners access to their application information. The customer chooses what information to share, and to whom it can be provided. For example, a PC manufacturer may opt to permit customers to track the progress of their order. The web service offers a simple three-stage service to clients:

1   quote

2   book

3   track

With Yellow Live/Voice, Yellow Freight became the first transportation company to offer live voice capability through its website. This service allows customers to have real-time audio conversations with customer-service representatives by downloading voice-enabling software. Customers who use a computer equipped with a microphone and speakers can engage in two-way audio communication, while those whose computers lack a microphone can type text questions and then listen to audio feedback from customer service.

E-Channels, which includes Yellow Live/Voice, helps customers stay connected to Yellow Freight via the Internet. This service allows customers to track shipments sent through Yellow Freight from any mobile phone that has wireless Internet capabilities. Customers can also track shipments using a palmtop organiser. These features grant customers greater options and control over how, when, from where and how often they access information about their shipments.

Yellow Freight's e-commerce services provide customers with greater control over their accounts and efficiency in shipping. The entire shipping process, from price quotes to collection to tracking, can now be accomplished on-line. By expanding the options available to customers who need to track their shipments, Yellow Freight has gained a competitive advantage in the global shipping industry.

Source: 'E-channels', Yellow Freight, www.yellowfreight.com/ecommerce/echannels/, accessed 17 January 2002; 'The first Internet-based live voice ecommerce service in the transportation industry', Yellow Freight, press release, 18 September 2000, www.yellowfreight.com/aboutyellow/newsroom/pressreleases/pr_archive/pr_091800.html; the Yellow Freight website, www.yellowfreight.com, accessed 17 January 2002; www.myyellow.com, accessed 19 April 2004.

Creating growth opportunities

Solutions create fresh opportunities for increasing the amount of business or share-of-wallet that a company receives from its customer base. An expanded portfolio of service-intensive offerings makes this possible. Often, services represent a far larger market opportunity than the core product market. To illustrate, Deere & Company, the agricultural equipment manufacturer, found that the proportion of each euro farmers spend on equipment has been declining for years and that the bulk of that spending now goes for services. Moreover, by centring on that profit pool, Deere is tapping into a market opportunity that is 10 times larger than the equipment market. To that end, Deere provides a range of services for its customers (for example, health insurance and banking) and is employing innovative technologies to make the farmer's life easier and more productive. For example, Deere is experimenting with global positioning systems (GPS) and biosensors on its combines. C. K. Prahalad and Venkat Ramaswamy describe the initiative:

> *Imagine driverless combines and tractors with onboard sensors that can measure the oil content of grain or distinguish between weeds and crops. The benefits are enormous. Farmers can ration herbicide according to soil conditions. GPS-guided steering ensures repeatable accuracy, eliminates overtreating of crops … thereby reducing time, fuel, labour, and chemical costs.… Farmers can be more productive, minimising the cost per acre.* [*]

Sustaining differentiation and customer loyalty

As farmers view more and more products as commodities, business marketers who emphasise solutions can sustain differentiation more effectively than rivals who maintain a strict focus on the core product offering. Why? According to Mohanbir Sawhney, "Solutions offer many more avenues for differentiation than products because they include a variety of services that can be customised in many unique ways for individual customers." [*] Likewise, by developing a rich network of relationships with members of the customer organisation, co-creating solutions with the customer, and becoming directly connected to the customer's operations, they enhance customer loyalty and throw up severe barriers to competing firms when they attempt to persuade the customer to switch suppliers.

8.3 BUSINESS SERVICE MARKETING: SPECIAL CHALLENGES

The development of marketing programmes for both products and services can be approached from a common perspective; yet the relative importance and form of various strategic elements differ between products and services. The underlying explanation for these strategic differences, asserts Henry Assael, lies in the distinctions between a product and a service:

> *Services are intangible; products are tangible. Services are consumed at the time of production, but there is a time lag between the production and consumption of products. Services cannot be stored; products can. Services are highly variable; most products are highly standardised. These differences produce differences in strategic applications that often stand many product marketing principles on their head.* [*]

Thus, success in the business service marketplace begins with understanding the meaning of *service*.

8.3.1 Services are different

There are inherent differences between goods and services, providing a unique set of marketing challenges for service businesses and for manufacturers that provide services as a core offering. Put simply, services are deeds, processes, and performances. [*] For example, a management consultant's core offerings are primarily deeds and actions performed for customers. The most basic, and universally recognised, difference between goods and services is *intangibility*. Services are more intangible than manufactured goods, and manufactured goods are more tangible than services. Because services are actions or performances, they cannot be seen or touched in the same way that consumers sense tangible goods.

8.3.2 Tangible or intangible?

Figure 8.3 provides a useful tool for understanding the product-service definitional problem. The continuum suggests that there are very few *pure products* or *pure services*. For example, a personal computer is a physical object made up of tangible elements that facilitate the work of an individual and an organisation. In addition to the computer's physical design and performance characteristics, the quality of technical service support is an important dimension of the marketing programme. Thus, most market offerings comprise a combination of tangible and intangible elements.

Whether an offering is classified as a good or as a service depends on how the organisational buyer views it—whether the tangible or the intangible elements dominate. On one end of the spectrum, grease and oil are tangible-dominant; the essence of what is being bought is the physical product. Management seminars, on the other hand, are intangible-dominant because what is being bought—professional development, education, learning—has few, if any, tangible properties. A convention hotel is in the middle of the continuum because the buyer receives an array of both tangible elements (meals, beverages, notepads, and so on) and intangible benefits (courteous personnel, fast check-ins, meeting room ambiance, and so forth).

The concept of tangibility is especially useful to the business marketer because many business offerings are composed of product and service combinations. The key management task is to evaluate carefully (from the buyer's standpoint) which elements dominate. The more the market offering is characterised by intangible elements, the more difficult it is to apply the standard marketing tools that were developed for products. The business marketer must focus on specialised marketing approaches appropriate for services.

The concept of tangibility also helps the manager focus clearly on the firm's *total market offering*.* In addition, it helps the manager recognise that a change in one element of the market offering may completely change the offering in the customer's view. For example, a business marketer who decides to hold spare-parts inventory at a central location and use overnight delivery to meet customer requirements must refocus marketing strategy. The offering has moved toward the intangible end of the continuum because of the intangible benefits of reduced customer inventory and fast transportation. This new "service," which is less tangible, must be

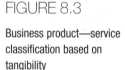

FIGURE 8.3

Business product—service classification based on tangibility

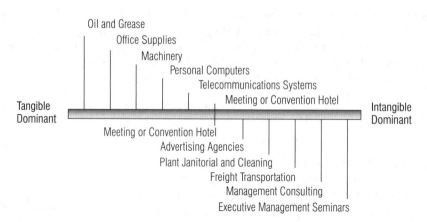

Source: Adapted from G. Lynn Shostack, "Breaking Free from Product Marketing," *Journal of Marketing* 41 (April 1977): p. 77. Published by the American Marketing Association.

TABLE 8.2 Unique service characteristics

Characteristics	Examples	Marketing Implications
Simultaneous production and consumption	Telephone conference call; management seminar; equipment repair	Direct-seller interaction requires that service be done "right"; requires high-level training for personnel; requires effective screening and recruitment
Nonstandardised output	Management advice varies with the individual consultant; merchandise damages vary from shipment to shipment	Emphasises strict quality control standards; develop systems that minimise deviation and human error; prepackage the service; look for ways to automate
Perishability: inability to store or stockpile	Unfilled airline seats; an idle computer technician; unrented warehouse space	Plan capacity around peak demand; use pricing and promotion to even out demand peaks and valleys; use overlapping shifts for personnel
Lack of ownership	Use of railway wagon; use of consultant's know-how; use of mailing list	Focus promotion on the advantages of nonownership: reduced labour, overhead, and capital; emphasise flexibility

carefully explained, and the intangible results of lower inventory costs must be made more concrete to the buyer through an effective promotion programme.

In summary, business services are market offerings that are predominantly intangible. However, few services are totally intangible—they often contain elements with tangible properties. In addition to tangibility, business services have other important distinguishing characteristics that influence how they are marketed. Table 8.2 summarises the core characteristics that further delineate the nature of business services.

8.3.3 Simultaneous production and consumption

Because services are generally *consumed as they are produced*, a critical element in the buyer–seller relationship is the effectiveness of the individual who actually provides the service—the IBM technician, the DHL driver, the KPMG consultant. From the service firm's perspective, the entire marketing strategy may rest on how effectively the individual service provider interacts with the customer. Here the actual service delivery takes place, and the promise to the customer is kept or broken. This critical point of contact with the customer is referred to as **interactive** or **real-time marketing**. Recruiting, hiring, and training personnel assume special importance in business service firms.

8.3.4 Service variability

Observe in Table 8.2 that service is *nonstandardised*, meaning that the quality of the service output may vary each time it is provided.* Services vary in the amount of equipment and labour used to provide them. For example, a significant human element is involved in teaching an executive seminar compared with providing overnight airfreight service. Generally, the more labour involved in a service, the less uniform the output. In these labour-intensive cases, the user may also find it difficult to judge the quality before the service is provided. Because of uniformity problems, business service providers must focus on finely tuned quality-control programmes, invest in "systems" to minimise human error, and seek approaches for automating the service.

INSIDE BUSINESS MARKETING

Do Service Transition Strategies Pay Off?

To improve their competitive position in the era of intense global competition and the increasing commoditisation that characterises many product markets, a host of manufacturing firms have added services to their existing product offerings. If successful, such service transition strategies could make the firm's value proposition more unique, difficult for rivals to duplicate, and valuable to customers, thereby enhancing profitability and firm value. Do these service transition strategies pay off? A recent study by Eric Fang and his colleagues provides the answers.

- Before they can expect positive effects on firm value, business marketing firms should recognise that service transition strategies typically require achieving a critical mass in sales, estimated to be 20 to 30 per cent of total sales.

- Transitioning to services is significantly more effective for companies that offer services related to their core product business. Sales of unrelated services demonstrate little impact on firm value.

- Adding services to a core product offering increases firm value for companies in slow growth and turbulent industries. However, "firms in high growth industries can destroy firm value by shifting their focus . . . to service initiatives. In stable (low turbulence) industries, adding services has a negative effect on firm value."

Eric (Er) Fang, Robert W. Palmatier, and Jan-Benedict E. M. Steenkamp, "Effect of Service Transition Strategies on Firm Value," *Journal of Marketing*, 72 (September 2008): pp. 1–14.

8.3.5 Service perishability

Generally, services *cannot be stored*; that is, if they are not provided at the time they are available, the lost revenue cannot be recaptured. Tied to this characteristic is the fact that demand for services is often unpredictable and widely fluctuating. The service marketer must carefully evaluate capacity—in a service business, **capacity** is a substitute for inventory. If capacity is set for peak demand, a "service inventory" must exist to supply the highest level of demand. As an example, some airlines that provide air shuttle service between New York, Washington, and Boston offer flights that leave every hour. If, on any flight, the plane is full, another plane is brought to the terminal—even for one passenger. An infinite capacity is set so that no single business traveller is dissatisfied. Obviously, setting high-capacity levels is costly, and the marketer must analyse the cost versus the lost revenue and customer goodwill that might result from maintaining lower capacity.

8.3.6 Nonownership

The final dimension of services shown in Table 8.2 is that the service buyer uses, but *does not own*, the service purchased. Essentially, payment for a service is a payment for the use of, access to, or hire of items. Renting or leasing is "a way for customers to enjoy use of physical goods and facilities that they cannot afford to buy, cannot justify purchasing, or prefer not to retain after use."[*] The service marketer must feature the advantages of nonownership in its communications to the marketplace. The key benefits to emphasise are reductions in staff, overhead, and capital from having a third party provide the service.

Although there may be exceptions, these characteristics provide a useful framework for understanding the nature of business services and isolating special marketing strategy requirements. The framework suggests that different types of service providers should pursue different types of strategies because of the intangibility and heterogeneity of their services. In this case, providers of professional services (consulting, tax advising, accounting, and so on) should develop marketing strategies that emphasise word-of-mouth communication, provide tangible evidence, and employ value pricing to overcome the issues created by intangibility and heterogeneity.[*]

8.4 SERVICE QUALITY

Quality standards are ultimately defined by the customer. Actual performance by the service provider or the provider's perception of quality are of little relevance compared with the customer's perception. "Good" service results when the service provider meets or exceeds the customer's expectations.[*] As a result, many management experts argue that service companies should carefully position themselves so that customers expect a little less than the firm can actually deliver. The strategy: underpromise and overdeliver.

8.4.1 Dimensions of service quality

Because business services are intangible and nonstandardised, buyers tend to have greater difficulty evaluating services than evaluating goods. Because they are unable to depend on consistent service performance and quality, service buyers may perceive more risk.[*] As a result, they use a variety of prepurchase information sources to reduce risk. Information from current users (word of mouth) is particularly important. In addition, the evaluation process for services tends to be more abstract, more random, and more heavily based on symbology rather than on concrete decision variables.[*]

Research provides some valuable insights into how customers evaluate service quality. From Table 8.3 note that customers focus on five dimensions in evaluating service quality: reliability, responsiveness, assurance, empathy, and tangibles. Among these dimensions, reliability—delivery on promises—is the most important to customers. High-quality service performance is also shaped by the way frontline service personnel provide it. To the customer, service quality represents a responsive employee, one who inspires confidence and one who adapts to the customer's unique needs or preferences and delivers the service in a professional manner. In fact, the performance of employees who are in contact with the customer may compensate for temporary service quality problems (for example, a problem reoccurs in a recently repaired photocopier).[*] By promptly acknowledging the error and responding quickly to the problem, the service employee may even strengthen the firm's relationship with the customer.

TABLE 8.3 The dimensions of service quality

Dimension	Description	Examples
Reliability	Delivering on promises	Promised delivery date met
Responsiveness	Being willing to help	Prompt reply to customers' requests
Assurance	Inspiring trust and confidence	Professional and knowledgeable staff
Empathy	Treating customers as individuals	Adapts to special needs of customer
Tangibles	Representing the service physically	Distinctive materials: brochures, documents

Source: Adapted from Valarie A. Zeithaml, Mary Jo Bitner, and Dwayne D. Gremler, *Services Marketing: Integrating Customer Focus across the Firm*, 5th ed. (Boston: McGraw-Hill Irwin, 2009), pp. 116–120.

8.4.2 Customer satisfaction and loyalty

Four components of a firm's offering and its customer-linking processes affect customer satisfaction:

1   The basic elements of the product or service that customers expect all competitors to provide;

2   Basic support services, such as technical assistance or training, that make the product or service more effective or easier to use;

3   A recovery process for quickly fixing product or service problems;

4   Extraordinary services that so excel in solving customers' unique problems or in meeting their needs that they make the product or service seem customised.*

Leading service firms carefully measure and monitor customer satisfaction because it is linked to customer loyalty and, in turn, to long-term profitability.* Xerox, for example, regularly surveys more than 400 000 customers regarding product and service satisfaction using a 5-point scale from 5 (high) to 1 (low). In analysing the data, Xerox executives made a remarkable discovery: Very satisfied customers (a 5 rating) were far more loyal than satisfied customers. Very satisfied customers, in fact, were *six times* more likely to repurchase Xerox products than satisfied customers.

8.4.3 Service recovery

Business marketers cannot always provide flawless service. However, the way the firm responds to a client's service problems has a crucial bearing on customer retention and loyalty. **Service recovery** encompasses the procedures, policies, and processes a firm uses to resolve customer service problems promptly and effectively. For example, when IBM receives a customer complaint, a specialist who is an expert in the relevant product or service area is assigned as "resolution owner" of that complaint. On being assigned a customer complaint or problem, the IBM specialist must contact the customer within 48 hours (except in the case of severe problems, where the required response is made much faster). Larry Schiff, a marketing strategist at IBM, describes how the process works from there:

> They introduce themselves as owners of the customer's problem and ask: What's it going to take for you to be very satisfied with the resolution of this complaint? ... Together with the customer, we negotiate an action plan and then execute that plan until the customer problem is resolved. The problem only gets closed when the customer says it is closed, and we measure this [that is, customer satisfaction with problem resolution] as well.*

Service providers who satisfactorily resolve service failures often see that their customer's level of perceived service quality rises. One study in the ocean-freight-shipping industry found that clients who expressed higher satisfaction with claims handling, complaint handling, and problem resolution have a higher level of overall satisfaction with the shipping line.* Therefore, business marketers should develop thoughtful and highly responsive processes for dealing with service failures. Some studies have shown that customers who experienced a service failure and had it corrected to their satisfaction have greater loyalty to the supplier than those customers who did not experience a service failure!

8.4.4 Zero defections

The quality of service provided to business customers has a major effect on customer "defections"—customers who do not come back. Service strategists point out that customer defections have a powerful effect on the bottom line.* As a company's relationship with a customer lengthens, profits rise—and generally rise considerably. For example, one service firm found that profit from a fourth-year customer is triple that from a first-year customer. Many additional benefits accrue to service companies that retain their customers: They can charge more, the cost of doing business is reduced, and the long-standing customer provides "free" advertising. The implications are clear: Service providers should carefully track customer defections and recognise that continuous improvement in service quality is not a cost but, say Frederick Reichheld and W. Earl Sasser, "an investment in a customer who generates more profit than the margin on a one-time sale."*

8.4.5 Return on quality

A difficult decision for the business-services marketing manager is to determine how much to spend on improving service quality. Clearly, expenditures on quality have diminishing returns—at some point, additional expenditures do not increase profits. To make good decisions on the level of expenditures on quality, managers must justify quality efforts on a financial basis, knowing where to spend on quality improvement, how much to spend, and when to reduce or stop the expenditures. Roland Rust, Anthony Zahorik, and Timothy Keiningham have developed a technique for calculating the "return on investing in quality."* Under this approach, service quality benefits are successively linked to customer satisfaction, customer retention, market share, and, finally, to profitability. The relationship between expenditure level and customer-satisfaction change is first measured by managerial judgement and then through market testing. When the relationship has been estimated, the return on quality can be measured statistically. The significant conclusion is that quality improvements should be treated as investments: They must pay off, and spending should not be wasted on efforts that do not produce a return.

8.5 SERVICE PACKAGES

The **service package** can be thought of as the product dimension of service, including decisions about the essential concept of the service, the range of services provided, and the quality and level of service. In addition, the service package must consider some unique factors—the personnel who perform the service, the physical product that accompanies the service, and the process of providing the service.* A useful way to conceptualise the service product is shown in Figure 8.4.

8.5.1 Customer-benefit concept

Services are purchased because of the benefits they offer, and a first step in either creating a service or evaluating an existing one is to define the **customer-benefit concept**—that is, evaluate the core benefit the customer derives from the service. Understanding the customer-benefit concept focuses the business marketer's attention on those attributes—functional, effectual, and psychological—that must be not only offered but also tightly monitored from a quality-control standpoint. For example, a sales manager selecting a resort hotel for an annual sales meeting is purchasing a core benefit that could be stated as "a successful meeting." The hotel marketer must then assess the full range of service attributes and components necessary to provide a successful meeting. Obviously, a wide variety of service elements come into play: (1) meeting-room size, layout, environment, acoustics; (2) meals; (3) comfortable and quiet sleeping rooms; (4) audiovisual equipment; and (5) staff responsiveness.

FIGURE 8.4

Conceptualising the service product

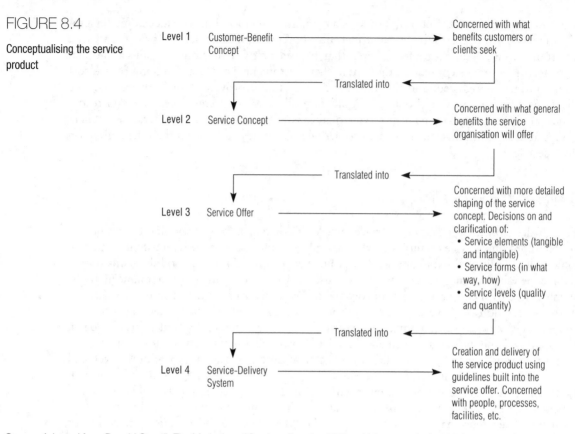

Source: Adapted from Donald Cowell, *The Marketing of Services* (London: William Heinemann, Ltd., 1984), p. 100.

8.5.2 Service concept

Once the customer-benefit concept is understood, the next step is to articulate the **service concept,** which defines the general benefits the service company will provide through the bundle of goods and services it sells to the customer. The service concept translates the customer-benefit concept into the range of benefits the service marketer will *provide*. For a hotel, the service concept might specify the benefits that it will develop: flexibility, responsiveness, and courteousness in providing meeting rooms; a full range of audiovisual equipment; flexible meal schedules; message services; professional personnel; and climate-controlled meeting rooms.

8.5.3 Service offer

Intimately linked with the service concept is the **service offer,** which spells out in more detail those services to be offered; when, where, and to whom they will be provided; and how they will be presented. The service elements that make up the total service package, including both tangibles and intangibles, must be determined. The service offer of the hotel includes a multitude of tangible elements (soundproof meeting rooms, projection equipment, video players, slide projectors, flip charts, refreshments, heating and air-conditioning, meals) and intangible elements (attitude of meeting-room setup personnel, warmth of greetings from desk clerks and bellhops, response to unique requests, meeting-room ambiance). Generally, management finds it easier to manage the tangible (equipment and physical) elements of the service than to control the intangible elements.

8.5.4 Service delivery system

The final dimension of the service product is the service delivery system—how the service is provided to the customer. The delivery system includes carefully conceived jobs for people; personnel with capabilities and attitudes necessary for successful performance; equipment, facilities, and layouts for effective customer work flow; and carefully developed procedures and processes aimed at a common set of objectives.[*] Thus, the service delivery system should provide a carefully designed blueprint that describes how the service is rendered for the customer.

For physical products, manufacturing and marketing are generally separate and distinct activities; for services, these two activities are often inseparable.[*] The service performance and the delivery system both create the product and deliver it to customers. This feature of services underscores the important role of people, particularly service providers, in the marketing process. Technicians, repair personnel, and maintenance engineers are intimately involved in customer contact, and they decidedly influence the customer's perception of service quality. The business service marketer must pay close attention to both people and physical evidence (tangible elements such as uniforms) when designing the service package.

8.5.5 Service personnel

A first step in creating an effective service package is to ensure that all personnel know, understand, and accept the customer-benefit concept. As Donald Cowell states, "So important are people and their quality to organisations and ... services that 'internal marketing' is considered to be an important management role to ensure that all staff are customer conscious."[*] In short, the attitudes, skills, knowledge, and behaviour of service personnel have a critical effect on the customer's level of satisfaction with the service.

8.6 HYBRID OFFERINGS[*]

To advance revenue and profit growth, many traditional manufacturers are creating hybrid offerings that combine products and services into innovative value propositions for customers. A **hybrid offering** represents a combination of one or more goods and one or more services that together offer more customer benefits than if the good and service were available separately.[*] For example, a manufacturer of ATM machines drew on its deep knowledge of consumer usage of its machines across its installed base and developed services for improving cash management and productivity in retail banking operations. While such offerings can provide a strong differential advantage, many manufacturing firms struggle when they venture into the services sphere. Recent research provides a valuable framework for identifying the unique resources that should be leveraged and for defining the distinctive capabilities that should be developed to create successful strategies for hybrid offerings (see Figure 8.5).

8.6.1 Unique resources manufacturing firms can leverage

Compared to pure service firms, manufacturers possess four distinct resources that can be particularly valuable in developing hybrid offerings.

Installed base product usage and process data

The installed base of products at customer organisations represents a unique asset for most manufacturing firms. For example, if a firm provides maintenance and repair services to its

FIGURE 8.5

Manufacturer-specific resources and capabilities for successful hybrid offerings

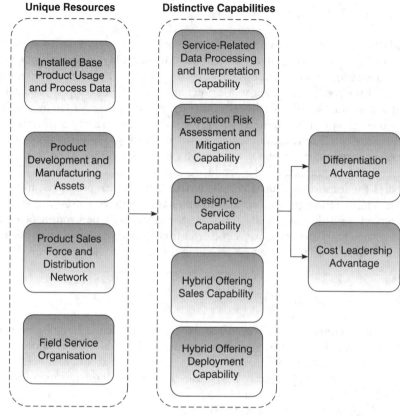

Source: Wolfgang Ulaga and Werner J. Reinartz, Hybrid Offerings: How Manufacturing Firm's Combine Goods and Services Successfully *Journal of Marketing*, 75 (November 2011), forthcoming.

installed base, product usage data can be systematically gathered and used to tailor service offerings that advance customers' goals. Many goods, from elevators and earthmoving equipment to heating and air conditioning (HVAC) systems for buildings and shopping malls, are equipped with smart technologies that can capture usage data and facilitate control from a remote location. An equipment manufacturer explains:

> *Today, our forklift trucks are equipped with a multitude of data sensors. We remote-monitor operations on a real-time basis, 24/7, which allows us to collect data on how many hours the forklift truck runs per day, how many hours of downtime the equipment endures, etc. We consolidate all that data in an online database.* [*]

Product development and manufacturing assets

The stock of unique assets represented in a firm's R&D and manufacturing infrastructure can be leveraged to achieve a competitive advantage over direct competitors and pure service players in developing superior hybrid offerings. For example, a tyre manufacturer developed a new tyre casing that allowed it to regroove and remould its tyres more frequently than those of its competitors. This innovation lowered the total cost of ownership for trucking company customers because the tyres provided tens of thousands of miles more of wear than with any competitive offerings.

Product sales force and distribution network

Business-to-business firms generally rely on a direct sales force and/or work with channel partners to cover sales territories. By enabling access to a full range of buying influentials in

TABLE 8.4 Classification scheme of business services for hybrid offerings

		Service Recipient	
		Service Oriented Toward the Supplier's Good	**Service Oriented Toward the Customer's Process**
Nature of the Value Proposition	**Supplier's Promise to Perform a Deed (input-based)**	**1. Product Life Cycle Services (PLS)** **Definition:** Services to facilitate the customer's access to the supplier's good and ensure its proper functioning during all states of the life cycle. **Examples:** Delivery of industrial cables. Inspection of an ATM machine. Regrooving of an industrial tyre. Recycling of a power transformer. **Primary Distinctive Capabilities:** Hybrid offering deployment capability. Design-to-service capability.	**3. Process Support Services (PSS)** **Definition:** Services to assist customers in improving their own business processes. **Examples:** Energy efficiency audit for a commercial building. Logistics consulting for material-handling processes in a warehouse. **Primary Distinctive Capabilities:** Service-related data processing and interpretation capability. Hybrid offering deployment capability. Hybrid offering sales capability.
	Supplier's Promise to Achieve Performance (output-based)	**2. Asset Efficiency Services (AES)** **Definition:** Services to achieve productivity gains from assets invested by customers. **Examples:** Remote monitoring of a jet engine. Welding robot software customisation. **Primary Distinctive Capabilities:** Service-related data processing and interpretation capability. Execution risk assessment and mitigation capabilities. Hybrid offering sales capabilities.	**4. Process Delegation Services (PDS)** **Definition:** Services to perform processes on behalf of the customers. **Examples:** The fleet management on behalf of a trucking company. Petrol and chemicals supply management for a semiconductor manufacturer. **Primary Distinctive Capabilities:** Service-related data processing and interpretation capability. Executive risk assessment and mitigation capabilities. Design-to-service capability. Hybrid offering sales capabilities. Hybrid offering deployment capability.

Source: Adapted from Wolfgang Ulaga and Werner J. Reinartz, ''Hybrid Offerings: How Manufacturing Firm's Combine Goods and Services Successfully,'' *Journal of Marketing*, 75 (November 2011), forthcoming.

customer organisations, the sales force provides a unique resource for developing and implementing strategies for hybrid offerings. Channel intermediaries can likewise represent a unique resource in the market but some manufacturers report difficulty in capturing the full potential of their dealer network for growing service revenue.

Field service organisation

Most manufacturers have developed a field organisation to deliver and install products as well as to provide service to customers. Research indicates that manufacturers typically earn 45 per cent of gross profits from the aftermarket, though it accounts for only 24 per cent of revenue.[*] The field service network provides a key resource for delivering after-sales services in a cost efficient manner but also provides an opportunity for pursuing new and more ambitious hybrid offerings.

These four resources represent the critical inputs that can be used to develop the distinctive capabilities that best-practice firms apply in developing profitable hybrid offerings (see Figure 8.5).

8.6.2 Distinctive capabilities for launching hybrid offerings

Superior resources and capabilities enable a firm to achieve competitive advantage through differentiated offerings or lower relative cost. Based on case studies and depth interviews with senior executives in manufacturing firms, Wolfgang Ulaga and Warren J. Reinartz identify five capabilities that are particularly critical to the successful launch of hybrid offerings:[*]

1   **Service-related data processing and interpretation capability** is the manufacturer's capacity to gather, analyse, and interpret installed base product usage and process data to help business customers reduce costs and/or increase productivity. For example, an industrial equipment manufacturer that instals electric motors in commercial buildings, used by customers to monitor energy consumption, drew on this rich data source to develop distinctive skills in facility management. Energy efficiency consulting services for business customers became a new source of revenue generation for the company.

2   **Execution risk assessment and mitigation capability** concerns the manufacturer's capacity to evaluate the likelihood that agreed-upon outcomes of hybrid offerings will be achieved and then to design and implement safeguarding mechanisms to meet performance commitments and to maintain internal profit targets. For example, a manufacturer of in-flight entertainment systems for commercial airlines thoroughly examined product usage and process data from the installed base of customers to develop reliable outcome expectations and performance guarantees.

3   **Design-to-service capability** is the manufacturer's capacity to integrate the product and service elements of the offering *early* in the development process to tap the full potential for revenue generation and/or cost reduction. To illustrate, by reengineering its offset printing presses, a manufacturer enabled its service technicians to perform first-level maintenance remotely, thereby reducing costs and increasing service responsiveness.

4   **Hybrid offering sales capability** is ''the manufacturer's capacity to reach key decision makers in the customer organisation, coordinate key contacts in the customer and vendor firms, sell hybrid offering value through specific documentation and communication tools, and align the sales force with both the field organisation and channel partners to increase hybrid offering revenues.''[*]

5   **Hybrid offering deployment capability** is the manufacturer's capacity to use flexible offering platforms that can standardise production and delivery processes while providing a menu of options to adapt to individual customers' needs. For example, a company offers six different maintenance packages for printers to cover the needs of retail banking customers. In describing the offerings, a manager observes: ''we build 'service boxes.'''[*]

8.6.3 Classifying services for hybrid offerings

From Table 8.4, observe that business services can be classified on two dimensions to identify four good-service combinations. The first dimension identifies whether the service is directed at the supplier's good or is targeted on the customer's process. A second dimension for classifying services for hybrid offerings concerns whether the supplier promises to perform a deed (input-based) or to achieve a performance outcome (output-based). Different resources and distinctive capabilities are needed to successfully deploy strategies for each of the resulting business service categories.

Product life cycle services

Product life cycle services (PLS) refers to services that facilitate the customer's access to a manufacturer's product and ensure its desired functioning during all stages of its useful life from delivery, installation, and maintenance to recycling or disposal. Since these services are directly tied to the supplier's product, the value proposition represents a promise to perform a deed on behalf of the customer. While PLS, such as timely maintenance and repair, are expected by business customers, they can assume a valuable role in building the firm's reputation as a trusted service provider in the market.

Asset efficiency services

To achieve a differential advantage, some manufacturers create distinctive value-added services that are directly tied to their products. **Asset efficiency services (AES)** are services that are designed to provide customers with productivity gains on their asset investments. Rather than promising to perform a deed as with PLS, the value proposition for AES goes one step further and promises a level of performance related to asset productivity. For example, a manufacturer of in-flight entertainment systems makes this commitment: "We guarantee availability of 98.5 per cent of video screens up and running in an aircraft."[*] To succeed with AES, manufacturers must possess distinctive capabilities for assessing and managing product failure risks.

Process support services

Process support services (PSS) are services provided by a manufacturer that assist customers in increasing the efficiency of their own business processes. Rather than focusing on the manufacturer's product, PSS centres on the customer's processes (for example, a manufacturer of material handling equipment offers warehouse optimisation and logistics consulting to customers). To succeed with PSS, manufacturers report that fundamental changes are required in the sales approach and organisation to reach a different set of buying influentials in the customer organisation as well as to assist and train customer personnel in achieving process improvements. Often, there is a need to add specialised technicians to the field service organisation and dedicated PSS salespersons to the sales force.

Process delegation services

Process delegation services (PDS) represent those services where a manufacturer performs specific processes on behalf of the customer (for example, DuPont not only supplies the paint but also manages Ford Paint shops). Other examples include fly-by-the-hour agreements for commercial jet engines or the fleet management of tyres for a trucking enterprise. Unlike PSS where the supplier promises to perform a deed, the value proposition for PDS involves a promise to achieve a particular level of process performance (that is, output-based).

In contrast to outsourcing arrangements, PDS typically involves an integrated mix of product and service elements, a highly customised offering tailored to specific customer requirements, and often, a complex gain-sharing agreement. From Table 8.4, observe that manufacturers must master the full range of distinctive capabilities to succeed in the PDS category. For that reason, the availability of PDS are rather limited in many business market sectors and are only offered by the market leaders.

SUMMARY

Customer satisfaction represents the culmination of a set of customer experiences with the business-to-business firm. A customer experience map provides a powerful platform for defining the most critical customer–company interactions, uncovering customer expectations, and spotting opportunities to create value and strengthen customer loyalty. Rather than selling individual products and services, leading-edge business-to-business firms focus on what customers really want—solutions. To design a solution, the business marketing manager begins by analysing a customer problem and then identifies the products and services required to solve that problem. Because solutions can be more readily customised for individual customers, they provide more avenues for differentiation than products can offer.

Business customers view a solution as a set of customer-company relational processes that involve: (1) customer requirements definition, (2) customisation and integration of goods and/or services, (3) their deployment, and (4) postdeployment customer support. To deliver effective solutions, the business marketer should develop appropriate mechanisms for coordinating the activities of different organisation units that contribute to different stages of the customer solution development process. Ultimately, solution effectiveness depends on supplier as well as customer behaviours.

Business services are distinguished by their intangibility, linked production and consumption, lack of standardisation, perishability, and use as opposed to ownership. Together, these characteristics have profound effects on how services should be marketed. Buyers of business services focus on five dimensions of service quality: reliability, responsiveness, assurance, empathy, and tangibles. Because of intangibility and lack of uniformity, service buyers have significant difficulty in comparing and selecting service vendors. Service providers must deliver on promises, inspire trust and confidence, and provide tangible evidence (for example, documented savings) to create satisfied customers. A key first step in creating strategies for a service is to define the customer-benefit concept and develop the related service concept. Next, the service offer is detailed and a blueprint for the service delivery system is developed.

Many manufacturers are creating hybrid offerings to generate a new platform for revenue and profit growth. A hybrid offering represents a combination of one or more goods and one or more services that together offer more customer benefits than if the good and service were available separately. Building on unique resources, such as product usage and process data from the installed base of products, and building distinctive capabilities, such as the capability to integrate product and service elements early in the development process, manufacturers are developing four types of hybrid offerings: (1) product life cycle services, (2) asset efficiency services, (3) process support services, and (4) process delegation services.

DISCUSSION QUESTIONS

1   Identify and discuss the distinguishing characteristics of services. What problems do these characteristics present to marketers?

2   What is the significance of 'tangibles' in service industries?

3   How does the Company-Customer Relationship vary from a product to a solutions perspective and how can it impact the overall strategy?

4 Discuss the development of a marketing strategy for a university. What marketing decisions should be made in developing this strategy?

5 Name the different dimensions of service quality and discuss their relevance and impact on the overall strategy.

INTERNET EXERCISES

1 SAP AG, a leading enterprise software and business management company, provides online collaborative services that enable more effective management of all project information. Go to http://www.sap.com and to its relevant services and support area and describe the service solutions SAP provides for a new business enterprise.

REFERENCES

Assael, Henry, *Marketing Management: Strategy and Action* (Boston: Kent Publishing, 1985), p. 693.

Brown, Stephen W., Gustafsson, Anders, and Witell, Lars, "Beyond Products," *The Wall Street Journal* (June 22, 2009), pp. R7–R8.

Challagalla, Goutam, Venkatesh, R., and Kohli, Ajay K., "Proactive Postsales Service: When and Why Does it Pay Off?" *Journal of Marketing* 73 (March 2009): pp. 70–87.

Clemes, Michael, Mollenkopf, Diane, and Burn, Darryl, "An Investigation of Marketing Problems across Service Typologies," *Journal of Services Marketing* 14 (no. 6–7, 2000): p. 568.

Cohen, Morris A., Agrawal, Narendra, and Agraval, Vipul, "Winning in the Aftermarket," *Harvard Business Review* 84 (May 2006): pp. 129–138.

Cowell, Donald, *The Marketing of Services* (London: William Heinemann, 1984), p. 73.

Davidow, William H., and Uttal, Bro, "Service Companies: Focus or Falter," *Harvard Business Review* 67 (July–August 1989): p. 84.

Dibb, Sally, Simkin, Lyndon, Pride, Bill, and Ferrell, O.C., *Marketing Concepts & Strategies*, 6th ed. (Cengage, 2012).

Doole, Isobel, and Lowe, Robin, *International Marketing Strategy* 6th ed. (Cengage, 2012).

Durvasula, Srinivas, Lysonski, Steven, and Mehta, Subhash C., "Business-to-Business Marketing: Service Recovery and Customer Satisfaction Issues with Ocean Shipping Lines," *European Journal of Marketing* 34 (no. 3–4, 2000): p. 441.

Frei, Francis X., "The Four Things a Service Business Must Get Right," *Harvard Business Review* 86 (April 2008): pp. 70–80.

Gronroos, "Christian, Relationship Marketing: Strategic and Tactical Implications," *Management Decision*, 34 (no. 3, 1996): pp. 5–14.

Gulati, Ranjay, "Silo Busting: How to Execute on the Promise of Customer Focus," *Harvard Business Review* 85 (May 2007): pp. 98–108.

Heskett, James L., *Managing in the Service Economy* (Boston: Harvard Business School Press, 1986), p. 20.

Heskett, James L., Jones, Thomas O., Loveman, Gary W., Sasser Jr., W. Earl and Schlesinger, Leonard A., "Putting the Service-Profit Chain to Work," *Harvard Business Review* 72 (March–April 1994): pp. 164–174.

Jones, Thomas O., and Sasser Jr., W. Earl, "Why Satisfied Customers Defect," *Harvard Business Review* 73 (November–December 1995): p. 90.

Leonhardt, David, "The FedEx Economy," *The New York Times*, October 8, 2005, p. B1.

Lovelock, Christopher, and Gummesson, Evert, "Whither Services Marketing? In Search of a New Paradigm and Fresh Perspectives," *Journal of Services Research* 7 (August 2004): p. 36.

Meyer, Christopher, and Schwager, Andre, "Understanding Customer Experiences," *Harvard Business Review* 85 (February 2007): pp. 116–127.

Moutinho, Luiz, and Southern, Geoffrey, *Strategic Marketing Management: A process Based Approach* (Cengage, 2012).

Peppers, Don, and Rogers, Martha, *Return on Customer: Creating Maximum Value from Your Scarcest Resource* (New York: Currency Doubleday, 2005), p. 144.

Prahalad, C.K., and Ramaswamy, Venkat, *The Future of Competition: Co-Creating Unique Value with Customers* (Boston: Harvard Business School Press, 2004), pp. 93–94.

Reichheld, Frederick F., *Loyalty Rules! How Today's Leaders Build Lasting Relationships* (Boston: Harvard Business School Press, 2001).

Reichheld, Frederick F., and Sasser, W. Earl, "Zero Defections: Quality Comes to Services," *Harvard Business Review* 68 (September–October 1990): p. 105.

Rickard, Davidx, "Winning by Understanding the Full Customer Experience," The Boston Consulting Group, Inc., 2006, p. 1, http://www.bcg.com accessed May 15, 2008.

Rust, Roland T., Lemon, Katherine N., and Zeithaml, Valarie A., "Return on Marketing: Using Customer Equity to Focus Marketing Strategy," *Journal of Marketing* 68 (January 2004): pp. 109–127.

Rust, Roland T., Zahorik, Anthony J., and Keiningham, Timothy L., "Return on Quality (ROQ): Making Service Quality Financially Accountable," *Journal of Marketing* 59 (April 1995): pp. 58–70.

Sawhney, Mohanbir, "Going beyond the Product: Defining, Designing, and Delivering Customer Solutions," Working Paper, Kellogg School of Management, Northwestern University, December 2004, pp. 1–10.

Sawhney, Mohanbir, Balasubramanian, Sridhar, and Krishnan, Vish V., "Creating Growth with Services," *MIT Sloan Management Review* 45 (Winter 2004): pp. 34–43.

Schiff, Larry, "How Customer Satisfaction Improvement Works to Fuel Business Recovery at IBM," *Journal of Organizational Excellence* 20 (Spring 2001): p. 12.

Shankar, Venkatesh, Berry, Leonard L., and Detzel, Thomas, "A Practical Guide to Combining Products and Services," *Harvard Business Review* 87 (November 2009): pp. 94–99.

Sharma, Arun, Krishnan, R., and Grewal, Dhruv, "Value Creation in Markets: A Critical Area of Focus for Business to-Business Markets," *Industrial Marketing Management* 30 (June 2001): pp. 391–402.

Steward, Michelle D., Walker, Beth A., Hutt, Michael D., and Kumar, Ajith, "The Coordination Strategies of High Performing Salespeople: Internal Working Relationships that Drive Success," *Journal of the Academy of Marketing Science* 38 (October 2010): pp. 550–566.

Tuli, Kapil, Kohli, Ajay, and Bharadwaj, Sundar G., "Rethinking Customer Solutions: From Product Bundles to Relational Processes, *Journal of Marketing* 7 (July 2007): pp. 1–17.

Tuli, Kohli, and Bharadwaj, "Rethinking Customer Solutions," p. 14.

Ulaga, Wolfgang, and Reinartz, Warren J., "Hybrid Offerings: How Manufacturing Firms Combine Goods and Services Successfully," *Journal of Marketing* 75 (6), 5–23 (November 2011)

van Weele, Arjan, *Puchasing and Supply Chain Management: Analysis Strategy, Planning and Practice*, 5th ed. (Cengage, 2010).

Vargo, Stephen L., and Lusch, Robert F., "Evolving to a New Dominant Logic for Marketing," *Journal of Marketing* 68 (January 2004): pp. 1–18.

Verhage, Bronis J., *Marketing: A Global Perspective* (Cengage, 2013).

Zeithaml, Valarie A., "How Consumer Evaluation Processes Differ between Goods and Services," in *Marketing of Services*, James H. Donnelly and William R. George, eds. (Chicago: American Marketing Association, 1981), pp. 200–204.

Zeithaml, Valarie A., Berry, Leonard R., and Parasuraman, A., "Communication and Control Processes in the Delivery of Service Quality," *Journal of Marketing* 52 (April 1988): pp. 35–48.

Zeithaml, Valarie A., Bitner, Mary Jo, and Gremler, Dwayne D., *Services Marketing: Integrating Customer Focus across the Firm*, 5th ed. (Boston: McGraw-Hill Irwin, 2009), p. 2.

Zeithaml, Valarie A., Parasuraman, A., and Berry, Leonard R., "Problems and Strategies in Services Marketing," *Journal of Marketing* 49 (Spring 1985): p. 34.

CHAPTER 9
MANAGING INNOVATION AND NEW INDUSTRIAL PRODUCT DEVELOPMENT

CHAPTER OBJECTIVES

The long-term competitive position of most organisations is tied to their ability to innovate—to provide existing and new customers with a continuing stream of new products and services. Innovation is a high-risk and potentially rewarding process. After reading this chapter, you will understand:

1 The different forms and steps development projects can take

2 The characteristics of the disruptive innovation model

3 The barriers to successful innovation and how to overcome them

4 The factors that decide the success of new products

With his American swagger and his hair bleached white, Tony Fadell stood out at button-down Philips Electronics, where he led an in-house operation designing ... consumer electronics devices. It was there that he came up with the idea of marrying a Napster-like music store with a hard drive-based MP3 player. He shopped the concept around the Valley before Apple's Jon Rubenstein snapped it up and put Fadell in charge of the engineering team that built the first iPod.*

Once prototypes were developed, CEO Steve Jobs worked closely with the team and was instrumental in moulding the shape, feel, and design of the device.* Through product innovations from the iPod to the iPhone and iPad and through strategic foresight and the careful management of its brand, Apple has transformed itself from a niche computer company to one of the most valuable enterprises in the world.*

Many firms derive much of their sales and profits from recently introduced products. Indeed, best-practice firms generate about 48 per cent of sales and 45 per cent of profits from products commercialised in the past five years.* But the risks of product innovation are high; significant investments are involved, and the likelihood of failure is high. With shortening product life cycles and accelerating technological change, speed and agility are central to success in the innovation battle.

This chapter examines product innovation in the business marketing environment. The first section provides a perspective on the firm's management of innovation. Second, product innovation is positioned within a firm's overall technological strategy. Third, key dimensions of the new-product-development process are examined. Attention centres on the forces that drive successful new product performance in the firm. The final section of the chapter explores the determinants of new product success and timeliness.

9.1 THE MANAGEMENT OF INNOVATION

Management practices in successful industrial firms reflect the realities of the innovation process itself. James Quinn asserts that "innovation tends to be individually motivated, opportunistic, customer responsive, tumultuous, nonlinear, and interactive in its development. Managers can plan overall directions and goals, but surprises are likely to abound."* Clearly, some new-product-development efforts are the outgrowth of deliberate strategies (intended strategies that become realised), whereas others result from emergent strategies (realised strategies that, at least initially, were never intended).* Bearing little resemblance to a rational, analytical process, many strategic decisions involving new products are rather messy, disorderly, and disjointed processes around which competing organisational factions contend. In studying successful innovative companies such as Sony, Vodafone, and Hewlett-Packard, Quinn characterised the innovation process as controlled chaos:

Many of the best concepts and solutions come from projects partly hidden or "bootlegged" by the organisation. Most successful managers try to build some slack or buffers into their plans to hedge their bets.... They permit chaos and replications in early investigations, but insist on much more formal planning and controls as expensive development and scale-up proceed. But even at these later stages, these managers have learned to maintain flexibility and to avoid the tyranny of paper plans.*

Some new products result from a planned, deliberate process, but others follow a more circuitous and chaotic route.* Why? Research suggests that strategic activity within a large organisation falls into two broad categories: induced and autonomous strategic behaviour.*

9.1.1 Induced strategic behaviour

Induced strategic behaviour is consistent with the firm's traditional concept of strategy. It takes place in relationship to its familiar external environment (for example, its customary markets).

By manipulating various administrative mechanisms, top management can influence the perceived interests of managers at the organisation's middle and operational levels and keep strategic behaviour in line with the current strategy course. For example, existing reward and measurement systems may direct managers' attention to some market opportunities and not to others. Examples of induced strategic behaviour or deliberate strategies might emerge around product-development efforts for existing markets.

9.1.2 Autonomous strategic behaviour

During any period, most strategic activity in large, complex firms is likely to fit into the induced behaviour category. However, large, resource-rich firms are likely to possess a pool of entrepreneurial potential at operational levels, which expresses itself in autonomous strategic initiatives. Imagine a company that encourages its technical employees to devote 15 per cent of their work time to developing their own ideas. Through the personal efforts of individual employees, new products are born. For example,

- Gary Fadell is the engineering genius behind the iPod.

- Michimosa Fujino championed the HondaJet that may shake up the small-jet business with the same value proposition—high fuel efficiency and sleek design—that the first-generation Honda Civic used to rattle auto manufacturers 30 years ago.[*]

"Civic of the sky"

Senior executives at Honda and industry analysts alike believe that the HondaJet can quickly gain 10 per cent of the small-jet market and turn a profit in three to four years. Compared to the popular Cessna Citation CJ1+ that seats four to six passengers, the HondaJet is priced at €2.75 million, €660 000 below the Cessna, uses about 22 per cent less fuel, has 20 per cent more passenger cabin space, and boasts the fit and finish of a luxury car.

Now in his mid-forties, Mr. Fujino has tirelessly promoted his idea for two decades. He succeeded in keeping the project alive by nurturing ties to senior executives and by tying his risk-taking to Honda's broader efforts to rekindle a spirit of innovation. Although formal reviews of the jet project have been intense and even "ugly" at times, he persevered because, behind the scenes, some senior executives enthusiastically supported his efforts. A crucial turning point for the project came at a critical board meeting where Mr. Fujino was presenting the idea. After an awkward start and what he describes as a "cold glaze" from some board members, "he was able to drive home the jet's potential when he analogised it to Honda's breakthrough car, calling the jet a 'Civic of the sky.'"[*]

Autonomous strategic behaviour is conceptually equivalent to entrepreneurial activity and introduces new categories of opportunity into the firm's planning process. Managers at the product-market level conceive of market opportunities that depart from the current strategy course, then engage in product-championing activities to mobilise resources and create momentum for further development of the product. Emphasising political rather than administrative channels, product champions question the firm's current concept of strategy and, states Robert Burgelman, "provide top management with the opportunity to rationalise, retroactively, successful autonomous strategic behaviour."[*] Through these political mechanisms, successful autonomous strategic initiatives, or emergent strategies, can become integrated into the firm's concept of strategy.

Clayton M. Christensen and Michael E. Raynor observe:

Emergent strategies result from managers' responses to problems or opportunities that were unforeseen in the analysis and planning stages of the deliberate strategy making process. When the efficacy of that strategy ... is recognised, it is possible to formalise it, improve it, and exploit it, thus transforming an emergent strategy into a deliberate one.[*]

9.1.3 Product championing and the informal network

Table 9.1 highlights several characteristics that may distinguish induced from autonomous strategic behaviour. Autonomous strategic initiatives involve a set of actors and evoke strategic dialogue different from that found in induced initiatives. An individual manager, the product champion, assumes a central role in sensing an opportunity and in mobilising an informal network to explore the idea's technical feasibility and market potential. A **product champion** is an organisation member who creates, defines, or adopts an idea for an innovation and is willing to assume significant risk (for example, position or prestige) to successfully implement the innovation.[*]

Compared with induced strategic behaviour, autonomous or entrepreneurial initiatives are more likely to involve a communication process that departs from the regular work flow and the hierarchical decision-making channels. The decision roles and responsibilities of managers in this informal network are poorly defined in the early phases of the strategy-formulation process but become more formalised as the process evolves. Note in Table 9.1 that autonomous strategic behaviour entails a creeping commitment toward a particular strategy course. By contrast, induced strategic initiatives are more likely to involve administrative mechanisms that encourage a more formal and comprehensive assessment of strategic alternatives at various levels in the firm's planning hierarchy.

TABLE 9.1   Induced versus autonomous strategic behaviour: selected characteristics of the marketing strategy formulation process

	Induced	**Autonomous**
Activation of the strategic decision process	An individual manager defines a market need that converges on the organisation's concept of strategy.	An individual manager defines a market need that diverges from the organisation's concept of strategy.
Nature of the screening process	A formal screening of technical and market merit is made using established administrative procedures.	An informal network assesses technical and market merit.
Type of innovation	Incremental (e.g., new product development for existing markets uses existing organisational resources).	Major (e.g., new product development projects require new combinations of organisational resources).
Nature of communication	Consistent with organisational work flow.	Departs from organisational work flow in early phase of decision process.
Major actors	Prescribed by the regular channel of hierarchical decision making.	An informal network emerges based on mobilisation efforts of the product champion.
Decision roles	Roles and responsibilities for participants in the strategy formulation process are well defined.	Roles and responsibilities of participants are poorly defined in the initial phases but become more formalised as the strategy formulation process evolves.
Implications for strategy	Strategic alternatives are considered and commitment to a particular strategic course evolves.	Commitment to a particular strategic course emerges in the early phases through the sponsorship efforts of the product champion.

Source: Adapted from Michael D. Hutt, Peter H. Reingen, and John R. Ronchetto Jr., "Tracing Emergent Processes in Marketing, Strategy Formation," *Journal of Marketing* 52 (January 1988): pp. 4–19. See also Clayton M. Christensen and Michael E. Raynor, *The Innovator's Solution: Creating and Sustaining Successful Growth* (Boston: Harvard Business School Press, 2003), pp. 213–231.

9.1.4 Conditions supporting corporate entrepreneurship[*]

Entrepreneurial initiatives cannot be precisely planned but they can be nurtured and encouraged. First, the availability of appropriate rewards can enhance a manager's willingness to assume the risks associated with entrepreneurial activity. Second, senior management can assume an instrumental role in fostering innovation by promoting entrepreneurial initiatives and encouraging calculated risk-taking. Third, resource availability, including some slack time, is needed to provide entrepreneurs with some degrees of freedom to explore new possibilities. Fourth, an organisational structure supporting corporate entrepreneurship provides the administrative mechanisms that bring more voices to the innovation process across the firm and allow ideas to be evaluated, selected, and implemented.[*]

What motivates entrepreneurs?

Recent research identifies two additional dimensions that motivate corporate entrepreneurs: (1) intrinsic motivation (the drive originating within oneself) and (2) work design (for example, the availability of challenging projects; opportunities to interact directly with customers and other entrepreneurs). Matthew R. Marvel and his research colleagues describe what technical corporate entrepreneurs desire in their job:

> They want their innovative efforts to be connected to customer problems that need to be solved—and important customer problems at that. To understand these problems, they need contact with customers. To get breakthrough ideas on how to solve these problems, they also need contact with other world-class technologists.[*]

9.2 MANAGING TECHNOLOGY

Technological change, Michael Porter asserts, is "a great equaliser, eroding the competitive advantage of even well-entrenched firms and propelling others to the forefront. Many of today's great firms grew out of technological changes that they were able to exploit."[*] Clearly, the long-run competitive position of most business-to-business firms depends on their ability to manage, increase, and exploit their technology base. This section explores the nature of development projects, the disruptive innovation model, and the defining attributes of successful innovators in fast-changing high-technology markets.

9.2.1 Classifying development projects

A first step in exploring the technology portfolio of a firm is to understand the different forms that development projects can take. Some development projects centre on improving the manufacturing process, some on improving products, and others on both process and product improvements. All of these represent commercial development projects. By contrast, research and development is the precursor to commercial development. A firm's portfolio can include four types of development projects.[*]

1   **Derivative projects** centre on incremental product enhancements (for example, a new feature), incremental process improvements (for example, a lower-cost manufacturing process), or incremental changes on both dimensions.
    Illustration: A feature-enhanced or cost-reduced Canon colour copier.

2   **Platform projects** create the design and components shared by a set of products. These projects often involve a number of changes in both the product and the manufacturing process.

Illustrations: A common motor in all Bosch hand tools; multiple applications of Intel's microprocessor.

3   **Breakthrough projects** establish new core products and new core processes that differ fundamentally from previous generations.
    Illustrations: Computer discs and fibre-optic cable created new product categories.

4   **Research and development** is the creation of knowledge concerning new materials and technologies that eventually leads to commercial development.[*]
    Illustration: Alcatel-Lucent's development of communications technology that underlies its networking systems used by diverse customers such as retailers, banks, and hotel chains.

9.2.2 A product-family focus

A particular technology may provide the foundation or platform for several products. For example, Honda applies its multivalve cylinder technology to power-generation equipment, cars, business jets, motorcycles, and lawn mowers.[*] Products that share a common platform but have different specific features and enhancements required for different sets of consumers constitute a **product family**.[*] Each generation of a product family has a platform that provides the foundation for specific products targeted to different or complementary markets. By expanding on technical skills, market knowledge, and manufacturing competencies, entirely new product families may be formed, thereby creating new business opportunities.

Strategists argue that a firm should move away from planning that centres on single products and focus instead on families of products that can grow from a common platform. Consider Apple's stream of innovations—its operating system first helped it to gain market share in desktop and laptop computers.

> *From there, new products and services appeared to just fall into place—the iTunes Store for purchasing music; new iPod models for different purposes; video playback on the iPod combined with the distribution of video content from the iTunes store; and finally, the iPhone …*[*]

The move toward a product-family perspective requires close interfunctional working relationships, a long-term view of technology strategy, and a multiple-year commitment of resources. Although this approach offers significant competitive leverage, Steven Wheelwright and Kim Clark note that companies often fail to invest adequately in platforms: "The reasons vary, but the most common is that management lacks an awareness of the strategic value of platforms and fails to create well-thought-out platform projects."[*]

9.2.3 The disruptive innovation model[*]

Special insights into innovation management come from examining the rate at which products are improving and customers can use those improvements. For example, when personal computers were first introduced in the early 1980s, typists often had to pause for the Intel 286 chip to catch up. But today, only the most demanding customers can fully use the speed and performance of personal computers. For many products, from Excel spreadsheets to application-enriched handsets and information appliances, few customers absorb the performance features that innovating companies include as they introduce new and improved products.

Overshooting

Figure 9.1 shows, first, a rate of improvement in a given product or technology that customers can use, represented by the dotted line, sloping slightly upward across the chart. Second, for a

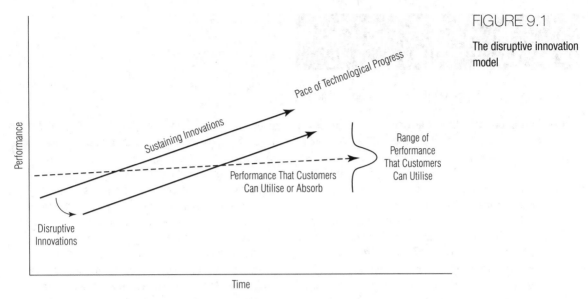

FIGURE 9.1

The disruptive innovation model

given product, innovating firms offer a trajectory of improvement as they develop new and improved versions over time. The pace of technological progress usually outstrips the ability of many, if not most, customers to keep up with it (see the steeply sloping solid lines in Figure 9.1). Therefore, as companies strive to make better products they can sell at higher profit margins to the most demanding customers, they overshoot and provide much more performance than mainstream customers are able to use.

Sustaining versus disruptive innovation

Third, from Figure 9.1, a distinction is made between a sustaining innovation and a disruptive innovation. According to Clayton M. Christensen and Michael E. Raynor, "A sustaining innovation targets demanding, high-end customers with better performance than what was previously available (for example, incremental product improvements or breakthrough products)."[*] A disruptive innovation represents a product or service that is not as good as currently available alternatives. "But disruptive technologies offer other benefits—typically, they are simpler, more convenient, and less expensive products that appeal to new or less-demanding customers."[*]

Disruptive strategy examples

Once a disruptive product or service gains a foothold, the improvement cycle begins and eventually it intersects with the needs of more demanding customers. For example, Xerox held a commanding position in the high-speed photocopier business until Canon's simple tabletop copier disrupted that strategy in the early 1980s. Likewise, easyJet disrupted established airlines; Amazon.com disrupted traditional bookstores; Ryman disrupted small stationery stores and distributors of office supplies; and Google disrupted directories of all sorts, including Yellow Pages.

Types of disruptive strategies

Disruptive strategies can take two forms: low-end disruptions and new-market disruptions. Table 9.2 describes the characteristics of these strategies and contrasts them with a strategy geared to sustaining innovations. Note, for example, that the targeted customers for low-end disruption are *overserved customers*, whereas new-market disruptions target *nonconsumption*— customers who historically lacked the resources to buy and use the product.

B2B TOP PERFORMERS

Flying low cost with frills or no frills

Over the last decade there has been a huge growth in low cost airlines around the world. The Irish airline Ryanair has been particularly successful. The no frills airlines followed a model pioneered in the US by South West Airlines. To do this the company cuts the 'included' service to the bone. Food on board has to be paid for, there is no seat allocation and seat bookings and check-in are made on the Internet and charged. Payment by most types of credit and debit cards incur extra costs. Destination airports are often not the closest airport to the flier's destination and appear to be chosen because landing charges are less. The compensation for 'no frills' is low prices. The pricing model is based on yield management software that is designed to maximise the revenue achieved on each flight, by rewarding early customers with low prices and charging high prices to latecomers. This model contrasts with the full service airlines which have traditionally tried to maintain high ticket prices, even when running the plane half-full, and have focused on alliances with other airlines to ensure that long-haul passengers have a seamless service.

The chief executive of Ryanair, Michael O'Leary, is outspoken and combative and has attacked any moves by stakeholders to add costs to the business model, restrict the airline's activities or criticise its activities – governments putting green taxes on flights, airport authorities increasing landing charges and pressure groups criticising the contribution to carbon emissions. Although the basic price of a flight might be very low, the cost to the customer can be much higher when taxes are taken into account. Moreover Ryanair adds other charges, for example, for payment by credit card and for carrying luggage over a certain weight.

Many competitors have followed the example and the no frills airlines have transformed regional air travel where distances are short.

Low-end strategy tests

For a low-end disruptive strategy to succeed, two requirements must be met:

1   There should be customers at the low end of the market who are eager to purchase a "good-enough" product if they could acquire it at a lower price.

2   The company must be able to create a business model that can yield attractive profits at the discount prices that are needed to attract customers at the low end of the market.
Example: easyJet drew customers away from the major carriers.

New-market strategy tests

For new-market disruptions, at least one and generally both of these requirements must be met:

1   A large population can be defined who have historically lacked the money, equipment, or skill to acquire this product or service for themselves.

2   Present customers need to go to an inconvenient location to use the product or service.

A final litmus test

Once an innovation passes the tests that apply to low-end or new-market disruptions, a final critical test remains: The innovation must be disruptive to all the significant competitive firms in the industry. If one or more of the significant industry players is pursuing the strategy, the odds will be stacked against the new entrant.

TABLE 9.2 Alternative approaches to creating new-growth businesses

Dimensions	Sustaining Innovations	Low-End Disruptions	New-Market Disruptions
Targeted performance of the product or service	Incremental or breakthrough improvement in attributes most valued by the industry's most demanding customers	Performance that is good enough to meet performance requirements at the low end of the mainstream market	Lower performance on key attributes but enhanced performance on new attributes, particularly simplicity and convenience
Targeted customers	Targets the most profitable customers in the mainstream markets who are willing to pay a premium for improved performance	Serves over-served customers in the low end of the mainstream market	Targets customers who historically lacked the money or skill to buy and use the product (i.e., nonconsumers)
Profitability of the business model	Improves or maintains profit margins by exploiting the existing processes, cost structure, and current competitive advantages	Uses a new operating or financial approach or both, that can earn attractive profits at the discount prices required to win business at the low end of the market	Business model must make money at lower price per unit sold and at unit production volumes that initially will be small

Source: Reprinted by permission of the Harvard Business Review. From "Three Approaches to Creating New Growth Business" in The Innovator's Solution by Clayton Christensen, p. 51. Copyright © 2003 by the Harvard Business School Publishing Corporation; all rights reserved.

9.2.4 Illustration: A new-market disruption[*]

One principle for developing disruptive ideas is to "do what competitors won't." For instance, Salesforce.com has pursued a strategy that leaders in the customer relationship (CRM) software market found unappealing. Before Salesforce.com entered the market, both of these formidable rivals sold relatively expensive solutions that required customisation and installation to ensure proper integration with the customer's other software packages. Customers also were charged an ongoing fee for maintenance of the installed software.

Adopting a different approach

Salesforce.com provides customers with access to programmes that reside on centralised host computers. Users access these databases through the Web for a modest monthly fee. While customers often find these hosted solutions to be occasionally slower and somewhat more difficult to readily integrate with other applications, they are flexible, easy to use, and quite economical—all defining characteristics of a disruptive innovation.

Scott D. Anthony and his colleagues observe that "Salesforce.com used several tactics that made its competitors unwilling or uninterested in immediately responding:

- It started with nonconsumption (that is, selling to small customers purchasing their first CRM software).
- It targeted a customer its competitors considered undesirable (that is, small and medium-sized businesses that were the least profitable for rivals).
- It used a different distribution channel (that is, on the Web).
- It created a business model that did not depend on a revenue stream of vital importance to incumbents."[*]

9.2.5 Innovation winners in high-technology markets

In rapidly changing industries with short product life cycles and quickly shifting competitive landscapes, a firm must continually innovate to keep its offerings aligned with the market. A firm's ability to cope with change in a high-velocity industry is a key to competitive success. Shona Brown and Kathleen Eisenhardt provide an intriguing comparison of successful versus less successful product innovation in the computer industry.[*] Successful innovators were firms that were on schedule, on time to the market, and on target in addressing customer needs. The study found that firms with a successful record of product innovation use different organisational structures and processes than their competitors. In particular, four distinguishing characteristics marked the innovation approach of successful firms.

Limited structure

Creating successful products to meet changing customer needs requires flexibility, but successful product innovators combine this flexibility with a few rules that are never broken. First, strict priorities for new products are established and tied directly to resource allocation. This allows managers to direct attention to the most promising opportunities, avoiding the temptation to pursue too many attractive opportunities. Second, managers set deadlines for a few key milestones and always meet them. Third, responsibility for a limited number of major outcomes is set. For example, at one firm in Cape Town, engineering managers were responsible for product schedules while marketing managers were responsible for market definition and product profitability. Although successful firms emphasised structure for a few areas (for example, priorities or deadlines), less successful innovators imposed more control—lockstep, checkpoint procedures for every facet of new product development—or virtually no structure at all. Successful firms strike a balance by using a structure that is neither so rigid as to stiffly control the process nor so chaotic that the process falls apart.

Real-time communication and improvisation

Successful product innovators in the computer industry emphasise real-time communication within new-product-development teams *and* across product teams. Much of the communication occurs in formal meetings, but there is also extensive informal communication throughout the organisation. Clear priorities and responsibilities, coupled with extensive communications, allow product developers to improvise. "In the context of jazz improvisation, this means creating music while adjusting to the changing musical interpretations of others. In the context of product innovation, it means creating a product while simultaneously adapting to changing markets and technologies."[*]

More formally, then, **improvisation** involves the design and execution of actions that approach convergence with each other in time.[*] The shorter the elapsed time between the design and implementation of an activity, the more that activity is improvisational. Successful firms expect constant change, and new product teams have the freedom to act. One manager noted: "We fiddle right up to the end" of the new-product-development process. Real-time communications among members of the product development team, coupled with limited structure, provide the foundation for such improvisation.

Experimentation: Probing into the future

Some firms make a large bet on one version of the future, whereas others fail to update future plans in light of changing competition. Creators of successful product portfolios did not invest in any one version of the future but, instead, used a variety of low-cost probes to create options. Examples of low-cost probes include developing experimental products for new markets, entering into a strategic alliance with leading-edge customers to better understand future needs, or conducting regular planning sessions dedicated to the future. In turbulent industries, strategists cannot accurately predict which of many possible versions of the future will arrive. Probes create more possible responses for managers when the future does arrive while lowering the probability of being surprised by unanticipated futures.

Time pacing

Successful product innovators carefully manage the transition between current and future projects, whereas less successful innovators let each project unfold according to its own schedule. Successful innovators, like Intel, practice time pacing—a strategy for competing in fast-changing markets by creating new products at predictable time intervals.[*] Organisation members carefully choreograph and understand transition processes. For example, marketing managers might begin work on the definition of the next product while engineering is completing work on the current product and moving it to manufacturing. Time pacing motivates managers to anticipate change and can have a strong psychological impact across the organisation. "Time pacing creates a relentless sense of urgency around meeting deadlines and concentrates individual and team energy around common goals."[*]

9.3 THE NEW-PRODUCT-DEVELOPMENT PROCESS

To sustain their competitive advantage, leading-edge firms such as Canon, Microsoft, and Unilever make new product development a top management priority. They directly involve managers and employees from across the organisation to speed actions and decisions. Because new product ventures can represent a significant risk as well as an important opportunity, new product development requires systematic thought. The high expectations for new products are often not fulfiled. Worse, many new industrial products fail. Although the definitions of failure are somewhat elusive, research suggests that 40 per cent of industrial products fail to meet objectives.[*] Even though there may be some debate over the number of failures, there is no debate that a new product rejected by the market constitutes a substantial waste to the firm and to society.

This section explores: (1) the forces that drive a firm's new product performance, (2) the sources of new product ideas, (3) cross-functional barriers to successful innovation, and (4) team-based processes used in new product development. A promising method for bringing the "voice of the consumer" directly into the development process is also explored.

9.3.1 What drives a firm's new product performance?

A benchmarking study sought to uncover the critical success factors that drive a firm's new product performance.[*] It identified three factors (Figure 9.2): (1) the quality of a firm's new-product-development process, (2) the resource commitments made to new product development, and (3) the new product strategy.

Process

Successful companies use a high-quality new-product-development process—they give careful attention to executing the activities and decision points that new products follow from the idea stage to launch and beyond. The benchmarking study identified the following characteristics among high-performing firms:

- The firms emphasised upfront market and technical assessments before projects moved into the development phase.

FIGURE 9.2 **The major drivers of a firm's new product performance**

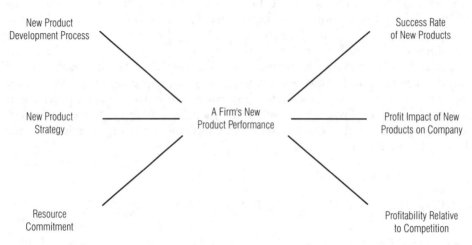

Source: Adapted from Robert G. Cooper and Elko J. Kleinschmidt, "Benchmarking Firms' New Product Performance and Practices," *Engineering Management Review* 23 (Fall 1995): pp. 112–120.

- The process featured complete descriptions of the product concept, product benefits, positioning, and target markets before development work was initiated.

- Tough project go/kill decision points were included in the process, and the kill option was actually used.

- The new product process was flexible—certain stages could be skipped in line with the nature and risk of a particular project.

Detailed upfront homework on the product concept, the likely market response, and the product's technical feasibility, along with a thorough business and financial assessment, are important dimensions of the process successful product creators follow.

Resource commitments

Adequate resources were invested in new product development in top-performing firms. Three ingredients were important here:

1 Top management committed the resources necessary to meet the firm's objectives for the total product effort.

2 R&D budgets were adequate and aligned with the stated new product objectives.

3 The necessary personnel were assigned and were relieved from other duties so that they could give full attention to new product development.

Research suggests that rather than being imposed by top management, the creative potential of new-product-development teams "is likely to be more fully realised when they are given the flexibility—within a broad strategic directive—to determine their own project controls and especially to pursue their own processes and procedures."[*]

New product strategy

A clear and visible new product strategy was another driver of a firm's new product perform-ance (see Figure 9.2). Successful firms like Unilever set aggressive new product performance goals (for example, x per cent of company sales and profit from new products) as a basic corpo-rate goal and communicate it to all employees. In turn, Robert Cooper and Elko Kleinschmidt report that successful firms centred development efforts on clearly defined arenas—particular product, market, and technology domains—to direct the new product programme:

> The new product strategy specifies "the arenas where we'll play the game," or perhaps more important, where we won't play ... what's in bounds and out of bounds. Without arenas defined, the search for new product ideas or opportunities is unfocused.[*]

9.3.2 Anticipating competitive reactions[*]

Two-thirds of new product introductions trigger reactions by competitors. Consequently, busi-ness marketers can improve the odds of new-product-launch success by implementing a strong **competitor orientation** before and during the launch. Here the new product strategist develops detailed scenarios that provide a guide for countering different competitive responses. Competi-tors are strongly motivated to react when: (1) the new product represents a major threat to their market and (2) the market is experiencing a high rate of growth. Competitors are also more inclined to react when extensive marketing communications by the innovating firm enhance the visibility of the new product introduction.

Alternatively, if the new product introduction does not pose a direct challenge to the competi-tor's market, a reaction is less likely. Recent research suggests that radically new products or products that target niche markets are less likely to spawn competitive responses.

9.3.3 Sources of new product ideas

The business marketer should be alert to new product ideas and their sources, both inside and outside the company. Internally, new product ideas may flow from salespersons who are close to customer needs, from R&D specialists who are close to new technological developments, and from top management who know the company's strengths and weaknesses. Externally, ideas may come from channel members, such as distributors or customers, or from an assessment of competitive moves.

Eric von Hippel challenges the traditional view that marketers typically introduce new prod-ucts to a passive market.[*] His research suggests that the customers in the business market often develop the idea for a new product and even select the supplier to make that product. The cus-tomer is responding to the perceived *capability* of the business marketer rather than to a specific physical product. This points up the need for involving customers in new product development and promoting corporate capability to consumers (idea generators).

Lead users

Because many industrial product markets for high technology and, in particular, capital equip-ment consist of a small number of high-volume buying firms, special attention must be given to the needs of **lead users**. These include a small number of highly influential buying organisations that are consistent early adopters of new technologies.[*] Lead users face needs that are general in the marketplace, but they confront these needs months or years before most of that marketplace encounters them. In addition, they are positioned to benefit significantly by obtaining a solution that satisfies those needs. For example, if an automobile manufacturer wanted to design an innovative braking system, marketing managers might secure insights from auto racing teams, who have a strong need for better brakes. In turn, they might look to a related field like aerospace, where antilock braking systems were first developed so that military aircraft could land on short runways.[*]

The lead user method

Lead user projects are conducted by a cross-functional team that includes four to six managers from marketing and technical departments; one member serves as project leader. Team members typically spend 12 to 15 hours per week on the projects, which are usually completed in four to six weeks. Lead user projects proceed through five phases (Figure 9.3).

Customer visits

A popular approach among business marketers for gaining new product insights is customer visits. Here a cross-functional team visits a customer organisation to secure a firsthand account of customer needs. Based on a carefully crafted interview guide, in-depth interviews are conducted with key buying influentials to uncover user problems, needs, and desires. "The whole idea is to observe how customers use the product, to see firsthand how it fits into their business process, and to ask open-ended questions about their operations and business goals."[*]

Web-based methods for improving customer inputs to design

Recognising the ability of customers to innovate, many firms have developed tools that invite customers to design their own products. With these innovative toolkits, customers are given an array of features that can be configured, as desired, to create their own customised products. These toolkits often incorporate engineering and cost modules. To illustrate, if a customer wishes to change the length of a lorry bed, the design tool automatically computes the additional

FIGURE 9.3 The lead user method

Phase	Central Focus	Description
Phase 1	Laying the Foundation	The team identifies target markets and secures support from internal stakeholders for the type and level of innovations desired.
Phase 2	Determining the Trends	The team talks to experts in the field who have a broad view of emerging technologies and pioneering applications in the particular area.
Phase 3	Identifying Lead Users	The team begins a networking process to identify lead users at the leading edge of the target market and to gather information that might contribute to breakthrough products.
Phase 4	Developing and Assessing Preliminary Product Ideas	The team begins to shape product ideas and to assess market potential and fit with company interests.
Phase 5	Developing the Breakthroughs	To design final concepts, the team hosts a workshop bringing together lead users with other in-house managers. After further refinement, the team presents its recommendations to senior management.

Source: Adapted with modifications from Eric von Hippel, Stefan Thomke, and Mary Sonnack, "Creating Breakthroughs at 3M," *Harvard Business Review* 77 (September–October 1999), p. 52.

cost and the associated changes that will be required in both the transmission and the engine. For aesthetic compatibility, the design tool might even modify the shape of the cab. Likewise, many software companies encourage users to add custom-designed modules to their standard products and then commercialises the best of those components.*

9.4 DETERMINANTS OF NEW PRODUCT PERFORMANCE AND TIMELINESS

What factors are most important in determining the success or failure of the new product? Why are some firms faster than others in moving projects through the development process? Let's review the available evidence.

9.4.1 The determinants of success

Both strategic factors and a firm's proficiency in carrying out the new-product-development process determine new product success.* (See Figure 9.4.)

Strategic factors

Research suggests that four strategic factors appear to be crucial to new product success. The level of product advantage is the most important. **Product advantage** refers to customer perceptions of product superiority with respect to quality, cost–performance ratio, or function relative to competitors. Successful products offer clear benefits, such as reduced customer costs, and are of higher quality (for example, more durable) than competitors' products. A study of more than 100 new product projects in the chemical industry illustrates the point. Here, Robert Cooper and Elko Kleinschmidt assert, "The winners are new products that offer high relative product quality, have superior price/performance characteristics, provide good value for the money to the customer, are superior to competing products in meeting customer needs, [and] have unique attributes and highly visible benefits that are easily seen by the customer."*

Marketing synergy and technical synergy are also pivotal in new product outcomes. **Marketing synergy** is the fit between the needs of the project and the firm's resources and skills in

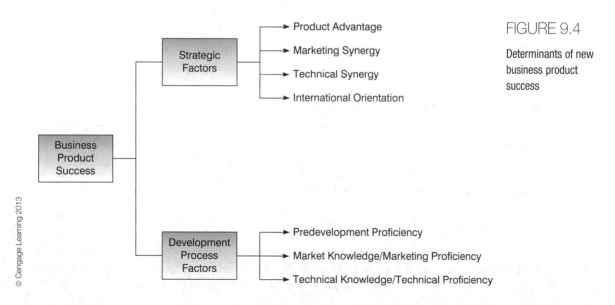

FIGURE 9.4

Determinants of new business product success

marketing (for example, personal selling or market research). By contrast, **technical synergy** concerns the fit between the needs of the project and the firm's R&D resources and competencies. New products that match the skills of the firm are likely to succeed.

In addition to the preceding three factors, an **international orientation** also contributes to the success of product innovation.[*] New products designed and developed to meet foreign requirements and targeted at world or nearest-neighbour export markets outperform domestic products on almost every measure, including success rate, profitability, and domestic and foreign market shares. Underlying this success is a strong international focus in market research, product testing with customers, trial selling, and launch efforts.

Development process factors

New product success is also associated with particular characteristics of the development process. **Predevelopment proficiency** provides the foundation for a successful product. Predevelopment involves several important tasks such as initial screening, preliminary market and technical assessment, detailed market research study, and preliminary business/financial analysis. Firms that are skilled in completing these upfront tasks are likely to experience new product success.

Market knowledge and **marketing proficiency** are also pivotal in new product outcomes. As might be expected, business marketers with a solid understanding of market needs are likely to succeed. Robert Cooper describes the market planning for a successful product he examined: "Market information was very complete: there was a solid understanding of the customer's needs, wants, and preferences; of the customer's buying behaviour and price sensitivity; of the size and trends of the market; and of the competitive situation. Finally, the market launch was well planned, well targeted, proficiently executed, and backed by appropriate resources."[*]

Technical knowledge and **technical proficiency** are other important dimensions of the new-product-development process. When technical developers have a strong base of knowledge about the technical aspects of a potential new product, and when they can proficiently pass through the stages of the new-product-development process (for example, product development, prototype testing, pilot production, and production start-up), these products succeed.

9.4.2 Fast-paced product development

Rapid product development offers a number of competitive advantages. To illustrate, speed enables a firm to respond to rapidly changing markets and technologies. Moreover, fast product development is usually more efficient because lengthy development processes tend to waste resources on peripheral activities and changes.[*] Of course, although an overemphasis on speed may create other pitfalls, it is becoming an important strategic weapon, particularly in high-technology markets.

Matching the process to the development task

How can a firm accelerate product development? A major study of the global computer industry provides some important benchmarks.[*] Researchers examined 72 product development projects of leading U.S., European, and Asian computer firms. The findings suggest that multiple approaches are used to increase speed in product development. Speed comes from properly matching the approach to the product development task at hand.

Compressed strategy for predictable projects

For well-known markets and technologies, a **compression strategy** speeds development. This strategy views product development as a predictable series of steps that can be compressed. Speed comes from carefully planning these steps and shortening the time it takes to complete each one. This research indicates that the compressed strategy increased the speed of product development for products that had predictable designs and that were targeted for stable and mature markets. Mainframe computers fit into this category—they rely on proprietary hardware, have more predictable designs from project to project, and compete in a mature market.

Experiential strategy for unpredictable projects

For uncertain markets and technologies, an **experiential strategy** accelerates product development. The underlying assumption of this strategy, explain Kathleen Eisenhardt and Behnam Tabrizi, is that "product development is a highly uncertain path through foggy and shifting markets and technologies. The key to fast product development is, then, rapidly building intuition and flexible options in order to learn quickly about and shift with uncertain environments."[*]

Under these conditions, speed comes from multiple design iterations, extensive testing, frequent milestones, and a powerful leader who can keep the product team focused. Here real-time interactions, experimentation, and flexibility are essential. The research found that the experiential strategy increased the speed of product development for unpredictable projects such as personal computers—a market characterised by rapidly evolving technology and unpredictable patterns of competition.

SUMMARY

Product innovation is a high-risk and potentially rewarding process. Sustained growth depends on innovative products that respond to existing or emerging consumer needs. Effective managers of innovation channel and control its main directions but have learned to stay flexible and expect surprises. Within the firm, marketing managers pursue strategic activity that falls into two broad categories: induced and autonomous strategic behaviour.

New-product-development efforts for existing businesses or market-development projects for the firm's present products are the outgrowth of induced strategic initiatives. In contrast, autonomous strategic efforts take shape outside the firm's current concept of strategy, depart from the current course, and centre on new categories of business opportunity; middle managers initiate the project, champion its development, and, if successful, see the project integrated into the firm's concept of strategy. Corporate entrepreneurs thrive in a culture where senior managers promote and reward innovative behaviour, encourage risk-taking, and provide the administrative mechanisms to screen, develop, and implement new product ideas.

The long-run competitive position of most business marketing firms depends on their ability to manage and increase their technological base. Core competencies provide the basis for products and product families. Each generation of a product family has a platform that serves as the foundation for specific products targeted at different or complementary market applications. Because companies keep working to make better products, they can sell at higher profit margins to the most demanding customers, and they often overshoot the needs of mainstream customers. A sustaining innovation provides demanding high-end customers with improved performance, whereas disruptive innovations target new or less-demanding customers with an easy-to-use, less expensive alternative that is "good enough." Disruptive strategies take two forms: low-end and new-market disruptions.

Firms that are successful innovators in turbulent markets combine limited structures (for example, priorities, deadlines) with extensive communication and the freedom to improvise on current projects. These successful product creators also explore the future by experimenting with a variety of low-cost probes and build a relentless sense of urgency in the organisation by creating new products at predictable time intervals (i.e., time pacing).

Effective new product development requires a thorough knowledge of customer needs and a clear grasp of the technological possibilities. Lead user analysis and customer visits often uncover valuable new product opportunities. Top-performing firms execute the new-product-development process proficiently, provide adequate resources to support new product objectives, and develop clear new product strategy. Both strategic factors and the firm's proficiency in executing the new-product-development process are critical to the success of industrial products. Fast-paced product development can provide an important source of competitive advantage. Speed comes from adapting the process to the new-product-development task at hand.

DISCUSSION QUESTIONS

1   A company that makes wheat flour has a large share of the consumer market with several premium brands containing wheat flour. The company is now considering developing a powder that can be mixed with water to make a delicious vegetable sauce. Of course, this product will have to compete with other

vegetable sauces on the market. Develop a detailed proposal for a concept test for this new product.

2 A discontinuous innovation involves the introduction of a completely new product. This is a relatively rare phenomenon in business. Give some examples of this kind of innovation and explain why they are so rare. How do you assess the future for new products?

3 Do you think the risk associated with the development of new products will increase during the next ten years? Why or why not?

4 Compare and contrast different approaches to organising the new product development process. As a marketing consultant, which one would you suggest for a family owned business specialising in making tools? Which one would you recommend for a large multinational corporation?

5 Comment on the following statement. 'In this firm we never worry about a new product that fails because we don't reach our profitability objectives. We only need to worry if we don't recover our production and marketing costs.'

INTERNET EXERCISE

1 Rolls Royce started off in 1884 as an electrical and mechanical business established by Henry Royce. Today, the firm is best known for its luxury cars and has branched successfully into several different business markets. Go to http://www.rolls-royce.com and identify its major product lines.

REFERENCES

Anthony, Scott D., Johnson, Mark W., Sinfield, Joseph V., and Altman, Elizabeth J., *The Innovator's Guide to Growth: Putting Disruptive Innovation to Work* (Boston: Harvard Business Press, 2008), pp. 125–126.

Athaide, Gerard A., and Stump, Rodney L., "A Taxonomy of Relationship Approaches during Technology Development in Technology-Based, Industrial Markets," *Journal of Product Innovation Management* 16 (September 1999): pp. 469–482.

Beaulieu, Joseph, "The Moat around Apple's iOS Platform Continues to Widen," April 20, 2011, Morningstar, Inc., p. 1, http://www.morningstar.com, accessed May 25, 2011.

Bonner, Joseph M., Ruekert, Robert W., and Walker Jr., Orville C., "Upper Management Control of New Product Development Projects and Project Performance," *Journal of Product Innovation Management* 19 (May 2002): p. 243.

Brown, Shona L., and Eisenhardt, Kathleen M., "The Art of Continuous Change: Linking Complexity Theory and Time-Paced Evolution in Relentlessly Shifting Organizations," *Administrative Science Quarterly* 42 (March 1997): pp. 1–34.

Burgelman, Robert A., "A Process Model of Internal Corporate Venturing in the Diversified Major Firm," *Administrative Science Quarterly* 28 (April 1983a): pp. 223–244.

Burgelman, Robert A., "Corporate Entrepreneurship and Strategic Management: Insights from a Process Study," *Management Science* 29 (December 1983b): p. 1352.

Calantone, Roger, "Product Innovativeness Dimensions and Their Relationship with Product Advantage, Product Financial Performance, and Project Protocol," *Journal of Product Innovation Management* 27 (December 2010): pp. 991–1006.

Christensen, Clayton M., and Raynor, Michael E., *The Innovator's Solution: Creating and Sustaining Successful Growth* (Boston: Harvard Business School Press, 2003), pp. 215–216.

Cooper, Robert G., *Winning at New Products: Accelerating the Process from Idea to Launch* (Reading, MA: Addison-Wesley, 1993), p. 27.

Cooper, Robert G., "Perspective: The Stage-Gate® Idea to Launch Process—Update, What's New, and NextGen Systems," *Journal of Product Innovation Management* 25 (May 2008): pp. 213–232.

Cooper, Robert G., and Edgett, Scott J., "Maximizing Productivity in Product Innovation," *Research Technology Management* 51 (March–April 2008): pp. 47–58.

Cooper, Robert G., and Edgett, Scott J., "Developing a Product Innovation and Technology Strategy for Your Business," *Research Technology Management* 53 (May–June 2010): pp. 33–40.

Cooper, Robert G., and Kleinschmidt, Elko J., "Major New Products: What Distinguishes the Winners in the Chemical Industry?" *Journal of Product Innovation Management* 10 (March 1993): p. 108.

Cooper, Robert G., and Kleinschmidt, Elko J., "Determinants of Timeliness in Product Development," *Journal of Product Innovation Management* 11 (November 1994): pp. 381–417.

Cooper, Robert G., and Kleinschmidt, Elko J., "Benchmarking Firms' New Product Performance and Practices," *Engineering Management Review* 23 (Fall 1995): pp. 112–120.

Cooper, Robert G., Edgett, Scott J., and Kleinschmidt, Elko J., "Benchmarking Best NPD Practices–I," *Research Technology Management* 47 (January–February 2004a): pp. 31–43.

Cooper, Robert G., Edgett, Scott J., and Kleinschmidt, Elko J., "Benchmarking Best NPD Practices–II," *Research Technology Management* 47 (May–June 2004b): pp. 50–59.

Cooper, Robert G., Edgett, Scott J., and Kleinschmidt, Elko J., "Benchmarking Best NPD Practices–III," *Research Technology Management* 47 (November–December 2004c): pp. 43–55.

de Brentani, Ulrike, Kleinschmidt, Elko J., and Salomo, Soren, "Success in Global New Product Development: Impact of Strategy and the Behavioral Environment of the Firm," *Journal of Product Innovation Management* 27 (March 2010): pp. 143–160.

Debruyne, Marion, Moenart, Rudy, Griffin, Abbie, Hart, Susan, Hultink, Erik Jan, and Robben, Henry "The Impact of New Product Launch Strategies on Competitive Reaction in Industrial Markets," *Journal of Product Innovation Management* 19 (March 2002): pp. 159–170.

Dibb, Sally, Simkin, Lyndon, Pride, Bill, and Ferrell, O.C., *Marketing Concepts & Strategies*, 6th ed. (Cengage, 2012).

Doole, Isobel, and Lowe, Robin, *International Marketing Strategy* 6th ed. (Cengage, 2012).

Edward F. McQuarrie, *Customer Visits: Building a Better Market Focus* (Armonk, NY: M.E. Sharpe, 2008).

Eisenhardt, Kathleen M., and Brown, Shona L., "Time Pacing: Competing in Markets That Won't Stand Still," *Harvard Business Review* 76 (March–April 1998): pp. 59–69.

Eisenhardt, Kathleen M., and Tabrizi, Behnam N., "Accelerating Adaptive Processes: Product Innovation in the Global Computer Industry," *Administrative Science Quarterly* 40 (March 1995): pp. 84–110.

Erickson, Tamara J., Magee, John F., Roussel, Philip A., and Saad, Komol N., "Managing Technology as Business Strategy," *Sloan Management Review* 31 (Spring 1990): pp. 73–83.

Fortune, "After Steve Jobs: Apple's Next CEO—Tony Fadell (2)," June 26, 2008, http://money.cnn.com/galleries/2008/fortune/0806/gallery.apple_jobs_successors.fortune/2.html, accessed July 16, 2008.

Gertz, Dwight L., and Baptista, João P.A. *Grow to Be Great: Breaking the Downsizing Cycle* (New York: The Free Press, 1995), pp. 92–103.

Hamel, Gary, "The Why, What, and How of Management Innovation," *Harvard Business Review* 84 (February 2006): pp. 72–84.

Hargadon, Andrew, *How Breakthroughs Happen: The Surprising Truth about How Companies Innovate* (Boston: Harvard Business School Press, 2003), pp. 168–182.

Hauser, John, Tellis, Gerald J., and Griffin, Abbie, "Research on Innovation: A Review and Agenda for Marketing Science," *Marketing Science* 25 (November–December 2006): p. 707.

Hutt, Michael D., Reingen, Peter H., and Ronchetto Jr., John R., "Tracing Emergent Processes in Marketing Strategy Formation," *Journal of Marketing* 52 (January 1988): pp. 4–19.

Kahney, Leander, "Inside Look at Birth of iPod," July 21, 2004, http://www.wired.com/gadgets/mac/news/2004/07/64286, accessed June 3, 2008.

Kelly, Donna, and Lee, Hyunsuk, "Managing Innovation Champions: The Impact of Project Characteristics on the Direct Manager Role," *Journal of Product Innovation Management* 27 (December 2010): pp. 1007–1019.

Kleinschmidt, Elko J., and Cooper, Robert G., "The Performance Impact of an International Orientation on Product Innovation," *European Journal of Marketing* 22 (9, 1988): pp. 56–71.

Maidique, Modesto A., "Entrepreneurs, Champions, and Technological Innovations," *Sloan Management Review* 21 (Spring 1980): pp. 59–70.

Martin, Dick, *Secrets of the Marketing Masters* (New York: AMACOM, 2009), p. 85.

Marvel, Griffin, Hebda, and Vojak, "Examining the Technical Corporate Entrepreneurs' Motivation," p. 764.

Marvel, Matthew R., Griffin, Abbie, Hebda, John, and Vojak, Bruce, "Examining the Technical Corporate Entrepreneurs' Motivation: Voices from the Field," *Entrepreneurship Theory and Practice*, 31 (September 2007): pp. 753–768.

Meyer, Marc H., and Utterback, James M., "The Product Family and the Dynamics of Core Capability," *Sloan Management Review* 34 (Spring 1993): pp. 29–47.

Mintzberg, Henry, and James A. Walton, "Of Strategies, Deliberate and Emergent," *Strategic Management Journal* 6 (July–August 1985): pp. 257–272.

Montoya-Weiss, Mitzi M., and Calantone, Roger, "Determinants of New Product Performance: A Review and Meta-Analysis," *Journal of Product Innovation Management* 11 (November 1994): pp. 397–417.

Moorman, Christine, and Miner, Anne S., "The Convergence of Planning and Execution: Improvisation in New Product Development," *Journal of Marketing* 62 (July 1998): p. 3.

Moutinho, Luiz, and Southern, Geoffrey, *Strategic Marketing Management: A process Based Approach* (Cengage, 2012).

Nevens, T. Michael, Summe, Gregory L., and Uttal, Bro, "Commercializing Technology: What the Best Companies Do," *Harvard Business Review* 60 (May–June 1990): pp. 154–163.

Porter, Michael E., "Technology and Competitive Advantage," *Journal of Business Strategy* 6 (Winter 1985): p. 60.

Prahalad, C. K., "Weak Signals versus Strong Paradigms," *Journal of Marketing Research* 32 (August 1995): pp. iii–vi.

Quinn, James B., "Managing Innovation: Controlled Chaos," *Harvard Business Review* 63 (May–June 1985): p. 83.

Shirouzu, Norihiko, "Mr. Fujino's Bumpy Flight Lands Honda in the Jet Age," *The Wall Street Journal*, June 18, 2007, pp. B1 and B3.

Sood, Ashish, and Tellis, Gerard J., "Technological Evolution and Radical Innovation," *Journal of Marketing* 69 (July 2005): pp. 152–168.

Thomke, Stephen, and von Hippel, Eric, "Customers as Innovators: A New Way to Create Value," *Harvard Business Review* 80 (April 2002): pp. 74–81.

van Weele, Arjan, *Puchasing and Supply Chain Management: Analysis Strategy, Planning and Practice*, 5th ed. (Cengage, 2010).

Verhage, Bronis J., *Marketing: A Global Perspective* (Cengage, 2013).

von Hippel, Eric, "Get New Products from Customers," *Harvard Business Review* 60 (March–April 1982): pp. 117–122.

von Hippel, Eric, *The Sources of Innovation* (New York: Oxford University Press, 1988).

von Hippel, Eric, Thomke, Stefan, and Sonnack, Mary, "Creating Breakthroughs at 3M," *Harvard Business Review* 77 (September–October 1999): pp. 47–57.

Walker, Beth A., Kapelianis, Dimitri, and Hutt, Michael D., "Competitive Cognition," *MIT Sloan Management Review* 46 (Summer 2005): pp. 10–12.

Wheelwright, Steven C. and Clark, Kim B., "Creating Project Plans to Focus Product Development," *Harvard Business Review* 70 (March–April 1992): pp. 70–82.

CHAPTER 10
MANAGING
BUSINESS
MARKETING
CHANNELS

CHAPTER OBJECTIVES

The channel of distribution is the marketing manager's bridge to the market. Channel innovation represents a source of competitive advantage that separates market winners from market losers. The business marketer must ensure that the firm's channel is properly aligned to the needs of important market segments. At the same time, the marketer must also satisfy the needs of channel members, whose support is crucial to the success of business marketing strategy. After reading this chapter, you will understand:

1   How to examine different types of channel

2   The characteristics of multichannel strategies

3   The crucial steps in the channel process

4   Requirements for successful channel management

Go to Market Strategy, an influential book by Lawrence G. Friedman, aptly describes the central focus of a channel strategy in the business market:

> *The success of every go-to-market decision you make, indeed your ability to make smart go-to-market decisions at all, depends on how well you understand your customers.... You must build an accurate customer fact-base that clarifies who the customers are in your target market, what they buy, how they buy it, how they want to buy it, and what would motivate them to buy more of it from you.*[*]

The channel component of business marketing strategy has two important and related dimensions. First, the channel structure must be designed to accomplish marketing objectives. However, selecting the best channel to accomplish objectives is challenging because: (1) the alternatives are numerous, (2) marketing goals differ, and (3) business market segments are so various that separate channels must often be used concurrently. The ever-changing business environment requires managers to periodically reevaluate the channel structure. Stiff competition, new customer requirements, and the rapid growth of online resources are among the forces that create new opportunities and signal the need for fresh channel strategies. Customers want simple and fast online transactions for some purchases but require highly complex solutions designed by an experienced sales team for others. Often, business-to-business firms need to develop a flexible multi-channel approach that can seamlessly handle each transaction cost effectively.[*]

Second, once the channel structure has been specified, the business marketer must manage the channel to achieve prescribed goals. To do so, the manager must develop procedures for selecting intermediaries, motivating them to achieve desired performance, resolving conflict among channel members, and evaluating performance. This chapter provides a structure for designing and administering the business marketing channel.

10.1 THE BUSINESS MARKETING CHANNEL

The link between manufacturers and customers is the **channel of distribution**. The channel accomplishes all the tasks necessary to effect a sale and deliver products to the customer. These tasks include making contact with potential buyers, negotiating, contracting, transferring title, communicating, arranging financing, servicing the product, and providing local inventory, transportation, and storage. These tasks may be performed entirely by the manufacturer or entirely by intermediaries, or they may be shared between them. The customer may even undertake some of these functions; for example, customers granted certain discounts might agree to accept larger inventories and the associated storage costs.

Fundamentally, channel management centres on these questions: Which channel tasks will be performed by the firm, and which tasks, if any, will be performed by channel members? Figure 10.1 shows various ways to structure business marketing channels. Some channels are **direct**—the manufacturer must perform all the marketing functions needed to make and deliver products. The manufacturer's direct sales force and online marketing channels are examples. Others are **indirect**; that is, some type of intermediary (such as a distributor or dealer) sells or handles the products.

A basic issue in channel management, then, is how to structure the channel so that the tasks are performed optimally. One alternative is for the manufacturer to do it all.

10.1.1 Direct channels

Direct distribution, common in business marketing, is a channel strategy that does not use intermediaries. The manufacturer's own sales force deals directly with the customer, and the

FIGURE 10.1

B2B marketing channels

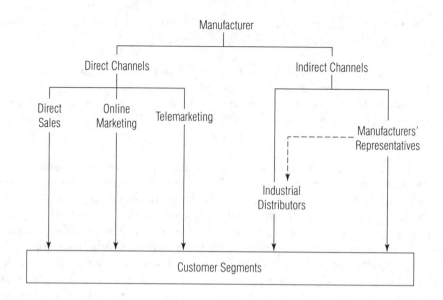

manufacturer has full responsibility for performing all the necessary channel tasks. Direct distribution is often required in business marketing because of the nature of the selling situation or the concentrated nature of industry demand. The direct sales approach is feasible when: (1) the customers are large and well defined, (2) the customers insist on direct sales, (3) sales involve extensive negotiations with upper management, and (4) selling has to be controlled to ensure that the total product package is properly implemented and to guarantee a quick response to market conditions.

A direct sales force is best used for the most complex sales opportunities: highly customised solutions, large customers, and complex products. Customised solutions and large customer accounts require professional account management, deep product knowledge, and a high degree of selling skill—all attributes a sales representative must possess. Also, when risk in a purchase decision is perceived as high and significant expertise is required in the sale, customers demand a high level of personal attention and relationship building from the direct sales force as a precondition for doing business. However, according to Lawrence Friedman and Timothy Furey, "in the broad middle market and small-customer market, where transactions are generally simpler, other channels can do a more cost-effective job—and can often reach more customers."[*]

Surprisingly, many firms use their Web sites only for promotional purposes and not yet as a sales channel. Business marketing firms can use E-channels as: (1) information platforms, (2) transaction platforms, and (3) platforms for managing customer relationships. The effect on the business increases as a firm moves from level one to level three.

10.1.2 Indirect channels

Indirect distribution uses at least one type of intermediary, if not more. Business marketing channels typically include fewer types of intermediaries than do consumer-goods channels. Indirect distribution accounts for a large share of sales in Europe. Manufacturers' representatives and industrial distributors account for most of the transactions handled in this way. Indirect distribution is generally found where: (1) markets are fragmented and widely dispersed, (2) low transaction amounts prevail, and (3) buyers typically purchase a number of items, often different brands, in one transaction.[*] For example, IBM's massive sales organisation concentrates on large corporate, government, and institutional customers. Industrial distributors effectively and efficiently serve literally thousands of other IBM customers—small to medium-sized

INSIDE BUSINESS MARKETING

Tesco's multi-channel approach to market leadership

The Internet has changed the way in which consumers shop. In the past, those seeking to replenish their kitchen cupboards, fridges and freezers would usually visit their local supermarket or hypermarket. Now, these same consumers can visit the Internet and order their groceries for direct delivery to their homes. The concept is seen to be particularly attractive to professional, highearning, ABC1 men and women who work long hours and have limited leisure time, but many other consumers increasingly buy their groceries online. Indeed, the most visited websites each week are those operated by Tesco, Asda, Sainsbury's and Ocado. **Tesco.com** is one service that allows customers to buy their groceries direct over the Internet. Consumers can access the Tesco website at Tesco.com and select their purchase items. Their orders are then compiled by a team of in-store sales assistants for delivery to consumers' homes at a time of their choosing. So large is the Internet part of the grocery market that many supermarket retailers now operate fully 'dark stores', where no consumers visit and only teams of staff operate picking online orders for home delivery. Assorting within such stores into clusters or product categories is particularly important for operations staff, just as it is within normal stores for consumers requiring similar products to be grouped together.

Initially, the Tesco.com concept was trialled in 11 stores in two major UK cities. The company's preliminary research showed that around 200 000 consumers were using the service offered by these 11 stores and that this was increasing by 10 000 every week. Before long, the obvious popularity of Internet shopping prompted Tesco to roll out Tesco.com to other parts of the UK. By the end of the first year, the company offered the service from 100 Tesco stores. Careful consideration has been given to the marketing of the Internet shopping service. The sight of the Tesco.com logo displayed by the company's delivery vans has become familiar to those living in the areas where the service is offered. In addition, the retailer is using a combination of local poster and in-store advertising, direct mail and an Internet campaign to promote the Tesco.com operation. Today, Tesco is the most used website of all e-tailers.

Increasing familiarity with shopping on the Internet looks set to increase the demand for services like Tesco. com. A whole generation of young adults is emerging that has grown up with the convenience and reassurance of web-based shopping. How substantial a part of Tesco's business the service will become remains to be seen. However, Tesco management clearly understands that retaining its market-leading position means being ready to respond to changing shopping needs. There had been concerns in certain quarters that the large retailers would reduce investment in their stores and the in-store customer experience, but such fears seem unfounded. At the moment, the largest supermarket companies are opening new stores faster than ever before in their history. Another concern expressed by the pundits was that a substantial shift in grocery shopping from the supermarkets to the Internet could damage scale advantages and affect profitability. In fact, for Tesco, online retailing is supporting its portfolio of stores.

In common with many retailers, Tesco has a multi-channel operation. Tesco Extra is an edge-of-town hypermarket business offering mixed merchandise on top of groceries and Tesco Superstores are large grocery-led supermarkets, often on edge-of-town retail parks. The town centre and suburbs are not ignored in Tesco's multi-channel strategy: Tesco Express is a large chain of C-stores (convenience stores) often mini-marts in the suburbs and Tesco Metro are town centre supermarkets focusing on groceries. These storebased propositions are joined by Tesco.com, providing home deliveries of everything found in a Tesco Extra hypermarket and more. Some consumers may prefer just one of these options, while others will use a mix of Tesco stores depending on their whereabouts, the occasion and time of shopping, and may prefer the web and Tesco.com. Tesco's management must understand the different customer profiles that its concepts attract and engage accordingly with these consumers in order to build loyalty.

Sources: *Marketing: Concepts and Strategies*, 5th edition and Tesco, 2011.

organisations. These channel partners assume a vital role in IBM's strategy on a global scale. IBM offers a high level of support to its channel partners, including co-marketing opportunities, customer lead generation, extensive training, and technical assistance. (See a complete description of IBM's channel outreach programme at http://www.ibm.com/partnerworld.)

10.1.3 Integrated multichannel models*

Leading business marketing firms use multiple sales channels to serve customers in a particular market. The goal of a multichannel model is to coordinate the activities of many channels, such as field sales representatives, channel partners, call centres, and the Web, in order to enhance the total customer experience and profitability. Consider a typical sales cycle that includes the following tasks: lead generation, lead qualification, negotiation and sales closure, fulfilment, and customer care and support (Figure 10.2). In a multichannel system, different channels can perform different tasks within a single sales transaction with a customer. For example, business marketing firms might use a call centre and direct mail to generate leads, field sales representatives to close sales, business partners (for example, industrial distributors) to provide fulfilment (that is, deliver or install product), and a Web site to provide post-sale support.

Managing customer contact points

Figure 10.3 shows a particular multichannel strategy that a number of leading firms use to reach the vast middle market composed of many small and medium-sized businesses. First, the channels are arranged from top to bottom in terms of their *relative cost of sales* (that is, direct sales is the most expensive, whereas the Internet is the least). By shifting any selling tasks to lower-cost channels, the business marketer can boost profit margins and reach more customers, in more markets, more efficiently.

Business partner's key role Returning to Figure 10.3, observe the central role of business partners across the stages of the sales cycle. Low-cost, direct-to-customer channels—like the

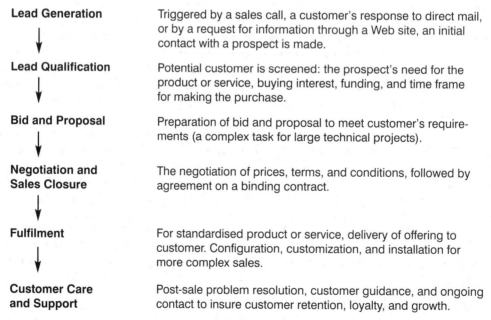

FIGURE 10.2 Typical sales cycle: Tasks performed throughout the sales process

Lead Generation

Triggered by a sales call, a customer's response to direct mail, or by a request for information through a Web site, an initial contact with a prospect is made.

Lead Qualification

Potential customer is screened: the prospect's need for the product or service, buying interest, funding, and time frame for making the purchase.

Bid and Proposal

Preparation of bid and proposal to meet customer's requirements (a complex task for large technical projects).

Negotiation and Sales Closure

The negotiation of prices, terms, and conditions, followed by agreement on a binding contract.

Fulfilment

For standardised product or service, delivery of offering to customer. Configuration, customization, and installation for more complex sales.

Customer Care and Support

Post-sale problem resolution, customer guidance, and ongoing contact to insure customer retention, loyalty, and growth.

Source: Adapted from Lawrence G. Friedman, *Go to Market Strategy: Advanced Techniques and Tools for Selling More Products, to More Customers, More Profitably* (Boston: Butterworth-Heinemann, 2002), pp. 234–236.

1. Consider the relative cost of alternative sales channels.

> Direct sales – most expensive
> Business partners
> Telechannels
> Direct mail
> Internet – least expensive

2. Employ business partners to cover SMB customers and perform the <u>primary</u> sales tasks.

3. Fully utilise other sales channels to lend direct <u>support</u> across the sales cycle.

> Lead generation from telechannels, direct mail and the internet
> Sales closure support from direct sales rep, as required
> Customer care from internet

SMB = small and medium-sized

FIGURE 10.3

Multichannel integration map: Simple example of high-coverage partnering model

Source: Adapted with modifications from Lawrence G. Friedman, *Go to Market Strategy: Advanced Techniques and Tools for Selling More Products, to More Customers, More Profitably* (Boston: Butterworth-Heinemann, 2002), p. 243. Copyright 2002.

Internet—are used to generate sales leads, which are then given to channel partners. These partners are then expected to complete the sales cycle but can secure assistance from Oracle's sales representatives to provide guidance and support (when needed) in closing the sale. By emphasising the partner channel for middle-market customers, Oracle can significantly increase market coverage and penetration while enjoying higher profit margins and lower selling costs. Moreover, this allows the sales force to concentrate on large enterprise customers.

This provides just one example of how a firm can coordinate and configure sales cycle tasks across various sales channels to create an integrated strategy for a particular market. Any firm that serves a variety of markets requires distinctly different multichannel models to serve customers in those markets. To illustrate, a company might serve key corporate accounts through sales representatives and the middle market through channel partners, call centres, and the Internet.

Customer Relationship Management (CRM) systems

Many business marketing firms pursue very complex market coverage strategies and use *all* of the alternative paths to the market we have discussed. For example, Toshiba sells directly through a field sales organisation to large enterprises; through channel partners and resellers to the government, education, and the midsize business market; and through retail stores to the small business and home market. This multichannel mix features many points of contact that Toshiba must manage and coordinate to ensure a "singular" customer experience across channels. CRM systems provide a valuable tool for coordinating sales channel activities and managing crucial connections and handoffs between them. Lawrence Friedman, a leading sales strategy consultant, notes:

> *Channel coordination used to be a difficult, messy problem involving the tracking and frequent loss of hand-written memos, voice mails, paper lists of sales leads, and dog-eared customer history files. CRM has ushered in a new era of IT-driven channel coordination, enabling electronic transmission of leads and customer histories from one channel to another, with no loss of information or sales information falling through the cracks.[*]*

10.2 PARTICIPANTS IN THE BUSINESS MARKETING CHANNEL

Channel members assume a central role in the marketing strategies of business-to-business firms, large and small. A channel management strategy begins with an understanding of the intermediaries that may be used. Primary attention is given to two: (1) industrial distributors and (2) manufacturers' representatives. They handle a sizable share of business-to-business sales made through intermediaries.

10.2.1 Distributors

Industrial distributors are the most pervasive and important single force in distribution channels. Distributors are heavily used for MRO (maintenance, repair, and operations) supplies, with many industrial buyers reporting that they buy as much as 75 per cent of their MRO supplies from distributors. Generally, about 75 per cent of all business marketers sell *some* products through distributors. What accounts for the unparalleled position of the distributor in the industrial market?

Distributors are generally small, independent businesses serving narrow geographic markets. Sales average almost €1.5 million, although some top €2.25 billion. Net profits are relatively low as a percentage of sales (4 per cent); return on investment averages 11 per cent. The typical order is small, and the distributors sell to a multitude of customers in many industries. The typical distributor is able to spread its costs over a sizable group of vendors—it stocks goods from between 200 and 300 manufacturers. A sales force of outside and inside salespersons generates orders. *Outside salespersons* make regular calls on customers and handle normal account servicing and technical assistance. *Inside salespersons* complement these efforts, processing orders and scheduling delivery; their primary duty is to take telephone orders. Most distributors operate from a single location, but some approach the "supermarket" status with as many as 400 branches.

Compared with their smaller rivals, large distributors seem to have significant advantages. Small distributors are typically unable to achieve the operating economies larger firms enjoy. Large firms can automate much of their operations, enabling them to significantly reduce their sales and general administrative expenses, often to levels approaching 10 per cent of sales.

Distributor responsibilities

Table 10.1 shows industrial distributors' primary responsibilities. The products they sell—cutting tools, abrasives, electronic components, ball bearings, handling equipment, pipe, maintenance equipment, and hundreds more—are generally those that buyers need quickly to avoid production disruptions. Thus, the critical elements of the distributor's function are to have these products readily available and to serve as the manufacturer's selling arm.

Distributors are full-service intermediaries; that is, they take title to the products they sell, and they perform the full range of marketing functions. Some of the more important functions

TABLE 10.1 Key distribution responsibilities

Responsibility	Activity
Contact	Reach all customers in a defined territory through an outside sales force that calls on customers or through an inside group that receives telephone orders
Product availability	Provide a local inventory and include all supporting activities: credit, just-in-time delivery, order processing, and advice
Repair	Provide easy access to local repair facilities (unavailable from a distant manufacturer)
Assembly and light manufacturing	Purchase material in bulk, then shape, form, or assemble to user requirements

are providing credit, offering wide product assortments, delivering goods, offering technical advice, and meeting emergency requirements. Not only are distributors valuable to their manufacturer-suppliers but their customers generally view them favourably. Some purchasing agents view the distributor as an extension of their "buying arms" because they provide service, technical advice, and product application suggestions.

A Service Focus To create more value for their customers, many large distributors have expanded their range of services. Value is delivered through various supply chain and inventory management services, including automatic replenishment, product assembly, in-plant stores, and design services. The most popular services involve helping customers design, construct, and, in some cases, operate a supply network. Other value-adding activities include partnerships in which the distributor's field application engineers work at a customer's site to help select components for new product designs. To reap the profits associated with these important services, many distributors now charge separate fees for each unique service.

Classification of distributors

To select the best distributor for a particular channel, the marketing manager must understand the diversity of distributor operations. Industrial distributors vary according to product lines and user markets. Firms may be ultraspecialised (for example, selling only to municipal water works), or they may carry a broad line of generalised industrial products. However, three primary distributor classifications are usually recognised.

1 **General-line distributors** cater to a broad array of industrial needs. They stock an extensive variety of products and could be likened to the supermarket in consumer-goods markets.

2 **Specialists** focus on one line or on a few related lines. Such a distributor may handle only power transmission equipment—belts, pulleys, and bearings. The most common specialty is fasteners, although specialisation also occurs in cutting tools, power transmission equipment, pipes, valves, and fittings. There is a trend toward increased specialisation as a result of increasing technical complexity of products and the need for higher levels of precision and quality control.

3 A **combination house** operates in two markets: industrial and consumer. Such a distributor might carry electric motors for industrial customers and hardware and automotive parts to be sold through retailers to final consumers.

Choosing a distributor

The selection of a distributor depends on the manufacturer's requirements and the needs of target customer segments. The general-line distributor offers the advantage of one-stop purchasing. If customers do not need a high level of service and technical expertise, the general-line distributor is a good choice. The specialist, on the other hand, provides the manufacturer with a high level of technical capability and a well-developed understanding of complex customer requirements. Specialists handle fasteners, for instance, because of the strict quality-control standards that users impose.

Manufacturers and their distributors are finding the Internet to be a major catalyst for stimulating collaboration. A recent poll asked distributors which business strategies would have the largest effect on them in the future, and the top two were collaboration with supply chain partners and new information technologies.[*] E-collaboration includes sales and services, ordering and billing, technical training and engineering, Internet meetings, auctions, and exchanges. These results suggest that Internet collaboration is a critical strategic force in managing channel relationships.

The distributor as a valuable partner

The quality of a firm's distributors is often the difference between a highly successful marketing strategy and an ineffective one. Customers prize good distributors, making it all the more necessary to strive continually to engage the best in any given market. Distributors often provide the only economically feasible way of covering the entire market.

In summary, the industrial distributor is a full-service intermediary who takes title to the products sold; maintains inventories; provides credit, delivery, wide product assortment, and technical assistance; and may even do light assembly and manufacturing. Although the distributor is primarily responsible for contacting and supplying present customers, industrial distributors also solicit new accounts and work to expand the market. They generally handle established products—typically used in manufacturing operations, repair, and maintenance—with a broad and large demand.

Industrial distributors are a powerful force in business marketing channels, and all indications point to an expanded role for them. The manufacturer's representative is an equally viable force in the business marketing channel.

10.2.2 Manufacturers' representatives

For many business marketers who need a strong selling job with a technically complex product, **manufacturers' representatives**, or reps, are the only cost-effective answer. In fact, Erin Anderson and Bob Trinkle note that the one area untouched by the outsourcing boom is field selling in the business-to-business area. They contend that many companies could benefit by using outsourced sales professionals, namely, manufacturers' reps, to augment or even replace the field sales force.[*] Reps are salespeople who work independently (or for a rep company), represent several companies in the same geographic area, and sell noncompeting but complementary products.

The rep's responsibilities

A rep neither takes title to nor holds inventory of the products handled. (Some reps do, however, keep a limited inventory of repair and maintenance parts.) The rep's forte is expert product knowledge coupled with a keen understanding of the markets and customer needs. Reps are usually limited to defined geographical areas; thus, a manufacturer seeking nationwide distribution usually works with several rep companies. Compared with a distributor channel, a rep generally gives the business marketer more control because the firm maintains title and possession of the goods.

The rep-customer relationship

Reps are the manufacturers' selling arm, making contact with customers, writing and following up on orders, and linking the manufacturer with the industrial end users. Although paid by the manufacturer, the rep is also important to customers. Often, a rep's efforts during a customer emergency (for example, an equipment failure) mean the difference between continuing or stopping production. Most reps are thoroughly experienced in the industries they serve—they can offer technical advice while enhancing the customer's leverage with suppliers in securing parts, repair, and delivery. The rep also provides customers with a continuing flow of information on innovations and trends in equipment, as well as on the industry as a whole.

Commission basis

Reps are paid a commission on sales; the commission varies by industry and by the nature of the selling job. Commissions typically range from a low of 2 per cent to a high of 18 per cent for selected products. The average commission rate is 5.3 per cent.[*] Percentage commission compensation is attractive to manufacturers because they have few fixed sales costs. Reps are paid only when they generate orders, and commissions can be adjusted based on industry conditions.

Because reps are paid on commission, they are motivated to generate high levels of sales—another fact the manufacturer appreciates.

Experience

Reps possess sophisticated product knowledge and typically have extensive experience in the markets they serve. Most reps develop their field experience while working as salespersons for manufacturers. They are motivated to become reps by the desire to be independent OEM and to reap the substantial monetary rewards possible on commission.

When reps are used

- *Large and Small Firms*: Small and medium-sized firms generally have the greatest need for a rep, although many large firms—for example, AkzoNobel, Siemens, and Intel—use them. The reason is primarily economic: Smaller firms cannot justify the expense of maintaining their own sales forces. The rep provides an efficient way to obtain total market coverage, with costs incurred only as sales are made. The quality of the selling job is often very good as a result of the rep's prior experience and market knowledge.

- *Limited Market Potential*: The rep also plays a vital role when the manufacturer's market potential is limited. A manufacturer may use a direct sales force in heavily concentrated business markets, where the demand is sufficient to support the expense, and use reps to cover less-dense markets. Because the rep carries several lines, expenses can be allocated over a much larger sales volume.

- *Servicing Distributors*: Reps may also be employed by a firm that markets through distributors. When a manufacturer sells through hundreds of distributors across Europe, reps may sell to and service those distributors.

B2B TOP PERFORMERS

Why Intel Uses Reps

Intel has a strong corporate brand, an experienced corporate sales force, and long-standing relationships with broad-line distributors such as Arrow Electronics. Intel also uses manufacturers' representatives. Why?

After purchasing a business unit from Digital Equipment Corporation in 1998, Intel realised that several product lines from the acquired unit provided promising market potential, particularly in networking and communications. Specifically, the product lines could spur profitable growth in embedded applications market segments, such as medical equipment and point-of-sale terminals, where the proper application function is based on microprocessors and network connections. At Intel, however, marketing managers argued that the go-to-market strategy that has proved so successful in the PC market would not be suitable for original equipment manufacturers (OEMs) in these sectors.

George Langer, Intel's worldwide representative programme manager, explains:

> There was no sales organisation, few customer relationships, and more than a few OEMs who questioned Intel's renewed interest in the embedded segments. Intel did not have existing capability to get these product lines in front of appropriate customers. The customer base was large and diverse. (This was not the PC OEM customer base where Intel had nurtured strong relationships over time.) And, finally, the value of the Intel brand was not clearly associated with communications, embedded, and networking market segments. Intel turned to outsourced selling [that is, manufacturers' reps].

Source: Erin Anderson and Bob Trinkle, *Outsourcing the Sales Function: The Real Cost of Field Sales* (Mason, Ohio: Thomson Higher Education, 2005), pp. 74–75.

- *Reducing Overhead Costs*: Sometimes the commission rate paid to reps exceeds the cost of a direct sales force, yet the supplier continues to use reps. This policy is not as irrational as it appears. Assume, for example, that costs for a direct sales force approximate 8 per cent of sales and that a rep's commission rate is 11 per cent. Using reps in this case is often justified because of the hidden costs of a sales force. First, the manufacturer does not provide fringe benefits or a fixed salary to reps. Second, the costs of training a rep are usually limited to those required to provide product information. Thus, using reps eliminates significant overhead costs.

Multiple paths to market

A wide array of factors influences the choice of intermediaries, with the tasks they perform being of prime importance.

Different market segments The primary reason for using more than one type of intermediary for the same product is that different market segments require different channel structures. Some firms use three distinct approaches. Large accounts are called on by the firm's own sales force, distributors handle small repeat orders, and manufacturers' reps develop the medium-sized firm market.

How customers buy Like size of accounts, differences in purchase behaviour may also dictate using more than one type of intermediary. If a firm produces a wide line of industrial products, some may require high-calibre selling to numerous buying influences in a single buyer's firm. When this occurs, the firm's own sales force will focus on the more complex buying situations, whereas the distributors will sell standardised products from local stocks.

10.3 CHANNEL DESIGN

Channel design is the dynamic process of developing new channels where none existed and modifying existing channels. The business marketer usually deals with modification of existing channels, although new products and customer segments may require entirely new channels. Regardless of whether the manager is dealing with a new channel or modifying an existing one, channel design is an active rather than a passive task. Effective distribution channels do not simply evolve; rather, they are developed by management, which takes action on the basis of a well-conceived plan that reflects overall marketing goals. Business firms formulate their marketing strategies to appeal to selected market segments, to earn targeted levels of profits, to maintain or increase sales and market share growth rates, and to achieve all this within specified resource constraints. Each element of the marketing strategy has a specific purpose.

Channel design is best conceptualised as a series of stages that the business marketing manager must complete to be sure that all important channel dimensions have been evaluated (Figure 10.4). The result of the process is to specify the structure that provides the highest probability of achieving the firm's objectives.* Note that the process focuses on channel structure and not on channel participants. **Channel structure** refers to the underlying framework: the number of channel levels, the number and types of intermediaries, and the linkages among channel members. Selection of individual intermediaries is indeed important—it is examined later in the chapter.

10.3.1 Step 1: Define customer segments

The primary goal of the distribution channel is to satisfy end-user needs, so the channel design process should begin there. Step 1 is about defining target market segments and isolating the customer buying and usage behaviour in each segment (what they buy, how they buy, and how they put their purchases to use).

FIGURE 10.4

The channel design process

Source: Adapted from V. Kasturi Rangan, *Transforming Your Go-to-Market Strategy: The Three Disciplines of Channel Management* (Boston: Harvard Business Press, 2006), pp. 73–94.

Some business marketers err by considering their channel partners as "customers and rarely looking beyond them." To inform the channel design process, however, the marketing strategist should centre on the importance of the product from the customer's perspective. V. Kasturi Rangan observes:

Producers of agricultural channels, for example, should target farmers and not dealers. Producers of engineering plastics (pellets) for automobile bumpers, on the other hand, should focus on the auto manufacturer and not the consumer, because that is where the product has value in the eyes of the end user.... Other features of the automobile (not bumpers) are more salient [in the choice decision at the consumer level]. [*]

10.3.2 Step 2: Identify customers' channel needs by segment

Identifying and prioritising the channel function requirements for customers in each market segment is next. This information should be elicited directly from a sample of present or potential customers from each segment. Table 10.2 provides a representative list of channel functions that may be more or less important to customers in a particular segment. For example, large customers for information-technology products might rank product customisation, product quality assurance, and after-sales service as their top three needs, whereas small customers may prioritise product information, assortment, and availability as their most important needs. The business marketing manager should also probe customers on other issues that might provide strategy insights. For instance, how sensitive are customers to a two-hour versus six-hour service response time, or how much value do they perceive in a three-year versus one-year warranty?

10.3.3 Step 3: Assess the firm's channel capabilities

Once customer requirements have been isolated and prioritised, an assessment is made of the strengths and weaknesses of the firm's channel. The central focus is on identifying the gaps between what customers in a segment desire and what the channel is now providing. Customers base their choice of a channel not on a single element, but on a complete bundle of benefits (that is, channel functions). To that end, the business-to-business firm should identify particular channel functions, like after-sales support or availability, where action could be taken to enhance the customer value proposition.

TABLE 10.2 Channel functions aligned with customer needs

Channel Function	Customer Needs
1. Product Information	Customers seek more information for new and/or technically complex products and those that are characterised by a rapidly changing market environment.
2. Product Customisation	Some products must be technically modified or need to be adapted to meet the customer's unique requirements.
3. Product Quality Assurance	Because of its importance to the customer's operations, product integrity and reliability might be given special emphasis by customers.
4. Lot Size	For products that have a high unit value or those that are used extensively, the purchase represents a sizable euro outlay and a significant financial decision for the customer.
5. Assortment	A customer may require a broad range of products, including complementary items, and assign special value to one-stop shopping.
6. Availability	Some customer environments require the channel to manage demand uncertainty and support a high level of product availability.
7. After-Sales Services	Customers require a range of services from installation and repair to maintenance and warranty.
8. Logistics	A customer organisation may require special transportation and storage services to support its operations and strategy.

Source: Adapted from V. Kasturi Rangan, Melvyn A. J. Menezes, and E. B. Maier, "Channel Selection for New Industrial Products: A Framework, Method, and Application," *Journal of Marketing* 56 (July 1992): pp. 72–74.

10.3.4 Step 4: Benchmark to competitors

What go-to-market strategies are key competitors using? In designing a channel, cost considerations prevent the business marketer from closing all the gaps on channel capabilities that may appear. However, a clear direction for strategy is revealed by understanding the channel offerings of competitors. For example, an aggressive competitor that goes to market with its own team of account managers and dedicated service specialists might demonstrate special strength in serving large corporate customers. However, countless opportunities exist for smaller rivals to counter this strategy by developing special channel offerings tailored to small and medium-sized customers.

10.3.5 Step 5: Create channel solutions for customers' latent needs

Sometimes, a review of competitor offerings can alert the marketer to opportunities for new offerings that may have special appeal to customers. "At other times, customers' needs may be latent and unarticulated, and it is the channel steward's responsibility to tap into and surface those requirements."* Based on such an assessment, a provider of information-technology equipment created an entirely new channel option for the small and medium-sized customer segment. Rather than selling equipment, this new channel takes responsibility for installing, upgrading, and maintaining the equipment at the customers' locations for an ongoing service fee.

10.3.6 Step 6: Evaluate and select channel options

Channel decisions must ultimately consider the cost-benefit trade-offs and the estimated profitability that each of the viable channel options presents.* Some of the channel gaps that are uncovered in this assessment can be closed by the independent actions and investments of the business-to-business firm (for example, adding to the service support staff or the sales force). For the most part, however, the greatest progress will come from the channel partners (for example, distributors or reps) working together and discussing how channel capabilities can be aligned to customer needs. "The idea is to enhance the value delivered to customers through collaborative action among channel partners. If the partners can agree on how to pull it off and, indeed, accomplish their redefined tasks,"[*] they will squarely respond to customer needs and advance the performance of the channel. One important implication of the framework is that the design of the channel must change as customer and competitor behaviour changes. Rather than a static structure, channel management is an ongoing process involving continuous adjustments and evolution.

10.3.7 Crucial points in channel transformation

Marketing channels are often thought of as a series of product and information flows that originate with the business-to-business firm. In his rich and compelling perspective of the channel design process, V. Kasturi Rangan turns this notion on its head (see Figure 10.5):

> *The starting point is the customer, and the customer's demand-chain requirements. The channel is constructed to meet this core need. Roles, responsibilities, and rewards are allocated as a consequence of this need, and not the other way around.*[*]

10.4 CHANNEL ADMINISTRATION

Once a particular business-to-business channel structure is chosen, channel participants must be selected, and arrangements must be made to ensure that all obligations are assigned. Next, channel members must be motivated to perform the tasks necessary to achieve channel objectives. Third, conflict within the channel must be properly controlled. Finally, performance must be controlled and evaluated.

10.4.1 Selection of channel members

Why is the selection of channel members (specific companies, rather than *type*, which is specified in the design process) part of channel management rather than an aspect of channel design?

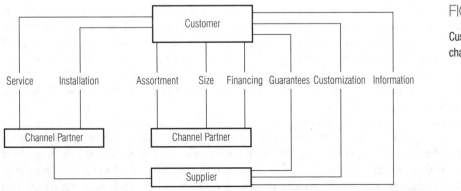

FIGURE 10.5

Customers drive the channel design process

Source: V. Kasturi Rangan, *Transforming Your Go-to-Market Strategy: The Three Disciplines of Channel Management* (Boston: Harvard Business Press, 2006), p. 91.

The primary reason is that intermediary selection is an ongoing process—some intermediaries choose to leave the channel, and the supplier terminates others. Thus, selection of intermediaries is more or less continuous. Performance of individual channel members must be evaluated continually. The manufacturer should be prepared to move quickly, replacing poor performers with potentially better ones. Including the selection process in ongoing channel management puts the process in its proper perspective.

Securing good intermediaries

The marketer can identify prospective channel members through discussions with company salespeople and existing or potential customers, or through trade sources, such the Verified Directory of Manufacturers' Representatives. Once the list of potential intermediaries is reduced to a few names, the manufacturer uses the selection criteria to evaluate them. For example, the McGraw-Edison Company uses an intensive checklist to compare prospective channel members; important criteria are market coverage, product lines, personnel, growth, and financial standing.

The formation of the channel is not at all a one-way street. The manufacturer must now persuade the intermediaries to become part of the channel system. Some distributors evaluate potential suppliers just as rigorously as the manufacturers rate them—using many of the same considerations. Manufacturers must often demonstrate the sales and profit potential of their product and be willing to grant the intermediaries some territorial exclusivity. Special efforts are required to convince the very best rep in a market to represent a particular manufacturer's product. Those efforts must demonstrate that the manufacturer will treat the rep organisation as a partner and support it.

10.4.2 Motivating channel members

Distributors and reps are independent and profit oriented. They are oriented toward their customers and toward whatever means are necessary to satisfy customer needs for industrial products and services. Their perceptions and outlook may differ substantially from those of the manufacturers they represent. As a consequence, marketing strategies can fail when managers do not tailor their programmes to the capabilities and orientations of their intermediaries. To manage the business marketing channel effectively, the marketer must understand the intermediaries' perspective and devise ways to motivate them to perform in a way that enhances the manufacturer's long-term success. The manufacturer must continually seek support from intermediaries, and the quality of that support depends on the motivational techniques used.

A partnership

Channel member motivation begins with the understanding that the channel relationship is a *partnership*. Manufacturers and intermediaries are in business together; whatever expertise and assistance the manufacturer can provide to the intermediaries improves total channel effectiveness. One study of channel relationships suggested that manufacturers may be able to increase the level of resources directed to their products by developing a trusting relationship with their reps; by improving communication through recognition programmes, product training, and consultation with the reps; and by informing the reps of plans, explicitly detailing objectives, and providing positive feedback.[*]

Another study of distributor-manufacturer working partnerships recommended similar approaches. It also suggested that manufacturers and their distributors engage in joint annual planning that focuses on specifying the cooperative efforts each firm requires of its partner to reach its objectives and that periodically reviews progress toward objectives.[*] The net result is trust and satisfaction with the partnership as the relationship leads to meeting performance goals.

Dealer advisory councils

One way to enhance the performance of all channel members is to facilitate the sharing of information among them. Distributors or reps may be brought together periodically with the manufacturer's management to review distribution policies, provide advice on marketing strategy, and supply industry intelligence.[*] Intermediaries can voice their opinions on policy matters and are brought directly into the decision-making process. However, for dealer councils to be effective, the input of channel members must have a meaningful effect on channel policy decisions.

Margins and commission

In the final analysis, the primary motivating device is compensation. The surest way to lose intermediary support is compensation policies that do not meet industry and competitive standards. Reps or distributors who feel cheated on commissions or margins shift their attention to products generating a higher profit. The manufacturer must pay the prevailing compensation rates in the industry and must adjust the rates as conditions change.

Intermediaries' compensation should reflect the marketing tasks they perform. If the manufacturer seeks special attention for a new industrial product, most reps require higher commissions. As noted earlier in the chapter, many industrial distributors charge separate fees for the value-added services they provide. For this approach to work effectively, it is critical that the client understands the value it is receiving for the extra charges.

Building trust

The very nature of a distribution channel—with each member dependent on another for success—can invite conflict. Conflict can be controlled in various ways, including channel-wide committees, joint goal setting, and cooperative programmes involving a number of marketing strategy elements. To compete, business marketers need to be effective at cooperating within a network of organisations—the channel. For example, an IBM executive who led the team that developed the first IBM PC in 1981 also drove the decision to sell it through dealers and later through the channel. Soon after the introduction of the PC, an executive with American Express Travel Related Services approached the IBM executive with an idea to sell the PCs directly to American Express card members. The IBM executive refused—he wanted the *channel* to get the sale. As a result, IBM secured the commitment and trust of its channel partners, setting the stage for many other strategy initiatives.[*]

Successful cooperation results from relationships in which the parties have a strong sense of communication and trust. Robert M. Morgan and Shelby D. Hunt suggest that relationship commitment and trust develop when: (1) firms offer benefits and resources that are superior to what other partners could offer; (2) firms align themselves with other firms that have similar corporate values; (3) firms share valuable information on expectations, markets, and performance; and (4) firms avoid taking advantage of their partners.[*] By following these prescriptions, business marketers and their channel networks can enjoy sustainable competitive advantages over their rivals and their networks.

SUMMARY

Channel strategy is an exciting and challenging aspect of business marketing. The challenge derives from the number of alternatives available to the manufacturer in distributing business products. The excitement results from the ever-changing nature of markets, user needs, and competitors.

Channel strategy involves two primary management tasks: designing the overall structure and managing the operation of the channel. Channel design includes evaluating distribution goals, activities, and potential intermediaries. Channel structure includes the number, types, and levels of intermediaries to be used. A central challenge is determining how to create a strategy that effectively blends e-commerce with traditional channels. Business marketing firms use multiple sales channels to serve customers in a particular market segment: company salespersons, channel partners, call centres, direct mail, and the Internet. The goal of a multichannel strategy is to coordinate activities across those channels to enhance the customer's experience while advancing the firm's performance.

The primary participants in business marketing channels are distributors and reps. Distributors provide the full range of marketing services for their suppliers, although customer contact and product availability are their most essential functions. Manufacturers' representatives specialise in selling, providing their suppliers with quality representation and with extensive product and market knowledge. The rep is not involved with physical distribution, leaving that burden to the manufacturers.

The central objective of channel management is to enhance the value delivered to customers through the carefully orchestrated activities of channel partners. The channel design process hinges on deep knowledge of customer needs, and the channel structure must be adjusted as customer or competitor behaviour changes. Selection and motivation of channel partners are two management tasks vital to channel success. The business marketing manager may need to apply interorganisational management techniques to resolve channel conflict. Conflict can be controlled through a variety of means, including channel-wide committees, joint goal setting, and cooperative programmes that demonstrate trust and commitment.

DISCUSSION QUESTIONS

1   Compare and contrast the five major types of marketing channels for business to business products.

2   What role do distributors play in the industrial distribution process?

3   Explain the main differences between direct and indirect channels of distribution and analyse the advantages and disadvantages of each one.

4   Why might a company choose to use more than one marketing channel?

5   Why might consumers blame intermediaries for distribution inefficiencies?

INTERNET EXERCISES

The fortunes of many manufacturers depend on their dealer network, particularly producers of construction equipment. Take a look at two such companies' websites, and examine what they say about their dealer network and parts/service support: **www.caterpillar.com** and **www.jcb.com**

1 In the context of these websites, how important to these businesses is the chosen route to market: the dealer network?

2 In terms of delivering customer service, what is the role in the marketing channel of these dealerships?

REFERENCES

Anderson, Erin A., and Trinkle, Bob, *Outsourcing the Sales Function: The Real Cost of Field Sales* (Mason, Ohio: Thomson Higher Education, 2005.

Anderson, Erin, Lodish, Leonard M., and Weitz, Barton A., "Resource Allocation in Conventional Channels," *Journal of Marketing Research* 24 (February 1987): p. 95.

Anderson, James C., and Narus, James A., "A Model of Distribution Firm and Manufacturing Firm Working Partnerships," *Journal of Marketing* 54 (January 1990): p. 56.

Corey, E. Raymond, Cespedes, Frank V., and Rangan, V. Kasturi, *Going to Market: Distribution Systems for Industrial Products* (Boston: Harvard University Press, 1989), p. 26.

Davie, Christopher, Stephenson, Tom, and Valdivieso de Uster, Maria, "Three Trends in Business-to-Business Sales," *McKinsey Quarterly* (May 2010), pp. 1–4, http://www.mckinsey.com, accessesd May 20, 2011.

Dibb, Sally, Simkin, Lyndon, Pride, Bill, and Ferrell, O.C., *Marketing Concepts & Strategies*, 6th ed. (Cengage, 2012).

Doole, Isobel, and Lowe, Robin, *International Marketing Strategy* 6th ed. (Cengage, 2012).

Elliott, Heidi, "Distributors, Make Way for the Little Guys," *Electronic Business Today* 22 (September 1996): p. 19.

Friedman, Lawrence G., *Go to Market: Advanced Techniques and Tools for Selling More Products, to More Customers, More Profitably* (Boston: Butterworth-Heinemann, 2002), p. 116.

Friedman, Lawrence G., and Furey, Timothy R., *The Channel Advantage* (Boston: Butterworth-Heinemann, 1999), p. 84.

Harper, Doug, "Councils Launch Sales Ammo," *Industrial Distribution* 80 (September 1990): pp. 27–30.

McQuiston, Daniel H., "A Conceptual Model for Building and Maintaining Relationships between Manufacturers' Reps and Their Principals," *Industrial Marketing Management* 30 (February 2001): pp. 165–181.

Morgan, Robert M., and Hunt, Shelby D., "The Commitment-Trust Theory of Relationship Marketing," *Journal of Marketing* 58 (July 1994): pp. 20–38.

Moutinho, Luiz, and Southern, Geoffrey, *Strategic Marketing Management: A process Based Approach* (Cengage, 2012).

Narus, James A. and Anderson, James C. "Turn Your Distributors into Partners," *Harvard Business Review* 64 (March–April 1986): p. 68.

O'Heir, Jeff "The Advocates: They Raised Their Voices to Legitimize the Channel," *Computer Reseller News*, June 17, 2002, p. 51.

Rangan, V. Kasturi, *Transforming Your Go-to-Market Strategy: The Three Disciplines of Channel Management* (Boston: Harvard Business Press, 2006), pp. 73–88.

Sharma, Arun, and Mehrotra, Anuj, "Choosing an Optimal Mix in Multichannel Environments," *Industrial Marketing Management* 36 (January 2007): pp. 21–28.

Tuttle, Al, "E-Collaboration: Build Trust and Success," *Industrial Distribution* 92 (June 1, 2002): p. 59.

van Weele, Arjan, *Puchasing and Supply Chain Management: Analysis Strategy, Planning and Practice*, 5th ed. (Cengage, 2010).

Verhage, Bronis J., *Marketing: A Global Perspective* (Cengage, 2013).

CHAPTER 11
SUPPLY CHAIN
MANAGEMENT

CHAPTER OBJECTIVES

When suppliers fail to deliver products or services as promised, buyers search for a new supplier. Organisational buyers assign great importance to supply chain processes that eliminate the uncertainty of product delivery. Supply chain management assures that product, information, service, and financial resources all flow smoothly through the entire value-creation process. Business marketers invest considerable financial and human resources in creating supply chains to service the needs and special requirements of their customers. After reading this chapter, you will understand:

1   The role of supply chain management in business marketing strategy

2   The importance of integrating both firms and functions throughout the entire supply chain

3   The critical role of logistics activities in achieving supply chain management goals

4   The importance of achieving high levels of logistics service performance while simultaneously controlling the cost of logistics activities

Bill Copacino, a leading strategy consultant, puts the importance of supply chain management in focus:[*]

> *In almost every industry, supply chain management has become a much more important strategic and competitive variable. It affects all of the shareholder value levers—cost, customer service, asset productivity, and revenue generation. Yet we are seeing a growing gap in performance between the leading and the average companies. The best are getting better faster than the average companies across almost every industry. The leading supply chain performers are applying new technology, new innovations, and new process thinking to great advantage. The average-performing companies and the laggards have a limited window of opportunity in which to catch up.*

Who are the leading supply chain performers? Gartner, Inc., examines this question with its annual ranking of the top 25 chains headquartered in Europe.[*] Topping the most recent list are three companies also listed in the global Garter Supply Chain Top 25—Unilever, Inditex and H & M Hennes & Mauritz.

Supply chain management (SCM) is a technique for linking a manufacturer's operations with those of all of its strategic suppliers and its key intermediaries and customers to enhance efficiency and effectiveness. Central to SCM are the coordination and collaboration activities performed with partners, which may include suppliers, intermediaries, third-party service providers, and customers.

SCM can advance a firm's financial performance in two fundamental ways: revenue enhancement and cost reduction.[*] First, by creating a more responsive supply chain to meet customer requirements and deliver on promises, successful SCM helps a company to win new customers and win more business (and increase revenue) from existing customers. Second, by integrating processes from procurement and manufacturing to logistics, successful SCM lowers costs across the entire enterprise, advancing profitability.

This chapter describes the nature of SCM, isolates the factors that lead to successful supply chain strategies, and demonstrates how logistics management is a key driver of supply chain success. Once the strategic role of SCM has been highlighted, the chapter examines how logistics processes form the core of the SCM strategy. The logistical elements are described in terms of their interface within the distribution channel and how they must be integrated to create desired customer service standards and responsive business marketing strategies.

11.1 SUPPLY CHAIN MANAGEMENT: A TOOL FOR COMPETITIVE ADVANTAGE

As business is becoming more and more competitive, purchasing and supply chain management are increasingly recognised by top managers as key business drivers. Again and again it appears that purchasing professionals and supply managers can contribute significantly not only to the company's bottom line, but also to its top line. Since most companies today spend more than half of their sales turnover on purchased parts and services, efficient and constructive relationships with suppliers are key to the company's short-term financial position and long-term competitive power.[*]

11.1.1 Supply chain management goals

SCM is both a boundary- and function-spanning endeavour. The underlying premise of SCM is that waste reduction and enhanced supply chain performance come only with both intrafirm and interfirm functional integration, sharing, and cooperation. Therefore, each firm within the supply chain must tear down functional silos and foster true coordination and integration of marketing, production, procurement, sales, and logistics. Furthermore, actions, systems, and processes among *all* the supply chain participants must be integrated and coordinated. Firm-wide integration is a necessary, but not sufficient, condition for achieving the full potential benefits of SCM. Integration must be taken to a higher plane so that functions and processes are coordinated across all the organisations in the supply chain. SCM is undertaken to achieve four major goals: waste reduction, time compression, flexible response, and unit cost reduction.[*]

Waste reduction

Firms that practise SCM seek to reduce waste by minimising duplication, harmonising operations and systems, and enhancing quality. With respect to duplication, firms at all levels in the supply chain often maintain inventories. Efficiencies can be gained for the chain as a whole if the inventories can be centralised and maintained by just a few firms at critical points in the distribution process. With a joint goal of reducing waste, supply chain partners can work together to modify policies, procedures, and data-collection practices that produce or encourage waste.[*] Typically, waste across the supply chain manifests itself in excess inventory. Effective ways to address this issue are through postponement and customisation strategies, which push the final assembly of a completed product to the last practical point in the chain. Dell provides an excellent illustration of how to reduce waste through effective "waste" management strategies. The company's build-to-order model produces a computer only when there is an actual customer order. Dell works with its suppliers to achieve a system where inventory turns are measured in hours rather than days. Because Dell does not maintain stocks of unsold finished goods, it has no need to conduct "fire sales." The result: Waste has been eliminated both on the component side and on the finished-goods side.

Time compression

Another critical goal of SCM is to compress order-to-delivery cycle time. When production and logistics processes are accomplished in less time, everyone in the supply chain is able to operate more efficiently, and a primary result is reduced inventories throughout the system. Time compression also enables supply chain partners to more easily observe and understand the cumulative effect of problems that occur anywhere in the chain and respond quickly. Reduced cycle time also speeds the cash-to-cash cycle for all chain members, enhancing cash flow and financial performance throughout the system. Time compression means that information and products flow smoothly and quickly, thus permitting all parties to respond to customers in a timely manner while maintaining minimal inventory. Many industrial distributors, like W.W. Grainger, have designed supply chains that are able to respond to customer orders with "same-day" delivery, allowing customers to reduce inventories and to rest assured that timely delivery support is available to solve unexpected problems.

Flexible response

The third goal of SCM is to develop flexible response throughout the supply chain. Flexible response in order handling, including how orders are handled, product variety, order configuration, order size, and several other dimensions, means that a customer's unique requirements can be met cost-effectively. To illustrate, a firm that responds flexibly can configure a shipment in almost any way (for example, different pallet patterns or different product assortments) and do it quickly without problems for the customer. Flexibility also may mean customising products in the warehouse to correspond to a customer's need for unique packaging and unitisation. The key to flexibility is to meet individual customer needs in a way that the customer views as cost-effective and the supply chain views as profitable.

Unit cost reduction

The final goal of SCM is to operate logistics in a manner that reduces cost per unit for the end customer. Firms must determine the level of performance the customer desires and then minimise the costs of providing that service level. The business marketer should carefully assess the balance between level of cost and the degree of service provided. The goal is to provide an appropriate value equation for the customer, meaning that cost in some cases is higher for meaningful enhancements in service. Cost cutting is not an absolute, but the SCM approach is focused on driving costs to the lowest possible level for the level of service requested. For example, shipping product in full truckload quantities weekly is less expensive than shipping pallet quantities every day; however, when a customer like Honda wants daily deliveries to minimise inventories, the SCM goal is to offer daily shipments at the lowest possible cost. SCM principles drive down costs because they focus management attention on eliminating activities that unnecessarily add cost, such as duplicate inventories, double and triple handling of the product, unconsolidated shipments, and uncoordinated promotions, such as special sales.

Hau Lee, an internationally recognised expert, points out that supply chain efficiency is necessary, but it is not enough to ensure that firms do better than their rivals. Only companies that build agile, adaptable, and aligned supply chains get ahead of the competition.[*] Efficient supply chains often become uncompetitive because they do not adapt to changes in market structures: Supply chains need to keep adapting so that they can adjust to changing customer needs. In addition, low-cost supply chains are not always able to respond to sudden and unexpected changes in markets—like a shift in resource availability or the effect of a natural disaster. Finally, excellent supply chain companies align the interests of all the firms in their supply chain with their own—if any company's interests differ from those of the other organisations in the supply chain, its actions do not maximise the chain's performance.

11.1.2 Benefits to the final customer

A well-managed supply chain ultimately creates tangible benefits for customers throughout the supply chain. When the supply chain reduces waste, improves cycle time and flexible response, and minimises costs, these benefits should flow through to ultimate customers. Thus, a key focus of the supply chain members is monitoring how much the customer is realising these important benefits and assessing what may be preventing them from doing so. A supply chain's customer can be viewed on several dimensions, and it is important to focus on each. A producer of electronic radio parts views the radio manufacturer as an absolutely critical customer, but the auto manufacturer that installs the radio in a car is equally important, if not more so, and ultimately the final buyer of the automobile must be satisfied. So, different demands, desires, and idiosyncrasies of customers all along the supply chain must be understood and managed effectively.

11.1.3 The financial benefits perspective

Innovative supply chain strategies that couple physical goods movement with financial information sharing can open the door to greater end-to-end supply chain cost savings, better balance sheets, lower total costs, higher margins, and a more stable supply chain with everyone sharing the savings.[*] When supply chain partners are achieving their goals and the benefits are flowing through to customers, supply chain members should succeed financially. The most commonly reported benefits for firms that adopt SCM are lower costs, higher profit margins, enhanced cash flow, revenue growth, and a higher rate of return on assets. Because activities are harmonised and unduplicated, the cost of transportation, order processing, order selection, warehousing, and inventory is usually reduced. A study to validate the correlation between supply chain integration and business success shows that best-practice SCM companies have a 45 per cent

INSIDE BUSINESS MARKETING

Steel Shortages at Nissan

One of the most competitive arenas in business is the relationship between automotive companies and their steel suppliers. Since steel makes up an important part of a car's cost price, and since many steel suppliers exist in the global marketplace, buyers of automotive companies are relentlessly looking for opportunities to reduce steel prices and costs. In its endeavour to pay competitive prices for steel, Nissan in Japan decided in 2004 to reduce its number of steel suppliers to just two companies: Nippon Steel and JFE Steel. By allocating its huge volume to just two suppliers, the company was able to realise considerable price reductions.

The markets for commodities like steel are characterised by supply and demand. Since the relationship between supply and demand may vary over time, the negotiation position between market parties is subject to change. Buyers' markets, where automotive manufacturers are in the lead, may change into times where supply is scarce and where, conversely, steel suppliers are in the lead. Experienced steel buyers are aware of this business cycle with its downturns and upswings. As an automotive manufacturer, you have to be careful not to upset steel suppliers in an economic downturn, since this may backfire in times when suppliers are in the lead and when you are in desperate need of certain steel volumes.

This became painfully clear to Nissan in late 2004 when, despite being Japan's second-biggest carmaker, it needed to suspend operations at three of its four domestic plants. Earlier, in September that year, Nissan introduced a series of new automotive models in Japan which, of course, required higher steel volumes. Demand for new models, including the Tiida compact car and Fuga sedan, was high and started to outstrip the company's projections. As a result Nissan sought more steel from its suppliers – Nippon Steel and JFE Steel – however both were at that time operating at full capacity to meet booming demand at home and in China and were unable to comply to Nissan's requests for delivery. Steel prices had also been rising due to tight raw material supplies and the surge in demand from the Chinese economy. Given the less attractive prices which would be paid by Nissan, both companies were not willing to change their capacity commitments at the cost of losing other more profitable customers. As a result Nissan had to skip production of over 25 000 vehicles in the next year.[*]

total supply chain cost advantage over their median supply chain competitors.[*] Cash flows are improved because the total cycle time from raw materials to finished product is reduced. The leading firms also enjoy greater cash flow—they have a cash-to-order cycle time exactly half that of the median company. On the other hand, recent evidence suggests that the stock market punishes firms that stumble in SCM. For example, one study showed that supply chain glitches can result in an 8.6 per cent drop in stock price on the day the problem is announced and up to a 20 per cent decline within 6 months.[*]

11.1.4 Information and technology drivers

Supply chains could not function at high levels of efficiency and effectiveness without powerful information systems. Many of the complex Internet supply chains maintained by companies like Hewlett-Packard and Cisco could not operate at high levels without sophisticated information networks and interactive software. The Internet—and Internet technology—is the major tool business marketers rely on to manage their lengthy and integrated systems. In addition, a host of software applications play a key role in helping a supply chain operate at peak efficiency.

Supply chain software

SCM software applications provide real-time analytical systems that manage the flow of products and information through the supply chain network.[*] Of course, many supply chain functions are coordinated, including procurement, manufacturing, transportation, warehousing, order entry, forecasting, and customer service. Much of the software is focused on each one of the different functional areas (for example, inventory planning or transportation scheduling). However, the trend is to move toward software solutions that integrate several or all of these functions. The result is that firms can work with a comprehensive "supply chain suite" of software that manages flow across the supply chain while including all of the key functional areas. Several firms producing Enterprise Resource Planning (ERP) software—such as SAP or Oracle—have developed applications that attempt to integrate functional areas and bridge gaps across the supply chain.

SCM software creates the ability to transmit data in real time and helps organisations *transform* supply chain processes into competitive advantages. Equipping employees with portable bar code scanners that feed a centralised database, FedEx is a *best-practices* leader at seamlessly integrating a variety of technologies to enhance all processes across an extended supply chain.[*] The company uses a real-time data transmission system (via the bar code scanners used for every package) to assist in routing, tracking, and delivering packages. The information recorded by the scanners is transmitted to a central database and is made available to *all* employees and customers. Each day FedEx's communications network processes nearly 400 000 customer service calls and tracks the location, pickup time, and delivery time of 2.5 million packages! FedEx is electronically linked so tightly with some customers that when the customer receives an order, FedEx's server is notified to print a shipping label, generate an internal request for pickup, and then download the label to the customer's server. The label, with all the needed customer information, is printed at the customer's warehouse and applied to the package just before FedEx picks it up. This tight electronic linkage adds significant efficiency to the customer's supply chain process and allows FedEx to deliver on its promises.[*]

11.2 SUCCESSFULLY APPLYING THE SUPPLY CHAIN MANAGEMENT APPROACH

The design of the firm's supply chain often depends on the nature of the demand for its products. Marshall Fisher suggests that products can be separated into two categories: "functional" items, like paper, maintenance supplies, and office furniture, for example; or "innovative" items, like smart phones, computer notepads, or other high-tech products. The importance of this distinction is that functional items require different supply chains than do innovative products.[*]

Functional products typically have predictable demand patterns, whereas innovative products do not. The goal for functional products is to design a supply chain with efficient physical distribution; that is, it minimises logistics and inventory costs and assures low-cost manufacturing. Here, the key information sharing takes place within the supply chain so that all participants can effectively orchestrate manufacturing, ordering, and delivery to minimise production and inventory costs.

Innovative products, on the other hand, have less predictable demand, and the key concern is reacting to short life cycles, avoiding shortages or excess supplies, and taking advantage of high profits during peak demand periods. Rather than seeking to minimise inventory, supply chain decisions centre on the questions of where to *position* inventory, along with production capacity, in order to hedge against uncertain demand. The critical task is to capture and distribute timely information on customer demand to the supply chain. When designing the supply chain, firms should concentrate on creating *efficient* processes for functional products and *responsive* processes for innovative products.

11.2.1 Successful supply chain practices

Most successful supply chains have devised approaches for participants to work together in a partnering environment. Supply chains are not effective and, in reality, are *not* supply chains

Risk Analysis by the Ministry of Defence

If a supplier does not fulfill his obligations in the realisation of complex and extensive projects, this can lead to considerable damages or loss for a military organisation. To limit the risk of problems as much as possible, the Ministries of Defence of several European countries sometimes carry out an analysis of the risks related to doing business with suppliers for strategic projects. In general, three categories of risks are distinguished:

1   Technical risk regarding the suitability/ professionalism of the management, the means of production, the skills, tools and testing equipment of the company in question for the manufacture of the required goods and services, which must meet the agreed requirements and must be delivered within the agreed term.

2   Quality risk with regard to the quality management of the company in general and the quality control system of the project in question in particular.

3   Financial risk related to the degree in which the company is considered to function soundly and effectively for the duration of the project. Of importance in this respect are: financial condition, investment elasticity and a solid financial condition in the near future.

In large and technologically complex projects the risks can be so large that additional measures and arrangements are required. These measures should consist of at least periodical preventive audits aimed at assessing the technical capacity and quality control (the so-called 'preaward survey'), to be conducted by the military; and the financial status of the company in question, to be conducted by the accounting department. This latter analysis concerns the actual and the anticipated results of the company activities (such as turnover and company results) and ratio analysis of several financial parameters (such as liquidity and solvency).[*]

when the participants are adversaries. Supply chain partnerships form the foundation. Highly effective supply chains feature integrated operations across supply chain participants, timely information sharing, and delivering added value to the customer. As testimony to the importance of supply chain partnerships, the Malcolm Baldrige National Quality Award Committee recently made "key supplier and customer partnering and communication mechanisms" a separate category that it would use to recognise the best companies in the United States.[*] In considering the economic value created across *the supply chain*, one expert observes, "You should go for the best return on net assets for the supply chain, and trade off costs between income statements and balance sheets to see that *everybody* shares in that gain."[*] For the supply chain partners to work as a unit, this enlightened perspective of collaboration is mandatory.

For the supply chain partnership to succeed, the partners need to clearly define their strategic objectives, understand where their objectives converge (and perhaps diverge), and resolve any differences.[*] Because the supply chain strategy drives all the important processes in each firm as well as those that connect the firms, managers in both organisations must participate in key decisions and support the chosen course. Once key participants specify and endorse supply chain strategies, performance metrics can be established to track how well the supply chain is meeting its common goals. The metrics used to measure performance are tied to the strategy and must be linked to the performance evaluation and reward systems for employees in each of the participating firms. Without this step, individual managers would not be motivated to accomplish the broad goals of the supply chain.

11.3 LOGISTICS AS THE CRITICAL ELEMENT IN SUPPLY CHAIN MANAGEMENT

Nowhere in business marketing strategy is SCM more important than in logistics.

Logistics management includes the management of materials planning, the supply of raw materials and other purchased goods, internal transportation, storage and physical distribution. It may also include, in some companies, reverse logistics, i.e. recycling packaging materials and surplus materials.

Effective business marketing demands efficient, systematic delivery of finished products to channel members and customers. The importance of this ability has elevated the logistics function to a place of prominence in the marketing strategy of many business marketers.

11.3.1 Distinguishing between logistics and supply chain management

Logistics is the critical element in SCM. In fact, there is considerable confusion over the difference between the discipline of SCM and logistics. As discussed, SCM is focused on the *integration of* all *business processes* that add value for customers.

The 1990s witnessed the rising importance of time-based competition, rapidly improving information technology, expanding globalisation, increasing attention to quality, and the changing face of interfirm relationships. These trends combined to cause companies to expand their perspective on logistics to include all the firms involved in creating a finished product and delivering it to the buyer or user on time and in perfect condition. For example, the supply chain for electric motors would include raw material suppliers, steel fabricators, component parts manufacturers, transportation companies, the electric motor manufacturer, the distributor of electric motors, the warehouse companies that store and ship components and finished products, and the motor's ultimate buyer. Figure 11.1 graphically depicts such a supply chain. The SCM concept is an integrating philosophy for coordinating the total flow of a supply channel from supplier to ultimate user. Logistics is critical, however, to business marketers, because regardless of the orientation to the entire supply chain, the firm relies on its logistics system to deliver product in a timely, low-cost manner.

11.3.2 Managing flows

The significance of the supply chain perspective in logistical management is that the business marketing manager focuses attention on the performance of *all participants* in the supply chain.

FIGURE 11.1 **Supply chain for electric motors**

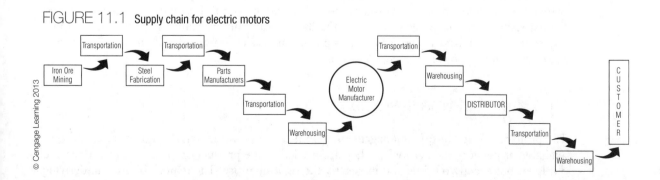

The manager also coordinates their efforts to enhance the timely delivery of the finished product to the ultimate user at the lowest possible cost. Inherent in the supply chain approach is the need to form close *relationships* with the supply chain participants, including vendors, transportation suppliers, warehousing companies, and distributors. The focus of logistics in the SCM for business marketers is the *flow of product* through the supply chain, with *timely information* driving the entire process.

Product flow in the reverse direction is also important in business supply chains. Many companies, like Xerox and Canon, routinely remanufacture products that are worn out or obsolete. Effective linkages and processes must be in place to return such products to a facility in order to remanufacture or retrofit them. If the reverse supply chains are operating effectively, companies can sometimes realise higher margins on the remanufactured products than they do on new items.*

11.4 THE STRATEGIC ROLE OF LOGISTICS

In the past, logistics was viewed simply as a cost of doing business but today, many companies view logistics as a critical strategic weapon that can add value to customer relationships. For many business marketers, logistics is their *primary* marketing tool for gaining and maintaining competitive superiority. These firms typically recognise that logistics performance is an important part of marketing strategy, and they exploit their logistics competencies. Companies that incorporate logistics planning and management into long-term business strategies can achieve significant benefits, which create real value for the company. To illustrate, Nucor Steel enjoys strong customer loyalty because it can deliver steel to a construction site within a 2- to 4-hour window and offload the truck in the sequence in which the steel beams will be used on the job! This advantage is significant because storage space is limited at most construction sites in urban areas. This strong value-added service allows Nucor to achieve higher levels of profitability than its competitors.

11.4.1 Sales-marketing-logistics integration

The rising value of logistics as a strategic marketing weapon has fostered the integration of the sales, marketing, and logistics functions of many business marketers. In progressive firms, unified teams of sales, production, logistics, information systems, and marketing personnel develop integrated logistics programmes to offer to potential customers. Teams of specialists from each area make sales calls and tailor logistics solutions to customer problems. United Stationers, one of the largest U.S. office products distributors, brings operations and salespeople together to meet with the company's resellers in an effort to create customer-responsive logistics service. As a result of its efforts, United guarantees customers that orders placed by 7:00 p.m. will be received before noon on the following day. Customers can dial into United's mainframe computer and place orders electronically. The company considers all of its logistics personnel to be part of the sales function. Some firms have taken the integration even further. Baxter Healthcare warehouse workers team up with warehouse personnel at the hospitals that Baxter serves. During visits to the customer warehouse, the Baxter warehouser evaluates the operation, looking for ways to improve packing so that shipments are easier to unload and unpack. As a result, Baxter warehousers have become salespeople.

11.4.2 Just-in-time systems

The principle of **just-in-time management** (JIT) means that all materials and products become available at the very moment when they are needed in the production process, not sooner and not later, but exactly on time and in exactly the right quantity. The major objective underlying this approach is to continuously tackle and solve manufacturing bottlenecks within, and interface problems between, consecutive steps in the supply chain processes. Incoming inspection, buffer stock, and extensive quality control procedures on incoming materials are primarily considered as 'waste'. The basic idea is to strive continuously to reduce and eliminate these often 'hidden' costs in the factory.

JIT implies that nothing is produced if there is no demand. The production process is 'pulled' by customer orders. The 'customer' is in fact the organisational entity which is 'next-in-line'. This concept, therefore, may relate to other departments within the company itself. However, it may also relate to external customers, outside the organisation. When no customer orders have been received, manufacturing activities will come to an end and the spare time is used to do minor repairs/maintenance, housekeeping or prepare for materials planning. The spare time may also be used to discuss how to improve on the work currently being conducted within the organisational entity ('small group activities'). No production, therefore, does not imply that the time is used unproductively.

Because they contract out a considerable amount of work, many large Japanese producers work closely with a limited number of suppliers (which are sometimes organised in supplier networks or supplier associations). The bulk of the materials requirements are sourced from these suppliers. It is not uncommon that one manufacturer is responsible for more than 50 per cent of a supplier's turnover. At the same time this same supplier may deliver 80 per cent of the manufacturer's specific materials requirements. This leads, in contrast to many European manufacturers, to a large interdependence between manufacturers and suppliers. As a result Japanese manufacturers are able to benefit much more from the supplier's expertise and capabilities. Another aspect is that Japanese manufacturers in general focus on assembly only. All component manufacturing is outsourced to specialised suppliers. Since the producer frequently represents a large share of the supplier's turnover, a maximum effort by the supplier is ensured. Obviously, there is some risk involved for suppliers when engaging in this type of relationship: if there is no market demand for the customer's product, there will be less work for the supplier. In this way part of the business's economic risk is transferred to the suppliers. However, if the producer can guarantee a certain production volume for a number of years, it becomes appealing for the supplier to invest in new technology. Japanese supplier relations, generally, are characterised by their long-term orientation (3 to 5-year contracts).*

Elements of a logistical system

Table 11.1 presents the controllable variables of a logistical system. Almost no decision on a particular logistical activity can be made without evaluating its effect on other areas. The system of warehouse facilities, inventory commitments, order-processing methods, and transportation linkages determines the supplier's ability to provide timely product availability to customers. As a result of poor supplier performance, customers may have to bear the extra cost of higher inventories, institute expensive priority-order-expediting systems, develop secondary supply sources, or, worst of all, turn to another supplier.

11.4.3 Total-cost approach

In the management of logistical activities, two performance variables must be considered: (1) total distribution costs and (2) the level of logistical service provided to customers. The logistical system must be designed and administered to achieve that combination of cost and service levels that yields maximum profits. Logistical costs vary widely for business marketers, depending on the nature of the product and on the importance of logistical service to the buyer. Logistical costs can consume 16 to 36 per cent of each sales euro at the manufacturing level, and logistical activities can consume more than 40 per cent of total assets. Thus, logistics can have a significant effect on corporate profitability. How, then, can the marketer manage logistical costs?

TABLE 11.1   Controllable elements in a logistics system

Elements	Key Aspects
Customer service	The "product" of logistics activities, *customer service* relates to the effectiveness in creating time and place utility. The level of customer service provided by the supplier has a direct impact on total cost, market share, and profitability.
Order processing	Order processing triggers the logistics process and directs activities necessary to deliver products to customers. Speed and accuracy of order processing affect costs and customer service levels.
Logistics communication	Information exchanged in the distribution process guides the activities of the system. It is the vital link between the firm's logistics system and its customers.
Transportation	The physical movement of products from source of supply through production to customers is the most significant cost area in logistics, and it involves selecting modes and specific carriers as well as routing.
Warehousing	Providing storage space serves as a buffer between production and use. Warehousing may be used to enhance service and to lower transportation costs.
Inventory control	Inventory is used to make products available to customers and to ensure the correct mix of products is at the proper location at the right time.
Packaging	The role of packaging is to provide protection to the product, to maintain product identity throughout the logistics process, and to create effective product density.
Materials handling	Materials handling increases the speed of, and reduces the cost of, picking orders in the warehouse and moving products between storage and the transportation carriers. It is a cost-generating activity that must be controlled.
Production planning	Utilised in conjunction with logistics planning, production planning ensures that products are available for inventory in the correct assortment and quantity.
Plant and warehouse location	Strategic placement of plants and warehouses increases customer service and reduces the cost of transportation.

Source: Adapted from James R. Stock and Douglas M. Lambert, *Strategic Logistics Management*, 5th ed. (Homewood, IL: McGraw-Hill, 2000).

The **total-cost,** or trade-off, **approach** to logistical management guarantees to minimise total logistical costs in the firm and within the channel. The assumption is that costs of individual logistical activities are interactive; that is, a decision about one logistical variable affects all or some of the others. Management is thus concerned with the efficiency of the entire system rather than with minimising the cost of any single logistical activity. The interactions among logistical activities (that is, transportation, inventory, warehousing) are described as cost trade-offs because a cost increase in one activity is traded for a large cost decrease in another activity, the net result being an overall cost reduction.

11.5 CALCULATING LOGISTICS COSTS

11.5.1 Activity-based costing

The activity-based costing (ABC) technique is used to precisely measure the costs of performing specific activities and then trace those costs to the products, customers, and channels that consumed the activities.[*] This is a powerful tool in managing the logistics operations of a supply chain. ABC provides a mechanism to trace the cost of performing logistics services for the customers that use these services, making it easier to assess the appropriate level of customer service to offer. Firms using ABC analysis can obtain more accurate information about how a particular customer or a specific product contributes to overall profitability.[*]

11.5.2 Total cost of ownership

Total cost of ownership (TCO) determines the total costs of acquiring and then using a given item from a particular supplier. The approach identifies costs—often buried in overhead or general expenses—that relate to the costs of holding inventory, poor quality, and delivery failure.[*] A buyer using TCO explicitly considers the costs that the supplier's logistics system either added to, or eliminated from, the purchase price and would take a long-term perspective in evaluating cost.[*] Thus, a supplier particularly efficient at logistics might be able to reduce the buyer's inventory costs and the buyer's expenses of inspecting inbound merchandise. As a result, the total cost of ownership from that supplier would be lower than the cost from other suppliers that were not able to rapidly deliver undamaged products. Increasing acceptance of the TCO approach will cause logistics efficiency to become an even more critical element of a business marketer's strategy.

11.6 BUSINESS-TO-BUSINESS LOGISTICAL SERVICE

Many studies have shown that logistics service is often just as important as product quality as a measure of supplier performance. In many industries, a quality product at a competitive price is a given, so customer service is the key differentiator among competitors. In one industry, for example, purchasing managers begin the buying process by calling suppliers with the best delivery service to see whether they are willing to negotiate prices. Because it is so important to customers, reliable logistics service can lead to higher market share and higher profits. A study by Bain and Company showed that companies with superior logistics service grow 8 per cent faster, collect a 7 per cent price premium, and are 12 times as profitable as firms with inferior service levels.[*] These facts, together with the extensive spread of just-in-time manufacturing, make it clear that logistical service is important to organisational buyers.

Logistical service relates to the availability and delivery of products to the customer. It comprises the series of sales-satisfying activities that begin when the customer places the order and that end when the product is delivered. Responsive logistical service satisfies customers and creates the opportunity for closer and more profitable buyer-seller relationships.[*] Logistical service includes whatever aspects of performance are important to the business customer (Table 11.2). These service elements range from delivery time to value-added services, and each of these elements can affect production processes, final product output, costs, or all three.

11.6.1 Logistics service impacts on the customer

Supplier logistical service translates into product availability. For a manufacturer to produce or for a distributor to resell, industrial products must be available at the right time, at the right place, and in usable condition. The longer the supplier's delivery time, the less available the product; the more inconsistent the delivery time, the less available the product. For example, a reduction in the supplier's delivery time permits a buyer to hold less inventory because needs can be met rapidly. The customer reduces the risk that the production process will be interrupted. Consistent delivery enables the buyer to programme more effectively—or routinise—the purchasing process, thus lowering buyer costs. Consistent delivery-cycle performance allows

TABLE 11.2 Common elements of logistics service

Elements	Description
Delivery time	The time from the creation of an order to the fulfilment and delivery of that order encompasses both order-processing time and delivery or transportation time.
Delivery reliability	The most frequently used measure of logistics service, delivery reliability focuses on the capability of having products available to meet customer demand.
Order accuracy	The degree to which items received conform to the specification of the order. The key dimension is the incidence of orders shipped complete and without error.
Information access	The firm's ability to respond to inquiries about order status and product availability.
Damage	A measure of the physical conditions of the product when received by the buyer.
Ease of doing business	A range of factors, including the ease with which orders, returns, credits, billing, and adjustments are handled.
Value-added services	Such features as packaging, which facilitates customer handling, or other services such as prepricing and drop shipments.

Source: Reprinted with permission from Jonathon L. S. Byrnes, William C. Copacino, and Peter Metz, "Forge Service into a Weapon with Logistics," *Transportation and Distribution*, Presidential Issue 28 (September 1987): p. 46.

buyers to cut their level of buffer or safety stock, thereby reducing inventory cost. However, for many business products, such as those that are low in unit value and relatively standardised, the overriding concern is not inventory cost but simply having the products. A malfunctioning €0.71 bearing could shut down a whole production line.

11.6.2 Determining the level of service

Buyers often rank logistics service right behind "quality" as a criterion for selecting a vendor. However, not all products or all customers require the same level of logistical service. Many made-to-order products—such as heavy machinery—have relatively low logistical service requirements. Others, such as replacement parts, components, and subassemblies, require extremely demanding logistical performance. Similarly, customers may be more or less responsive to varying levels of logistical service.

Profitable levels of service

In developing a logistical service strategy, business marketing strategists should assess the profit impact of the service options that they provide to customers. In nearly all industries, firms provide numerous supply chain services such as next-day delivery, customised handling, and specialised labelling. However, few companies actually trace the true costs of specialised services and the resulting effect on customer profitability.

To combat this unhealthy situation, some companies are now using *cost-to-serve* analytics to address the problem; among them are Dow Chemical, Eastman Chemical, and Georgia-Pacific (GP). GP used total-delivered-cost analysis to improve the performance of a major customer account.[*] By incorporating cost-to-serve data into the calculation of gross margin, GP's supply chain team determined that the costs to provide this customer with expedited transportation and distribution services were significantly reducing the account's profitability. In a top-to-top meeting with the customer, GP used the data to expose the root causes of the high costs and poor service, which included last-minute, uncoordinated promotional planning and purchasing across the customer's major business units and the customer's unwillingness to share inventory levels and positioning. Once confronted with the data, customers are often willing to collaborate on ways to improve service, reduce costs, and restore profitability.

To recap, service levels are developed by assessing customer service requirements. The sales and cost of various service levels are analysed to find the service level generating the highest profits. The needs of various customer segments dictate various logistical system configurations. For example, when logistical service is critical, industrial distributors can provide the vital product availability, whereas customers with less rigorous service demands can be served from factory inventories.

11.6.3 Logistics impacts on other supply chain participants

A supplier's logistical system directly affects a distributor's ability to control cost and service to end users. Delivery time influences not only the customer's inventory requirements but also the operations of channel members. If a supplier provides erratic delivery service to distributors, the distributor is forced to carry higher inventory in order to provide a satisfactory level of product availability to end users.

Inefficient logistics service to the distributors either increases distributor costs (larger inventories) or creates shortages of the supplier's products at the distributor level. Neither result is good. In the first instance, distributor loyalty and marketing efforts will suffer; in the second, end users will eventually change suppliers. In some industries, distributors are expanding their role in the logistics process, which makes them even more valuable to their suppliers and customers. In the chemical industry, for example, the role of distributors is completely transforming as they offer logistics solutions—JIT delivery, repackaging, inventory management—to their customers.[*] The logistics expertise distributors provide enables their vendors (manufacturers) to focus on their own core competencies of production and marketing.

11.7 BUSINESS-TO-BUSINESS LOGISTICAL MANAGEMENT

The elements of logistics strategy are part of a system, and as such, each affects every other element. The proper focus is the total-cost view. Although this section treats the decisions on facilities, transportation, and inventory separately, these areas are so intertwined that decisions in one area influence the others.

11.7.1 Logistical facilities

The strategic development of a warehouse provides the business marketer with the opportunity to increase the level of delivery service to buyers, reduce transportation costs, or both. Business firms that distribute repair, maintenance, and operating supplies often find that the only way to achieve desired levels of delivery service is to locate warehouses in key markets. The warehouse circumvents the need for premium transportation (air freight) and costly order processing by keeping products readily available in local markets.

Serving other supply chain members

The nature of the business-to-business (B2B) supply chain affects the warehousing requirements of a supplier. Manufacturers' representatives do not hold inventory, but distributors do. When manufacturers' reps are used, the supplier often requires a significant number of strategically located warehouses. On the other hand, a supply chain using distributors offsets the need for warehousing.

Obviously, local warehousing by the distributor is a real service to the supplier. A few well-located supplier warehouses may be all that is required to service the distributors effectively.

Outsourcing the warehousing function

Operating costs, service levels, and investment requirements are essential considerations regarding the type of warehouse to use. The business firm may either operate its own warehouses or turn them over to a "third party"—a company that specialises in performing warehousing services. The advantages of third-party warehousing are flexibility, reduced assets, and professional management—the firm can increase or decrease its use of space in a given market, move into or out of any market quickly, and enjoy an operation managed by specialists. Third-party warehousing may sometimes supplement or replace distributors in a market.

Many third-party warehouses provide a variety of logistical services for their clients, including packaging, labelling, order processing, and some light assembly. Saddle Creek Corporation, a third-party warehouse company based in Lakeland, Florida, maintains warehouse facilities in a number of major markets. Clients can position inventories in all these markets while dealing with only one firm. Also, Saddle Creek can link its computer with the suppliers' computers to facilitate order processing and inventory updating. The Saddle Creek warehouse also repackages products to the end-user's order, labels, and arranges for local delivery. A business marketer can ship standard products in bulk to the Saddle Creek warehouse—gaining transportation economies—and still enjoy excellent customer delivery service. The public or contract warehouse is a feasible alternative to the distributor channel when the sales function can be economically executed either with a direct sales force or with reps.

11.7.2 Transportation

Transportation is usually the largest single logistical expense, and with continually rising fuel costs, its importance will probably increase. Typically, the transportation decision involves evaluating and selecting both a mode of transportation and the individual carrier(s) that will ensure the best performance at the lowest cost. Mode refers to the type of carrier—rail, truck, water, air, or some combination of the four. Individual carriers are evaluated on rates and delivery performance.[*] The supply chain view is important in selecting individual carriers. Carriers become an integral part of the supply chain, and close relationships are important. One study found evidence that carriers' operating performance improved when they were more involved in the relationship between buyer and seller.[*] By further integrating carriers into the supply chain, the entire supply chain can improve its competitive position. In this section we consider: (1) the role of transportation in industrial supply chains and (2) the criteria for evaluating transportation options.

Transportation and logistical service

A business marketer must be able to effectively move finished inventory between facilities to channel intermediaries and to customers. The transportation system is the link that binds the logistical network together and ultimately results in timely delivery of products. Efficient warehousing does not enhance customer service levels if transportation is inconsistent or inadequate.

Effective transportation service may be used in combination with warehouse facilities and inventory levels to generate the required customer service level, or it may be used in place of them. Inventory maintained in a variety of market-positioned warehouses can be consigned to one centralised warehouse when rapid transportation services exist to deliver products from the central location to business customers. Xerox is one company that uses premium airfreight service to offset the need for high inventories and extensive warehouse locations. The decision on transportation modes and particular carriers depends on the cost trade-offs and service capabilities of each. It is interesting that in the age of next-day delivery and express airfreight services, barges that weave their way through a maze of rivers, lakes, and channels are thriving.[*] A barge trip that takes 17 hours would take a train 4 hours and a truck 90 minutes for a similar trip. Although very slow (averaging 15 miles per hour), the barge offers huge cost advantages compared with truck and rail. For products such as limestone, coal, farm products, and petroleum, the slow and unglamorous barge is an effective logistics tool.

Transportation performance criteria

Cost of service is the variable cost of moving products from origin to destination, including any terminal or accessory charges. The cost of service may range from as little as €0.0075 per tonne-mile via water to as high as €0.375 per tonne-mile via airfreight. The important aspect of selecting the transportation mode is not cost per se but cost relative to the objective to be achieved. Bulk raw materials generally do not require prepaid delivery service, so the cost of anything other than rail or water transportation could not be justified. On the other hand, although airfreight may be almost 10 times more expensive than motor freight, the cost is inconsequential to a customer who needs an emergency shipment of spare parts. The cost of premium (faster) transportation modes may be justified by the resulting inventory reductions.

Speed of service refers to the elapsed time to move products from one facility (plant or warehouse) to another facility (warehouse or customer plant). Again, speed of service often overrides cost. Rail, a relatively slow mode used for bulk shipments, requires inventory buildups at the supplier's factory and at the destination warehouse. The longer the delivery time, the more inventory customers must maintain to service their needs while the shipment is in transit. The slower modes involve lower variable costs for product movement, yet they result in lower service levels and higher investments in inventory. The faster modes produce just the opposite effect. Not only must a comparison be made between modes in terms of service but various carriers within a mode must be evaluated on their "door-to-door" delivery time.

Service consistency is usually more important than average delivery time, and all modes of transportation are not equally consistent. Although air provides the lowest average delivery time, generally it has the highest variability in delivery time relative to the average. The wide variations in modal service consistency are particularly critical in business marketing planning. The choice of transportation mode must be made on the basis of cost, average transit time, and consistency if effective customer service is to be achieved.

In summary, because business buyers often place a premium on effective and consistent delivery service, the choice of transportation mode is an important one—one where cost of service is often secondary. However, the best decision on transportation carriers results from a balancing of service, variable costs, and investment requirements. The manager must also consider the transportation requirements of ordinary, versus expedited (rush order), shipments.

11.7.3 Inventory management

Inventory management is the buffer in the logistical system. Inventories are needed in business channels because:

1 Production and demand are not perfectly matched;

2 Operating deficiencies in the logistical system often result in product unavailability (for example, delayed shipments, inconsistent carrier performance);

3 Business customers cannot predict their product needs with certainty (for example, because a machine may break down or there may be a sudden need to expand production).

Inventory may be viewed in the same light as warehouse facilities and transportation: It is an alternative method for providing the level of service customers require, and the level of inventory is determined on the basis of cost, investment, service required, and anticipated revenue.

Quality focus: Eliminate inventories

Today's prevalent total-quality-management techniques and just-in-time management principles emphasise the reduction or outright elimination of inventories. Current thinking suggests that inventories exist because of inefficiencies in the system: Erratic delivery, poor forecasting, and ineffective quality-control systems all force companies to hold excessive stocks to protect themselves from delivery, forecasting, and product failure. Instead, improved delivery, forecasting, and manufacturing processes should eliminate the need to buffer against failures and uncertainty. Information technology involving bar coding, scanner data, total quality processes, better transportation management, and more effective information flow among firms in the supply chain have made it possible to control inventories more carefully and reduce them to the lowest possible levels.

The Internet connectivity that unites the supply chain from an information standpoint has permitted substantial inventory reductions in several industries. One recent study showed that average inventory turnover for manufacturers has increased from 8 to more than 12 times per year.[*] Much of the credit for this improvement is attributed to more information sharing among the supply chain members, sophisticated inventory management software, and generally higher levels of supply chain coordination. Successful business marketing managers must develop quality processes that in themselves reduce or eliminate the need to carry large inventories, while coordinating and integrating a supply chain system that can function effectively with almost no inventory.

11.7.4 Third-party logistics

Using **third-party logistics firms** to perform logistics activities represents an important trend among business-to-business firms. These external firms perform a wide range of logistics functions traditionally performed within the organisation. Most companies use some type of third-party firm, whether for transportation, warehousing, or information processing. The strategic decision to outsource logistics is often made by top management. The functions the third-party company performs can encompass the entire logistics process or selected activities within that process. Third parties can perform the warehousing; they may perform the transportation function (for example, a truck line like Schneider National); or they may perform the entire logistics process from production scheduling to delivery of finished products to the customer (for example, Ryder Dedicated Logistics). Third parties enable a manufacturer or distributor to concentrate on its core business while enjoying the expertise and specialisation of a professional logistics company. The results are often lower costs, better service, improved asset utilisation, increased flexibility, and access to leading-edge technology. Recently, some firms have advocated the use of "Fourth-Party Logistics"—firms that own no assets but serve to manage several third parties that are employed to perform various logistics functions.[*]

Despite the advantages of third-party logistics firms, some firms are cautious because of reduced control over the logistics process, diminished direct contact with customers, and the problems of terminating internal operations. In analysing the most effective and efficient way to accomplish logistics cost and service objectives, the business marketing manager should carefully consider the benefits and drawbacks of outsourcing part or all logistics functions to third-party providers. In an interesting application of third-party logistics, Caterpillar (the manufacturer of earthmoving equipment) formed a logistics services company to manage the parts distribution for other manufacturers.[*] The company applies the knowledge gained from its own experiences in distributing 300 families of products that require over 530 000 spare parts. Caterpillar transfers knowledge from the company's internal operations to customers and vice versa.

Towards a sustainable environment: 'People, planet, profit'

Corporate social responsibility today is a prime topic on the agenda of many top managers. In 2007 the Dutch minister of Healthcare and Environmental Policy announced that all purchases

INSIDE BUSINESS MARKETING

Zara's Global Stretch: One Size Fits All?

Thanks to this unrivalled capability for delivering the goods (or 'instant fashion' as it has been dubbed), Zara, the clothing wing of Spain's Inditex, has beaten the odds to become a leading international brand. By mid-2011, Zara's value was estimated at a staggering €32 billion; impressive for a company founded on a mere €30! Its designs have even attracted a blossoming style icon, the UK's Duchess of Cambridge, who was spotted in a £49.95 blue dress from Zara shortly after her globally televised royal wedding. Meanwhile Harvard Business School has praised the company in a recent study for putting the customer-focused approach to operations.

The fashion giant's marketing success is based on the *vertical integration* of design, 'just-in-time' production, delivery and sales through a fast-expanding chain of trendy stores offering affordable fashion in hot demand regionally. This achievement comes at a time when low-cost Chinese imports increasingly challenge the European fashion business. And although – when it comes to marketing inexpensive fashion products in the casual wear retail sector – speed is vital, the 'one size fits all' principle does not apply. Instead, Zara relies on one of the most successful logistics operations on the globe to match supply with demand.

About three hundred young designers, most of them recruited straight from the world's best design schools, work at the company's headquarters in La Coruña in Galicia, a relatively deprived area in the north of Spain. The designers keep in regular touch with Zara store managers – who hold frequent staff meetings to discuss local trends –to determine the bestsellers and customer preferences. The garments are then produced, mostly in Spain, Portugal and Morocco, which Inditex calls its 'proximity'. The logistical efficiency allows Zara more flexibility. The chosen textiles are prepared domestically, then transported to local co-operatives, where the clothes are stitched together. Finally, the finished products are shipped across Europe and globally by truck or plane. Limited batches prevent any unnecessary surplus stock and increase customers' perceived exclusivity of the items. When lines are sold out, they are substituted rapidly with fresh alternatives instead of 'more of the same' stock. It's the ultimate marketing technique to attract frequent shoppers to the stores. European customers, in fact, visit Zara stores an average of seventeen times a year, nearly six times as much as other fashion stores.

To put this into perspective, Hennes & Mauritz (H&M) of Sweden launches about 3000 new items per year; Zara, meanwhile, produces around 11 000 – nearly four times this. A new Zara product is delivered to stores within five weeks after its design; for a new version of an existing model, the required time is reduced to only four-teen days. Thanks to this effective method of fine-tuning the new product development process, all store managers actually influence the designs that the company will introduce. It also prevents Zara from having to discount slow-selling products, as is common among other retailers. And by spending only about 10 per cent of what most competitors spend on IT, and less than 0.3 per cent of sales revenues on advertising (as opposed to an average of 4 per cent spent by its rivals), Zara manages to keep its retail prices low.

Today, only about one-third of the company's production – mostly basic products – is outsourced to Asia. Hence, the company is not affected as much by Asia's rising costs. But Zara still is a global company: it has over five thousand stores in about eighty nations, sixty per cent of them in Europe. Zara's marketing approach, sometimes referred to as an *oil stain strategy*, involves opening a few test stores in a new country first, to develop a better insight into local consumers, before further penetrating that particular market. It should be noted, however, that Zara sells the same products in various countries for different prices. The same products will cost nearly twice as much in Western Europe as in Japan, for example. Experts wonder how much longer Zara can continue to do this, especially now that it is increasing its *online* sales across the world.[*]

made by the government from 2010 need to meet sustainable and environmental requirements. The intention is clear, but a major question is how to define sustainable purchasing. What does the government actually mean when they refer to corporate social responsibility and responsible purchasing?

Sustainability seems to be used as a general, container concept. It clearly has different aspects. Most of the time it is referred to as corporate social responsibility (CSR). Sometimes it is referred to as sustainability. The idea is to develop business solutions in such a way that requirements of the current world population are met without doing harm to the needs of future generations. This is a far from simple issue. Sustainable development is aimed at developing a better world. Sustainable purchasing, therefore, is about buying for a better future world. These concepts today are widely adopted by the Western world. As a consequence, companies just going for their economic benefits only are not accepted by the general public any more. The traditional *shareholder* focus had made way for a *stakeholder* focus which has a much wider scope. Sustainable profitability can only be achieved if the company is able to balance the interests of customers, employees, the environment, and its shareholders, i.e. serving the needs of 'People, Planet, Profit'. This idea was expressed by Carroll (1991) in his famous sustainability pyramid.

For this reason large companies pay a lot of attention to sustainability. A company like DSM, for example, articulated some years ago as a major objective developing a top position in chemical industry on the issue of sustainability. This can be understood, if one considers the environmental damage that is usually caused by this type of company. As these chemical companies have now become very visible to the general public, they need to pay attention to environmental concerns. In their corporate social responsibility policies they pay interest to three major stakeholders: 'People, Planet, Profit'.

The 'People' aspect includes all activities that are focused on providing good labour conditions to employees and a labour climate in which individual employees are able to develop their skills and competencies. This explains the great interest today for safety, health, and environment (SHE) within companies and suppliers. The 'Planet' aspect includes all activities that are focused on an efficient use of natural sources of energy, raw materials and of other natural resources. Waste disposal, reuse of scrap and surplus materials, and reverse logistics are part of the 'Planet' aspect. The 'Profit' aspect provides guidelines for sustainable financial development of a company, measured over a longer period of time. When improving profitability, the idea is that the company keeps a good eye on the interests of all stakeholders concerned, like customers, shareholders, employees and suppliers. For a bank like Treodos Bank, this may imply that investments are only made in companies that offer sustainable solutions to the environment. Investing in heavy polluting industries, or companies that manufacture weapons for the defence industry may not be in line with the bank's sustainability principles.

The basic idea is that business decisions are continuously tested against these three principles. Another company which has paid attention to sustainability is TNT Post (see memo 17.2). In 2006 this company started to operate two new Boeing 747 airplanes, to allow for a weekly transport schedule between the Far East and Europe. As a result of this decision, the fuel consumption of the company almost doubled! How do you explain this to your stakeholders? How do you communicate this message to your employees? Peter Bakker, the CEO of TNT, is of the opinion that there is only one option: you need to demonstrate that TNT acts responsibly in its operations by showing that the company pursues the best possible efficiency in its business operations with regard to the use of fossil fuels and energy. As the memo shows, TNT actively takes responsibility for managing its supply chain and imposing sustainability requirements on its suppliers and other business partners.

SUMMARY

Leading business marketing firms demonstrate superior capabilities in supply chain management. SCM focuses on improving the flow of products, information, and services as they move from origin to destination. A key driver to SCM is coordination and integration among all the participants in the supply chain, primarily through sophisticated information systems and management software. Reducing waste, minimising duplication, reducing cost, and enhancing service are the major objectives of SCM. Firms successful at managing the supply chain understand the nature of their products and the type of supply chain structure required to meet the needs of their customers. In particular, effective supply chains integrate operations, share information, and above all, provide added value to customers.

Logistics is the critical function in the firm's supply chain because logistics directs the flow and storage of products and information. Successful supply chains synchronise logistics with other functions such as production, procurement, forecasting, order management, and customer service. The systems perspective in logistical management cannot be stressed enough—it is the only way to assure management that the logistical function meets prescribed goals. Not only must each logistical variable be analysed in terms of its effect on every other variable but the sum of the variables must be evaluated in light of the service level provided to customers. Logistics elements throughout the supply chain must be integrated to assure smooth product flow. Logistical service is critical in the buyer's evaluation of business marketing firms and generally ranks second only to product quality as a desired supplier characteristic.

Logistics decisions must be based on cost trade-offs among the logistical variables and on comparisons of the costs and revenues associated with alternative levels of service. The optimal system produces the highest profitability relative to the capital investment required. Three major variables—facilities, transportation, and inventory—form the basis of logistical decisions B2B logistics managers face. The business marketer must monitor the effect of logistics on all supply chain members and on overall supply chain performance. Finally, the strategic role of logistics should be carefully evaluated: Logistics can often provide a strong competitive advantage.

DISCUSSION QUESTIONS

1 Describe how firms that practice SCM can reduce waste.

2 How does a best-practices leader such as FedEx use technology to support its SCM?

3 Give an example of how logistics service can impact the customer in a B2B relationship.

4 Why might transportation by barge be a more popular logistical tool than an express airfreight service for a company selling limestone?

5 What are the benefits and drawbacks of employing third-party logistics firms?

INTERNET EXERCISES

1 Take a look at the website of David Watson Transport, a UK-based transportation company. Discuss what types of B2B Company might use David Watson Transport; and what types of B2B company might not.

REFERENCES

Bowman, Robert J., "Does Wall Street Really Care about the Supply Chain?" *Global Logistics and Supply Chain Strategies* (April 2001): pp. 31–35.

Boyson, Sandor, and Corsi, Thomas, "The Real-Time Supply Chain," *Supply Chain Management Review* 5 (January–February 2001): p. 48.

Brewer, Peter C., and Speh, Thomas W., "Using the Balanced Scorecard to Measure Supply Chain Performance," *Journal of Business Logistics* (Spring 2000): p. 75.

Brewer, Peter C. and Speh, Thomas W., "Adapting the Balanced Scorecard to Supply Chain Management," *Supply Chain Management Review* 5 (March–April 2001): p. 49.

Copacino, Bill, "Supply Chain Challenges: Building Relationships," *Harvard Business Review* 81 (July 2003): p. 69.

Dibb, Sally, Simkin, Lyndon, Pride, Bill, and Ferrell, O.C., *Marketing Concepts & Strategies*, 6th ed. (Cengage, 2012).

Doole, Isobel, and Lowe, Robin, *International Marketing Strategy* 6th ed. (Cengage, 2012).

Drakšaite, Aura, and Snieška, Vytautas, "Advanced Cost Saving Strategies of Supply Chain Management in Global Markets," *Economics and Management* (2008): p. 113

Ellram, Lisa, "Activity-Based Costing and Total Cost of Ownership: A Critical Linkage," *Journal of Cost Management* 8 (Winter 1995): p. 22.

Ferguson, Brad, "Implementing Supply Chain Management," *Production and Inventory Management Journal* (Second Quarter, 2000): p. 64.

Ferrin, Bruce and Plank, Richard E., "Total Cost of Ownership Models: An Exploratory Study," *Journal of Supply Chain Management* 38 (Summer 2002): p. 18.

Fisher, Marshall, "What Is the Right Supply Chain for Your Product?" *Harvard Business Review* 75 (March–April 1997): p. 106.

Foster, Thomas A., "Time to Learn the ABCs of Logistics," *Logistics* (February 1999): p. 67.

Gamble, Richard H., "Financing Supply Chains," http://businessfinancemag.com (June 2002): p. 35.

"Garter Announces Ranking of Top European Supply Chain Organizations for 2012", September 18, 2012, Garter, accessed at http://www.gartner.com/newsroom/id/2163615 on August 21, 2013

Holcomb, Mary Collins, "Customer Service Measurement: A Methodology for Increasing Customer Value through Utilization of the Taguchi Strategy," *Journal of Business Logistics* 15 (1, 1994): p. 29.

Kahl, Steven, "What's the 'Value' of Supply Chain Software?" *Supply Chain Management Review* 3 (Winter 1999): p. 61.

LaLonde, Bernard J., and Pohlen, Terrance L., "Issues in Supply Chain Costing," *International Journal of Logistics Management* 7 (1, 1996): p. 3.

Lee, Hau L., "The Triple-A Supply Chain," *Harvard Business Review* 82 (October 2004): pp. 102–112.

Liker, Jeffrey K., and Choi, Thomas Y., "Building Deep Supplier Relationships," *Harvard Business Review* 82 (December 2004): p. 104.

Marsh, Peter, "A Moving Story of Spare Parts," *The Financial Times*, August 29, 1997, p. 8.

Mathews, Anna Wilde, "Jet-Age Anomalies, Slowpoke Barges Do Brisk Business," *The Wall Street Journal*, May 15, 1998, p. B1.

Maurer, Andreas, Wieland, Sandra, Wallenburg, Carl Marcus, and Springinklee, Martin, "Achieving Supply Chain Advantage," November 2010, The Boston Consulting Group, pp. 1–9, http://www.bcg.com, accessed June 25, 2011.

McConville, Daniel J., "More Work for Chemical Distributors," *Distribution* 95 (August 1996): p. 63.

Richard, Pierre J., and Devinney, Timothy M., "Modular Strategies: B2B Technology and Architectural Knowledge," *California Management Review* 47 (Summer 2005): pp. 86–113.

Rudzki, Robert A., "Supply Chain Management Transformation: A Leader's Guide," *Supply Chain Management Review* 12 (March 2008): p. 14.

Sharma, Arun, Grewal, Dhruv, and Levy, Michael, "The Customer Satisfaction/Logistics Interface," *Journal of Business Logistics* 16 (2, 1995): p. 1.

Speh, Thomas W., *Changes in Warehouse Inventory Turnover* (Chicago: Warehousing Education and Research Council, 1999).

Stock, James, Speh, Thomas W., and Shear, Herbert, "Many Happy (Product) Returns," *Harvard Business Review* 80 (July 2002): p. 14.

Van Hoek, Remko, "When Good Customers Are Bad," *Harvard Business Review* 83 (September 2005): p. 19.

van Weele, Arjan, *Puchasing and Supply Chain Management: Analysis Strategy, Planning and Practice*, 5th ed. (Cengage, 2010).

Verhage, Bronis J., *Marketing: A Global Perspective* (Cengage, 2013).

Vitasek, Kate, Manrodt, Karl B., and Abbott, Jeff, "What Makes a LEAN Supply Chain?" *Supply Chain Management Review* 9 (October 2005): pp. 39–45.

CHAPTER 12
PRICING STRATEGIES
FOR BUSINESS
MARKETS

CHAPTER OBJECTIVES

Understanding how customers define value is the essence of the pricing process. Pricing decisions complement the firm's overall marketing strategy. The diverse nature of the business market presents unique problems and opportunities for the price strategist. After reading this chapter, you will be able to

1   Explain the significance of price to customers and its relationship to other marketing variables

2   Understand the role of the pricing mechanism and the meaning of the demand curve

3   Compare two opposite pricing strategies for new products

4   Systematically develop a pricing strategy, including pricing objectives

5   Identify the most widely used types of discounts and allowances

6   Discuss common cost-based approaches to pricing and their advantages, constraints and risks

7   Understand the concepts of demand-oriented pricing and price elasticity of demand

8   Recognise the nature of price competition in different types of market structures

Price matters greatly to a business customer because it influences operating costs and costs of goods sold, and these costs affect the customer's selling price and profit margin. When purchasing major equipment, an industrial buyer views the price as the amount of investment necessary to obtain a certain level of return or savings. Such a purchaser is likely to compare the price of a machine with the value of the benefits that the machine will yield. A while ago, Caterpillar lost market share to foreign competitors because its prices were too high. A business buyer does not compare alternative products by price alone, though; other factors, such as product quality and supplier services, are also major elements in the purchase decision. For example, one study found that in the buying decision process for mainframe computer software operating systems, intangible attributes, such as the seller's credibility and understanding of the buyer's needs, were very important in the buyer's decision process.[*]

This chapter is divided into four parts. The first analyses key determinants of the industrial pricing process and provides an operational approach to pricing decisions. The second examines pricing policies for new and existing products, emphasising the need to actively manage a product throughout its life cycle. The third provides a framework to guide strategy when a competitor cuts prices. The final section examines an area of particular importance to the business marketer: competitive bidding.

12.1 THE PRICING PROCESS IN BUSINESS MARKETS

There is no easy formula for pricing an industrial product or service. The decision is multidimensional: The interactive variables of demand, cost, competition, profit relationships, and customer usage patterns each assumes significance as the marketer formulates the role of price in the firm's marketing strategy. Pertinent considerations, illustrated in Figure 12.1, include: (1) pricing objectives, (2) demand determinants, (3) cost determinants, and (4) competition.

While more than one strategy path can be followed to achieve profitable results, all successful pricing strategies demonstrate three principles.[*] They are:

● *Value based* and reflect a clear understanding of how a firm's products or services create value for customers

● *Proactive* and anticipate disruptive events such as a competitive threat, negotiations with customers, or a technological change

● *Profit-driven* and judge success based on bottom-line performance, rather than the level of revenue generated

FIGURE 12.1

Key components of the price-setting decision process

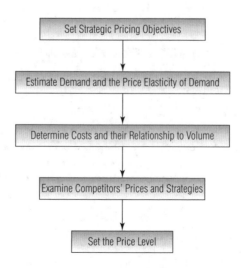

© Cengage Learning 2013

12.1.1 Price objectives

The pricing decision must be based on objectives congruent with marketing and overall corporate objectives. The marketer starts with principal objectives and adds collateral pricing goals: (1) achieving a target return on investment, (2) achieving a market share goal, or (3) meeting competition. Many other potential pricing objectives extend beyond profit and market share goals, taking into account competition, channel relationships, and product-line considerations.

Because of their far-reaching effects, pricing objectives must be established with care. Each firm faces unique internal and external environmental forces. Contrasting the strategies of DuPont and Dow Chemical illustrates the importance of a unified corporate direction. Dow's strategy focuses first on pricing low-margin commodity goods *low* to build a dominant market share and then on maintaining that dominant share. DuPont's strategy, on the other hand, emphasises higher-margin specialty products. Initially, these products are priced at a *high* level, and prices are reduced as the market expands and competition intensifies.

Similarly, when Apple launched products, such as the iPhone or iPad, critics claimed that the price of each was far too high. However, the firm's strategists understood that a hard-core group of technology adopters would embrace the products and assign a high value to the unique differentiation of Apple's offerings. By meeting the needs of sophisticated technology adopters, Apple established a high benchmark for value for its products, providing latitude for planned price adjustments over time. Each firm requires explicit pricing objectives that are consistent with its corporate mission.

12.1.2 Demand determinants

A strong market perspective is fundamental in pricing. The business market is diverse and complex. A single industrial product can be used in many ways; each market segment may represent a unique application for the product and a separate usage level. The importance of the industrial good in the buyer's end product also varies by market segment. Therefore, potential demand, sensitivity to price, and potential profitability can vary markedly across market segments. To establish an effective pricing policy, marketers should focus first on the value a customer places on a product or service. This reverses the typical process that gives immediate attention to the product cost and the desired markup.[*]

Differentiating through value creation

Value-based strategies seek to move the selling proposition from one that centres on current prices and individual transactions to a longer-term relationship built around value and lower total cost in use. Importantly, recent research suggests that benefits have a greater effect on perceived value to business customers than sacrifices (price and costs). Ajay Menon, Christian Homburg, and Nikolas Beutin note: Contrary to the general belief in a cost-driven economy, "we encourage managers to emphasise benefits accruing from a relationship and not focus solely on lowering the price and related costs when managing customer value."[*] A better way is to provide unique add-on benefits by building trust, demonstrating commitment and flexibility, and initiating joint working relationships that enhance customer value and loyalty.

In support, recent research by Wolfgang Ulaga and Andreas Eggert indicates that relationship benefits display a stronger potential for differentiation in key supplier relationships than cost considerations.[*] Based on a best-practice profile for companies seeking key supplier status, the researchers identify service support and personal interaction as core differentiators, followed by a supplier's know-how and its ability to improve a customer's time to market. Product quality and delivery performance, along with acquisition cost and operation costs, display a moderate potential to help the awarding of key supplier status to a business-to-business firm by a customer. Interestingly, price shows the weakest potential for differentiation. A specific approach for designing value-based strategies is highlighted in the next section.

Capturing value[*]

How organisational buyers evaluate the economic value of the total offering determines the appropriateness of a pricing strategy. Two competitors with similar products may ask different prices because buyers perceive their total offerings as unique. In the eyes of the organisational buyer, one firm may provide more value than another.

Economic value represents the cost savings and/or revenue gains that customers realise by purchasing the firm's product instead of the next-best alternative (the reference value). Some product or service features are quite similar across competitive offerings in a category (that is, points of parity) whereas others might be unique to a particular firm's brand (that is, points of differentiation). **Commodity value,** then, is the value that a customer assigns to product features that resemble those of competitors' offerings. By contrast, **differentiation value** is the value associated with product features that are unique and different from competitors'. Importantly, the price-per-unit of value that organisational buyers are willing to pay a firm for differentiating features is greater than the price-per-unit of value that they would pay for commodity features. "That's because refusal to pay a supplier's price for differentiating features means that the buyer must forgo those features. Refusal to pay a supplier's price for commodity features means simply that the customer must buy them elsewhere," says Gerald E. Smith and Thomas T. Nagle.[*] Recall that best-practice business-to-business firms create distinctive value propositions that isolate those product and service features that matter the most to customers, demonstrate the value of their unique elements, and communicate that value in a manner that clearly conveys a deep understanding of the customer's business priorities.[*]

Isolating value drivers in key customer segments

Exploratory methods such as depth interviews are required for identifying and measuring value. For example, depth interviews can be used to probe customer needs and problems and for learning how your products or services could address these problems. The goal here is to first identify the most significant drivers of value for customers in each market segment (see Figure 12.2). Economic value embodies both cost and revenue drivers. **Cost drivers** create value by providing economic savings while **revenue drivers** add incremental value by facilitating revenue or margin expansion.[*] For example, consider the value that Sonoco, a packaging supplier, provided for Lance, the snack food maker. One improvement involved the use of flexographic painted

FIGURE 12.2

A value-based approach for pricing

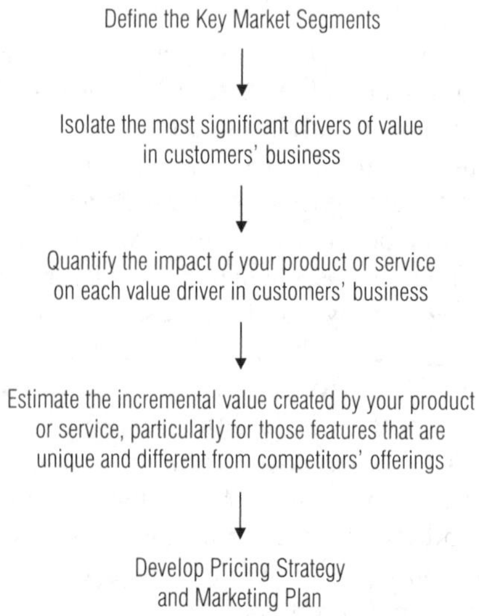

Define the Key Market Segments

↓

Isolate the most significant drivers of value
in customers' business

↓

Quantify the impact of your product or service
on each value driver in customers' business

↓

Estimate the incremental value created by your product
or service, particularly for those features that are
unique and different from competitors' offerings

↓

Develop Pricing Strategy
and Marketing Plan

Source: Adapted from Gerald E. Smith and Thomas T. Nagle, "How Much Are Customers Willing to Pay," *Marketing Research* 14 (Winter 2002): pp. 20–25.

packaging film on some of Lance's key brands.* These efforts drastically reduced Lance's packaging costs (cost driver) and, by enhancing the appeal of the products, spawned a growth in sales (revenue driver).

Second, once the business marketing strategist has identified the most important value drivers for customers, attention then turns to quantifying the impact of the firm's product or service on the customer's business model. To illustrate, a medical equipment company developed a new surgical product. Based on depth interviews with surgical teams at key hospitals, value research found that this product could reduce the length of a particular surgical procedure from 55 minutes to 40 minutes, freeing up precious time in capacity-constrained operating rooms.* In addition to estimating the value of the product, the study also revealed ways in which surgical procedures could be more tightly scheduled to capture the full value potential of the new product.

Third, the strategist should compare the firm's product or service to the next-best alternative, isolating those features that are unique and different from competitors. Does the product provide favourable points of difference that provide value that a customer cannot access elsewhere? How much value does each of these features create for the customer? Finally, by understanding how customers actually use a product or service and realise value from its use, the business marketer is ideally equipped to set the price and develop a responsive marketing strategy. "Suppliers cannot expect a fair return on their supplier value if they cannot persuasively prove it to the customer's own satisfaction."*

12.1.3 Value-based pricing illustrated

The UK government announced plans to commence the use of value-based pricing by the NHS. This system will replace the Pharmaceutical Price Regulation Scheme (PPRS), which has been in place since 1957*. This will be undertaken by the National Institute for Health and Care Excellence (NICE).

This new approach will price drugs based on their benefits, not just to individual patients, but also to society as a whole.

Health Minister Lord Howe described how, "We want to make sure we get the best possible outcomes for all NHS patients with the resources we have. "We cannot simply spend more and more on drugs – this would mean spending less and less elsewhere. That's why we have asked NICE to look at the impact that drugs can have on people's ability to work or contribute to the economy and society. A drug that brings a lot of extra benefits may justify the NHS paying more, but equally the NHS might pay less for a drug that does not deliver wider benefits."*

As the NHS case illustrates, the business marketing strategist can secure benefits to the company and its customers by emphasising a value-based approach.

Elasticity varies by market segment

Price elasticity of demand measures the degree to which customers are sensitive to price changes. Specifically, **price elasticity of demand** refers to the rate of percentage change in quantity demanded attributable to a percentage change in price. Price elasticity of demand is not the same at all prices. A business marketer contemplating a change in price must understand the elasticity of demand. For example, total revenue (price times quantity) increases if price is decreased and demand is price elastic, whereas revenue falls if the price is decreased and demand is price inelastic. Many factors influence the price elasticity of demand—the ease with which customers can compare alternatives and switch suppliers, the importance of the product in the cost structure of the customer's product, and the value that the product represents to a customer.

Satisfied customers are less price sensitive

Recent research demonstrates that highly satisfied customers are less sensitive to prices, compared with those who have a moderate level of customer satisfaction.* This relationship is particularly strong for purchase decisions that involve a high level of product/service complexity and a high degree of customisation. Thus, reduced customer price sensitivity represents an important payoff to a business marketer for developing a customised solution for the customer.

Search behaviour and switching costs

The price sensitivity of buyers increases—and a firm's pricing latitude decreases—to the degree that:

- Organisational buyers can easily shop around and assess the relative performance and price of alternatives. Purchasing managers in many firms use information technology to track supplier prices on a global basis.

- The product is one for which it is easy to make price comparisons. For example, it is easier to compare alternative photocopiers than it is to compare specialised manufacturing equipment options.

- Buyers can switch from one supplier to another without incurring additional costs. Low switching costs allow a buyer to focus on minimising the cost of a particular transaction.[*]

End use

Important insights can be secured by answering this question: How important is the business marketer's product as an input into the total cost of the end product? If the business marketer's product has an insignificant effect on cost, demand is likely inelastic. Consider this example:

> A manufacturer of precision electronic components was contemplating an across-the-board price decrease to increase sales. However, an item analysis of the product line revealed that some of its low-volume components had exotic applications. A technical customer used the component in an ultrasonic testing apparatus that was sold for €6000 a unit. This fact prompted the electronics manufacturer to raise the price of the item. Ironically, the firm then experienced a temporary surge of demand for the item as purchasing agents stocked up in anticipation of future price increases.[*]

Of course, the marketer must temper this estimate by analysing the costs, availability, and suitability of substitutes. Generally, when the industrial product is an important but low-cost input into the end product, price is less important than quality and delivery reliability. When, however, the product input represents a larger part of the final product's total cost, changes in price may have an important effect on the demand for both the final product and the input. When demand in the final consumer market is price elastic, a reduction in the price of the end item (for example, a personal computer) that is caused by a price reduction of a component (for example, a microprocessor) generates an increase in demand for the final product (personal computer) and, in turn, for the industrial product (microprocessor).

End-market focus

Because the demand for many industrial products is derived from the demand for the product of which they are a part, a strong end-user focus is needed. The marketer can benefit by examining the trends and changing fortunes of important final consumer markets. Different sectors of the market grow at different rates, confront different levels of competition, and face different short-run and long-run challenges. A downturn in the economy does not fall equally on all sectors. Pricing decisions demand a two-tiered market focus—on organisational customers and on final-product customers. Thus, business marketers will have more success in raising prices to customers who are prospering than to customers who are hard pressed.

Value-based segmentation

The value customers assign to a firm's offering can vary by market segment because the same industrial product may serve different purposes for different customers. This underscores the important role of market segmentation in pricing strategies. Take Sealed Air Corporation, the innovative supplier of protective packaging, including coated air bubbles.[*] The company recognised that for some applications, substitutes were readily available. But for other applications, Sealed Air had an enormous advantage—for example, its packaging materials offered superior cushioning for heavy items with long shipping cycles. By identifying those applications where the firm had a clear advantage and understanding the unique value differential in each setting, marketing managers were ideally equipped to tackle product-line expansion and pricing decisions and to ignite Sealed Air's remarkable revenue growth for nearly two decades.

12.1.4 Cost determinants

Business marketers often pursue a strong internal orientation; they base prices on their own costs, reaching the selling price by calculating unit costs and adding a percentage profit. A strict cost-plus pricing philosophy overlooks customer perceptions of value, competition, and the interaction of volume and profit. Many progressive firms, such as Canon, Toyota, and the NHS, use target costing to capture a significant competitive advantage.

Target costing[*]

Target costing features a design-to-cost philosophy that begins by examining market conditions: The firm identifies and targets the most attractive market segments. It then determines what level of quality and types of product attributes are required to succeed in each segment, given a predetermined target price and volume level. According to Robin Cooper and Regine Slagmulder, to set the target price, the business marketer has to understand the customer's perception of value: "A company can raise selling prices only if the perceived value of the new product exceeds not only that of the product's predecessor, but also that of competing products."[*]

Once the target selling price and target profit margins have been established, the firm calculates the allowable cost. The strategic cost-reduction challenge isolates the profit shortfall that occurs if the product designers are unable to achieve the allowable cost. The value of distinguishing the allowable cost from the target cost lies in the pressure that this exercise exerts on the product-development team and the company's suppliers. To transmit the competitive cost pressure it faces to its suppliers, the firm then breaks down the target price of a new product into a cascade of target costs for each component or function. For example, the major functions of an automobile include the engine, transmission, cooling system, and audio system.

A profit-management tool

Toyota used target costing to reduce the price of its recently modified Camry model and did so while offering as standard equipment certain features that were expensive options on the model it replaced. Similarly, Canon used target costing to develop its breakthrough personal copier that transformed the photocopier industry.[*] Rather than a cost-control technique, Japanese managers who pioneered the approach view target costing as a profit-management tool. As Robin Cooper and W. Bruce Chew assert, "The task is to compute the costs that must not be exceeded if acceptable margins from specific products at specific price points are to be guaranteed."[*]

Classifying costs[*]

The target costing approach stresses why the marketer must know which costs are relevant to the pricing decision and how these costs fluctuate with volume and over time; they must be considered in relation to demand, competition, and pricing objectives. Product costs are crucial in projecting the profitability of individual products as well as of the entire product line. Proper classification of costs is essential.

The goals of a cost-classification system are to: (1) properly classify cost data into their fixed and variable components and (2) properly link them to the activity causing them. The manager can then analyse the effects of volume and, more important, identify sources of profit. The following cost concepts are instrumental in the analysis:

1   **Direct traceable or attributable costs:** Costs, fixed or variable, are incurred by and solely for a particular product, customer, or sales territory (for example, raw materials).

2   **Indirect traceable costs:** Costs, fixed or variable, can be traced to a product, customer, or sales territory (for example, general plant overhead may be indirectly assigned to a product).

3   **General costs:** Costs support a number of activities that cannot be objectively assigned to a product on the basis of a direct physical relationship (for example, the administrative costs of a sales district).

General costs rarely change because an item is added or deleted from the product line. Marketing, production, and distribution costs must all be classified. When developing a new line or when deleting or adding an item to an existing line, the marketer must grasp the cost implications:

●   What proportion of the product cost is accounted for by purchases of raw materials and components from suppliers?

●   How do costs vary at differing levels of production?

●   Based on the forecasted level of demand, can economies of scale be expected?

●   Does our firm enjoy cost advantages over competitors?

●   How does the "experience effect" impact our cost projections?

12.1.5 Competition

As competition increases in virtually every product and market, the likely response of the competitors to a firm's pricing strategy becomes increasingly important. An attempt should be made to forecast how competitors might react to a change in pricing strategy by analysing the market and product factors which affect them, consumer perceptions of their product offers and their internal cost structures. Competitors' pricing strategies will be affected by such issues as their commitment to particular products and markets, and the stance that they might have adopted in the past during periods of fierce competition.

Before implementing pricing strategies and tactics, therefore, it is essential to estimate the likely consumer and competitor response by evaluating similar situations which have arisen in other markets or countries. The responses of competitors who adopt a global strategic approach are likely to be more easily predicted than a competitor adopting a multidomestic strategy. It is useful to consider how these factors have affected the competitive responses of a number of companies such as Gillette, Kodak and Philip Morris.[*]

Hypercompetitive rivalries

Some strategy experts emphasise that traditional patterns of competition in stable environments is being replaced by hypercompetitive rivalries in a rapidly changing environment.[*] In a stable environment, a company could create a fairly rigid strategy designed to accommodate long-term conditions. The firm's strategy focused on sustaining its own strategic advantage and establishing equilibrium where less-dominant firms accepted a secondary status.

In hypercompetitive environments, successful companies pursue strategies that create temporary advantage and destroy the advantages of rivals by constantly disrupting the market's equilibrium. For example, Intel continually disrupts the equilibrium of the microprocessor industry sector, and Apple stirs up the consumer electronics industry with its innovative products. Moreover, the Internet provides customers with real-time access to a wealth of information that drives the prices of many products lower. Leading firms in hypercompetitive environments constantly seek out new sources of advantage, further escalating competition and contributing to hypercompetition.

Consider the hypercompetitive rivalries in high-technology markets. Firms that sustain quality and that are the first to hit the next-lower strategic price point enjoy a burst of volume and an expansion of market share. For example, Hewlett-Packard has ruthlessly pursued the next-lower price point in its printer business, even as it cannibalised its own sales and margins.[*]

Gauging competitive response

To predict the response of competitors, the marketer can first benefit by examining the cost structure and strategy of both direct competitors and producers of potential substitutes. The marketer can draw on public statements and records (for example, annual reports) to form rough estimates. Competitors that have ascended the learning curve may have lower costs than those just entering the industry and beginning the climb. An estimate of the cost structure is valuable when gauging how well competitors can respond to price reductions and when projecting the pattern of prices in the future.

Under certain conditions, however, followers into a market may confront lower initial costs than did the pioneer. Why? Some of the reasons are highlighted in Table 12.1. By failing to recognise potential cost advantages of late entrants, the business marketer can dramatically overstate cost differences.

The market strategy competing sellers use is also important here. Competitors are more sensitive to price reductions that threaten those market segments they deem important. They learn of price reductions earlier when their market segments overlap. Of course, competitors may choose not to follow a price decrease, especially if their products enjoy a differentiated position. Rather than matching competitors' price cuts, one successful steel company reacts to the competitive challenge by offering customised products and technical assistance to its customers.[*] Later in the chapter, special attention is given to this question: How should you respond to price attacks by competitors?

TABLE 12.1 Selected cost comparison issues: Followers versus the pioneer

Technology/economies of scale	Followers may benefit by using more current production technology than the pioneer or by building a plant with a larger scale of operations.
Product/market knowledge	Followers may learn from the pioneer's mistakes by analysing the competitor's product, hiring key personnel, or identifying through market research the problems and unfulfiled expectations of customers and channel members.
Shared experience	Compared with the pioneer, followers may be able to gain advantages on certain cost elements by sharing operations with other parts of the company.
Experience of suppliers	Followers, together with the pioneer, benefit from cost reductions achieved by outside suppliers of components or production equipment.

Source: Adapted from George S. Day and David B. Montgomery, "Diagnosing the Experience Curve," *Journal of Marketing* 47 (Spring 1983): pp. 48–49.

The manager requires a grasp of objectives, demand, cost, competition, and legal factors (discussed later) to approach the multidimensional pricing decision. Price setting is not an act but an ongoing process.

12.2 PRICING ACROSS THE PRODUCT LIFE CYCLE

What price should be assigned to a distinctly new industrial product or service? When an item is added to an existing product line, how should it be priced in relation to products already in the line?

12.2.1 Pricing new products

Establishing the correct launch price for a product or service can reset market price expectations and boost the profit trajectory across the remainder of that offering's life cycle.[*] The strategic decision of pricing new products can be best understood by examining the policies at the boundaries of the continuum—from **skimming** (high initial price) to **penetration** (low initial price). Consider again the pricing strategies of DuPont and Dow Chemical. Whereas DuPont assigns an initial high price to new products to generate immediate profits or to recover R&D expenditures, Dow follows a low-price strategy with the objective of gaining market share.

In evaluating the merits of skimming versus penetration, the marketer must again examine price from the buyer's perspective. This approach, asserts Joel Dean, "recognises that the upper limit is the price that will produce the minimum acceptable rate of return on the investment of a sufficiently large number of prospects."[*] This is especially important in pricing new products because the potential profits to buyers of a new machine tool, for example, will vary by market segment, and these market segments may differ in the minimum rate of return that will induce them to invest in the machine tool.

Skimming

A skimming approach, appropriate for a distinctly new product, provides an opportunity to profitably reach market segments that are not sensitive to the high initial price. As a product ages, as competitors enter the market, and as organisational buyers become accustomed to evaluating and purchasing the product, demand becomes more price elastic. Joel Dean refers to the policy of skimming at the outset, followed by penetration pricing as the product matures, as **time segmentation**.[*] Skimming enables the marketer to capture early profits, then reduce the price to reach more price-sensitive segments. It also enables the innovator to recover high developmental costs more quickly.

Robert Dolan and Abel Jeuland demonstrate that during the innovative firm's monopoly period, skimming is optimal if the demand curve is stable over time (no diffusion) and if production costs decline with accumulated volume. A penetration policy is optimal if there is a relatively high repeat purchase rate for nonconsumer durables or if a consumer durables's demand is characterised by diffusion.[*]

Penetration

A penetration policy is appropriate when there is: (1) high price elasticity of demand, (2) strong threat of imminent competition, and (3) opportunity for a substantial reduction in production costs as volume expands. Drawing on the experience effect, a firm that can quickly capture substantial market share and experience can gain a strategic advantage over competitors. The feasibility of this strategy increases with the potential size of the future market. By taking a large share of new sales, a firm can gain experience when the growth rate of the market is large. Of course, the value of additional market share differs markedly between industries and often among products, markets, and competitors in an industry.[*] Factors to be assessed in determining the value of additional market share include the investment requirements, potential benefits of experience, expected market trends, likely competitive reaction, and short- and long-term profit implications.

Product-line considerations

The contemporary business-to-business firm with a long product line faces the complex problem of balancing prices in the product mix. Firms extend their product lines because the demands for various products are interdependent or because the costs of producing and marketing those items are interdependent, or both.[*] A firm may add to its product line—or even develop a new product line—to fit more precisely the needs of a particular market segment. If both the demand and the costs of individual product-line items are interrelated, production and marketing decisions about one item inevitably influence both the revenues and costs of the others.

Are specific product-line items substitutes or complements? Will changing the price of one item enhance or retard the usage rate of this or other products in key market segments? Should a new product be priced high at the outset to protect other product-line items (for example, potential substitutes) and to give the firm time to revamp other items in the line? Such decisions require knowledge of demand, costs, competition, and strategic marketing objectives.

INSIDE BUSINESS MARKETING

Business-to-business pricing using EVC analysis

Analysing economic value to the customer (EVC) is a useful aid to setting prices for business-to-business organisations. This example concerns the pricing of panel presses, which are supplied to the car parts business. The analysis focuses on the market leader and two other competitors.

The analysis begins by considering a reference product against which the costs of competing products are compared.

In this case, the market leader is used as the reference product. In this example, a car parts company buying the panel press from the market leader would expect to pay the following costs. The purchase price of the press is £60 000. Start-up costs, such as installation charges, staff training and lost production during installation, are £20 000, and postpurchase costs, including operating costs such as labour, servicing/maintenance and power, are £130 000. This means that, over its life cycle, the panel press will cost the car parts company a total of £210 000. Companies competing with the market leader present the customer with a different profile of costs. Company A has, by incorporating a number of new design features managed to cut the start-up costs for a comparable panel press to £10 000 and reduced post-purchase costs to £105 000. This means that the total costs for the press are £35 000 less than those for the market leader. The result is that Company A's press offers the customer an EVC of £210 000 less £115 000, which equals £95 000. Assuming that Company A charged a purchase price of £95 000 for the panel press, the customer would face total life-cycle costs that were equivalent to the market leading product. If, however, Company A decided to offer the panel press at a purchase price of only £80 000, the lower life-cycle costs of the product would give the customer a considerable financial incentive to buy.

Consider the position of a second competitor, Company B, with similar start-up and post-purchase costs to the market leader. This company has, through certain technological advances, increased the rate at which the press can be operated, potentially increasing productivity and therefore revenue for the customer. As a result, the press has the potential to offer an additional £50 000 profit contribution over the presses of the market leader and Company A. The EVC associated with this is £110 000, because this is the highest price the customer may be expected to pay.[*]

12.3 RESPONDING TO PRICE ATTACKS BY COMPETITORS[*]

Rather than emphasising the lowest price, most business marketers prefer to compete by providing superior value. However, across industries, marketing managers face constant pressure from competitors who are willing to use price concessions to gain market share or entry into a profitable market segment. When challenged by an aggressive competitor, many managers immediately want to fight back and match the price cut. However, because price wars can be quite costly, experts suggest a more systematic process that considers the long-run strategic consequences versus the short-term benefits of the pricing decision. Managers should never set the price simply to meet some immediate sales goal, but, instead, to enhance long-term project goals. George E. Cressman Jr. and Thomas T. Nagle, consultants from the Strategic Pricing Group, Inc., observe: "Pricing is like playing chess; players who fail to envision a few moves ahead will almost always be beaten by those who do."[*]

12.3.1 Evaluating a competitive threat

Figure 12.3 provides a systematic framework for developing a strategy when one or more competitors have announced price cuts or have introduced new products that offer more value to at least some of your customers. To determine whether to reduce price to meet a competitor's challenge, you should address four important questions:

FIGURE 12.3 Evaluating a competitive threat

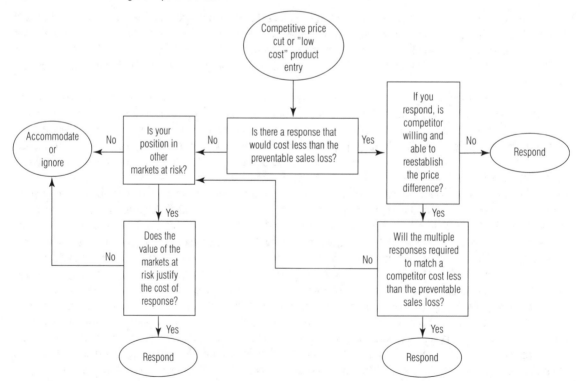

Source: Reprinted from Business Horizons 45(2), George E. Cressman, Jr. and Thomas T. Nagle, "How to Manage an Aggressive Competitor," p. 25, copyright © 2002, with permission from Elsevier.

1   *Is there a response that would cost you less than the preventable sales loss?* (See centre of Figure 12.3.) Before responding to a competitor's price reduction, the marketing strategist should ask: Do the benefits justify the costs? If responding to a price change is less costly than losing sales, a price move may be the appropriate decision. On the other hand, if the competitor threatens only a small slice of expected sales, the revenue loss from ignoring the threat may be much lower than the costs of retaliation. Indeed, when the threat centres on a small segment of customers, the cost of reducing prices for all customers to prevent the small loss is likely to be prohibitively expensive.

    If a price response is required, the strategist should focus the firm's competitive retaliation on the most cost-effective actions. The cost of retaliating to a price threat can be reduced by incorporating one or more of the following elements into the pricing action:

- Centre reactive price cuts only on those customers likely to be attracted to the competitor's offer (for example, rather than cutting the price of its flagship Pentium chip, Intel offered the lower-priced Cerrus chip for the cost-conscious market segment).
- Centre reactive price cuts on a particular geographic region, distribution channel, or product line where the competitor has the most to lose from a price reduction.
- Capitalise on any competitive advantages to increase the value of your offer as an alternative to matching the price (for example, a firm that has better-quality products can respond by offering a longer warranty period to customers).
- Raise the cost to the competitor related to its discounting. (For example, if the competitor's price reduction is limited only to new customers and not the firm's existing customers, "retaliate by educating the competitor's existing customers that they are being treated unfairly."[*])

2   *If you respond, is the competitor willing and able to merely reduce the price again to restore the price difference?* Matching a price cut will be ineffective if the competitor simply reestablishes the differential by a further price reduction. According to Cressman and Nagle, to determine the appropriate course, the strategist should attempt to understand why the competitor chose to compete on price in the first place: "If the competitor has little market share relative to the share that could be gained with a price advantage, and has no other way to attract customers, then there is little to lose from bringing the price down as low as necessary to gain sales."[*] This is especially true when competitors have made huge investments in areas such as R&D that largely represent sunk costs. Under such conditions, accommodation—market share loss—is less costly than fighting a price war.

3   *Will the multiple responses that may be required to match the competitor's price still cost less than the avoidable sales loss?* A single response is rarely enough to stop price moves by competitors that are struggling to establish a market position. Price competition is particularly likely in industries where entry requires a significant investment in fixed manufacturing capacity. Rather than idling manufacturing capacity, a competitor may be willing to aggressively pursue sales that will make at least some contribution to covering fixed costs. If competitors are likely to continue to cut prices, the best strategy for the defender is to:

- Allow the competitor to win where it is least damaging to profitability, such as in more price-sensitive, lower-margin customer segments (for example, government contracts).
- Create barriers that make it more difficult for competitors to reach less price-sensitive, more profitable customer segments (for example, build switching costs by developing unique solutions for the most valued customers).

4   *Is your position in other markets (product or geographic) at risk if the competitor increases market share? Does the value of all the markets that are at risk justify the cost of the strategy response?* Before responding with a price reduction, the business marketer must clearly define the long-run strategic benefits as well as the risks of a particular strategy response. The benefits might include additional sales in a particular market in the future, or immediate sales gains of complementary

products (such as software, peripherals, and services associated with the sale of a computer), or a lower cost of future sales resulting from increased volume. The risks are that a targeted price reduction will spread to other markets, creating a downward price spiral that undermines profitability.

12.3.2 Understanding the rules of competitive strategy

Dealing effectively with an aggressive competitor requires more than a willingness to fight—it requires a competitive strategy and an understanding of when the appropriate response to a competitor's price cut is to ignore it, accommodate it, or retaliate. George E. Cressman and Thomas T. Nagle offer these guidelines for competitive strategy development:

● Never participate in a competitive engagement you cannot win. Fight those battles where you have competitive strength, and avoid those where you are clearly at a disadvantage.

● Always participate in competitive engagements from a position of advantage. Don't fight by competitors' rules (which they select for their advantage); use what is advantageous for you.[*]

12.4 COMPETITIVE BIDDING

A significant volume of business commerce is transacted through competitive bidding. Rather than relying on a specific list price, the business marketer must develop a price, or a bid, to meet a customer's particular product or service requirements.

Government and other public agencies buy almost exclusively through competitive bidding. Competitive bidding in private industry centres on two types of purchases. One type includes nonstandard materials, complex fabricated products where design and manufacturing methods vary, and products made to the buyer's specifications. This type has no generally established market level. Competitive bids enable the purchaser to evaluate the appropriateness of the prices.[*] The second type is the reverse auction, where many sellers bid for an order from a single buyer. GE, for example, uses reverse auctions to buy both direct (for example, standard component parts) and indirect materials (for example, maintenance items, office supplies), making roughly a third of its total purchasing expenditures in this fashion. Typically, reverse auctions are best suited for product categories that buyers view as commodities.[*] Competitive bidding may be either closed or open.

12.4.1 Closed bidding

Closed bidding, often used by business and governmental buyers, involves a formal invitation to potential suppliers to submit written, sealed bids. All bids are opened and reviewed at the same time, and the contract is generally awarded to the lowest bidder who meets desired specifications. The low bidder is not guaranteed the contract—buyers often make awards to the lowest responsible bidder; the ability of alternative suppliers to perform remains part of the bidding process.

Online sealed bid format

A sealed bid format is also used for online auctions. The term *sealed* means that only one supplier and the buyer have access to the details of the bid. According to Sandy Jap:

> *The bid process is asynchronous in the sense that the buyer and supplier take turns viewing the bid. The buyer posts the RFP (request for purchase) electronically, the supplier*

submits a bid, and the buyer views the submitted bid. The buyer then either makes a decision after viewing all bids or, if multiple rounds of bidding are involved, may respond to the supplier, who then resubmits a new bid.

12.4.2 Open bidding

Open bidding is more informal and allows suppliers to make offers (oral and written) up to a certain date. The buyer may deliberate with several suppliers throughout the bidding process. Open bidding may be particularly appropriate when specific requirements are hard to define rigidly or when the products and services of competing suppliers vary substantially.

In some buying situations, prices may be negotiated. Complex technical requirements or uncertain product specifications may lead buying organisations first to evaluate the capabilities of competing firms and then to negotiate the price and the form of the product-service offering. Negotiated pricing is appropriate for procurement in both the commercial and the governmental sectors of the business market.

Online open bid format

When conducted online, open bidding takes a different form. Here suppliers are invited to bid simultaneously during a designated time period for the contract. In contrast to the sealed-bid format, all suppliers and the buyer view the bids at the same time. The goal, of course, is to push the price down. Sandy Jap, who has conducted extensive research on reverse auctions, argues that the open-bid format, when used regularly, can damage buyer–supplier relationships:

> *This harm occurs because open-bid formats reveal pricing information to competition, which erodes the supplier's bargaining power. Open-bid formats also place a more explicit focus on price, a short-term variable that is usually the focus of transaction-oriented exchanges rather than relational exchanges. When buyers use an open-bid format amid a context in which relational exchanges are emphasised, they send an inconsistent message to suppliers and may foster distrust.*

Recent research on the use of online reverse auctions suggests that the larger the number of bidders, the larger the economic stakes, and the less visible the price in an auction, the more positive is the impact on the buyer–seller relationship.* However, large price drops over the course of the event have a detrimental effect on the buyer–seller relationship.

12.4.3 Strategies for competitive bidding

Because making bids is costly and time consuming, firms should choose potential bid opportunities with care. Contracts offer differing levels of profitability according to the bidding firm's related technical expertise, past experience, and objectives. Therefore, careful screening is required to isolate contracts that offer the most promise.* Having isolated a project opportunity, the marketer must now estimate the probabilities of winning the contract at various prices. Assuming that the contract is awarded to the lowest bidder, the chances of the firm winning the contract decline as the bid price increases. How will competitors bid?

In many industries, business marketers confront situations in which the supplier that wins the initial contract has the advantage in securing long-term follow-up business. To illustrate, suppliers bidding on contracts to meet the worldwide information-technology service needs of American Express often submit attractive bids to form an initial relationship with the centralised purchasing unit.* Although they may sacrifice some immediate profit, they see the low bid as an investment that will lead to improved efficiencies and a continuing stream of profitable follow-up business.

In pursuing this type of bidding strategy, the business marketer must carefully assess how likely it is that the initial contract will lead to follow-up business opportunities. For example, the purchase of an office automation system may bond the buyer to a particular seller, thus providing the potential for future business. The costs of switching to another supplier are high because the buyer has made investments in employee training and new business procedures, as well as in the equipment itself.* Such investments create inertia against change. By contrast, for more standardised purchases, such bonding does not occur because the buyer's costs of switching to another supplier are quite low. In determining the initial bid strategy, the business marketer should examine the strength of the buyer–seller relationship, the probability of securing additional business, and the expected return from that business.

SUMMARY

Setting the price

Price is the element of the marketing mix most easily and quickly changed, without substantial investment.

Accurate pricing is also one of the most effective ways for a firm to become more profitable. This makes pricing one of the most important marketing decisions. A customer orientation plays a key role in price determination. As we've seen, the selling price reflects the value that customers are willing to exchange for a desired product. This determines the upper limit of the range of possible prices. The lower limit depends on the product's cost.

Other considerations in pricing decisions are the company's strategy and objectives, competition, the effect on the product mix, the resellers' interests and finally legislation or ethics. The selling price is a major marketing tool, because it will influence sales – and therefore the firm's production volume. This in turn will affect the company's cost per unit, which again is one of the inputs in price determination, thus completing the circle. Hence, pricing is one of the most critical decisions in marketing strategy development.

Price mechanism and demand curve

The price of products and services affects both demand and supply. For example, a high price – with a large profit margin – may lead to many suppliers in the market, even if the total demand is limited. Due to increasing competition, prices will fall, causing demand to go up. The lower profit margins, however, also lead to a reduction in supply. As a result, prices can rise again; the cycle then repeats itself. This price mechanism is one of the driving forces of the economy: it measures the relative value of goods, making it possible to compare products with one another. It also stimulates or curbs production, and rations scarce products.

The demand curve provides a clear understanding of the relationship between price and demand. The demand curve for a particular product graphically illustrates how customer demand responds to a series of possible prices. Movement along the demand curve is the result of a price change: in a downward sloping demand curve, demand increases as the price decreases. On the other hand, a shift in the demand curve (either upward or downward) is the result of more fundamental market forces, such as changes in consumer tastes, income, the market size or availability of substitutes.

Pricing new products

In new product pricing, the innovating marketer's primary considerations in choosing between price skimming and penetration pricing are how quickly competitors can launch their own versions of the new product and the effect of their entry into the market. For a new product with a large potential market – one that is likely to attract competitors soon after the product's introduction – penetration pricing is usually the most appropriate strategy. The low selling price helps the firm to penetrate the market and gain a large market share quickly. It also tends to discourage potential competitors by making the market appear less attractive than with a price skimming strategy. Conditions for a penetration pricing strategy include sufficient production and distribution capacity, a sound financial position and a long product life cycle.

With a price skimming approach, the marketer charges the highest price that early adopters, who most want the product, are willing to pay. This allows management to 'skim the cream' from the target market – especially if the product is perceived as having unique advantages – and then reduce the price over time to appeal to the next most lucrative segments. A successful skimming strategy enables the company to recover its product development costs quickly and maximise profits across segments. Of course, a high introductory price, which often generates greater initial profits than would a lower price, will also encourage competitors to enter the market.

Pricing objectives

Using a systematic decision-making approach, the pricing objectives indicate what we intend to achieve through price setting. The pricing strategy, in turn, provides the framework within which we translate our pricing objectives into the actual market pricing tactics. In a business or marketing plan, pricing objectives should be formulated as specifically as possible, in such a way that there is a direct and measurable relationship with the price. Market driven firms often express their pricing objectives in terms of price perception, such as a desired change in price awareness or price acceptance.

Among large companies, the most common pricing objectives are profitability objectives, including target return on investment, profit maximisation and a desired gross profit margin. Other common pricing objectives are sales-related objectives, such as target market share and sales maximisation, and competitive effect objectives, such as meeting competition and value pricing.

Control over prices

In business transactions, few customers pay list price for merchandise. Most buyers get a discount – or reduction from the base price – from the supplier. The actual prices resellers pay depend both on the functions they perform in the channel of distribution and on their degree of control over prices. Retailers, for example, gain greater control over prices by linking their resale support to the profit margins granted by the supplier, by carrying competing products, and by creating loyalty for their own store brands. Manufacturers can increase their control over prices by allowing the resellers adequate profit margins, by creating a strong national brand image that justifies high prices and by printing a recommended retail price on their packaging.

By offering discounts, manufacturers can influence their customers' buying and marketing behaviour. These price cuts are typically offered to middlemen for volume purchases (either cumulative or noncumulative quantity discounts), off-season buying (seasonal discounts), early

payment of invoices (cash discounts) and for handling distribution-related functions in the trade channel that otherwise would be performed by the manufacturer (trade or functional discounts). When properly coordinated with their overall pricing strategy, price discounting can help a firm to build long-term relationships with customers and improve its competitive position. Like discounts, allowances help a company influence customer buying behaviour without formally reducing the list price of a product or service. Allowances are pricing adjustments that indirectly lower the price that a reseller or other customer pays in exchange for taking some action, such as participating in a programme, promoting a product or purchasing during a particular time period. The most widely used types are trade-in allowances, promotional allowances and rebates.

Corporations within which products are sold from one division to another must set the price of the goods transferred in terms of the revenues and costs to their business units. The transfer price can be based either on the product's market price or on its actual production costs per unit.

Cost-based price determination

The three major dimensions on which prices of products and services can be based are cost, demand and competition. The simplest and most commonly used method of price setting is cost-oriented pricing. With cost-plus pricing, management tries to allocate only those costs directly attributable to a specific product or output. The seller's costs are calculated, and this amount or a specific percentage of it is added to the item's production cost to establish its price. When costs, such as overheads, are difficult to determine, firms use mark-up pricing to establish a selling price.

Variable-cost pricing – or direct costing – enables a firm to temporarily price below its full costs but still to contribute to overhead and profit. The product's price is based on the variable costs only. The difference between the variable costs and the selling price is called the contribution margin. A major risk of using variable-cost pricing is that it may trigger a price war, resulting in reduced profits for all companies in the industry.

Break-even analysis is a means of determining the number of products or services that must be sold at a given price to generate sufficient revenue to equal total costs. Only sales above the break-even point will lead to profit. If we also take into account the expected demand for the product at various prices, a flexible break-even analysis is a useful tool. A break-even analysis may well be combined with another pricing method, target return-on-investment pricing. This allows marketers to determine a new product's price level to achieve a desired or target return on investment.

Demand-oriented pricing

The opposite of the cost-oriented price determination is demand-oriented pricing, also referred to as perceived-value or value-based pricing. Using this strategy, companies set prices at a level that the intended buyers are willing to pay, and then deduct their own as well as the resellers' customary profit margins. Correctly assessing consumers' interest in a product at different price levels requires an insight into the buyer's price sensitivity, making price elasticity of demand a fundamental concept in demand-oriented pricing.

The price elasticity of demand indicates the sensitivity of buyers to price changes in terms of the quantities they will purchase, and thus how responsive demand will be to a price increase or decrease. For instance, a price change that leads to a relatively small change in demand indicates an inelastic demand. Typically, buyers are less price sensitive when there are few substitute products, or when the total expenditure for the product is low relative to their income. Income elasticity of demand shows the relationship between an increase in consumers' disposable income and the corresponding change in consumption. Lastly, demand for a product may also be affected by another product's change in price. This phenomenon is called cross elasticity of demand.

When a firm establishes a series of prices for a type of product, it creates a price line. Price lining requires two determinations: the floor and ceiling of the price range are established, and a limited number of price points are set for the various items within that range. The same product can often be sold to buyers under more than one price. Price discrimination is the practice of charging different buyers different prices for goods of like grade and quality. The most common forms of price differentiation are based on customer type (e.g. student discounts), product form (gift packages), location (seating in concert hall) and time (post-season sale). Setting the right price is part science, part art. In using psychological pricing, firms take into consideration the psychology of prices and not just the economics. With some prestige products, the higher the price, the more consumers are willing to buy the product. Consumers are also more inclined to buy a product with an odd-numbered price than with an even-numbered price, especially if the amount is just under a particular threshold. No wonder so many companies have adopted an odd even pricing strategy.

Competition-oriented pricing

When a company uses its competitors' prices as the primary basis for price setting, it follows a strategy of competition-oriented pricing. Marketers have the option of pricing at the market (me-too pricing), above the market (premium pricing) or below the market (discount pricing).

Based on the number of sellers and the type of product, companies operate and set prices in four types of market structures: monopoly, oligopoly, monopolistic competition and pure competition. In an oligopoly, a few large suppliers account for a high percentage of the market, so every seller is highly sensitive to the marketing actions taken by its competitors, including pricing. Price cuts are usually copied by competitors, but price increases only if the market leader takes the initiative. This explains the price stability on this type of market as well as the shape of this (kinked) supply curve. The most common market form, which typifies retailing, is monopolistic competition. The marketer's main challenge here is to keep the brand distinctive and to appeal to a target market of loyal buyers through an effective product positioning strategy.

In the B2B market, several suppliers – through competitive bidding – may independently submit bids to a potential buyer for a specific product or service. The bidding company must take the cost of providing the service or product into account as well as the prices its rivals are expected to submit. All companies use the expected profit decision rule, recognising that as the bid price increases, the potential profit also increases but the probability its winning the contract decreases.[*]

DISCUSSION QUESTIONS

1 Why was Apple able to launch new products, such as the iPhone and iPad, at such high prices?

2 Explain the differences between economic value, commodity value and differentiation value.

3   How might Toyota use target costing to gain a competitive advantage?

4   Karen Sigurdsson is CEO of a gadget company that has recently expanded from Europe to African and the Middle East. The company has loyal customers in Europe, but are relatively unknown elsewhere.

Karen has employed you to assess the pricing strategy of her company. Discuss what pricing approach would be most viable for this business.

5   Why is the concept of EVC (economic value to the customer) important when setting prices in the B2B markets?

INTERNET EXERCISES

Choose the websites of key government departments, EU departments or of leading regulatory bodies and learn more about the ways in which their activities and powers impact on marketers and consumers. For example, log on to the websites for the Competition Commission and the Office of Fair Trading at: www.competition-commission.org.uk and www.oft.gov.uk

1   What are the implications of these organisations' powers and recommendations for marketers?

2   In what ways do the activities of these bodies impact on consumers?

REFERENCES

Anderson, James C., Kumar, Nirmalya, and Narus, James A., *Value Merchants: Demonstrating and Documenting Superior Value in Business Markets* (Boston: Harvard Business School Press, 2007).

Anderson, James C., Narus, James A., and van Rossum, Wouter, "Customer Value Propositions in Business Markets," *Harvard Business Review* 86 (March 2006): p. 93.

Anderson, James C., Wouters, Marc, and van Rossum, Wouter, "Why the Highest Price Isn't the Best Price," *MIT Sloan Management Review* 51 (Winter 2010): p. 72.

Baker, Walter L., Marn, Michael V., and Zowada, Craig C., "Do You Have a Long-Term Pricing Strategy?" *McKinsey Quarterly* (October 2010), pp. 1–7, http://www.mckinsey.com, accessed June 15, 2011.

Cooper, Robin, and Chew, W. Bruce, "Control Tomorrow's Costs through Today's Designs," *Harvard Business Review* 74 (January–February 1996): pp. 88–97.

Cooper, Robin, and Slagmulder, Regine, "Develop Profitable New Products with Target Costing," *Sloan Management Review* 40 (Summer 1999): pp. 23–33.

Cressman Jr., George E., and Nagle, Thomas T., "How to Manage an Aggressive Competitor," *Business Horizons* 45 (March–April 2002), pp. 23–30.

Dean, Joel, "Pricing Policies for New Products," *Harvard Business Review* 54 (November–December 1976): p. 151.

Deschamps, Jean-Phillippe, and Ranganath Nayak, P., *Product Juggernauts: How Companies Mobilize to Generate a Stream of Market Winners* (Boston: Harvard Business School Press, 1995), pp. 119–149.

Dibb, Sally, Simkin, Lyndon, Pride, Bill, and Ferrell, O.C., *Marketing Concepts & Strategies*, 6th ed. (Cengage, 2012).

Dolan, Robert J., "The Same Make, Many Models Problem: Managing the Product Line," in *A Strategic Approach to Business Marketing*, Robert E. Spekman and David T. Wilson, eds. (Chicago: American Marketing Association, 1985), pp. 151–159.

Dolan, Robert J., "How Do You Know When the Price Is Right?" *Harvard Business Review* 73 (September–October 1995): pp. 174–183.

Dolan, Robert J., and Jeuland, Abel P., "Experience Curves and Dynamic Demand Models: Implications for Optimal Pricing Strategies," *Journal of Marketing* 45 (Winter 1981): pp. 52–62.

Doole, Isobel, and Lowe, Robin, *International Marketing Strategy* 6th ed. (Cengage, 2012).

Eggert, Andreas, and Ulaga, Wolfgang, "Managing Customer Value in Key Supplier Relationships," *Industrial Marketing Management* 39 (November 2010): pp. 1346–1355.

Fernando, Surani and Moss, Abigail, 'UK value-based pricing will struggle to materialise as year-end deadline approaches', Financial Times Online, 13th March 2013, accessed at http://www.ft.com/cms/s/2/db268c82-8be8-11e2-b001-00144feabdc0.html#axzz2dGEMDrEz, on 29th August 2013

Hancock, Maryanne Q., John, Roland H., and Wojcik, Philip J., "Better B2B Selling," *The McKinsey Quarterly* (June 2005): pp. 1–8.

Ingenbleek, Paul, Debruyne, Marion, Frambach, Rudd T., and Verhallen, Theo M., "Successful New Product Pricing Practices: A Contingency Approach," *Marketing Letters* 14 (December 2004): pp. 289–304.

Jacobson, Robert, and Aaker, David A., "Is Market Share All That It's Cracked Up to Be?" *Journal of Marketing* 49 (Fall 1985): pp. 11–22.

Jap, Sandy D., "Online Reverse Auctions: Issues, Themes, and Prospects for the Future," *Journal of the Academy of Marketing Science* 30 (Fall 2002): p. 507.

Jap, Sandy, "The Impact of Online Reverse Auction Design on Buyer-Seller Relationships," *Journal of Marketing* 71 (January 2007): pp. 146–159.

Mendel, Arthur H., and Poueymirou, Roger, "Pricing," in *The Purchasing Handbook*, Harold E. Fearon, Donald W. Dobler, and Kenneth H. Killen, eds. (New York: McGraw-Hill, 1993), pp. 201–227.

Monroe, Kent B., Pricing: Making Profitable Decisions (New York: McGraw-Hill, 1979), pp. 52–57.

Moore, Geoffrey A., *Inside the Tornado: Marketing Strategies from Silicon Valley's Cutting Edge* (New York: HarperCollins, 1995), pp. 84–85.

Moutinho, Luiz, and Southern, Geoffrey, *Strategic Marketing Management: A process Based Approach* (Cengage, 2012).

Moyer, Reed, and Boewadt, Robert J., "The Pricing of Industrial Goods," *Business Horizons* 14 (June 1971): pp. 27–34.

Nagle, Thomas T., *The Strategy and Tactics of Pricing: A Guide to Profitable Decision Making* (Englewood Cliffs, NJ: Prentice Hall, 1987), p. 1.

'NICE Central to Value Based Pricing Of Medicines', accessed at http://www.nice.org.uk/newsroom/news/NICECentralToValueBasedPricingOfMedicines.jsp, on 29th August 2013

Reinartz, Werner, and Ulaga, Wolfgang, "How to Sell Services More Profitability," *Harvard Business Review* 86 (May 2008): pp. 91–96.

Rostky, George, "Unveiling Market Segments with Technical Focus Research," *Business Marketing* 71 (October 1986): pp. 66–69.

Sashi, C. M., and O'Leary, Bay, "The Role of Internet Auctions in the Expansion of B2B Markets," *Industrial Marketing Management* 31 (February 2002): pp. 103–110.

Sharma, Arun, Krishnan, R., and Grewal, Dhruv, "Value Creation in Markets: A Critical Area of Focus for Business-to-Business Markets," *Industrial Marketing Management* 30 (June 2001): pp. 397–398.

Shaw, J., Giglierano, J. and Kallis, J. (1989) 'Marketing complex technical products: the importance of intangible attributes', *Industrial Marketing Management* 18:45–53.Slatter, Stuart St. P., "Strategic Marketing Variables under Conditions of Competitive Bidding," *Strategic Management Journal* 11 (May–June 1990): pp. 309–317.

Smith, Gerald E., and Nagle, Thomas T., "How Much Are Customers Willing to Pay?" *Marketing Research* 14 (Winter 2002): pp. 20–25.

Smith, Gerald E., and Nagle, Thomas T., "A Question of Value," *Marketing Management* 14 (July/August 2005): pp. 38–43.

Ulaga, Wolfgang, and Eggert, Andreas, "Value-Based Differentiation in Business Relationships: Gaining and Sustaining Key Supplier Status," *Journal of Marketing* 70 (January 2006): pp. 119–136.

'Value-based pricing to be undertaken by NICE', National Health Executive Online, 21st June 2013, accessed at http://www.nationalhealthexecutive.com/NHS-Finance/value-based-pricing-to-be-undertaken-by-nice on 29th August 2013

van Weele, Arjan, *Puchasing and Supply Chain Management: Analysis Strategy, Planning and Practice*, 5th ed. (Cengage, 2010).

Verhage, Bronis J., *Marketing: A Global Perspective* (Cengage, 2013).

CHAPTER 13
BUSINESS
MARKETING
COMMUNICATIONS

CHAPTER OBJECTIVES

After reading this chapter, you will understand:

1   The decisions that must be made when forming a business advertising program

2   The business media options, including the important role of online advertising

3   The importance of communications in international companies

4   The role of personal selling and how to manage a sales force

Marketing communications are concerned with presenting and exchanging information with various stakeholders, both individuals and organisations to achieve specific results. This means not only that the information must be understood accurately but that, often, elements of persuasion are also required. In a domestic environment this process is difficult enough, but the management of both offline and online international marketing communications is made particularly challenging by a number of factors including the complexity of different market conditions, differences in media availability, languages, cultural sensitivities, regulations controlling advertising and sales promotions and the challenge of providing adequate resourcing levels.

A variety of approaches have been taken to define and describe the marketing mix area, which is concerned with persuasive communications. Some writers refer to the 'communications mix', others to the 'promotional mix' and others, for example Kotler (2002), use the two terms interchangeably to mean the same thing. Communications, embracing as it does the ideas of conveying information, is the most helpful term and implies the need for a two-way process in international marketing and is at the core of the digital media. It also includes internal communications between the organisation's staff, especially as organisations become larger, more diverse and complex. In addition 'internal staff' might include collaborative partners that add value to the organisation's offer and are part of the supply chain. Some online organisations encourage greater involvement of customers in the business and these situations redraw the boundaries between internal and external staff.*

13.1 BUSINESS-TO-BUSINESS (B2B) SOCIAL MEDIA

According to *The Marketer* magazine, B2B opportunities from social media are blossoming. American Express's B2B networking site *Openforum.com* is accessible to both new business customers and current Open Card members. It provides small and medium sized enterprises (SMEs) access to a wealth of advice and insight, including the views of Richard Branson and Seth Godin. Growing at 350 per cent year on year, the site quickly reached 10 000 Twitter followers. Intel's blog network allows readers to 'dig' or recommend its blogs on news sharing site Digg. Some Intel staff blogs have been recommended by over a thousand Digg users, providing a valuable platform for shaping opinion in Intel's markets, building reputation, and conveying a point of view favourable to supporting the company's marketing strategy. In a separate development, it is expected that many B2B social media gated communities will emerge, providing confidential business or issue 'chat rooms' for professionals in certain industries, similar to VuMedi for registered doctors. Social media applications are no longer only of interest to marketers addressing consumers.*

13.2 THE ROLE OF ADVERTISING

13.2.1 Integrated communication programs

Advertising and sales promotion are rarely used alone in the business-to-business setting but are intertwined with the total communications strategy—particularly personal selling. Personal and nonpersonal forms of communication interact to inform key buying influentials. The challenge for the business marketer is to create an advertising and sales promotion strategy that effectively blends with personal selling in order to meet sales and profit objectives. In addition, the advertising, online media, and sales promotion tools must be integrated; that is, a comprehensive program of media and sales promotion methods must be coordinated to achieve the desired results.

13.2.2 Increased sales efficiency

The effect of advertising on the marketing program's overall efficiency is evidenced in two ways. First, business suppliers frequently need to remind actual and potential buyers of their products or make them aware of new products or services. Although these objectives could be partially accomplished through personal selling, the costs of reaching a vast group of buyers would be prohibitive. Carefully targeted advertising extends beyond the salesperson's reach to unidentified buying influentials. A properly placed advertisement can reach hundreds of buying influentials for only a few cents each; the average cost of a business sales call is currently more than €150.14 Sales call costs are determined by the salesperson's wages, travel and entertainment costs, and fringe benefits costs. If these costs total €600 per day and a salesperson can make four calls per day, then each call costs €150. Second, advertising appears to make all selling activities more effective. Advertising interacts effectively with all communication and selling activities, and it can boost efficiency for the entire marketing expenditure.

13.2.3 Creating awareness

From a communications standpoint, the buying process takes potential buyers sequentially from unawareness of a product or supplier to awareness, to brand preference, to conviction that a particular purchase will fulfil their requirements, and, ultimately, to actual purchase. Business advertising often creates awareness of the supplier and the supplier's products. Sixty-one per cent of the design engineers returning an inquiry card from a magazine ad indicated that they were unaware of the company that advertised before seeing the ad.[*] Business advertising may also make some contribution to creating preference for the product—all cost-effectively.

In addition, advertising can create a corporate identity or image. Hewlett-Packard, Dell, IBM, and others use ads in general business publications such as *Business Week* and even television advertising to trumpet the value of their brand and to develop desired perceptions in a broad audience.[*]

13.2.4 What business-to-business advertising cannot do

To develop an effective communications program, the business marketing manager must blend all communication tools (online and print formats) into an integrated program, using each tool where it is most effective. Business advertising quite obviously has limitations. Advertising cannot substitute for effective personal selling—it must supplement, support, and complement that effort. In the same way, personal selling is constrained by its costs and should not be used to create awareness or to disseminate information—tasks quite capably performed by advertising.

For many purchasing decisions, advertising alone cannot create product preference—this requires demonstration, explanation, and operational testing. Similarly, conviction and actual purchase can be ensured only by personal selling. Advertising has a supporting role in creating awareness, providing information, and uncovering important leads for salespeople; that is how the marketing manager must use it to be effective.

13.3 MANAGING BUSINESS-TO-BUSINESS ADVERTISING

The advertising decision model in Figure 13.1 shows the structural elements involved in managing business-to-business advertising. First, advertising is only one component of the entire marketing strategy and must be integrated with other components to achieve strategic goals. The

FIGURE 13.1 The decision stages for developing the business-to-business advertising program

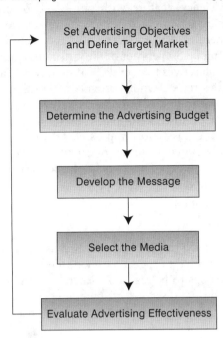

advertising decision process begins with formulating advertising objectives, which are derived from marketing goals. From this formulation the marketer can determine how much it has to spend to achieve those goals.

Then, specific communication messages are formulated to achieve the market behaviour specified by the objectives. Equally important is evaluating and selecting the media used to reach the desired audience. The result is an integrated advertising campaign aimed at eliciting a specific attitude or behaviour from the target group. The final, and critical, step is to evaluate the campaign's effectiveness.

13.3.1 Defining advertising objectives

Knowing what advertising must accomplish enables the manager to determine an advertising budget more accurately and provides a yardstick for evaluating advertising.

In specifying advertising goals, the marketing manager must realise that: (1) the advertising mission flows directly from the overall marketing strategy; advertising must fulfil a marketing strategy objective, and its goal must reflect the general aim and purpose of the entire strategy; and (2) the advertising program's objectives must respond to the roles for which advertising is suited: creating awareness, providing information, influencing attitudes, and reminding buyers of company and product existence.

13.3.2 Written objectives

An advertising objective must be measurable and realistic, and must specify what is to be achieved and when. The objective must speak in unambiguous terms of a specific outcome. The purpose is to establish a single working direction for everyone involved in creating, coordinating, and evaluating the advertising program. Correctly conceived objectives set standards for evaluating the advertising effort. A specific objective might be "to increase from 15 per cent (as measured in June 2012) to 30 per cent (by June 2013) the proportion of general contractors associating 'energy efficiency' feature with our brand of commercial air conditioners." The objective directs the manager to create a message related to the major product benefit, using media that reaches general contractors. The objective also provides a way to measure accomplishment (awareness among 30 per cent of the target audience).

Business advertising objectives frequently bear no direct relationship to specific euro sales targets. Although euro sales results would provide a "hard" measure of advertising accomplishment, it is often impossible to link advertising directly to sales.

Personal selling, price, product performance, and competitive actions have a more direct relationship to sales levels, and it is almost impossible to sort out advertising's impact. Thus, advertising goals are typically stated in terms of *communication goals* such as brand awareness, recognition, and buyer attitudes. These goals can be measured; it is presumed that achieving them stimulates sales volume.

Target audience

A significant task is specifying target audiences. Because a primary role of advertising is to reach buying influentials inaccessible to the salesperson, the business marketing manager must define the buying influential groups to be reached. Generally, each group of buying influentials is concerned with distinct product and service attributes and criteria, and the advertising must focus on these. Thus, the objectives must specify the intended audience and its relevant decision criteria.

Creative strategy statement

A final consideration is to specify the creative strategy statement. Once objectives and targets are established, the **creative strategy statement** provides guidelines for the company and advertising agency on how to position the product in the marketplace. Product position relates to how the target market perceives the product. For example, if the commercial air conditioners cited earlier currently have an unfavourable product position with regard to energy efficiency but recent product development efforts have advanced performance, the firm might use the following creative strategy statement: "Our basic creative strategy is to reposition the product from that of a reliable air conditioner to a high-performance, energy-efficient air conditioner."

All creative efforts—copy, theme, colour, and so forth—as well as media and tactics, should support the creative strategy statement. Planning an effective advertising campaign requires clearly defined objectives that provide a foundation for selecting media and measuring results.

13.3.3 Determining advertising expenditures

Collectively, business marketers spend billions of euros on media advertising annually, and the Web is winning a growing share of these euros. Typically, business marketers use a blend of intuition, judgment, experience, and, only occasionally, more advanced decision-oriented techniques to determine advertising budgets.

Rules of thumb

Often, because advertising is a relatively small part of the total marketing budget for business firms, the value of using sophisticated methods for advertising budgeting is not great. In these cases, managers tend to follow simple **rules of thumb** (for example, allocate 1 per cent of sales to advertising or match competition spending). Unfortunately, percentage-of-sales rules are all too pervasive throughout business marketing, even where advertising is an important element.

The fundamental problem with percentage-of-sales rules is that they implicitly make advertising a consequence rather than a determinant of sales and profits and can easily give rise to dysfunctional policies. Percentage-of-sales rules suggest that the business advertiser reduce advertising when sales volume declines, just when increased advertising may be more appropriate. Nevertheless, simple rules of thumb continue to be applied in budget decisions because they are easy to use and familiar to management.

Objective-task method

The task method for budgeting advertising expenditures relates advertising costs to the objective it is to accomplish. Because the sales euro results of advertising are almost impossible to measure, the task method focuses on the communications effects of advertising, not on the sales effects.

The **objective-task method** is applied by evaluating the tasks advertising will perform, analysing the costs of each task, and summing up the total costs to arrive at a final budget. The process can be divided into four steps:

1   Establish specific marketing objectives for the product in terms of such factors as sales volume, market share, profit contribution, and market segments.

2   Assess the communication functions that must be performed to realise the marketing objectives and then determine the role of advertising and other elements of the communications mix in performing these functions.

3   Define specific goals for advertising in terms of the measurable communication response required to achieve marketing objectives.

4   Estimate the budget needed to accomplish the advertising goals.

The task method addresses the major problem of the rule-of-thumb methods—funds are applied to accomplish a specific goal so that advertising is a *determinant* of those results, not a consequence. Using the task approach, managers allocate all the funds necessary to accomplish a specific objective rather than allocating some arbitrary percentage of sales. The most troubling problem with the method is that management must have some instinct for the proper relationship between expenditure level and communication response. It is difficult to know what produces a certain level of awareness among business marketing buying influentials. Will 12 two-page insertions in *Fortune* Magazine over the next six months create the desired recognition level, or will 24 insertions over one year be necessary?

Budgeting for advertising must not ignore the political and behavioural aspects of the process. Nigel Piercy's research suggests that firms pay insufficient attention to budgeting technique because they operate through structures and processes that are often political in nature.[*] Piercy suggests that what actually determines advertising budgets are the power "interests" in the company and the political behaviour of various parties in the budgeting process. An implication of this research is that the manager may be well served by focusing on budgeting as a political activity, and not simply as a technique-driven process.

Passing the threshold

Several communications are often needed to capture the attention of buyers, which complicates the budgeting decision. Research suggests that a brand must surpass a threshold level of awareness in the market before meaningful increases can be made to its brand preference share. A small advertising budget may not allow the marketer to move the firm's brand beyond a threshold level of awareness and on to preference. Eunsang Yoon and Valerie Kijewski warn that "the communications manager having limited marketing resources will then be in danger of making the mistake of stopping the program prematurely, thus wasting past investment, rather than pressing on to pass the threshold awareness level."[*]

Because budgeting is so important to advertising effectiveness, managers must not blindly follow rules of thumb. Instead, they should evaluate the tasks required and their costs against industry norms. With clear objectives and proper budgetary allocations, the next step is to design effective advertising messages.

13.3.4 Developing the advertising message

Message development is a complex, critical task in industrial advertising. Highlighting a product attribute that is unimportant to a particular buying group is not only a waste of advertising euros but also a lost opportunity. Both the appeal and the way that appeal is conveyed are vital to successful communication. Thus, creating business-to-business advertising messages involves determining advertising objectives, evaluating the buying criteria of the target audience, and analysing the most appropriate language, format, and style for presenting the message.

Perception

For an advertising message to be successful, an individual must first be exposed to it and pay attention to it. Thus, a business advertisement must catch the decision maker's attention. Once the individual has noticed the message, he or she must interpret it as the advertiser intended. Perceptual barriers often prevent a receiver from perceiving the intended message. Even though the individual is exposed to an advertisement, nothing guarantees that he or she processes the message.

In fact, the industrial buyer may read every word of the copy and find a meaning in it opposite to the one the advertiser intended.

The business advertiser must therefore contend with two important elements of perception: attention and interpretation. Buyers tend to screen out messages that are inconsistent with their own attitudes, needs, and beliefs, and they tend to interpret information in the light of those beliefs. Unless advertising messages are carefully designed and targeted, they may be disregarded or interpreted improperly.

Advertisers must put themselves in the position of the receivers to evaluate how the message appears to them. For example, technical ads were shown to create less desire in some readers to seek information because such ads suggest "more difficulty in operation." From a message-development viewpoint, the business advertiser must carefully tailor the technical aspects of promotional messages to the appropriate audience.

Focus on benefits

A business buyer purchases benefits—a better way to accomplish some task, a less expensive way to produce a final product, a solution to a problem, or a faster delivery time. Advertising messages need to focus on benefits that the target customer seeks and persuade the reader that the advertiser can deliver them.[*]

Messages that have direct appeals or calls to action are viewed to be "stronger" than those with diffuse or indirect appeals to action. Robert Lamons, an advertising consultant, observes: A good call to action can actually start the selling process. Promise a test report; offer a product demonstration; direct them to a special section of your Web site.... Compare how your product stacks up to others in the field. Everyone is super-busy these days, and if you can offer something that helps them expedite or narrow their search, you're giving them something money can't buy: free time.[*]

Understanding buyer motivations

Which product benefits are important to each group of buying influentials? The business advertiser cannot assume that a standard set of "classical buying motives" applies in every purchase situation. Many business advertisers often do not understand the buying motives of important market segments. Developing effective advertising messages often requires extensive marketing research in order to fully delineate the key buying criteria of each buying influencer in each of the firm's different target markets.

13.3.5 Selecting advertising media for business markets

Although the message is vital to advertising success, equally important is the medium through which it is presented. An integrated marketing communications program might include a blend of online, print, and direct-mail advertisements that deliver a consistent story across formats. Business-to-business media are selected by the target audience—the particular purchase-decision participants to be reached. Selection of media also involves budgetary considerations: Where are euros best spent to generate the customer contacts desired?

Online advertising

As business marketing strategists seek more effective ways to communicate with customers and prospects, they continue to shift more of the advertising budget to digital formats. For example, during a recent global interactive campaign, more than 220 000 visitors clicked through to a Hewlett-Packard microsite designed for small and mid-sized businesses.[*] A **microsite** is a specialised Web page a visitor lands on after clicking an online ad or e-mail. Similarly, both IBM and GE make extensive use of online videos to show how their products and services are helping customers around the world to solve business problems.

A Shift to Digital Online advertising spending by business-to-business firms exceeds €23.25 billion and will continue to grow at a rapid pace. Paid search engine advertising represents the prime format, accounting for over 45 per cent of total online spending, followed by display ads.[*] Experiencing particularly rapid spending growth is the rich media/video format, particularly the online video category. "Video is a particularly compelling way to tell a brand or product story that can be very useful for b-to-b communications, as these businesses tend to be more complex and can require additional explanation," according to Andreas Combuechen, CEO–chief creative officer of Atmosphere BBDO.[*]

Business publications

More than 2700 business publications carry business-to-business advertising. For those specialising in the pharmaceutical industry, *Drug Discovery & Development*, *Pharmaceutical Executive*, and *Pharmaceutical Technology* are a few of the publications available. Business publications are either horizontal or vertical.

Horizontal publications are directed at a specific task, technology, or function, whatever the industry. *Advertising Age*, *Purchasing*, and *Marketing News* are horizontal.

Vertical publications, on the other hand, may be read by everyone from floor supervisor to president within a specific industry. Typical vertical publications are *Chemical Business* or *Computer Gaming World*. If a business marketer's product has applications within only a few industries, vertical publications are a logical media choice. When many industries are potential users and well-defined functions are the principal buying influencers, a horizontal publication is effective.

Many trade publications are **requester publications,** which offer free subscriptions to selected readers. The publisher can select readers who are in a position to influence buying decisions and offer the free subscription in exchange for information such as title, function, and buying responsibilities. Thus, the advertiser can tell whether each publication reaches the desired audience.

Obviously, publication choice is predicated on a complete understanding of the range of purchase-decision participants and of the industries where the product is used. Only then can the target audience be matched to the circulation statements of alternative business publications.

Characteristics of an effective print Ad

Recent research on the effectiveness of business-to-business print ads provides strong evidence that the marketing strategist should emphasise a "rational approach" and provide a clear description of the product and the benefits it offers to customers.[*] The effectiveness of ads is also enhanced by detailing product quality and performance information in a concrete and logical manner.

Advertising cost

Circulation is an important criterion in the selection of publications, but circulation must be tempered by cost. First, the total advertising budget must be allocated among the various advertising tools, such as business publications, sales promotion, direct marketing (mail and e-mail), and online advertising. Of course, allocations to the various media options vary with company situation and advertising mission. The allocation of the business publication budget among various journals depends on their relative effectiveness and efficiency, usually measured in cost per thousand using the following formula:

$$\text{Cost per thousand} = \frac{\text{Cost per page}}{\text{Circulation in thousands}}$$

To compare two publications by their actual page rates would be misleading because the publication with the lower circulation is usually less expensive. The cost-per-thousand calculation should be based on circulation to the *target* audience, not the total audience. Although some publications may appear expensive on a cost per-thousand basis, they may in fact be cost-effective, with little wasted circulation.

B2B TOP PERFORMERS

Facebook can be a marketer's best friend

Founded in 2004, Facebook was initially created just to connect students at Harvard and other Ivy League universities; it soon expanded to include family, friends and colleagues. Since being opened to the general public, it has grown to support more than 500 million users worldwide. Although it still serves its original purpose, Facebook has acquired diverse new roles, even changing how people use the Internet. When conducting research, many people now seek recommendations from social media friends before conducting other kinds of searches. Facebook users share more than 5 billion pieces of Web content each week.

Marketing strategists say businesses now must worry about how to connect to consumers via social media. One of the ways is to create a fan page, of which Facebook has billions. The average user becomes a fan of four pages each month. Fan pages use widgets, which help companies keep track of information on who is becoming a fan of their page. Businesses can use widgets to learn about and track their customers in order to better understand and serve them. These pages are inexpensive and easy to produce, making them accessible to all businesses.

Businesses must tread carefully, however. Generally, Facebook users do not want to feel as if they are being subjected to sales pitches. In order to make fans feel connected to a company without making them feel like they are being pressured to buy something against their will, companies must dedicate time to responding to fan posts and providing relevant information. Problems aside, fan pages and other uses of widgets are a cheap way for companies to advertise their goods and services while also garnering information about consumers. Art Meets Commerce – a marketing firm commissioned to promote Broadway and Off-Broadway shows – has used Facebook with great success, as it is the company's number-one source of ticket sales. Given the popularity of fan pages and the low cost commitment, Facebook may be the future of advertising for some brands.

Some publications also have popular Web sites that advertisers can use to create integrated marketing communications.

Frequency and scheduling

Even the most successful business publication advertisements are seen by only a small percentage of the people who read the magazine; therefore, one-time ads are generally ineffective. Because a number of exposures are required before a message "sinks in," and because the reading audience varies from month to month, a schedule of advertising insertions is required. To build continuity and repetitive value, at least 6 insertions per year may be required in a monthly publication, and 26 to 52 insertions (with a minimum of 13) in a weekly publication.*

13.3.6 Direct marketing tools

Direct mail and e-mail are among the direct marketing tools available to the business marketer. Direct mail delivers the advertising message firsthand to selected individuals. Possible mailing pieces range from a sales letter introducing a new product to a lengthy brochure or even a product sample. Direct mail can accomplish all of the major advertising functions, but its real contribution is in delivering the message to a precisely defined prospect. In turn, says marketing consultant Barry Silverstein, direct *e-mail* can have a substantial effect on creating and qualifying customer leads, *if* some important rules are strictly followed: "always seek permission to send e-mail" and "always provide the recipient with the ability to 'opt out.'"*

Direct mail

Direct mail is commonly used for corporate image promotion, product and service promotion, sales force support, distribution channel communication, and special marketing problems.* In promoting corporate image, direct mail may help to establish a firm's reputation of technological leadership. On the other hand, product advertising by direct mail can put specific product information in the hands of buying influentials. For example, as part of a successful integrated marketing campaign to change perceptions of UPS from a ground shipping company to a supply chain leader, the firm used direct mail to target decision makers—from shipping managers to front-office administrators. The direct-mail strategy had strong results, achieving a 10.5 per cent response rate, with 36 per cent of those responders buying services.*

Direct e-mail

Because marketers are devoting a larger share of their advertising budgets to online marketing, IBM's customer relationship program, called *Focusing on You*, rests on a simple but powerful idea—ask customers what information they want and give it to them.* By giving the customer the choice, IBM learns about the customer's unique preferences and is better equipped to tailor product and service information to that customer's specific needs. The program relies on e-mail marketing, which is far less costly than direct mail. IBM found that sending customers traditional printed materials by mail was 10 times more expensive than email communications. Moreover, e-mail campaigns often yield higher responses than direct-mail campaigns, and the results are generated more quickly. For example, a third of all responses to a particular IBM e-mail campaign were generated in the first 24 hours!

Firms that plan to fully integrate direct e-mail into their marketing communications strategy should make a special effort to build their own e-mail list. Often such information is already available from the firm's customer relationship management (CRM) system. Remember that a goal of the CRM system is to integrate customer records from all departments, including sales, marketing, and customer service. As a result, if a customer responds to an e-mail (or direct-mail) campaign, the CRM system captures that information in a centralised database for all contact employees (salespersons, call centre employees, marketing managers) to retrieve.

Other ways to create an e-mail list include offering an e-mail alert service or e-mail newsletter, asking for e-mail addresses in direct-mail campaigns, and collecting e-mail addresses at trade shows.[*] Business marketers must also realise that the response to an e-mail campaign can be immediate, so they must be prepared to acknowledge, process, and fulfil orders before the e-mail campaign is launched.

13.4 MEASURING ADVERTING EFFECTIVENESS

The business advertiser rarely expects orders to result immediately from advertising.

Advertising is designed to create awareness, stimulate loyalty to the company, or create a favourable attitude toward a product. Even though advertising may not directly precipitate a purchase decision, advertising programs must be held accountable, and marketing managers are facing increased pressure to demonstrate the actual returns on marketing expenditures.[*] Research suggests that firms that are adept at marketing performance measurement generate greater profitability and stock returns than their competitors.[*] Thus, the business advertiser must be able to measure the results of current advertising in order to improve future advertising and evaluate the effectiveness of advertising expenditures against expenditures on other elements of marketing strategy.

13.4.1 Measuring impacts on the purchase decision

Measuring advertising effectiveness means assessing advertising's effect on what "intervenes" between the stimulus (advertising) and the resulting behaviour (purchase decision). The theory is that advertising can affect awareness, knowledge, and other dimensions that more readily lend themselves to measurement. In essence, the advertiser attempts to gauge advertising's ability to move an individual through the purchase decision process. This approach assumes, correctly or not, that enhancement of any one phase of the process or movement from one step to the next increases the ultimate probability of purchase.

Research suggests that business marketers should also measure the **indirect communication effects of advertising**.[*] This study revealed that advertising affects word-of-mouth communications (indirect effect), and such communications play an important role in buyer decision making. Similarly, the study showed that advertising indirectly affects buyers on the basis of its effect on overall company reputation and on the sales force's belief that advertising aids selling. The study suggested that advertising effectiveness measurements include a procedure for tracking and measuring advertising's effect on the indirect communication effects.

In summary, advertising effectiveness is evaluated against objectives formulated in terms of the elements of the buyer's decision process as well as some of the indirect communication effects. Advertising efforts are also judged, in the final analysis, on cost per level of achievement (for example, euros spent to achieve a certain level of awareness or recognition).

13.4.2 The measurement program

A sound measurement program entails substantial advanced planning. Figure 13.2 shows the basic areas of advertising evaluation. The advertising strategist must determine in advance what is to be measured, how, and in what sequence. A pre-evaluation phase is required to establish a benchmark for a new advertising campaign. For example, a pre-evaluation study would be conducted to capture the existing level of awareness a firm's product enjoys in a defined target market. After the advertising campaign, the evaluation study examines changes in awareness against this benchmark.

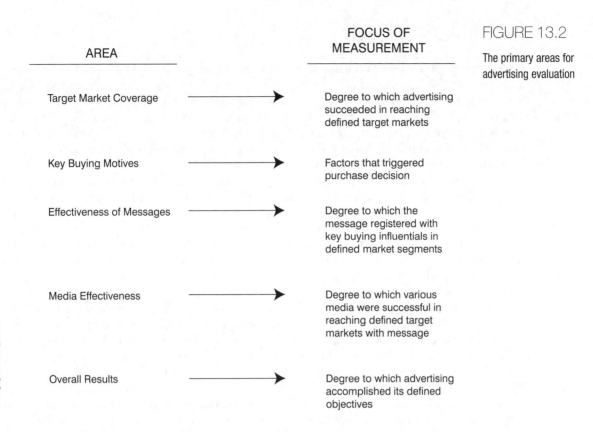

FIGURE 13.2

The primary areas for advertising evaluation

Five primary areas for advertising evaluation include: (1) markets, (2) motives, (3) messages, (4) media, and (5) results.

Web metrics

For online advertising, attention likewise centres on defined communication objectives. Was the ad designed to drive visitors to the Web site to view an online video or to download information on a new product?

This event is the "desired action," and the business marketing manager wants to measure site traffic to this action and evaluate all of the components of the Website that lead visitors to take this action. "Pulling in information from search marketing campaigns allows b-to-b marketers to better understand what visitors searched for to find their site and what text-based ads elicited the highest clickthrough and conversion (action) rates. In turn, these data can help marketers optimise their sites with language that resonates with their target audiences and customise their home pages with links that are most important to their visitors,"[*] says Jim Sterne, president, Target Media.

Evaluation is essential

The evaluation of business-to-business advertising is demanding and complex, but absolutely essential. Budgetary constraints are generally the limiting factors. However, professional research companies can be called on to develop field research studies. When determining the effect of advertising on moving a decision participant from an awareness of the product or company to a readiness to buy, the evaluations usually measure knowledge, recognition, recall, awareness, preference, and motivation. Measuring effects on actual sales are unfortunately seldom possible.

13.5 TRADE SHOWS

Trade shows and trade markets enable manufacturers or wholesalers to exhibit products to potential buyers, and so help the selling and buying functions. **Trade shows** are industry exhibitions that offer both selling and non-selling benefits.* On the selling side, trade shows let vendors identify prospects; gain access to key decision-makers; disseminate facts about their products, services and personnel; and actually sell products and service current accounts through contacts at the show.* Trade shows also allow a company to reach potential buyers who have not been approached through regular selling efforts. In fact, many trade show visitors have not recently been contacted by a sales representative of any company within the past year. Many of these individuals are, therefore, willing to travel several hundred miles to attend trade shows to learn about new goods and services. The non-selling benefits include opportunities to maintain the company image with competitors, customers and the industry; gather information about competitors' products and prices; and identify potential channel members.* Trade shows have a positive influence on other important marketing variables, such as maintaining or enhancing company morale, product testing and product evaluation.

Trade shows can permit direct buyer–seller interaction and may eliminate the need for agents. Companies exhibit at trade shows because of the high concentration of prospective buyers for their products. Studies show that it takes, on average, 5.1 sales calls to close an industrial business-to-business sale but less than 1 sales call (0.8) to close a trade show lead. The explanation for the latter figure is that more than half of the customers who purchase a product based on information gained at a trade show order the product by mail or by phone after the show. When customers use these more impersonal methods to gather information, the need for major sales calls to provide such information can be eliminated. Most manufacturers have sales and technical personnel who attend relevant trade shows in key target market territories. Birmingham's National Exhibition Centre (NEC) offers a 240-hectare (600-acre) site, with open display areas, plus 125 000 square metres (156 000 square yards) of covered exhibition space, hotels, parking for thousands of cars, plus rail and air links. Each year there are toy, fashion, giftware and antique trade fairs at the NEC, when trade customers can select merchandise for their next sales seasons. **Trade markets** are relatively permanent facilities that businesses can rent to exhibit products year round. At these markets, such products as furniture, home decorating supplies, toys, clothing and gift items are sold to wholesalers and retailers.*

Exhibitions and trade fairs are also an effective way of meeting many existing and potential customers from different countries. The cost of exhibiting at international trade fairs is very high when the cost of stand, space rental, sales staff time and travelling expenses are taking into account. It is for this reason that the selection of the most appropriate fairs for the industry is critical. Also important are the creative work for the stand, preparation of sales literature and selection of suitable personnel for the stand, bearing in mind the need to cultural and language empathy.

To obtain the maximum benefit from an exhibition it is essential to publicise the firm's attendance at the event to encourage potential customers to visit and also to ensure that all leads are followed up. Shimp (2006) explains that the real cost of exhibitions can be two or three times higher than the cost of the event itself.

An additional benefit of exhibitions is that they can provide experiential marketing, a rapidly growing communications approach also called customer experience marketing, in which customers obtain an engaging, entertaining and interactive brand experience. There are of course other ways of providing experiential marketing. For example, Apple operates stores in which customers can try out their products and Harley Davidson provides opportunities for visitors to ride its bikes.

Given the importance of context in many markets, such as Asia, experiential marketing, involving life experiences at events for external communications to customers and internal communications, were shown to be valuable (Whiteling 2007).

13.5.1 Planning trade-show strategy

To develop an effective trade-show communications strategy, managers must address four questions:

1 What functions should the trade show perform in the total marketing communications program?

2 To whom should the marketing effort at trade shows be directed?

3 What is the appropriate show mix for the company?

4 What should the trade-show investment-audit policy be? How should audits be carried out?[*]

Answering these questions helps managers crystallise their thinking about target audiences, about expected results, and about how funds should be allocated.

13.5.2 Managing the trade-show exhibit

To generate interest in an exhibit, business marketing firms run advertisements in business publications profiling new projects they will exhibit at the show. Tradeshow strategies should also be linked to interactive marketing communications. This enables many exhibitors to schedule appointments with prospects and customers during the show.

Sales personnel must be trained to perform in the trade-show environment. The selling job differs from the typical sales call in that the salesperson may have only 5 to 10 minutes to make a presentation. On a typical sales call, salespersons usually sell themselves first, then the company, and finally the product. At the trade show, the process is reversed.

There must be a system for responding effectively to inquiries generated at the show. Some business marketers find it effective to use a laptop to transmit information to corporate headquarters electronically. Headquarters staff then generate a letter and send out the required information by mail or e-mail. When prospects return to their offices after a show, the material is immediately available.

Improving sales efficiency

A study demonstrated the powerful way personal selling and trade shows work together in an integrated marketing communications strategy.[*] The results demonstrate that follow-up sales efforts generate higher sales productivity when customers had already been exposed to the company's products at a trade show. The return-on-sales figures are higher among show attendees than nonattendees, illuminating the positive effects of trade shows on customer purchase intentions. Although dramatically enhancing performance, however, trade shows can be extremely costly and must be carefully planned.

13.5.3 Personal selling

For many companies the first proactive communication tool to promote exports is personal selling. Selling is often used to gain the first few orders in a new market and as the main component of a push strategy to persuade distribution channel members, such as agents, distributors or retailers to stock the product. It is expensive, however.

The use of personal selling tends to be limited to situations in which benefits can be derived from two-way information flows, negotiations is required and when the revenue from the sale is sufficiently high to justify the costs. This is typically the case with business-to-business marketing.

In countries where labour costs are very low, personal selling is used to a greater extent than in high cost countries. This ranges from street and market trading to quite sophisticated multilevel distribution chains for business-to-business products. In high labour-cost countries personal selling of low unit cost products is used rarely, except for illegal trading, for example of drugs.

Effective selling in international business-to-business and consumer markets involves a wide range of tasks and skills, including product and market knowledge, listening and questioning skills. However, it is in the core selling activities of negotiation and persuasion that high-order expertise is required. It is likely that local people will be more effective than home-based representatives in understanding the subtleties of the negotiation process as they apply within the local business culture. They will have fluent language skills and an intimate knowledge of the culture of the country.

However, negotiation of high-value contracts may well require specialist technical knowledge, an understanding of the processes and systems and strict adherence to the firm's standards and values. For these reasons the company may well prefer to use staff from its head office to ensure that the sales people are well informed about the firm's capabilities and that their activities can be controlled.

This is particularly the case if the opportunities to make a sale are very infrequent (i.e. with capital goods) when high levels of technical skill and an understanding of the company's systems are needed but not easily learnt by new people. For example, Rolls-Royce use a complete team of UK-based engineers, accountants and sales people to sell aero engines to customers in foreign markets. Some of the team will make frequent visits, others will be based in close online and offline contact with the customer for a period of many months. The sheer complexity of the contracts means that only Rolls-Royce employees could understand the detail sufficiently to handle the negotiations. The high contract price provides sufficient revenue to pay for the costs of the UK-based sales team.

An alternative to employing local or head office sales staff (both have their advantages and disadvantages) is to employ expatriates, staff from the domestic country to work for extended periods in the host country in order to bridge the culture and company standards gap.

In practice the expatriate is like to experience a culture shock caused by living in a foreign culture where the familiar symbols, cues and everyday reassurances are missing, often causing feelings of frustration, stress and anxiety. The expatriate can respond to the situation in one of three ways. At one extreme, adjustment is made to the expatriate culture only. In effect the expatriate adjusts to the way of life of a ready-made cultural island within the host country and makes little attempt to adjust to the host culture.

At the other extreme the expatriate completely embraces the host culture and minimises contact with the expatriate community – and the firm, too. Ideally the expatriate adjusts to both the local culture and the expatriate culture. In this way the expatriate retains the home country's and firm's systems of values and beliefs, but is considerate and respectful towards the people of his or her host country and to their culture. It is this last option that is usually most beneficial for the firm's sales effort.

Whichever approach to selling is adopted it is through relevant training that firms aim to manage their sales staff's involvement with the firm and the market, and maintain their enthusiasm for selling. Honeycutt (2005) explains that global firms have a training culture, employ a more formal training curriculum and focus on 'soft' competencies, whereas local Singaporean firms used more on the job training and did not appear to understand how sales training could be used for competitive advantage. As the cost of personal selling is increasing, so firms are seeking ways of improving their cost-effectiveness by using more systematic ways of analysing customer requirements and carrying out the sales role, rather than relying on a good firm handshake for closing the deal.[*]

13.6 SALES ADMINISTRATION

Successful sales force administration involves recruiting and selecting salespersons, then training, motivating, supervising, evaluating, and controlling them. The industrial firm should foster an organisational climate that encourages the development of a successful sales force.

13.6.1 Recruitment and selection of salespersons

The recruiting process presents numerous trade-offs for the business marketer. Should the company seek experienced salespersons, or should it hire and train inexperienced individuals? The answer depends on the specific situation; it varies with the size of the firm, the nature of the selling task, the firm's training capability, and its market experience. Smaller firms often reduce training costs by hiring experienced and more expensive salespersons. In contrast, large organisations with a more complete training function can hire less experienced personnel and support them with a carefully developed training program.

A second trade-off is quantity versus quality. Often, sales managers screen as many recruits as possible when selecting new salespersons. However, this approach can overload the selection process, hampering the firm's ability to identify quality candidates.

13.6.2 Training

To prepare new salespersons adequately, the training program must be carefully designed. Periodic training is required to sharpen the skills of experienced salespersons, especially when the firm's environment is changing rapidly. Changes in business marketing strategy (for example, new products, new market segments) require corresponding changes in personal selling styles.

The salesperson needs a wealth of knowledge about the company, the product line, customer segments, competition, organisational buying behaviour, and effective communication skills.[*] All of these elements must be part of sales training programs. Compared with their counterparts, top-performing sales organisations train new salespeople in a broader range of areas: market knowledge, communication skills, listening techniques, complaint-handling skills, and industry knowledge.[*]

With the expansion in global marketing, firms need to include a sales training module that examines how to approach and respond to customers of different cultures. Such training would focus on the role of intercultural communication in developing global buyer–seller relationships.[*] Effective training builds the salesperson's confidence and motivation, thereby increasing the probability of success. In turn, training helps the business marketer by keeping personal selling in line with marketing program objectives. A successful training effort can reduce the costs of recruiting; many business-to-business firms have found that salesperson turnover declines as training improves. Clearly, a salesperson who is inadequately prepared to meet the demands of selling can quickly become discouraged, frustrated, and envious of friends who chose other career options. Effective training and capable first-line supervision can alleviate much of this anxiety, which is especially prevalent in the early stages of many careers.

13.6.3 Supervision and motivation

The sales force must be directed in a way that is consistent with the company's policies and marketing objectives. Critical supervisory tasks are continued training, counselling, assistance (for example, time management), and activities that help sales personnel plan and execute their work. Supervision also sets sales performance standards, fulfils company policy, and integrates the sales force with higher organisational levels.

Orville Walker, Gilbert Churchill, and Neil Ford define **motivation** as the amount of effort the salesperson "desires to expend on each of the activities or tasks associated with his (her) job, such as calling on potential new accounts, planning sales presentations, and filling out reports."[*] The model presented in Figure 13.3 hypothesises that a salesperson's job performance is a function of three factors: (1) level of motivation, (2) aptitude or ability, and (3) perceptions about how to perform his or her role. Each factor is influenced by personal variables (for example, personality), organisational variables (for example, training programs), and environmental variables (for example, economic conditions). Sales managers can influence some of the personal and organisational variables through selection, training, and supervision.

FIGURE 13.3 Determinants of a salesperson's performance

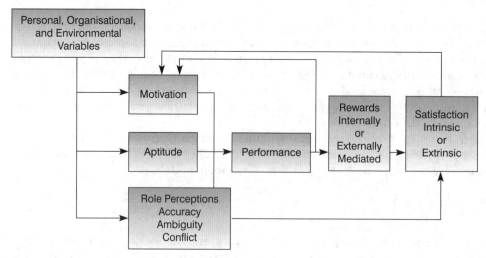

Source: Orville C. Walker Jr., Gilbert A. Churchill Jr., and Neil M. Ford, ''Motivation and Performance in Industrial Selling: Present Knowledge and Needed Research,'' *Journal of Marketing Research* 14 (May 1977): p. 158. Reprinted by permission of the American Marketing Association.

Motivation is related strongly to: (1) the individual's perceptions of the types and amounts of rewards from various degrees of job performance and (2) the value the salesperson places on these rewards. For a given level of performance, two types of rewards might be offered:

1 **Internally mediated rewards:** The salesperson attains rewards on a personal basis, such as feelings of accomplishment or self-worth.

2 **Externally mediated rewards:** Rewards are controlled and offered by managers or customers, such as financial incentives, pay, or recognition.

The rewards strongly influence salesperson satisfaction with the job and the work environment, which is also influenced by the individual's role perceptions. Job satisfaction declines when the salesperson's perception of the role is: (1) *inaccurate* in terms of the expectations of superiors, (2) characterised by *conflicting* demands among role partners (company and customer) that the salesperson cannot possibly resolve, or (3) surrounded by *uncertainty* because of a lack of information about the expectations and evaluation criteria of superiors and customers.

Hewlett-Packard's quarterly award for a salesperson who was particularly astute in converting an objection into an order to the elaborate sales award presentations at IBM.

Incentive plans can also be linked directly to important marketing strategy initiatives.

For example:

When ... FedEx wanted to encourage its salespeople to spend more time on three strategically important product lines, it gave salespeople goals for each of the three lines and provided them with weekly updates on their progress toward the goals. Salespeople earned certain bonuses and commissions if all three goals were achieved. The new incentive plan helped to ensure that the three key product lines got the majority of the sales force's attention.[*]

Direct link between job satisfaction and customer satisfaction

A recent study by Christian Homburg and Ruth M. Stock demonstrates a positive relationship between salespeople's job satisfaction and customer satisfaction.[*] Why? First, when they are exposed to a salesperson's positive emotions, customers experience a corresponding change in their own affective state. This phenomenon, rooted in the field of social psychology, is referred to as emotional contagion and has a positive influence on customer satisfaction. Second, the higher the salesperson's job satisfaction, the higher the quality of customer interaction, reflected by the salesperson's openness, flexibility, and customer orientation. The relationship between job satisfaction and customer satisfaction is particularly strong when customer interactions are frequent, customers assume a central role in the value-creation process, or innovative products or services are involved.

13.6.4 Evaluation and control

An ongoing sales management responsibility is to monitor and control the industrial sales force at all levels—national, regional, and district—in order to determine whether objectives are being attained and to identify problems, recommend corrective action, and keep the sales organisation in tune with changing competitive and market conditions.

Performance measures[*]

Sales managers use both behaviour-based and outcome measures of salesperson performance. When a sales force control system is more **behaviour based**, the sales manager monitors and directs the activities of salespeople, uses subjective measures to evaluate performance, and emphasises a compensation system with a large fixed component. Behaviour-based selling measures include the salesperson's knowledge of product applications and the company's technology, as well as the salesperson's clarity of presentations to customers. Behaviour-based control systems are a good match when salespeople lack experience, companies need to control how salespeople present their products and services, and when salespeople are asked to perform a number of non-sales activities (for example, assisting with new-product development).

By contrast, an **outcome-based** sales force control system involves less direct field supervision of salesperson activities and uses objective measures to evaluate performance and a compensation system with a large incentive component. Sales force outcome measures include sales results, market-share gains, new-product sales, and profit contributions. Outcome-based control fits when the skills and efforts of the sales force are the major determinants of sales results. "When sales reps make that big of a difference to the bottom line, it is worth it to give them autonomy and to pay them handsomely to do what they do," say Erin Anderson and Vincent Onyemah.[*]

Setting performance standards

The standards for evaluating salespersons offer ways to compare the performance of various salespersons or sales units (for example, districts), as well as for gauging the overall productivity of the sales organisation. Managerial experience and judgment are important in developing appropriate standards. Importantly, the standards must relate to overall marketing objectives. They must also take into account differences in sales territories, which can vary markedly in number and aggressiveness of competitors, level of market potential, and workload.

Evidence suggests that a strict reliance on outcome measures and incentive compensation plans may not produce the desired sales or marketing performance results: "The alleged automatic supervisory power of incentive pay plans has lulled some sales executives into thinking that important sales outcomes could be reasonably accomplished without intense management reinforcement in noncompensation areas."[*] Often more effective is a more balanced approach that assigns a more prominent role to field sales managers and emphasises behaviour-based measures.[*]

Behaviour-based measures also fit relationship selling—an important strategy in the business market. Relationship selling requires salespeople who have a team orientation and can focus on activities such as sales planning and sales support, as well as on goals such as customer satisfaction.

13.7 MANAGING THE SALES FORCE

Effective management of the business-to-business sales force is fundamental to the firm's success. Sales management refers to planning, organising, directing, and controlling personal selling efforts. Sales force decisions are tempered by overall marketing objectives and must be integrated with the other elements of the marketing mix. Forecasts of the expected sales response guide the firm in determining the total selling effort required (sales force size) and in organising and allocating the sales force (perhaps to sales territories). Techniques for estimating demand and forecasting sales are particularly valuable in sales planning. Sales management also involves the ongoing activities of selecting, training, deploying, supervising, and motivating sales personnel. Finally, sales operations must be monitored to identify problem areas and to assess the efficiency, effectiveness, and profitability of personal selling units.

This section considers strategic components of sales force management:

(1) methods for organising the sales force, (2) key account management, and (3) the distinctive characteristics of high-performing account managers.

13.7.1 Organising the personal selling effort

How should the sales force be organised? The appropriate form depends on such factors as the nature and length of the product line, the role of intermediaries in the marketing program, the diversity of the market segments served the nature of buying behaviour in each market segment, and the structure of competitive selling. The manufacturer's size and financial strength often dictate, to an important degree, the feasibility of particular organisational forms. The business marketer can organise the sales force by geography, product, or market. Large industrial enterprises that market diverse product lines may use all three.

Geographical organisation

The most common form of sales organisation in business marketing is geographical. Each salesperson sells all the firm's products in a defined geographical area. By reducing travel distance and time between customers, this method usually minimises costs. Likewise, sales personnel know exactly which customers and prospects fall within their area of responsibility.

The major disadvantage of the geographical sales organisation is that each salesperson must be able to perform every selling task for all of the firm's products and for all customers in the territory. If the products have diverse applications, this can be difficult. A second disadvantage is that the salesperson has substantial leeway in choosing which products and customers to emphasise. Sales personnel may emphasise products and end-use applications they know best. Of course, this problem can be remedied through training and capable first-line supervision. Because the salesperson is crucial in implementing the firm's segmentation strategy, careful coordination and control are required to align personal selling effort with marketing objectives.

Product organisation

In a product-oriented sales organisation, salespersons specialise in relatively narrow components of the total product line. This is especially appropriate when the product line is large, diverse, or technically complex and when a salesperson needs a high degree of application knowledge to meet customer needs. Furthermore, various products often elicit various patterns of buying behaviour. The salesperson concentrating on a particular product becomes more adept at identifying and communicating with members of buying centres.

A prime benefit of this approach is that the sales force can develop a level of product knowledge that enhances the value of the firm's total offering to customers. The product-oriented sales organisation may also help identify new market segments.

One drawback is the cost of developing and deploying a specialised sales force. A product must have the potential to generate a level of sales and profit that justifies individual selling attention. Thus, a "critical mass" of demand is required to offset the costs. In turn, several sales-persons may be required to meet the diverse product requirements of a single customer. To reduce selling costs and improve productivity, some firms have launched programs to convert product specialists into general-line specialists who know all the firm's products and account strategies. Often, as customers learn to use technology, they outgrow the need for product specialists and prefer working with a single salesperson for all products.

Market-centred organisation

The business marketer may prefer to organise personal selling effort by customer type. Owens-Corning recently switched from a geographical sales structure to one organised by customer type. Similarly, Hewlett-Packard successfully used this structure to strengthen its market position in retailing, financial services, and oil and gas exploration.[*] Sales executives at *Fortune* 500 companies that use sales teams believe they are better able to secure customers and improve business results by adopting a more customer-focused sales structure.[*]

By learning the specific requirements of a particular industry or customer type, the salesperson is better prepared to identify and respond to buying influentials. Also, key market segments become more accessible, thus providing the opportunity for differentiated personal selling strategies. The market segments must, of course, be sufficiently large to warrant specialised treatment.

13.7.2 Key account management[*]

Many business marketing firms find that a small proportion of customers (for example, 20 per cent) often account for a major share (for example, 80 per cent) of its business.

These customers possess enormous purchasing power by virtue of their size, and they are searching for ways to leverage their suppliers' capabilities to enhance the value they deliver to their own customers. In turn, many of these large buying firms have centralised procurement and expect suppliers to provide coordinated and uniform service support to organisational units that are geographically dispersed on a national or global scale. In exchange for a long-term volume commitment, these customers expect the business marketing firm to provide additional value-added services (for example, new-product-development assistance) and support (for example, just-in-time delivery) that may not be available to other customers.

Unique Value Propositions Customer prioritisation represents the degree to which firms prioritise customers by developing different value propositions for its top-tier versus bottom-tier customers. A recent study reveals that customer prioritisation leads to higher average customer profitability and a higher return on sales by: (1) positively affecting relationships with top-tier customers without affecting relationships with bottom-tier customers and (2) reducing marketing and sales costs.[*]

Key accounts versus regular accounts

A **key account** represents a customer who:

1 Purchases a significant volume as a percentage of a seller's total sales;

2 Involves several organisational members in the purchasing process;

3 Buys for an organisation with geographically dispersed units;

4 Expects a carefully coordinated response and specialised services such as logistical support, inventory management, price discounts, and customised applications.[*]

Rather than calling them "key accounts," some companies describe such customers as strategic accounts or national accounts.

Because a business seller often has fewer customers, personal contact with each customer is more feasible. Many business clients expect personalised service and come to depend on their supplier's personnel. This is one of the reasons why key account management is so important in many business markets. Key account management is the dedicated and close support for individual business customers whose volume of business is significant and warrants one-to-one handling. Some business products have technical features that are too numerous or too complex to explain through non-personal forms of promotion. Moreover, business purchases are frequently high in value, and must be suited to the job and available where and when needed; thus business buyers want reinforcement and personal assurances from sales personnel. Because business marketers depend on repeat purchases, sales personnel must follow up sales to make certain that customers know how to use the purchased items effectively, as well as to ensure that the products work properly.

Sales people need to perform the role of educators, showing buyers clearly how the product fits their needs. When the purchase of a product is critical to the future profitability of the business buyer, buying decision-makers gather extensive amounts of information about all alternative products and possible suppliers. To deal with such buyers successfully, the seller must have a highly trained salesforce that is knowledgeable not only about its own company's products but also about competitors' offerings. Besides, if sales representatives offer thorough and reliable information, they can reduce the buyer's uncertainty, as well as differentiate their company's product from the competition. Finally, the gathering of information lengthens the decision-making process. Thus it is important for sales people to be patient; to avoid pressuring their clients as they make important, new and complex decisions; and to continue providing information to their prospects throughout the entire process. The business development role is very important in business markets.[*]

13.7.3 National account success

Research suggests that successful national account units enjoy senior management support; have well-defined objectives, assignments, and implementation procedures; and are staffed by experienced individuals who have a solid grasp of their entire company's resources and capabilities and how to use them to create customer solutions.[*] Do key account management programs enhance profitability? Yes. A recent comprehensive study of US and German firms demonstrates the clear performance advantages that firms with active key account management programs enjoy over peers without them. In turn, the research also indicates that successful programs provide the key account manager with ready access to resources and support across functional areas.[*] Successful national account programs also adopt a strong relationship marketing perspective and consistently demonstrate their ability to meet the customer's immediate and future needs.

To this point, we have examined the central role of personal selling in business marketing strategy and alternative ways to align the sales force to customer segments. Attention now turns to key milestones in managing an engagement with a particular customer.

13.8 ISOLATING THE ACCOUNT MANAGEMENT PROCESS[*]

To explore the work that account managers perform, our focus is on complex sales situations in business markets, which are characterised by large euro values, protracted sales cycles, customised solutions, and the involvement of many organisational members on both the buying and selling sides. Frequently, in these sales situations an account manager is assigned to a particular set of customers and then assembles an ad hoc team as customer requirements or opportunities dictate. For example, large information-technology firms, such as IBM, reserve key account teams for a carefully chosen set of customers but rely on an assigned account manager to cover the majority of large-enterprise customers.

Assuming a central role in a particular engagement is the account manager who diagnoses what the customer needs, identifies the appropriate set of internal experts, recruits them onto the ad hoc team, and then orchestrates the selling centre's activities to deliver a solution that matches customer needs. Let's examine how high performing account managers undertake these activities and highlight how they differ from their peers. Recent studies that explored the characteristics of high-performing account managers at two *Fortune 500* firms provide some valuable insights.

13.8.1 Account management success

For complex sales situations, account manager performance is contingent on securing access to the right people and the right information to solve novel problems for the customer. Figure 13.4 highlights the key milestones in a customer engagement and emphasises the crucial role of relationship-building activities in the firm and in the client organisation. High performers excel at relationship building. Capitalising on these relationship connections, the account manager is

B2B TOP PERFORMERS

Oticon – The Strategy View

Around 1990, Oticon, a hearing aid manufacturer based in Copenhagen, was facing tough competition from larger companies who were capable of investing millions of US euros in facilities. They had to find a new way to compete, and they decided to adopt a strategy of 'reworking' their entire organisation. They decided to tackle the dangers of creeping bureaucracy by developing a paperless organisation, revolutionary at the time. But perhaps underlying this initiative was a more fundamental change in strategy from subscribing to the prescriptive strategy school to subscribing to the descriptive one.

Oticon's objectives were to active improvements on three fronts: creativity, speed and productivity. They identified four organisational changes that were needed to achieve the improvements:

- In employee outlook, a 'mono-job' to a 'multi-job' mentality.

- Organisationally, from a hierarchical structure to what the CEO called a 'spaghetti' organisation.

- Spatially, from a traditional individual-office layout to an open-plan office, including the introduction of mobile workplaces, again

predicting the concept of flexible workspaces by 'hot-desking'.

- A change in communication methods, and mentality, from writing (e-mails and memos) to talking.

The primary change was, therefore, from a task-based organisation to a project-oriented one.

Each employee might be involved in several projects, not limited by departmental boundaries, and doing different things in each. (The only paper record of the project would be a one-page description.)

The organisation changed from one driven by procedure to one driven by performance in completing the projects. The overall aim of the changes was to be 30 per cent more efficient in 3 years; hence it was called the '330 project'.

In summarising the changes, Lars Kolind, CEO, said that the new organisation was integrated, not structured, and that the open plan meant that there was no hiding place in bureaucracy for employees and that managers were on stage all the time. Some managers initially disliked this, but he preferred being able to go right to a problem and getting it solved. The greatest risk in any such project was not taking it all the way.[*]

FIGURE 13.4 The cycle of account management success

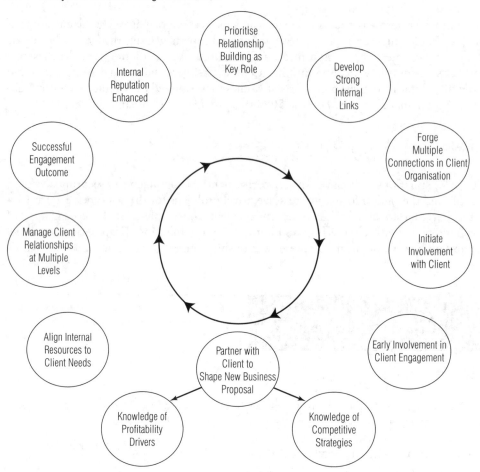

© Cengage Learning 2013

better equipped to design a business proposal that aligns the firm's capabilities to customer goals. Moreover, successful outcomes enhance the account manager's internal reputation, providing social capital the manager can invest in future customer engagements.

Building internal relationships

High-performing account managers form more cross-functional and cross-unit ties within the organisation than their colleagues. A diverse social network provides a manager with access to unique skills and knowledge. Account managers with ties to a number of distinct knowledge pools in the organisation can draw on a large array of skills, knowledge, and resources—thereby enhancing their customer responsiveness. Research suggests that top-performing salespeople are able to "navigate their own organisation to discover personnel, resources, or capabilities that may benefit them in specific sales situations."[*]

Aligning resources to client needs

In marshalling support and coordinating internal resources for a customer engagement, what sets high-performing salespeople apart? First, compared to lower performers, research indicates that high performers are more likely to consider relational as well as technical skills when identifying the set of internal experts who provide the best match for a particular customer engagement. This finding suggests that higher performers are more likely to recognise nuances of the customer relationship and identify team members who possess the interpersonal skills and technical orientation that best match the culture of the customer organisation and the characteristics (for example, personality) of key decision makers.

Second, higher performers are more successful than their colleagues in recruiting desired ad hoc team members. In addition to understanding "who knows what," success may hinge on the salesperson's ability to persuade the targeted internal experts to join and actively participate on the team. This finding highlights the vital importance of the internal relationship-building skills of successful salespeople. Not only do high performers have ready access to the experts who may be needed to capitalise on a customer opportunity, they are also more successful than their colleagues in attracting these experts to the ad hoc selling team.

Forging relationships within the customer organisation

Being centrally involved in a customer organisation's buying system improves an account manager's ability to understand the customer's requirements and business goals. Compared with their peers, high performers possess more cross-functional ties and a larger network of contacts within the customer organisation. Because complex sales situations involve a buying centre that includes participants from multiple levels of the organisational hierarchy and diverse units, an account manager's communication network must go beyond the focal purchasing unit.

Managing the customer engagement process

By developing a network of relationships both within the firm and within the customer organisation, an account manager is ideally equipped to manage the customer engagement process. Through these connections account managers receive vital information about emerging customer opportunities, customer requirements and solutions, and competitive challenges (see Figure 13.4).

Compared with low performers, high-performing account managers are more proactive in initiating involvement with the customer and tend to be involved in client engagements earlier in the purchasing process than their peers. Capitalising on this early involvement, high performers are also more inclined to take an active role in shaping the client's request for proposals (RFP). Compared to peers, they are better able to choreograph the activities of the client management process by determining the most appropriate time and sequence to deploy key members of the ad hoc team during the sales cycle.

Aligning and crafting

A successful client engagement hinges on both customer knowledge and competitive intelligence. High performers know more about client goals and the drivers of client profitability than low performers. When creating a customer solution, a salesperson must "act as a broker and assemble an ad hoc team of experts, coordinating the efforts of people who may not have met one another before."[*] Drawing on this knowledge allows them to align the capabilities of the firm to the goals of the customer. High-performing account managers develop sound competitive intelligence and use this knowledge to outmanoeuvre their rivals in a particular client engagement.

Enhanced internal reputation

By building a strong network of relationships within both the firm and the customer organisation, high-performing account managers—compared with their peers—are better able to diagnose customer requirements, mobilise internal experts, and choreograph the activities that are required to outmanoeuvre rivals and create the desired customer solution. Successful outcomes enhance the reputation of an account manager in the organisation, thereby strengthening internal working relationships and assuring ready access to the right people and right information for future engagements.

Best practices

The coordination of expertise is fundamental to the salesperson's role in the business market, particularly for high-opportunity and complex customer engagements. **Expertise coordination** is the process that a salesperson follows in diagnosing customer requirements and subsequently identifying, assembling, and managing an ad hoc team of internal experts who possess the knowledge and skills to deliver a superior customer solution.

The best practices of high-performing salespeople can provide a template for improving the client management process for complex sales situations. For example, depth interviews with high performers indicate that they make a finer-grained assessment of customer requirements that includes customer-related dimensions such as the culture of the organisation, the preferences and personalities of key decision makers with whom team members will interact, as well as key milestones in the buyer–seller relationship history. Such points could be accentuated in sales training and captured where possible in customer relationship management (CRM) systems. High performers also attribute their success to carefully choreographing the activities of key members of the team across the sales cycle. For example, some specialists are best deployed early in the process when contract negotiations are underway. Others may be of use behind the scenes and are deployed to the customer organisation as trouble shooters only if things go awry; still others may be best included from start to finish. Such best practices can be used to improve sales protocols and to refine sales training programs.

13.9 DEPLOYMENT ANALYSIS: A STRATEGIC APPROACH

To this point, our discussion has been concerned with: (1) recruiting and selection, (2) training, (3) motivating and supervising, and (4) evaluating and controlling. Poor decisions in one area can create a backlash in other areas. One critical sales management task remains: deploying the sales force. The objective is to form the most profitable sales territories, deploy salespersons to serve potential customers in those territories, and effectively allocate sales force time among those customers.

The size of the sales force establishes the level of selling effort that the business marketer can use. The selling effort is then organised by designating sales districts and sales territories. Allocation decisions determine how the selling effort is to be assigned to customers, prospects, and products. All these are illustrated in Table 13.1.

Proper deployment requires a multistage approach to find the most effective and efficient way to assign sales resources (for example, sales calls, number of salespersons, percentage of salesperson's time) across all of the **planning and control units** (**PCUs**) the firm serves

TABLE 13.1 Deployment decisions facing sales organisations

Type of Decision	Specific Development Decisions
Set total level of selling effort	Determine sales force size
Organise selling effort	Design sales districts
	Design sales territories
Allocate selling effort	Allocate effort to trading areas
	Allocate sales calls to accounts
	Allocate sales calls to prospects
	Allocate sales call time to products Determine length of sales call

Source: Reprinted from Industrial Marketing Management 11(3), Raymond LaForge and David W. Cravens, ''Steps in Selling Effort Deployment,'' p. 184, copyright © 1982, with permission from Elsevier.

(for example, prospects, customers, territories, districts, products).[*] Thus, effective deployment means understanding the factors that influence sales in a particular PCU, such as a territory.

13.9.1 Territory sales response

What influences the potential level of sales in a particular territory? Table 13.2 outlines eight classes of variables. This list shows the complexity of estimating sales response functions. Such estimates are needed, however, to make meaningful sales allocations.

Three territory traits deserve particular attention in sales response studies: potential, concentration, and dispersion.[*] **Potential** is a measure of the total business opportunity for all sellers in a particular market. **Concentration** refers to how much potential lies with a few larger accounts in that territory. If potential is concentrated, the salesperson can cover with a few calls a large proportion of the potential. Finally, if the territory is geographically **dispersed**, sales are probably lower because of time wasted in travel. Past research often centred on **territory workload—** the number of accounts. However, Adrian Ryans and Charles Weinberg report that workload is of questionable value in estimating sales response: "From a managerial standpoint, the recurrent finding of an association between potential and sales results suggests that sales managers should stress territory potential when making sales force decisions."[*]

13.9.2 Territory alignment[*]

The territory alignment decision affects the workspace for each member of the sales force, defining the particular customers whom they will serve as well as their immediate supervisor. Leading business consultants report that many business-to-business firms have significant imbalances in the territory alignments of their sales personnel. When territories are out of balance, too much sales effort is devoted to low-potential customers and too little to high-potential customers. As a result, "companies often leave millions of euros on the table."[*]

Sound territory alignment advances sales productivity and firm performance by:

- Promoting fair rewards (i.e., incentive pay) and boosting salesperson morale while balancing workload and opportunity (potential)

- Enhancing the coverage of customers and high-potential prospects

- Reducing travel time and costs (For example, after a sales territory realignment at industrial distributor W. W. Grainger, the company observed a 13.7 per cent reduction in salesperson travel

TABLE 13.2 Selected determinants of territory sales response

1 Environmental factors (e.g., health of economy)
2 Competition (e.g., number of competitive salespersons)
3 Company marketing strategy and tactics
4 Sales force organisation, policies, and procedures
5 Field sales manager characteristics
6 Salesperson characteristics
7 Territory characteristics (e.g., potential)
8 Individual customer factors

Source: Adapted from Adrian B. Ryans and Charles B. Weinberg, "Territory Sales Response," *Journal of Marketing Research* 16 (November 1979): pp. 453–465.

time that translated into a nearly €0.75 million reduction in travel expenses and an increase in selling time that contributed over €11.25 million in additional sales and €2.25 million in additional profits.)[*]

● Increasing company sales and profit

13.9.3 Developing the customer database

Alignment databases typically include a mix of internal and external information sources. Internal data sources may include customer purchasing activity, purchase frequency, cross-category buying, share-of-wallet, and marketing contacts by firm.

External data sources centre on the macrosegmentation characteristics of customers such as size of firm, industry, end market served as well as growth rate, credit rating, and office locations.

To develop initial workload measures, many companies first classify customers by segment and by historical sales volume. Next, the sales manager determines the frequency and desired length of each sales call for each account segment. By applying the frequency and sales call duration standards to each customer in the database, a customer account list can be converted into a workload database.

A number of territory alignment software programs, such as MAPS™ (ZS Associates), are available that combine a computerised map of territories with market, sales, and account workload data. A sales manager can use the software to evaluate the balance of workload and potential in the current alignment and experiment with possible changes to improve territory balance.

13.9.4 Sales resource opportunity grid

Deployment analysis matches sales resources to market opportunities. Planning and control units such as sales territories or districts are part of an overall portfolio, with various units offering various levels of opportunity and requiring various levels of sales resources. A sales resource opportunity grid can be used to classify the business-to-business firm's portfolio of PCUs.[*] In Figure 13.5, each PCU is classified on the basis of PCU opportunity and sales organisation strength.

PCU opportunity is the PCU's total potential for all sellers, whereas **sales organisation strength** includes the firm's competitive advantages or distinctive competencies within the PCU. By positioning all PCUs on the grid, the sales manager can assign sales resources to those that have the greatest level of opportunity and capitalise on the particular strengths of the sales organisation. For example, existing customers and prospects that are most appropriately positioned in the upper left cell of the grid represent the most attractive target, while those in the lower right cell represent the least attractive.

At various points in deployment decision making, the sales resource opportunity grid is important for screening the size of the sales force, the territory design, and the allocation of sales calls to customer segments. This method can isolate deployment problems or deployment opportunities worthy of sales management attention and further data analysis.

13.9.5 Isolating high-opportunity customers

Many firms find that salespeople spend more time than they should with low potential customer accounts. For example, a pharmaceutical firm found that the top 30 per cent of physicians write 90 per cent of the prescriptions for the classes of drugs that the company sells. These customers fall squarely in the top left quadrant of the sales resource opportunity grid. However, when the firm examined the actual sales calls being made by the sales force, they found that company

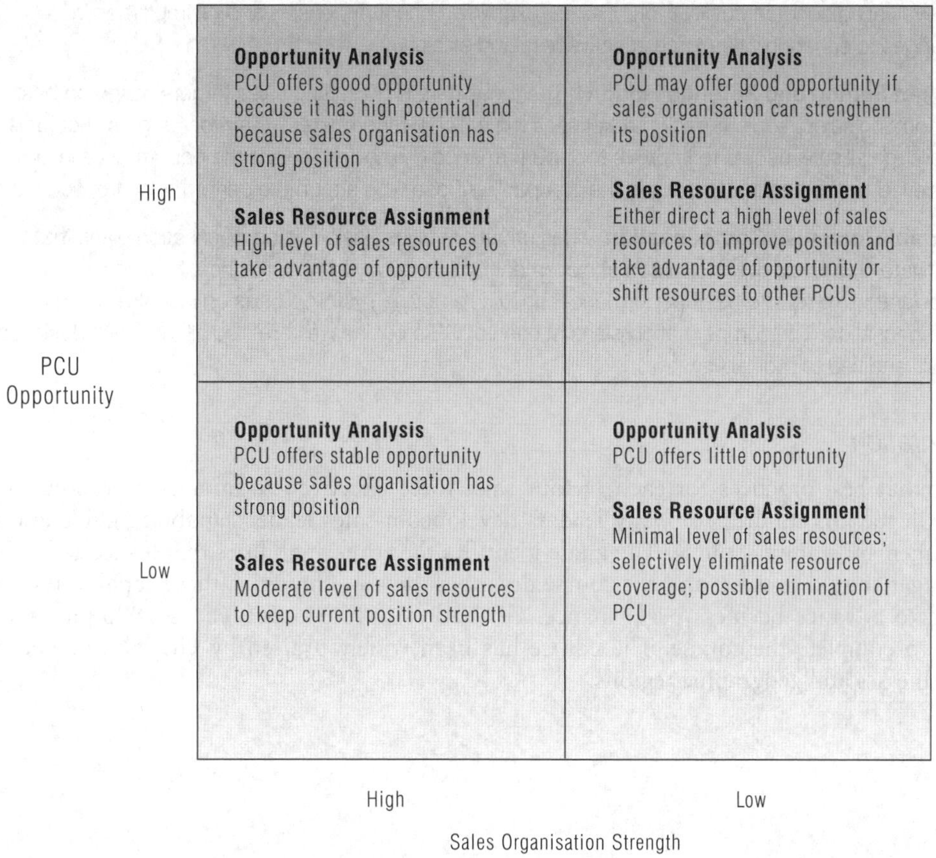

FIGURE 13.5

Sales resource opportunity grid

Opportunity Analysis
PCU offers good opportunity because it has high potential and because sales organisation has strong position

Sales Resource Assignment
High level of sales resources to take advantage of opportunity

Opportunity Analysis
PCU may offer good opportunity if sales organisation can strengthen its position

Sales Resource Assignment
Either direct a high level of sales resources to improve position and take advantage of opportunity or shift resources to other PCUs

Opportunity Analysis
PCU offers stable opportunity because sales organisation has strong position

Sales Resource Assignment
Moderate level of sales resources to keep current position strength

Opportunity Analysis
PCU offers little opportunity

Sales Resource Assignment
Minimal level of sales resources; selectively eliminate resource coverage; possible elimination of PCU

High

PCU Opportunity

Low

High   Low

Sales Organisation Strength

Source: Reprinted by permission of the publisher from "Steps in Selling Effort Deployment," by Raymond LaForge and David W. Cravens, *Industrial Marketing Management* 11 (July 1982): p. 187. Copyright © 1982 by Elsevier Science Publishing Co., Inc.

salespersons were directing nearly half of their time to less profitable physician segments (for example, lower left and right quadrants).[*]

13.9.6 GE's sales force effectiveness initiative[*]

Senior executives at GE surmised that, across the enterprise, the businesses that were driving organic growth were those that had been effective at utilising data, processes, and tools to support sales force decision making. To that end, the firm established four sales force effectiveness priorities that illustrate best practices for any firm, large or small, that competes in the business market.

1   **Customer Potential and Prioritisation**   Consistent with our discussion, defining customer and prospect potential represents a core requirement for sales force effectiveness. The GE framework for meeting this requirement includes three steps: (1) establishing a customer database, (2) calculating customer potential, and (3) prioritising customers and prospects. The relationship between account profiles (for example, customer firm's size and industry) and potential can be estimated by using managerial judgment and/or quantitative methods. Several GE businesses use regression analysis to determine the particular customer characteristics that are the best predictors of account potential.

2   **Territory Alignment**   To identify coverage gaps across territories and to better match sales resources with market opportunity, the GE process for accomplishing territory alignment involves:

(1) evaluating account quality (potential), (2) examining account density, and (3) implementing changes to enhance sales force effectiveness and efficiency.

3   **Target Setting and Potentialisation**   The focus here is on setting sales targets based on best-performing salespeople in each market sector in which GE competes. "Territory targets should challenge all salespeople to improve their performance by moving toward the performance level achieved by the best performers in the company—those who are on the performance frontier."*

4   **Variable Incentive Compensation**   This priority involves designing compensation plans that motivate high levels of salesperson achievement by linking pay to performance, by using accelerators to reward peak performance, and by removing systemic caps on incentive compensation. The compensation plans at each of GE's businesses are also aligned with business goals and tied to profitability.

Implementation

To ensure that best practices for each of four sales force effectiveness initiatives become well engrained in the GE culture, company leaders developed a sales leader capability guide and a sales management training course. The guide identifies the core capabilities that a successful GE sales manager should possess, and the course describes the ways in which these capabilities can be applied to advance business performance. GE leaders have encouraged its 5800-plus sales managers to complete the course. The course has been widely praised by GE sales managers across businesses and geographic regions.

SUMMARY

Personal selling is the process of informing customers and persuading them to purchase products through personal communication in an exchange situation. It is the most precise promotional method, but also the most expensive. The three general purposes of personal selling are finding prospects, convincing them to buy and keeping customers satisfied. It is particularly important in B2B.

Marketers must ensure their sales colleagues are fully conversant with their strategies and marketing plans, and that sales staff appreciate their role within the execution of marketing programmes. Internal marketing is very important in this respect. Not all customers are worth the same: some matter much more than others strategically and in terms of the volume of business or financial returns likely. Very important and large customers are deemed to be key accounts, particularly in business-to-business markets. Key account management is the process for effectively servicing and satisfying these accounts, to ensure mutually satisfactory ongoing relationships and volumes of business.

Sales promotion is an activity or material (or both) that acts as a direct inducement and offers added value to, or incentive to, buy the product to resellers, sales people or consumers. The ratchet effect is the stepped impact of using sales promotion and advertising together. Marketers use sales promotion to increase sales, to identify and attract new customers, to introduce a new product and to increase reseller inventories. Sales promotion methods fall into two general categories: consumer and trade. Consumer sales promotion techniques encourage consumers to buy from specific retail stores or dealerships or to try a specific product. These techniques include coupons, demonstrations, frequent user incentives – such as loyalty cards or trading stamps – point-of-sale (POS) materials, free samples, money refunds, premiums, price-off offers, and consumer contests and sweepstakes

The Internet, networked independent computers, is no longer just for computer buffs. Users are multiplying daily, including both consumers and businesses seeking to interact with prospective and current customers. Most businesses now have websites and recognise the potential for e-commerce. Scrambling and coding of credit card information has helped build consumer confidence in online purchase transactions. Websites are clearly flagged on much television and print advertising. In-company Internet networks – intranets – are enabling the rapid dissemination of routine communications, group communications, uniform computer applications, the latest software and information about product developments, and are assisting with internal marketing. Enabling frequent updating of messages, individually targeted communications and sales ordering, the Internet now features in most businesses' promotional mixes.

To be popular with consumers, research reveals that websites must offer interaction, obvious and easy navigation, topical content, relationship-building tools, search engine compliance, ease of use for first-time users and user-friendliness to experienced users, and security of use/payment. Increasingly, they should link to social media sites.

Digital marketing tools and techniques are used by marketers to improve their proposition to customers and overall competitiveness, with a value adding website and interrelated digital marketing techniques to drive traffic, conversion, positive experience and referrals. These techniques include website, online public relations, email, blogs/microblogs, social networks, podcasts, wikis and search engine management. An important aspect of digital is mobile marketing, which engages users of wireless devices with time and location sensitive, personalised information promoting goods, services and ideas, via apps, messaging, websites and social media communications. For consumers, the most visible change enabled by the digital era is the emergence of social media such as Facebook or YouTube, which permits so much sharing of material, perspectives and insights between consumers.

Direct marketing is a decision to do without marketing channel intermediaries and to focus most promotional resources on activities that deal directly with targeted customers, such as personal selling, telemarketing and direct mail. Now adopted by consumer goods producers, services, business companies, charities and even government departments, direct marketing has recently enjoyed rapid growth. This is likely to continue, with more direct mail, automated call centres, personal selling, door-to-door selling and leaflet dropping, direct response television advertising and use of the Internet with its associated technologies to contact potential customers. Direct marketing must be tailored to suit the behaviour and expectations of the target audience, while reflecting existing branding and other promotional mix designs.

DISCUSSION QUESTIONS

1   What roles does social media play in B2B marketing?

2   Why might it be a good idea for a B2B company to exhibit at a trade show?

3   Imagine you are a new marketing manager in a medium-sized B2B company. You have the option of employing a small salesforce, attending trade shows and seminars, developing limited advertising, constructing a website, and using direct mail.

Faced with a limited budged, how would you determine which aspects of the promotional mix should be utilised?

4   What is personal selling? How does personal selling differ from other types of promotional activity?

5   How should a sales manager establish criteria for selecting sales personnel? What are the general characteristics of a good sales person?

INTERNET EXERCISES

Most leading brands embrace a mix of promotional techniques, including advertising, sales promotions, publicity, the Web and the rest of the promotional mix. Pepsi is no exception.

Pepsi's *Pepsi World* award-winning website is an important part of the company's promotional activity, integrating advertising, sales promotions activity and publicity releases with customer involvement. Brand information, TV advertisements, music links, sports, promotions and street motion – there is much on offer on Pepsi's web pages. Log on to **www.pepsi.com/home**.

1   In what ways and with what messages is Pepsi engaging with customers through the pages of its website?

2   How do these approaches support the brand's positioning?

3   How do the web pages relate to the brand's television advertising?

REFERENCES

Aaker, David A., and Joachimsthaler, Erich, "The Lure of Global Branding," *Harvard Business Review* 77 (November–December 1999): pp. 137–144.

Alonzo, Vincent, "Selling Changes," *Incentive* 170 (September 1996): p. 46.

Anderson, Erin, and Onyemah, Vincent, "How Right Should the Customer Be?" *Harvard Business Review* 84 (July–August 2006): pp. 59–67.

Anderson, Erin, and Trinkle, Bob, *Outsourcing the Sales Function: The Real Costs of Field Sales* (Mason, OH: Thomson Higher Education, 2005).

Bagozzi, Richard P., "Performance and Satisfaction in an Industrial Sales Force: An Examination of Their Antecedents and Simultaneity," *Journal of Marketing* 44 (Spring 1980): pp. 65–77.

Bagozzi, Richard P., "Performance and Satisfaction in an Industrial Sales Force: A Causal Modeling Approach," in *Sales Management: New Developments from Behavioral and Decision Model Research*, Richard P. Bagozzi, ed. (Cambridge, MA: Marketing Science Institute, 1979), pp. 70–91.

Bomgar, "About Bomgar," http://www.bomgar.com, accessed August 1, 2011.

Bonoma, T.V. , "Get more out of your trade shows", *Harvard Business Review,* January- February 1983, pp. 75-83

Booker, Ellis, "Economic Slowdown Will Accelerate Online Shift," *B to B's Interactive Guide: 2008*, p. 3, http://www.btobonline.com, accessed August 1, 2008.

Brady, Diane, and Kiley, David, "Making Marketing Measure Up," *Business Week*, December 13, 2004, pp. 112–113.

Brown, Steven P., and Peterson, Robert A., "Antecedents and Consequences of Salesperson Job Satisfaction: Meta-Analysis and Assessment of Causal Effects," *Journal of Marketing Research* 30 (February 1993): pp. 63–77.

Brown, Steven P., Cron, William L., and Leigh, Thomas W., "Do Feelings of Success Mediate Sales Performance—Work Attitude Relationships?" *Journal of the Academy of Marketing Science* 21 (Spring 1993): pp. 91–100.

B-to-B, "B to B's Best Brands—Hewlett-Packard," B to B's Best: 2007, p. 26, http://www.btobonline.com, accessed June 15, 2008.

B-to-B, "eMarketer Projects U.S. Online Ad Spending Will Grow 20.2% This Year," *B to B*, June 8, 2011, http://www.btobonline.com, accessed August, 2011.

Bush, Victoria D., and Ingram, Thomas, "Adapting to Diverse Customers: A Training Matrix for International Marketers," *Industrial Marketing Management* 25 (September 1996): pp. 373–383.

Cannon, Joseph P., and Narayandas, Narakesari, "Relationship Marketing and Key Account Management," in Jagdish N. Sheth and Atul Parvatiyar, eds., *Handbook of Relationship Marketing* (Thousand Oaks, CA: Sage Publications, 2000), pp. 407–429.

Cespedes, Frank V., *Concurrent Marketing: Integrating Products, Sales, and Service* (Boston: Harvard Business School Press, 1995), p. 187.

Churchill Jr., Gilbert A., Ford, Neil M., and Walker Jr., Orville C., "Organizational Climate and Job Satisfaction in the Salesforce," *Journal of Marketing Research* 13 (November 1976): pp. 323–332.

Cort, Stanton G., Lambert, David R., and Garrett, Paula L., "Effective Business-to-Business Frequency: New Management Perspectives from the Research Literature," *Advertising Research Foundation Literature Review* (October 1983).

Cravens, David W. and LaForge, Raymond W., "Sales Force Deployment," in *Advances in Business Marketing*, vol. 1, Arch G. Woodside, ed. (Greenwich, CT: JAI Press, 1986), pp. 67–112.

Cravens, David W., Ingram, Thomas N., LaForge, Raymond W., and Young, Clifford E., "Behavior-Based and Outcome-Based Salesforce Control Systems," *Journal of Marketing* 57 (October 1993): p. 56.

Cron, William L., Dubinsky, Alan J., and Michaels, Ronald E., "The Influence of Career Stages on Components of Salesperson Motivation," *Journal of Marketing* 52 (January 1988): pp. 78–92.

Cron, William L., Marshall, Greg W., Singh, Jagdip, Spiro, Rosann, and Sujan, Harish, "Salesperson Selection, Training, and Development Trends: Implications, and Research Opportunities," *Journal of Personal Selling and Sales Management* 25 (Spring 2005): pp. 123–136.

Dibb, Sally, Simkin, Lyndon, Pride, Bill, and Ferrell, O.C., *Marketing Concepts & Strategies*, 6th ed. (Cengage, 2012).

Doole, Isobel, and Lowe, Robin, *International Marketing Strategy* 6th ed. (Cengage, 2012).

Edelman, David C., "Aligning with the Consumer Decision Journey," Idea in Practice, *Harvard Business Review* 89 (July 2011): pp. 1–4.

Edelman, David C., "Branding in the Digital Age: You're Spending Your Money in All the Wrong Places," *Harvard Business Review* 88 (December 2010): p. 2, http://www.hbr.org accessed July 25, 2011.

El-Ansary, Adel I., "Selling and Sales Management in Action: Sales Force Effectiveness Research Reveals New Insights and Reward-Penalty Patterns in Sales Force Training," *Journal of Personal Selling and Sales Management* 13 (Spring 1993): pp. 83–90.

Gopalakrishna, Srinath, and Lilien, Gary L., "A Three-Stage Model of Industrial Trade Show Performance," *Marketing Science* 14 (Winter 1995): pp. 22–42.

Gopalakrishna, Srinath, and Williams, Jerome D., "Planning and Performance Assessment of Industrial Trade Shows: An Exploratory Study," *International Journal of Research in Marketing* 9 (September 1992): pp. 207–224.

Herzog, Raymond E., "How Design Engineering Activity Affects Supplies," *Business Marketing* 70 (November 1985): p. 143.

Homburg, Christian, and Stock, Ruth M., "The Link between Salespeople's Job Satisfaction and Customer Satisfaction in a Business-to-Business Context: A Dyadic Analysis," *Journal of the Academy of Marketing Science* 32 (Spring 2004): pp. 144–158.

Homburg, Christian, Droll, Mathias, and Totzek, Dirk, "Customer Prioritization: Does It Pay Off and How Should It Be Implemented?" *Journal of Marketing* 72 (September 2008): pp. 110–128.

Homburg, Christian, Workman Jr., John P., and Jensen, Ove, "A Configurational Perspective of Key Account Management,"*Journal of Marketing* 66 (April 2002): pp. 38–60.

Hutt, Michael D., and Walker, Beth A., "A Network Perspective of Account Manager Performance," *Journal of Business & Industrial Marketing* 21 (7, 2006): pp. 466–473.

Johnston, Mark W., and Marshall, Greg W., *Sales Force Management* (New York: McGraw-Hill/Irwin, 2008).

Johnston, Mark W., Parasuraman, A., Futrell, Charles M., and Black, William C., "A Longitudinal Assessment of the Impact of Selected Organizational Influences on Salespeople's Organizational Commitment during Early Employment," *Journal of Marketing Research* 27 (August 1990): pp. 333–343.

Johnston, Wesley J., and Cooper, Martha C., "Industrial Sales Force Selection: Current Knowledge and Needed Research,"

Journal of Personal Selling and Sales Management 1 (Spring/Summer 1981): pp. 49–53.

Jones, Eli, "Leader Behavior, Work Attitudes, and Turnover of Salespeople: An Integrative Study," *Journal of Personal Selling and Sales Management* 16 (Spring 1996): pp. 13–23.

Krol, Carol, "E-Mail: Integrating Channels Key," B to B's Interactive Marketing Guide: 2008, p. 8, http://www.btobonline.com, accessed August 1, 2008.

LaForge, Raymond W., and Cravens, David W., "Steps in Selling Effort Deployment," *Industrial Marketing Management* 11 (July 1982): pp. 183–194.

Lamons, Robert, "Tips for Distinguishing Your Ads from Bad Ads," *Marketing News* (November 19, 2001): p. 10.

Lohtia, Ritu, Johnston, Wesley J., and Rab, Linda, "Business-to-Business Advertising: What Are the Dimensions of an Effective Print Ad?" *Industrial Marketing Management* 24 (October 1995): pp. 369–378.

Maddox, Kate, and Bulik, Beth Snyder, "Integrated Marketing Success Stories," *B2B* 89 (July 7, 2004): p. 23.

Marketo.com, "B2B Social Media," http://www.marketo.com, accessed August 1, 2011.

Martin, Dick, *Secrets of the Marketing Masters* (New York: AMACOM, 2009), p. 169.

McKee, Steve, "Five Common B2B Advertising Myths," *Business Week*, April 2007, http://www.businessweek.com, accessed July 29, 2008.

Morrall, Katherine, "Motivating Sales Staff with Rewards," *Bank Marketing* 28 (July 1996): pp. 32–38.

Moutinho, Luiz, and Southern, Geoffrey, *Strategic Marketing Management: A process Based Approach* (Cengage, 2012).

Moutinho, Luiz, and Southern, Geoffrey, *Strategic Marketing Management: A process Based Approach* (Cengage, 2012).

O'Sullivan, Dan, and Abela, Andrew V., "Marketing Performance Measurement Ability and Firm Performance," *Journal of Marketing* 71 (April 2007): pp. 79–93

Oliver, Richard L., "Behavior-and Outcome-Based Sales Control Systems: Evidence and Consequences of Price-Form and Hybrid Governance," *Journal of Personal Selling and Sales Management* 15 (Fall 1995): pp. 1–15.

Park, C. Whan, Roth, Martin S., and Jacques, Philip F., "Evaluating the Effects of Advertising and Sales Promotion Campaigns," *Industrial Marketing Management* 17 (May 1988): p. 130.

Piercy, Nigel, "Advertising Budgeting: Process and Structure as Explanatory Variables," *Journal of Advertising* 16 (2, 1987): p. 34.

Plouffe, Christopher R., and Barclay, Donald W., "Salesperson Navigation: The Intraorganizational Dimension of the Sales Role," *Industrial Marketing Management* 36 (May 2007): p. 529.

Powers, Todd M., and Menon, Anil, "Practical Measurement of Advertising Impact: The IBM Experience" in Roger A. Kerin and Rob O'Regan, eds., *Marketing Mix Decisions: New Perspectives and Practices* (Chicago: American Marketing Association 2008), pp. 77–109.

Pride ,Bill and Ferrell, O.C., *Marketing*, Cengage South-Western, 2012

Rosenbloom, B., *Marketing Channels: Management View*, Dryden Press (Hinsdale IL, (1987), p. 63

Russ, Frederick A., McNeilly, Kevin M., and Comer, James M., "Leadership, Decision-Making, and Performance of Sales Managers," *Journal of Personal Selling and Sales Management* 16 (Summer 1996): pp. 1–15.

Ryans, Adrian B., and Weinberg, Charles B., "Territory Sales Response," *Journal of Marketing Research* 16 (November 1979): pp. 453–465.

Ryans, Adrian B., and Weinberg, Charles B., "Territory Sales Response Models: Stability over Time," *Journal of Marketing Research* 24 (May 1987): pp. 229–233.

Sager, Jeffrey K., Futrell, Charles M., and Rajan Varadarajan, "Exploring Salesperson Turnover: A Causal Model," *Journal of Business Research* 18 (June 1989): pp. 303–326.

Schultz, Roberta J., and Evans, Kenneth R., "Strategic Collaborative Communication by Key Account Representatives," *Journal of Personal Selling and Sales Management* 22 (Winter 2002): pp. 23–32.

Silverstein, Barry, *Business-to-Business Internet Marketing*, 3rd ed. (Gulf Breeze, FL.: MAXIMUM Press, 2001a), p. 171.

Silverstein, Barry, *Internet Marketing for Information Technology Companies*, 2d ed. (Gulf Breeze, FL: MAXIMUM Press, 2001b), p. 107.

Steward, Michelle D., Walker, Beth A., Hutt, Michael D., and Kumar, Ajith, "The Coordination Strategies of High-Performing Salespeople: Internal Working Relationships that Drive Success," *Journal of the Academy of Marketing Science* 38 (October 2010): pp. 550–566.

Stock, Ruth Maria, "Interorganizational Teams as Boundary Spanners between Supplier and Customer Companies," *Journal of the Academy of Marketing Science* 34 (October 2006): pp. 588–599.

Taylor, Thayer C., "Hewlett-Packard," *Sales and Marketing Management* 145 (January 1993): p. 59.

Teas, R. Kenneth, and McElroy, James C., "Causal Attributions and Expectancy Estimates: A Framework for Understanding the Dynamics of Salesforce Motivation," *Journal of Marketing* 50 (January 1986): pp. 75–86;

Ustuner, Tuba, and Godes, David, "Better Sales Networks," *Harvard Business Review* 84 (July–August 2006): p. 108.

van Weele, Arjan, *Puchasing and Supply Chain Management: Analysis Strategy, Planning and Practice*, 5th ed. (Cengage, 2010).

Verhage, Bronis J., *Marketing: A Global Perspective* (Cengage, 2013).

Walker Jr., Orville C., Churchill Jr., Gilbert A., and Ford, Neil M., "Motivation and Performance in Industrial Selling: Present Knowledge and Needed Research," *Journal of Marketing Research* 14 (May 1977): pp. 156–168.

Workman Jr., John P., Homburg, Christian, and Jensen, Ove, "Intraorganizational Determinants of Key Account Management Effectiveness," *Journal of the Academy of Marketing Science* 31 (Winter 2003): pp. 3–21

Yip, George S., and Bink, Audrey J.M. "Managing Global Accounts," *Harvard Business Review* 84 (September 2007): pp. 103–111.

Yoon, Eunsang, and Kijewski, Valerie, "The Brand Awareness-to-Preference Link in Business Markets: A Study of the Semiconductor Manufacturing Industry," *Journal of Business-to-Business Marketing* 2 (4, 1995): pp. 7–36.

Zoltners, Andris A., and Lorimer, Sally E., "Sales Territory Alignment: An Overlooked Productivity Tool," *Journal of Personal Selling and Sales Management* 20 (Summer 2000): p. 139.

Zoltners, Andris A., and Sinha, Prabhakant, "Sales Territory Design: Thirty Years of Modeling and Implementation," *Marketing Science* 24 (Summer 2005): pp. 313–331.

PART V
EVALUATING
BUSINESS
MARKETING
STRATEGY AND
PERFORMANCE

14 Marketing Performance Measurement

CHAPTER 14
MARKETING
PERFORMANCE
MEASUREMENT

CHAPTER OBJECTIVES

Two business marketing managers facing identical market conditions and with equal resources to invest in marketing strategy could generate dramatically different results. Why? One manager might carefully monitor and control the performance of marketing strategy, whereas the other might not. The astute marketer evaluates the profitability of alternative segments and examines the effectiveness and efficiency of the marketing mix components to isolate problems and opportunities and alter the strategy as market or competitive conditions dictate. After reading this chapter, you will understand:

1   A system for converting a strategic vision into a concrete set of performance measures

2   The function and significance of marketing control in business marketing management

3   The components of the control process

4   The distinctive value of "dashboards" for evaluating marketing strategy performance

5   The importance of execution to the success of business marketing strategy

What stops chief marketing officers (CMOs) from getting a good night's sleep?

You worry about how much there is to do; and you worry that you may have taken a gamble that won't pay off.

—CMO, *Software Company*

Why are robust measurement systems an essential priority for CMOs?[*]

There's no way I would ever present to our CEO or executive committee without telling them, "€10 million was spent on marketing, and that gave us €100 million worth of business opportunities, as well as €50 million that's closed."

—CMO, *Consulting Company*

According to a study conducted by the Chief Marketing Officer (CMO) Council, chief marketing officers face intense pressure from bottom-line-focused CEOs and demanding corporate boards to improve the relevance, accountability, and performance of their organisations. Measuring marketing performance, quantifying and measuring marketing's worth, and improving marketing's efficiency and effectiveness continue to rank among the top challenges faced by marketers. The CMO Council study found that for today's marketers, proving marketing's value is the number-one challenge above other challenges, such as growing customer knowledge and extracting greater value and profitability from customers.[*] Thus, the critical importance of an effective control system that provides key measures of performance is highlighted for all business marketers, whether small or large.

Information generated by the marketing control system is essential for revising current marketing strategies, formulating new ones, and allocating funds. As Roland Rust and his colleagues note, "the effective dissemination of new methods of assessing marketing productivity to the business community will be a major step toward raising marketing's vitality in the firm and, more importantly, toward raising the performance of the firm itself."[*] While the effects of marketing investments play out over time, recent research provides evidence that brand equity, customer satisfaction, R&D, and product quality are all linked to firm value.[*] Thus, marketing control provides a critical foundation for diagnosing and advancing firm performance, and the assessment of marketing performance is as important as the formulation and execution of marketing strategy. Importantly, the requirements for an effective control system are strict—data must be gathered continuously on the appropriate performance measures. Thus, an effective marketing strategy is rooted in a carefully designed and well-applied control system. Such a system must also monitor the quality of strategy implementation. Gary Hamel asserts that "implementation is often more difficult than it need be because only a handful of people have been involved in the creation of strategy and only a few key executives share a conviction about the way forward."[*]

This chapter presents the rudiments of a marketing control system, beginning with a framework that converts strategy goals into concrete performance measures. Next, it examines the components of the control process. Finally, it examines the implementation skills that ultimately shape successful business marketing strategies.

14.1 A STRATEGY MAP: PORTRAIT OF AN INTEGRATED PLAN[*]

A strategy map provides a visual representation of the cause-and-effect relationships among the components of a company's strategy. Figure 14.1 provides the strategy map for Boise Office Solutions—a $3.5 billion distributor of office and technology products, office furniture, and paper products that developed a distinctive customer relationship strategy, emphasising customer solutions and personalised service. Leading firms widely use the strategy map concept, developed by

FIGURE 14.1   Creating boise office solutions' strategy map

Step 1: Define the Financial Objectives and Establish Growth and Productivity Goals

Increase Shareholder Value by:

- creating profitable customer revenue streams
- lowering operating costs

Step 2: Define the Customer Value Proposition for Target Segments

Boise created a new customer strategy defined by this strategic theme: *Create Distinctive Customer Value by Enhancing the Customer Relationship*

- shift from commodity to customer solution focus
- provide personalised, customised service
- offer seamless access across sales channels

Step 3: Establish the Time Line for Results

Break down financial goals into targets for particular processes:

- operations management—reduce the cost of servicing customers
- customer management—increase the number of relationship customers
- innovation management—create new offerings

Step 4: Identify the Critical Strategic Themes and Internal Processes with the Greatest Impact on the Strategy

Critical internal process objectives:

- operational excellence—move more customers to e-channel to enhance customer convenience and lower cost
- customer management—deliver personalised, proactive service and improve customer experience
- innovation management—create new tools for customers to apply to control spending

Step 5: Identify the Human, Information, and Organisational Resources Required to Support the Strategy

Align organisational members with the strategy:

- training—a specialised course on the initiative
- information technology (a new CRM system)
- incentives tied to strategy goals

Step 6: Develop an Action Plan and Provide Required Funding for Each of the Separate Initiatives (Strategic Themes)

Source: Adapted from Robert S. Kaplan and David P. Norton, *Strategy Maps: Converting Intangible Assets into Tangible Outcomes* (Boston: Harvard Business School Publishing, 2004), pp. 355–360.

Robert S. Kaplan and David P. Norton, because it isolates the interrelationships among four perspectives of a company that the authors refer to as a balanced scorecard[*]:

1   A **financial perspective** that describes the expected outcomes of the strategy, such as revenue growth, productivity improvements, or increased shareholder value

2   The **customer perspective** that defines how the firm proposes to deliver a competitively superior value proposition to targeted customers

3   The **internal perspective** that describes the business processes that have the greatest effect on the chosen strategy, such as customer relationship management, innovation management, or supply chain management

4   The **learning and growth perspective** that describes the human capital (personnel), information capital (information-technology systems), and organisational capital (climate) that must be aligned to the strategy to support value-creating internal processes

Using Boise Office Solutions as an illustrative case study, let's explore the six-step process that managers can use to build a tightly integrated strategy.[*]

14.1.1 Developing the strategy: The process

A strategy must provide a clear portrait that reveals how a firm will achieve its goals and deliver on its promises to customers, employees, and shareholders.[*] Boise Office Solutions sought a new strategy because the industry continued to consolidate and more and more of its customers viewed office products as a commodity. Without a fresh strategy, company executives believed that these challenging forces would continue to shrink profit margins and put increasing pressure on shareholder value. Likewise, in a service-driven, price-sensitive business, Boise managers were uncertain which customers might contribute the most value over time and how to allocate marketing budgets among the diverse customers that it served—from small businesses to large corporate accounts.[*]

Step 1: Define the financial objectives and establish growth and productivity goals

Strategy maps start with financial objectives for creating shareholder value through two paths: long-term revenue and short-term productivity. The long-term goal often establishes a stretch target that creates a value gap—the difference between a desired future state and current reality. Kaplan and Norton note that the size of the value gap must be established with care: "Executives must balance the benefits from challenging the organisation to achieve dramatic improvements in shareholder value with the realities of what can possibly be achieved."[*] So, specific targets for revenue growth and productivity improvements should be established along with a corresponding time line (for example, achieve revenue growth of 15 per cent by year 1 and 30 per cent by year 3).

Boise adopted a new customer strategy driven by this strategic theme: Create Distinctive Customer Value by Enhancing the Customer Relationship (see Figure 14.1). The financial objectives were to increase shareholder value by emphasising market segmentation and measuring revenue, profit contribution, and cost-to-serve by individual customer segment.

Step 2: Define the customer value proposition for target customer segments

Achieving revenue growth goals requires explicit attention to generating revenue from new customers or increasing revenue from existing customers. Thus, the most important component of strategy is to develop and clarify the value proposition for customers in targeted segments.

Boise adopted a customer solutions strategy that enhances value through one-to-one marketing, anticipates customers' needs to create customised service, and provides seamless access across sales channels (for example, sales force, Web, direct mail). A customer satisfaction survey assessed the core elements in the firm's new value proposition. The core objective, "to create distinctive value," was measured by:

- The number of customers retained in targeted segments;

- The number of new customers acquired;

- Estimates of the lifetime value of customers.

Step 3: Establish the time line for results

To develop a coordinated plan, the high-level financial goals must be broken down into targets for particular functions or internal processes, like innovation management, so that organisational members unite behind the strategy and are comfortable with the overall target.

For Boise, operations management processes would reduce the costs of servicing customers, the customer management process would increase the number of relationship customers, and the innovation processes would create new offerings such as contract purchase plans. A time line for performance targets guided the efforts in each group.

Step 4: Identify the critical strategic themes and internal processes with the greatest impact on the strategy

This step identifies the key processes in delivering the customer value proposition and reaching the company's financial objectives.

Boise's internal process objectives emphasised three themes (see Figure 14.1):

- *Operational excellence*: Rationalise operations by moving more customers to an e-commerce channel to provide more convenient customer access and lower costs per customer contact.

- *Customer management*: Leverage customer service by personalising the ordering process, making interactions easier for the customer, and meeting all the customer's needs in a single interaction.

- *Innovation management*: Redefine customer value expectations by creating new tools that customers can use to control spending on office supplies.

Once again, Boise developed measures—such as the percentage of customers in a target segment that used the e-commerce channel—for each of these themes. To illustrate, for operations, success at reaching cost reductions was measured by the percentage of business in targeted segments that came through e-channels; for innovation management, success was measured by the number of customers participating in new contract purchasing plans.

Step 5: Identify the human, information, and organisational resources required to support the strategy

The learning and growth objectives assess how ready the organisation is to support the internal processes that drive the strategy. This stage ensures that organisational members are aligned with the strategy and get with the training, information technology, and incentives to successfully implement it.

To introduce the strategy at Boise, every employee saw a video of the CEO describing the strategy, and more than 1000 employees attended a 6-hour course on the new customer management initiative. Moreover, the firm installed a comprehensive customer relationship management (CRM) system and provided 1500 customer service representatives and managers with 30 hours of training on it.[*] A video was likewise developed for customers to show them the benefits of the new strategy. Among the measures used were the percentage of employees trained for the new customer-centric strategy and the proportion of staff with incentives directly aligned to the strategy.

Step 6: Develop an action plan and provide required funding for each of the separate initiatives (strategic themes)

To reach financial targets and fulfil the strategic vision, several separate initiatives—involving different functions and processes in the company—must support the overall strategy in a coordinated fashion (see Figure 14.1). These initiatives create the performance results and form the foundation for successfully implementing the strategy. Rather than a series of stand-alone projects, these initiatives should be aligned to the overall strategy and managed as an integrated bundle of investments.

Strategy results

Boise's new strategy allowed the firm to reduce costs, boost growth, and offer even their most price-sensitive customers an integrated solution that delivered greater value than lower-priced competitors. In turn, customer retention improved dramatically, and sales from the firm's most valuable customers expanded. Don Peppers and Martha Rogers describe how the strategy achieves profit targets:

> *The firm now has good customer profitability data, which is yielding steady benefits on a customer-by-customer basis. For instance, relying on this data, Boise chose to discontinue working with one of its largest customers, a hospital group that apparently cost Boise money with every sale. And a senior executive visited another customer's headquarters, shared data to show that the company was one of Boise's least profitable accounts, and won a price increase over two years.* [*]

14.1.2 Maps: A tool for strategy making

Because a firm's strategy is based on developing a differentiated customer value proposition, the business marketing manager assumes a lead role in both strategy development and implementation. Fundamental to this role is the challenging job of coordinating activities across functions to create and deliver a superior solution for customers.

Translating objectives into results

The strategy map, coupled with the measures and targets from the balanced scorecard, provides a valuable framework for the strategist. First, the strategy map clearly describes the strategy, detailing objectives for the critical internal processes that create value and the organisational assets (for example, information technology, employee rewards) needed to support them. Second, the balanced scorecard translates objectives into specific measures and targets that guide critical components of the strategy. Third, to achieve financial or productivity goals, a set of well-integrated action plans must be designed that are carefully aligned to the overall strategy. Attention now turns to the central role of the control process in business marketing management.

14.2 MARKETING STRATEGY: ALLOCATING RESOURCES

All companies have limited resources. To target the whole of the market is usually unrealistic. The effectiveness of personnel and material resources can be greatly improved when they are more narrowly focused on a particular segment of customers. With limited resources, Saab and Porsche target only a few market segments compared with Ford or Toyota. Segmentation enables Saab and Porsche to identify homogeneous groups of customers at whom the Saab 95 or Porsche 911 models can be targeted. This maximises these companies' use of resources and marketing mix activities.

14.2.1 Guiding strategy formulation

Evaluation outcomes provide the foundation for integrating the market strategy formulation and the marketing control system. Results in the most recent operating period show how successful past marketing efforts were in meeting objectives. Performance below or above expectations then signals where funds should be reallocated. If the firm expected to reach 20 per cent of the OEM market but reached only 12 per cent, a change in strategy may be required. Performance information provided by the control system might demonstrate that sales personnel in the OEM market were reaching only 45 per cent of potential buyers; additional funds could be allocated to expand either the sales force or the advertising budget. On the other hand, since performance was below targets, as pointed out by the control system, the problem may not be with the strategy, but with the way it is being implemented. Thus, additional funds may be allocated to marketing efforts, but it may be necessary to also carefully examine how effectively the sales force is executing the sales strategy or whether the advertising was implemented effectively—perhaps the message is wrong or the advertising media were not appropriate.

14.2.2 Managing individual customers for profit[*]

Business marketers should also focus on revenues from individual customers and isolate the cost-to-serve them. For relationship customers, attention should be given to the share-of-wallet the firm is attracting. **Share-of-wallet** represents the portion of total purchases in a product and service category (for example, information technology) that a customer makes from the firm (for example, Hewlett-Packard).

For customers with a more transactional focus, the business marketer should:

- Develop a customer database that profiles the past purchasing patterns of customers;
- Determine the cost-to-serve each customer;
- Set a revenue target and profit goal;
- Develop a customer contact plan that details the sales channel (for example, direct sales, telesales, Web-based contact) to be used;
- Monitor performance results and the relative effectiveness of different sales channels.

Marketing managers must weigh the interactions among the strategy elements and allocate resources to create effective and efficient strategies. To do so, a system for monitoring past performance is an absolute necessity. In effect, the control system enables management to keep abreast of all facets of performance.

14.2.3 The marketing control process

Marketing control is a process management uses to generate information on marketing performance. Two major forms of control are: (1) control over efficient allocation of marketing effort and (2) comparison of planned and actual performance. In the first case, the business marketer may use past profitability data as a standard for evaluating future marketing expenditures. The second form of control alerts management to any differences between planned and actual performance and may also reveal reasons for performance discrepancies.

14.3 CONTROL AT VARIOUS LEVELS

The control process is universal in that it can be applied to any level of marketing analysis. For example, business marketers must frequently evaluate whether their general strategies are appropriate and effective. However, it is equally important to know whether the individual elements in the strategy are effectively integrated for a given market. Further, management must evaluate resource allocation within a particular element (for example, the effectiveness of direct selling versus that of industrial distributors). The control system should work in any of these situations. The four primary levels of marketing control are delineated in Table 14.1. In short, measures of marketing performance should be used both to assess the overall business success and to examine the health of particular products, markets, or distribution channels.[*]

14.3.1 Strategic control

Strategic control is based on a comprehensive evaluation of whether the firm is headed in the right direction. Strategic control focuses on assessing whether the strategy is being implemented as planned and whether it produces the intended results.[*] Because the business marketing environment changes rapidly, existing product/market situations may lose their potential, and new-product/market matchups provide important opportunities. Philip Kotler suggests that the firm periodically conduct a **marketing audit**—a comprehensive, periodic, and systematic evaluation of marketing operations that specifically analyses the market environment and the firm's internal marketing activities.[*] An analysis of the environment assesses company image, customer characteristics, competitive activities, regulatory constraints, and economic trends. Evaluating this information may uncover threats the firm can counter and future opportunities it can exploit.

An internal evaluation of the marketing system scrutinises marketing objectives, organisation, and implementation. In this way, management may be able to spot where existing products

TABLE 14.1 Levels of marketing control

Type of Control	Responsibility	Purpose of Control	Tools
Strategic control	Top management	To examine whether the company is pursuing its best opportunities with respect to markets, products, and channels	Marketing audit
Annual plan control	Top management, middle management	To examine whether the planned results are being achieved	Sales analysis; market-share analysis; expense-to-sales ratios; other ratios; attitude tracking
Efficiency and effectiveness control	Middle management	To examine how well resources have been utilised in each element of the marketing strategy to accomplish a specific goal	Expense ratios; advertising effectiveness measures; market potential; contribution margin analysis
Profitability control	Marketing controller	To examine where the company is making and losing money	Profitability by product territory, market segment, trade channel, order size

Source: Adapted from Philip Kotler, *Marketing Management: The Millennium Edition* (Englewood Cliffs, NJ: Prentice-Hall, 2000), p. 698.

could be adapted to new markets or new products could be developed for existing markets. The regular, systematic marketing audit is a valuable technique for evaluating the direction of marketing strategies.[*]

Marketing Performance Measurement (MPM) strategies[*]

Many firms are now *strategically* developing performance measurement approaches to evaluate their marketing efforts: They have developed a marketing operations area that concentrates on maintaining a set of pragmatic *marketing performance* objectives and measures that become the marketing performance measurement (MPM) system. Very simply, **marketing performance measurement** is a business strategy that provides performance feedback to the organisation regarding the results of marketing efforts, and it is often viewed as a specific form of market information processing for the organisation.[*]

For example, IBM maintains MPM from a central marketing operations function, providing its global marketing board with an integrated view across all business units. This process is part of marketing's strategic planning and resource management process, ensuring that the marketing measurement and specific metrics line up with the company's strategic and business objectives. IBM executives assert that MPM allows them to better align marketing priorities to business priorities and to connect marketing expenditures to business performance. Also, consistent use of common metrics under a common structure allows IBM to restructure programmes, shift emphasis on particular offerings, and move investments to higher-growth opportunities—in other words, to drive actionable results.

In a different approach, Intel identifies four top-level broad strategies each year. Then it determines key business strategies, marketing metrics, and targets, and puts these on a "dashboard." These metrics are monitored quarterly or monthly and do not usually change radically throughout the year. Lastly, Intel drills down to the project level and identifies tasks and management by objectives (MBOs), which are measured by activity (completed or not) or results. Intel's dashboard increases visibility, reinforces accountability, and facilitates execution of key marketing strategies. Intel marketing managers believe that the dashboard has allowed them to sharpen marketing strategies and to more clearly understand how marketing programmes can contribute to business success.

MPM guidelines and payoff

To effectively develop their MPM strategy, business marketing strategists should follow four important guidelines:

1   If the firm does not have an MPM process, it should begin slowly and should not aim for perfection.

2   The MPM should use relevant metrics that drive action.

3   All marketing groups and the sales department should be included in the MPM process.

4   The MPM process should become part of the weekly, monthly, quarterly, and annual reporting as well as a central component of the strategic planning process.

In a study conducted by Don O'Sullivan and Andrew V. Abela, MPM ability was shown to have a positive impact on firm performance in the high-tech sector.[*] The study found that firms with a strong MPM ability tend to outperform their competitors, as reported by senior marketers. The results also suggest that MPM ability has a positive influence on return on assets (ROA) and on stock returns. In addition, the research revealed that MPM ability has a significant, positive impact on CEO satisfaction with marketing. Development of MPM ability requires that marketers divert part of their budget and attention away from actual marketing programmes and toward measurement efforts.

14.3.2 Annual plan control

In **annual plan control**, the objectives specified in the plan become the performance standards against which actual results are compared. Sales volume, profits, and market share are the typical performance standards for business marketers. **Sales analysis** is an attempt to determine why actual sales varied from planned sales. Expected sales may not be met because of price reductions, inadequate volume, or both. A sales analysis separates the effects of these variables so that corrective action can be taken.

Market share analysis assesses how the firm is doing relative to competition. A machine-tool manufacturer's 10 per cent sales increase may, on the surface, appear favourable. However, if total machine-tool industry sales are up 25 per cent, a market-share analysis would show that the firm has not fared well relative to competitors.

Finally, **expense-to-sales ratios** are analyses of the efficiency of marketing operations—whether the firm is overspending or underspending. Frequently, industry standards or past company ratios provide standards of comparison. Total marketing expenses and expenses of each strategic marketing element are evaluated in relation to sales. These figures provide management with a basis for evaluating the company's performance.

14.3.3 Marketing control: The marketing performance dashboard

Many business marketers have adopted the practice of creating "dashboards" of key metrics that provide information on the performance of the marketing function. Dashboards may be configured in many ways, but they typically present marketers with a highly graphical capsule view of key performance and operational metrics.[*] A **marketing dashboard** is "a relatively small collection of interconnected key performance metrics and underlying performance drivers that reflect both short and long-term interests," informing decision making throughout the organisation.[*]

A marketing performance dashboard graphically depicts a company's marketing and operational performance through the use of simple gauges and scales. They represent graphical overlays on databases, providing managers with visual clues about what is happening in real time. Marketing dashboards are an appropriate visualisation of critical underlying performance data.[*] Business marketers are increasingly using dashboards because of the high level of attention senior management is devoting to marketing return-on-investment. Importantly, dashboards help companies improve performance because dashboard metrics centre on the key outcomes expected from the marketing function. For example, Tektronix, a company that provides test and measurement equipment to high-tech firms, demonstrates the striking improvements that a performance dashboard can facilitate. Over the first 5 years of using the system, the company has achieved a 125 per cent increase in responses to marketing programmes and has seen a 90 per cent increase in qualified sales leads. In addition, Tektronix has reduced its cost per lead by 70 per cent. Moreover, the company's marketing forecast accuracy now has a variance of 3 per cent, down from a variance of 50 per cent before the dashboard was developed.[*]

Which metrics matter?

The metrics to be included in a marketing dashboard will vary dramatically from one firm to the next, because each firm has different performance outcomes that are considered important.

> *Marketers must accept that there's no one-size-fits-all dashboard they can use; they must customise the tool for themselves. After establishing what the company's true business drivers are, management must cull the myriad possibilities down to the three or four key ones that will be the most fruitful to follow. At least one of these drivers, such as share of wallet, should indicate performance relative to competitors. At least one, such as loyalty,*

should clearly measure the customers' experience. And one, such as customers' average annual expenditures or lifetime value, should measure the growth of retained customers' business. Finally, any driver on the dashboard must be one the company can manipulate. It might be informative for a supplier of hospital beds to track the number of elective surgeries in the US, but the company can't influence that number, so it's not a useful metric for them to follow—they cannot "manipulate" the number of elective surgeries.

Isolating performance drivers

There is both art and science in the creation of effective marketing dashboards. However, an effective dashboard maps out the relationships between business outcomes and marketing performance. One of the great challenges is determining where all the relevant data reside: The marketer has to define what the key performance metrics are and think about where to get the actual data to populate those metrics, according to one expert who designs marketing dashboards. In addition, the information one really needs to make decisions almost always comes from multiple sources: internal sales and marketing data, as well as external partner or third-party data. A typical dashboard could include data from 6 to 10 sources, which presents a major challenge. Table 14.2 provides examples of the metrics used in the marketing dashboards by Cisco Systems, Cognos Corporation, and Adobe Systems. Note that each company employs a very different set of metrics. The dashboard elements for each firm reflect the importance that each particular element plays in the success of marketing strategy.

Desirable dashboard features

One expert in the development of marketing dashboards suggests that a good dashboard should accomplish several objectives. The dashboard should:

1 Foster decision making: the metrics should suggest a course of action to be followed;

2 Provide a unified view into marketing's value to the business;

3 Enable better alignment between marketing and the business;

4 Translate complex measures into a meaningful and coherent set of information.

Finally, a dashboard should be focused on two levels: The dashboard should: (a) report operations metrics that are internally focused and (b) reflect execution metrics that mirror marketplace performance.

TABLE 14.2 Marketing metrics: Selected company examples

Cognos Corp	Adobe Systems	Cisco Systems
Market share	Marketing activities: Ad reach; Web site hits	Image
Financial analyst firm rankings	Operational measures: Brand awareness	Brand perception
Average revenue per sales rep	Cost per sale; Programme-to-people ratio	Lead generation
Penetration of top global companies	Outcome-based metrics: Market share; Number of leads	Employee retention
Number of customers using a company solution year-to-date	Leading indicators: Brand loyalty; Lifetime value of a customer	Customer satisfaction

Source: Kelly Shermach, "Driving Performance," *Sales and Marketing Management* 157 (December 2005): p. 18; Kate Maddox, Sean Callahan, and Carol Krol, "Top Trends," *B to B* 90 (June 13, 2005): p. 24; and Sandra Swanson, "Marketers: James Richardson," *B to B* 90 (October 24, 2005): p. 10.

Operations metrics can include such measures as a marketing budget ratio, which tracks marketing investment as a per cent of total revenue; a programme-to-people ratio that determines the per cent of a marketing euro spent on programmes versus staff; and an awareness-to-demand ratio that evaluates the per cent of marketing investment focused on awareness-building versus demand-generation. Execution metrics, on the other hand, determine how effectively the marketing strategy is being executed. Here the measures include efficiency and effectiveness around implementation: Is awareness building? Are we developing preference? Is the company gaining consideration? Are leads being generated, opportunities identified and qualified? Are deals being closed? [*]

Marketing performance dashboards are powerful control tools that provide management at all levels of the company with vital data concerning just how well marketing strategy is performing and how much value the marketing function is adding to the firm.

B2B TOP PERFORMERS

Rice ... not all grains seem the same

Do you enjoy rice? Which brand and variety do you buy? In the rice isle of the supermarkets there are many brands, several of which offer similar varieties such as basmati or long grain, brown or white. However most households have a preference and purchase their favourite brand each time they require more rice. This is partly because of the branding adopted by the leading players, sometimes owing to the promo price deal, but often it stems from the segmentation strategies adopted by the leading brands.

Market leader Uncle Ben's, part of the Mars family of companies within Masterfoods, has been producing good tasting rice since the 1940s, but very much targeted at families or couples who are either in a hurry or needing the convenience of pre-prepared easy-to-cook rice in a variety of guises and cooking styles. Uncle Ben's brought rice to the attention of many consumers in the 1960s and 1970s, with generations now having grown up enjoying simple-cook rice out of the familiar orange packaging.

Recently Indian business Veetee launched its Dine In range of innovative plastic trays packed to show off the ready-cooked range of enticing rices: basmati, pilau, long grain, Thai jasmine, basmati and wild, Thai lime and herb and wholegrain; all ready to eat in two-minutes. Not aimed at scratch cooks or those prepared to boil on the hob, this range is targeting 'food cheats' who want an easy-to-prepare good looking product in no time at all so as to get on with their evening.

Further up the rice fixture will be found premium-priced Tilda, from another Indian food group based in the UK. While Tilda also has a microwave range, the bulk of its business is from dry rice, predominantly top-end dry basmati. Priced way above competitors, Tilda enjoys a strong market share and has legions of loyal users who are convinced they can discern a taste premium from the perfect looking aromatic basmati grains. Although far from complicated to cook, Tilda's appeal is more to scratch cooks and those who enjoy both cooking and consuming great tasting food. Not that Uncle Ben's or Veetee do not taste good, but their appeal is to consumers in a hurry or who are less confident cooks, seeking a value for money reliable rice.

Each of these leading rice brands has managed to differentiate what in many parts of the world is a basic commodity ... grains of rice. Each company, through recipes, packaging, product formulations, cooking methods, pricing and branding, has managed to appeal to a distinctive set of consumers. While they compete with retailers' own label rice ranges and with each other for many of the same consumers, each rice company has adopted a segmented approach to guide its product innovation, proposition development, marketing messages and consumer engagement programmes. Even in an apparent commodity market such as rice, segmentation has become firmly entrenched to direct the major players' strategies.

14.3.4 Efficiency and effectiveness control

Efficiency control examines how efficiently resources are being used in each element of marketing strategy (for example, sales force, advertising); **effectiveness control** evaluates whether the strategic component is accomplishing its objective. A good control system provides continuing data for evaluating the efficiency of resources used for a given element of marketing strategy to accomplish a given objective. Table 14.3 provides a representative sample of the types of data required. Performance measures and standards vary by company and situation, according to the goals and objectives in the marketing plan.

TABLE 14.3   Illustrative measures for efficiency and effectiveness control

Product

Sales by market segments

Sales relative to potential

Sales growth rates

Market share

Contribution margin

Percentage of total profits

Return on investment

Distribution

Sales, expenses, and contribution by channel type

Sales and contribution margin by intermediary type and individual intermediaries

Sales relative to market potential by channel, intermediary type, and specific intermediaries

Expense-to-sales ratio by channel, etc.

Logistics cost by logistics activity by channel

Communication

Advertising effectiveness by type of media

Actual audience/target audience ratio

Cost per contact

Number of calls, inquiries, and information requests by type of media

Euro sales per sales call

Sales per territory relative to potential

Selling expenses to sales ratios

New accounts per time period

Pricing

Price changes relative to sales volume

Discount structure related to sales volume

Bid strategy related to new contracts

Margin structure related to marketing expenses

General price policy related to sales volume

Margins related to channel member performance

14.3.5 Profitability control

The essence of **profitability control** is to describe where the firm is making or losing money in terms of the important segments of its business. A **segment** is the unit of analysis management uses for control purposes; it may be customer segments, product lines, territories, or channel structures. Suppose a business marketing firm focuses on three customer segments: health-care organisations, universities, and local government units. To allocate the marketing budget among the three segments, management must consider the profit contribution of each segment and its expected potential. Profitability control, then, provides a methodology for linking marketing costs and revenues with specific segments of the business.

Profitability by market segment

Relating sales revenues and marketing costs to market segments improves decision making. More specifically, say Leland Beik and Stephen Buzby,

> *For both strategic and tactical decisions, marketing managers may profit by knowing the effect of the marketing mix on the target segment at which marketing efforts are aimed. If the programmes are to be responsive to environmental change, a monitoring system is needed to locate problems and guide adjustments in marketing decisions. Tracing the profitability of segments permits improved pricing, selling, advertising, channel, and product management decisions. The success of marketing policies and programmes may be appraised by a dollar-and-cents measure of profitability by segment.* [*]

Profitability control, a prerequisite to strategy planning and implementation, has stringent information requirements. To be effective, the firm needs a marketing–accounting information system.

An activity-based cost system

The accounting system must first be able to link costs with the various marketing activities and must then attach these "activity" costs to the important segments to be analysed. The critical element in the process is to trace all costs to the activities (warehousing, advertising, and so on) for which the resources are used and then to the products or segments that consume them. [*] Such an **activity-based cost (ABC) system** reveals the links between performing particular activities and the demands those activities make on the organisation's resources. As a result, it can give managers a clear picture of how products, brands, customers, facilities, regions, or distribution channels both generate revenues and consume resources. [*] An ABC analysis focuses attention on improving activities that have the greatest effect on profits.

Robin Cooper and Robert Kaplan capture the essence of ABC:

> *ABC analysis enables managers to slice into the business many different ways—by product or group of similar products, by individual customer or client group, or by distribution channel—and gives them a close-up view of whatever slice they are considering. ABC analysis also illuminates exactly what activities are associated with that part of the business and how those activities are linked to the generation of revenues and the consumption of resources. By highlighting those relationships, ABC helps managers understand precisely where to take actions that drive profits. In contrast to traditional accounting, activity-based costing segregates the expenses of indirect and support resources by activities. It then assigns those expenses based on the drivers of the activities, rather than by some arbitrary percentage allocation.* [*]

ABC system illustrated [*]

ABC analysis highlights for managers where their actions will likely have the greatest effect on profits. The ABC system at Kanthal Corporation led to a review of profitability by size of customer. Kanthal, a manufacturer of heating wire, used activity-based costing to analyse its customer profitability and discovered that the well-known 80/20 rule (80 per cent of sales generated by 20 per cent of customers) was in need of revision. A 20/225 rule was actually operating: 20 per cent of customers were generating 225 per cent of profits. The middle 70 per cent of customers were hovering around the break-even point, and Kanthal was losing 125 per cent of its profits on 10 per cent of its customers.

The Kanthal customers generating the greatest losses were among those with the largest sales volume. Initially, this finding surprised managers, but it soon began to make sense. You cannot lose large amounts of money on a small customer. The large, unprofitable customers demanded lower prices, frequent deliveries of small lots, extensive sales and technical resources, and product changes. The newly revealed economics enabled management to change the way it did business with these customers—through price changes, minimum order sizes, and information technology—transforming the customers into strong profit contributors.

Using the ABC system

An ABC system requires the firm to break from traditional accounting concepts. Managers must refrain from allocating all expenses to individual units and instead separate the expenses and match them to the activity that consumes the resources.[*] Once resource expenditures are related to the activities they produce, management can explore different strategies for reducing the resource commitments. To enhance profitability, business marketing managers need to figure out how to reduce expenditures on those resources or increase the output they produce. For example, a sales manager would search for ways to reduce the number of sales calls on unprofitable customers or find ways to make the salesperson more effective with them. In summary, ABC systems enable the business marketing manager to focus on increasing profitability by understanding the sources of cost variability and developing strategies to reduce resource commitment or enhance resource productivity.

14.4 IMPLEMENTATION OF BUSINESS MARKETING STRATEGY

Many marketing plans fail because they are poorly implemented. Implementation is the critical link between strategy formulation and superior organisational performance.[*] **Marketing implementation** is the process that translates marketing plans into action assignments and ensures that such assignments are executed in a manner that accomplishes a plan's defined objectives.[*] Special implementation challenges emerge for the marketing manager because diverse functional areas participate in both developing and executing strategy.

14.4.1 The strategy-implementation fit

Thomas Bonoma asserts that "marketing strategy and implementation affect each other. Although strategy obviously affects actions, execution also affects marketing strategies, especially over time."[*] Although the dividing line between strategy and execution is a bit fuzzy, it is often not difficult to diagnose implementation problems and distinguish them from strategy deficiencies. Bonoma presents the following scenario:

> A firm introduced a new portable microcomputer that incorporated a number of features that the target market valued. The new product appeared to be well positioned in a rapidly growing market, but initial sales results were miserable. Why? The 50-person sales force had little incentive to grapple with a new unfamiliar product and continued to emphasise

the older models. Given the significant market potential, management had decided to set the sales incentive compensation level lower on the new machines than on the older ones. The older models had a selling cycle one-half as long as the new product and required no software knowledge or support. In this case, poor execution damaged good strategy.[*]

Marketing strategy and implementation affect each other. When both strategy and implementation are appropriate, the firm is likely to meet its objectives. Diagnosis becomes more difficult in other cases. For example, the cause of a marketing problem may be hard to detect when the strategy is on the mark but the implementation is poor. The business marketer may never become aware of the soundness of the strategy. Alternatively, excellent implementation of a poor strategy may give managers time to see the problem and correct it.

14.4.2 Implementation skills

Thomas Bonoma identifies four important implementation skills for marketing managers: (1) interacting, (2) allocating, (3) monitoring, and (4) organising.[*] Each assumes special significance in the business marketing environment.

Marketing managers are continually *interacting* with others both within and outside the corporation. Inside, a number of peers (for example, R&D personnel) over whom the marketer has little power often assume a crucial role in strategy development and implementation. Outside, the marketer deals with important customers, channel members, advertising agencies, and the like. The best implementers have good bargaining skills and the ability to understand how others feel.[*]

The implementer must also *allocate* time, assignments, people, euros, and other resources among the marketing tasks at hand. Astute marketing managers, says Bonoma, are "tough and fair in putting people and euros where they will be most effective. The less able ones routinely allocate too many euros and people to mature programmes and too few to richer ones."[*]

Bonoma asserts that marketing managers with good *monitoring* skills exhibit flexibility and intelligence in dealing with the firm's information and control systems: "Good implementers struggle and wrestle with their markets and businesses until they can simply and powerfully express the 'back of the envelope' ratios necessary to run the business, regardless of formal control system inadequacies."[*]

Finally, the best implementers are effective at *organising*. Sound execution often hinges on the marketer's ability to work with both the formal and the informal organisational networks. The manager customises an informal organisation to solve problems and facilitate good execution.

14.4.3 The marketing strategy centre: An implementation guide[*]

Diverse functional areas participate to differing degrees in developing and implementing business marketing strategy. Research and development, manufacturing, technical service, physical distribution, and other functional areas play fundamental roles. Ronald McTavish points out that "marketing specialists understand markets, but know a good deal less about the nuts and bolts of the company's operations—its internal terrain. This is the domain of the operating specialist. We need to bring these different specialists together in a 'synergistic pooling' of knowledge and viewpoint to achieve the best fit of the company's skills with the market and the company's approach to it."[*] This suggests a challenging and pivotal interdisciplinary role for the marketing manager in the business-to-business firm.

The marketing strategy centre provides a framework for highlighting this interdisciplinary role and for exploring key implementation requirements. Table 14.4 highlights important strategic topics examined throughout this textbook. In each case, nonmarketing personnel play active implementation roles. For example, product quality is directly or indirectly affected by several

TABLE 14.4 Interfunctional involvement in marketing strategy implementation: An illustrative responsibility chart

Decision Area	Marketing	Sales	Manufac-turing	R&D	Purcha-sing	Physical Distri-bution	Tech-nical Service	Strategic Business Unit	Corporate-Level Planner
Product/service quality									
Technical service support									
Physical distribution service									
National accounts management									
Channel relations									
Sales support									
Product/ service innovation									

© Cengage Learning 2013

Use the following abbreviations to indicate decision roles: R = responsible; A = approval; C = consult; M = implement; I = inform; X = no role in decision.

departments: manufacturing, research and development, technical service, and others. In turn, successful product innovation reflects the collective efforts of individuals from several functional areas. Clearly, effective strategy implementation requires well-defined decision roles, responsibilities, timetables, and coordination mechanisms.

On a global market scale, special coordination challenges emerge when selected activities such as R&D are concentrated in one country and other strategy activities such as manufacturing are dispersed across countries. Xerox, however, has been successful in maintaining a high level of coordination across such dispersed activities. The Xerox brand, marketing approach, and servicing procedures are standardised worldwide.[*]

The marketer's role

To ensure maximum customer satisfaction and the desired market response, the business marketer must assume an active role in the strategy centre by negotiating market-sensitive agreements and coordinating strategies with other members. While being influenced by other functional areas to varying degrees in the process, the marketer can potentially influence key areas such as the design of the logistical system, the selection of manufacturing technology, or the structure of a materials management system. Such negotiation with other functional areas is fundamental to the business marketer's strategic interdisciplinary role. Thus, the successful business marketing manager performs as an integrator by drawing on the collective strengths of the enterprise to satisfy customer needs profitably.

14.4.4 Looking back

Figure 14.2 synthesises the central components of business marketing management and highlights the material presented in this textbook. Part I introduced the major classes of customers that constitute the business market: commercial enterprises, governmental units, and institutions. The timely themes of organisational buying behaviour and customer relationship management provided the focus of Part II. Part III discussed the tools for assessing market opportunities; it explored techniques for identifying market segments and for forecasting sales. Functionally integrated marketing planning provides a framework for dealing with each component of the business marketing mix, as detailed in Part IV. Special attention was also given to the special challenges and unique opportunities that rapidly developing economies present for business-to-business firms.

FIGURE 14.2 A framework for business marketing management

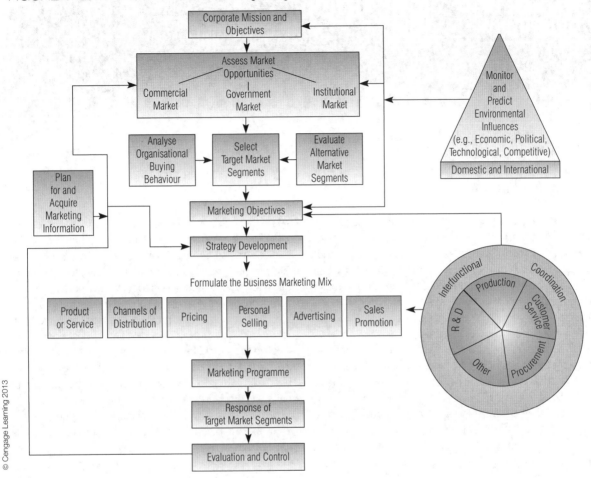

Once business marketing strategy is formulated, the manager must evaluate the response of target market segments to minimise any discrepancy between planned and actual results. This chapter, which constitutes Part V, explores the critical dimensions of the marketing control process, which is the final loop in the model presented in Figure 14.2: planning for and acquiring marketing information. Such information forms the core of the firm's management information system; it is derived internally through the marketing–accounting system and externally through the marketing research function. Evaluation and control enable the marketer to reassess business market opportunities and make adjustments as needed in business marketing strategy.

SUMMARY

Central to market strategy is the allocation of resources to each strategy element and the application of marketing efforts to segments. The marketing control system is the process by which the business marketing firm generates information to make these decisions. Moreover, the marketing control system is the means by which current performance can be evaluated and steps can be taken to correct deficiencies. Used in conjunction with the balanced scorecard, the strategy map converts a strategy vision into concrete objectives and measures, organised into four different perspectives: financial, customer, internal business process, and learning and growth. The approach involves developing a customer strategy, identifying target market segments, isolating the critical internal processes the firm must develop to deliver value to customers in these segments, and selecting the organisational capabilities needed to achieve customer and financial objectives. A strategy map provides a visual representation of a firm's critical objectives and the cause-and-effect relationships among them that drive superior organisational performance.

An effective control system has four distinct components. Strategic control, which is operationalised through the marketing audit, provides valuable information on the present and future course of the firm's basic product/market mission. Annual plan control compares annual with planned results to provide input for future planning. Efficiency and effectiveness control evaluates whether marketing strategy elements achieve their goals in a cost-effective manner. Finally, profitability control seeks to evaluate profitability by segment. Marketing dashboards are effective tools for helping managers to isolate and monitor key performance metrics while providing top management with a compact profile concerning the impact of marketing strategies on overall company performance.

Many business marketing plans fail because they are poorly executed. Marketing implementation is the process that translates marketing plans into action assignments and ensures that such assignments are executed in a timely and effective manner. Four implementation skills are particularly important to the business marketing manager: (1) interacting, (2) allocating, (3) monitoring, and (4) organising. Nonmarketing personnel play active roles in implementing business marketing strategy. This suggests a challenging and pivotal interdisciplinary role for the marketing manager.

DISCUSSION QUESTIONS

1   Pick a B2B company you are familiar with and create a strategy map based around their strategy.

2   What are the differences between efficiency control and effectiveness control?

3   Choose one example of a local, small scale B2B company; and one international B2B company. How might their profitability control differ?

4   What implementation skills should a marketing manager have and why?

5   Discuss why organisations should develop marketing strategies.

INTERNET EXERCISES

If you are working, look at your organisation's website or intranet. If you are studying, look at the intranet in your academic institution.

1 What elements of internal marketing are evident in the website's sections?

2 In what ways is the content attempting to control, coordinate and share information with employees or people within the organisation?

3 How else could the organisation communicate its marketing strategy and marketing plan intentions to internal stakeholders?

REFERENCES

Beik, Leland L., and Buzby, Stephen L., "Profitability Analysis by Market Segments," *Journal of Marketing* 37 (July 1973): p. 49.

Bonoma, Thomas V., "Making Your Marketing Strategy Work," *Harvard Business Review* 62 (March–April 1984): pp. 69–76.

Clark, Bruce H., "A Summary of Thinking on Measuring the Value of Marketing," *Journal of Targeting, Measurement and Analysis for Marketing* 9 (June 2001): p. 361.

Clark, Bruce H., Abela, Andrew V., and Ambler, Tim, "An Information Processing Model of Marketing Performance Measurement," *Journal of Marketing Theory and Practice* 14 (Summer 2006): p. 193.

Cooper, Robin, and Kaplan, Robert S., "Measure Costs Right: Make the Right Decisions," *Harvard Business Review* 66 (September–October 1988): p. 96.

Cooper, Robin, and Kaplan, Robert S., "Profit Priorities from Activity-Based Costing," *Harvard Business Review* 69 (May–June 1993): p. 130.

Cooper, Robin, and Kaplan, Robert S., "The Promise—and Peril—of Integrated Cost Systems," *Harvard Business Review* 76 (July–August 1998): pp. 109–118.

Cooper, Robin, and Chew, W. Bruce, "Control Tomorrow's Costs through Today's Designs," *Harvard Business Review* 74 (January–February 1996): pp. 88–97.

Dibb, Sally, Simkin, Lyndon, Pride, Bill, and Ferrell, O.C., *Marketing Concepts & Strategies*, 6th ed. (Cengage, 2012).

Doole, Isobel, and Lowe, Robin, *International Marketing Strategy* 6th ed. (Cengage, 2012).

Dougherty, Deborah, and Bowman, Edward H., "The Effects of Organizational Downsizing on Product Innovation," *California Management Review* 37 (Summer 1995): pp. 28–44.

Gerard, Michael, "The Best Technology Marketers Are Well Versed in MPM," *B to B* 93 (April 7, 2008): pp. 21–23.

Hamel, Gary, "Strategy as Revolution," *Harvard Business Review* 74 (July–August 1996): p. 82.

Hamel, Gary, and Välikangas, Liisa, "The Quest for Resilience," *Harvard Business Review* 81 (September 2003): pp. 52–63.

Hanssens, Dominique M., Rust, Roland T., and Srivastava, Rajendra K., "Marketing Strategy and Wall Street: Nailing Down Marketing's Impact," *Journal of Marketing* 73 (November 2009): pp. 115–118.

Hosford, Christopher, "Driving Business with Dashboards," *B to B* 91 (December 11, 2006): p. 18.

Hutt, Michael D., "Cross-Functional Working Relationships in Marketing," *Journal of the Academy of Marketing Science* 23 (Fall 1995): pp. 351–357.

Hutt, Michael D., and Speh, Thomas W., "The Marketing Strategy Center: Diagnosing the Industrial Marketer's Interdisciplinary Role," *Journal of Marketing* 48 (Fall 1984): pp. 53–61.

Hutt, Michael D., Walker, Beth A., and Frankwick, Gary L., "Hurdle the Cross-Functional Barriers to Strategic Change," *Sloan Management Review* 36 (Spring 1995): pp. 22–30.

Jacobs, Fred A., Johnston, Wesley, and Kotchetova, Natalia, "Customer Profitability: Prospective vs. Retrospective Approaches in a Business-to-Business Setting," *Industrial Marketing Management* 30 (June 2001): pp. 353–363.

Kaplan, Robert S., and Anderson, Steven R., "Time-Driven Activity-Based Costing," *Harvard Business Review* 82 (November 2004): pp. 131–138.

Kaplan, Robert S., and Norton, David P., "Using the Balanced Scorecard as a Strategic Management System," *Harvard Business Review* 74 (January–February 1996): pp. 75–85.

Kaplan, Robert S., and Norton, David P., "Having Trouble with Your Strategy? Then Map It," *Harvard Business Review* 78 (September–October 2000): pp. 167–176.

Kaplan, Robert S., and Norton, David P., *Strategy Maps: Converting Intangible Assets into Tangible Outcomes* (Boston: Harvard Business School Publishing, 2004).

Kaplan, Robert S., and Norton, David P., *The Execution Premium: Linking Strategy to Operations for Competitive Advantage* (Boston: Harvard Business Press, 2008), pp. 3–21.

Karpinski, Richard, "Making the Most of a Marketing Dashboard," *B to B* 91 (March 13, 2006): p. 17.

Kotler, Philip, *Marketing Management: The Millennium Edition* (Englewood Cliffs, NJ: Prentice Hall, 2000), pp. 708–709.

Kotler, Philip, "A Three-Part Plan for Upgrading Your Marketing Department for New Challenges," *Strategy and Leadership* 32 (May 2004): pp. 4–9.

Kotler, Philip, Gregor, William T., and Rogers III, William, "SMR Classic Reprint: The Marketing Audit Comes of Age," *Sloan Management Review* 20 (Winter 1989): pp. 49–62.

Krauss, Michael, "Marketing Dashboards Drive Better Decisions," *Marketing News* 39 (October 1, 2005): p. 7.

Maddox, Kate, "Tektronix Wins for Best Practices," *B to B* 90 (April 4, 2005): p. 33.

McGovern, Gail J., Court, David, Quelch, John A., and Crawford, Blair, "Bringing Customers into the Boardroom," *Harvard Business Review* 82 (November 2004): pp. 70–80.

McTavish, Ronald, "Implementing Marketing Strategy," *Industrial Marketing Management* 26 (November 5, 1988): p. 10.

Mokwa, Michael P., "The Strategic Marketing Audit: An Adoption/Utilization Perspective," *Journal of Business Strategy* 7 (Winter 1986): pp. 88–95.

Moutinho, Luiz, and Southern, Geoffrey, *Strategic Marketing Management: A process Based Approach* (Cengage, 2012).

Nath, Pravin, and Mahajan, Vijay, "Marketing in the C-Suite: A Study of Chief Marketing Officer Power in Firms' Top Management Teams," *Journal of Marketing* 75 (January 2010): pp. 60–77.

Noble, Charles H., and Mokwa, Michael P., "Implementing Marketing Strategies: Developing and Testing a Managerial Theory," *Journal of Marketing* 63 (October 1999): pp. 57–73.

O'Sullivan, Don, and Abela, Andrew V., "Marketing Performance Measurement Ability and Firm Performance," *Journal of Marketing* 71 (April 2007): p. 79.

Patterson, Laura, "Taking On the Metrics Challenge," *Journal of Targeting, Measurement and Analysis for Marketing* 15 (June 2007): p. 273.

Pauwels, Koen, Ambler, Tim, Clark, Bruce, LaPointe, Pat, Reibstein, David, Skiera, Bernd, Wierenga, Berend, and Wiesel, Thomas, "Dashboards and Marketing: Why, What, How and What Research Is Needed," *MSI Report #08-203*,May 2008 (Boston: Marketing Science Institute), p. 7.

Peppers, Don, and Rogers, Martha, *Return on Customer: A Revolutionary Way to Measure and Strengthen Your Business* (New York: Currency/Doubleday, 2005), pp. 133–134.

Porter, Michael E., "Changing Patterns of International Competition," *California Management Review* 28 (Winter 1986): pp. 9–40.

Rust, Roland T., Ambler, Tim, Carpenter, Gregory S., Kumar, V., and Srivastava, Rajendra K. "Measuring Marketing Productivity: Current Knowledge and Future Directions," *Journal of Marketing* 68 (October, 2004): 76–90.

Rust, Roland T., Lemon, Katherine N., and Narayandas, Das, *Customer Equity Management* (Upper Saddle River, NJ: Prentice Hall, 2005), pp. 426–428.

Srinivasan, Shuba, and Hanssens, Dominique M., "Marketing and Firm Value: Metrics, Methods, Findings, and Future Directions," *Journal of Marketing Research* 46 (June 2009): pp. 293–312.

van Weele, Arjan, *Puchasing and Supply Chain Management: Analysis Strategy, Planning and Practice*, 5th ed. (Cengage, 2010).

Verhage, Bronis J., *Marketing: A Global Perspective* (Cengage, 2013).

CASES

CHAPTER 1

Nynas: In the black and leading

For most people, oil is evident as a fuel for cars, heating and the generation of electricity, or as the basis for the plastics industry. What about the black surfaces of pavements, roads, driveways, car parks and school playgrounds? Bitumen is an oil-based product most of us take for granted, but it is a major part of the revenue for companies such as Shell, BP, Esso, Total, Colas or Lanfina. The leading bitumen player in the UK, Scandinavia and much of western Europe is Stockholm-based Nynas. In the UK, this relatively small player in the petrochemicals industry has overall market leadership in the bitumen market and is renowned for its innovative product development with polymer formulations.

Bitumen is one of the most ubiquitous materials made by industry, underfoot almost everywhere as a core ingredient of the macadams and asphalts in roads and pavements. There are numerous specialist applications too, such as the backing for carpet tiles, roofing felts, sealants for mighty dams and waterproofing for bridge decks. Inevitably this results in a diverse customer base for an organisation such as Nynas. In a market with competitors as large as Esso or Shell, Nynas's leadership has not occurred by accident. Nynas has established its enviable position by astutely utilising the resources required to develop innovative products, customer service schemes and flexible delivery capabilities in order to ensure customer satisfaction. At the heart of its business strategy is a desire to innovate, listen to customers and develop services that genuinely enable customers to be served properly.

Nynas believes it has several important edges over its rivals, as described below.

Customer dialogue

As a major producer with significant R&D technical support, Nynas's laboratories can determine a product formulation for most bitumen-based applications. Whether the customer is a local authority requiring a cost-effective thin surfacing for a housing estate's ageing pavements; a contractor such as Tarmac requiring 24-hour supply of high-quality, state-of-the-art bitumen for the construction of a new motorway; or a builder buying polymer-enhanced mastic asphalts to act as a waterproofing membrane for regency mews properties, Nynas can develop a quality bitumen-based product.

Consistent quality and innovative product development

Refineries in Belgium, Sweden and the UK, supported by a network of terminals and research laboratories across Europe, enable Nynas to continually improve its products and their performance. Customers do not want to have to resurface major roads or busy shopping centre pavements on a frequent basis. Specialist applications such as waterproofing dams or houses are time consuming, costly and inconvenient remedial activities that clients do not want to repeat in a hurry. Nynas has access to high-grade Venezuelan bitumen, not readily available to its major competitors, which gives it added flexibility in producing high-quality bitumen grades for specific applications. Whether it is for a routine commodity bulk job such as a school playground surface or an unusual requirement for waterproofing a royal building, Nynas has developed a reputation as being a leading supplier.

Logistical support

Users of bitumen often require deliveries at very short notice, in specific quantities and to guaranteed quality levels. These deliveries may be anywhere at any time. A contractor repairing a busy commuter route out of daylight hours needs on-time delivery of ready-to-use bitumen products. Repairs to a remote bridge still require guaranteed on-time delivery. Nynas's depots operate around the clock despatching computer monitored deliveries by tanker to clients as and when the customer has specified. Twenty-four hours a day, 365 days a year, Nynas prides itself on its high levels of responsiveness and reliability of delivery.

Nynas's composition of customers is varied. A major new road-building scheme will involve formal tendering and guarantees with penalties for inferior product or missed deliveries. The buying process of such customers will be highly formal, involving numerous managers, and functions as diverse as purchasing, technical support, construction, finance and logistical support. On both sides – customer and Nynas – cross-functional teams of scientists, engineers, managers and the field force will spend many months agreeing on the product requirements, contractual obligations, delivery requirements and application techniques. For other customers, the purchase is perhaps more of a routine re-buy, with only limited interaction and discussion between Nynas and the customer. On other occasions, the Nynas helpline may receive a midnight telephone call from a highways agency surveyor who has just discovered cracks in the surface of a major road and requires immediate assistance in both identifying the cause of the problem and rectifying the situation before commuters awake the next morning.

For a rather bland-looking substance such as bitumen, the market is diverse and challenging. Nynas has established its successful position in the European market for bitumen-based products by practising the best principles of marketing. The company strives to understand its customers' needs and to offer reliable products supported with effective customer service, round the clock. Product innovation is at the forefront of the company's strategy and, coupled with constantly improving ways of offering peace of mind to customers, provides an edge over rivals. Shrewd marketing analysis constantly monitors product changes, customers' expectations, competitors' activities and those aspects of the marketing environment – notably technological and regulatory forces – that will impact on the business's fortunes. Resources are allocated to match this thorough assessment of market opportunities and marketing requirements.

Questions for discussion

1 Who are Nynas's customers?

2 What types of business markets purchase the products made by Nynas?

3 Would most purchases of Nynas's products be new task, modified re-buy or straight re-buy?

Sources: Siobhan McKelvey and Willie Hunter, Nynas UK; Network magazine; the Nynas Annual Review.

CHAPTER 2

This time chose me

It is standard practice when seeking B2B suppliers to request a number of quotes. Three is the norm and upon receiving an invitation to tender, suppliers will very quickly try to assess whether or not they have been included 'just to make up numbers'. Tendering takes time, particularly if you want to have a good chance of securing the contract. But, if you are just making up numbers then the resource required to submit an attractive tender might be better focused elsewhere; particularly for SMEs, where resource is usually at a premium.

This situation is particularly noticeable in the print industry. There are a lot of printing firms around, many carrying very similar equipment and being capable of similar volume production runs. The trick in this industry is to keep the downtime on printers to a minimum and their utilisation at around a steady 70 per cent, which when you take into account cleaning, setting up and servicing machines, is quite a significant usage level.

So, if machines are idle, a low price will at least enable staff and operational costs to be covered. If space is limited then a higher price might encourage you to try and negotiate delivery times on other jobs to make space. In effect, pricing is not an absolute, it depends upon a range of circumstances and managing the variables is the skill of a good print operation.

A company called Webmart came into being in the mid 1990s and spotted the challenges that tender management was causing printers. Its solution to this was simple; create access to a broad range of printing solutions from a very large supplier base. This was eventually achieved by creating a negotiation-free platform to facilitate sales/deals without the need for sales people. Over 300 print suppliers have since signed up for this across the UK.

For buyers, the advantage is that they will be able to see the best print option at any particular moment in time and consistently be presented with highly competitive pricing options in what is in a very price driven market. For suppliers, the software behind the site enables them to manage their real-time pricing quickly and it has changed the nature of competition. All seem satisfied that they are drawing a good, steady and fair share of business this way.

Paul Johnston; Principal Lecturer, Sheffield Hallam University

Discussion questions

1 If you were a printer signed up for the Webmart service, what might the implications be for long term business development?

2 What other B2B suppliers might also benefit from this kind of sales enquiry/tendering platform?

CHAPTER 3

UIA

UIA Insurance is a mutual company with traditional roots in the trade union sector. Its business philosophy is anchored on socially responsible principles towards its members, customers, staff, partners and the community. UIA provides insurance to members of organisations in the not-for-profit sector and has maintained its in-house operations of its customer care centre. It also manages another trade union membership contact centre, UNISON Direct (*DM Business,* 2004).

The benefits of *not* outsourcing and handling the company's own call centre activities are cited as:

- Existing abilities in supporting implementation objectives across all business functions.
- Adequacy of its comprehensive staff-training programme.
- Facilitating speed and quality of communications and feedback between departments.

- Monitoring service quality such as enabling quick responses in resolving customer queries.
- Ensuring good customer care, thereby supporting the UIA brand.
- Facilitating efficiency and linkages in CRM processes.

Discussion questions

1   What is the consistency of the customer experience in UIA that supports CRM processes?

2   What are the potential risks to the customer relationship and the integrity of the brand by outsourcing to a second or third party?

CHAPTER 4

Marriott: Getting down to business with business travellers

Imagine marketing more than 3000 hotels and resorts under 16 brands in 68 countries which is the challenge facing Marriott, a multinational marketer that provides lodging services to millions of customers every day. The company, founded by J. Willard Marriott in 1927, started with a single root-beer stand and the 'spirit to serve'. Today, it achieves €8.25 billion in global sales from guest room revenue, meals, meeting and special-events and other services.

Each of Marriott's brands has its own positioning. The flagship Marriott brand stands for full service: properties have restaurants, meeting rooms, fitness centres, and other facilities. The JW Marriott brand is more up-market and the Ritz-Carlton brand is known for top quality service. Marriott's newest hotel brand is Edition, a chain of stylish luxury hotels. TownePlace Suites are mid-priced suite hotels for customers who plan an extended stay away from home. Fairfield Inn & Suites are for businesspeople and vacationers seeking value-priced accommodation.

Sluggish economic conditions have only intensified rivalry within the hyper-competitive hotel industry. Major hotel companies such as Accor, Hilton, Hyatt, InterContinental and Starwood all offer a wide range of hotel and resort brands for different customers' needs and tastes. In addition, local hotels and regional chains compete on the basis of location, ambience, price, amenities and other elements. To compete effectively in this pressured environment, Marriott is relying on extensive marketing research, expert segmentation and careful targeting.

Marriott uses a variety of research techniques to find out about customer needs and behaviour, including focus groups, online surveys, and in-room questionnaires. For example, when it conducted focus groups with customers who had stayed at its Marriott and Renaissance properties, it discovered some interesting differences. Renaissance customers said they like to open the curtains and look out of the window when they first enter their rooms. In contrast, Marriott guests said they get unpacked quickly and get right to work in their rooms. 'That's when we started making connections about the individual personalities that gravitate toward the Marriott brand,' says the vice president of marketing strategy. With this research in hand, marketers for the Marriott hotel brand targeted a segment they call 'achievers'; business travellers who feel driven to get a lot done in a short time. They created an advertising campaign to communicate that Marriott is about productivity and performance. The print and online adverts featured interviews with six real customers, who discussed their drive to accomplish personal and professional goals.

When Marriott looked at visitors who prefer Spring-Hill Suites, one of its suite hotel brands, it found a slightly different profile. These are business people who travel often and see a suite hotel as a place to spread out, feel refreshed, and take a break from the stress of being on the road. These customers are also heavy users of technology, especially mobile communication devices such as smartphones. In reaching out to this target market, Marriott uses mobile marketing as well as traditional media to get its message across. It invites business travellers to download its iPhone *app* and runs adverts designed especially for viewing on smartphone screens. Customers can click on the mobile advert to check room availability online or to speak with the reservations department.

Marriott also targets companies that need hotel space to hold meetings and seminars. In most cases, these companies bring in attendees from outside the immediate location, which means Marriott can fill more guest rooms during meetings. Meetings usually involve additional purchases, such as snacks or meals, another profitable reason to target businesses. Sales reps at major Marriott properties are ready to help companies plan employee workshops, supplier and distributor events and other meetings, for a handful to a ballroom full of people.

Studying the needs and buying patterns of companies that hold business meetings, Marriott's marketers have found that a growing number are interested in videoconferencing and other high-tech extras. To appeal to this segment, Marriott has equipped many of its meeting rooms with the latest in recording and communications technology. It has also partnered with AT&T and Cisco to offer 'virtual meeting' capabilities in its Marriott, JW Marriott, and Renaissance Hotels. This teleconferencing technology allows a group gathered in one of Marriott's hotel meeting rooms to collaborate with colleagues, clients or others anywhere in the world.

The segment of consumers and business travellers who care about the environment is sizable these days, and Marriott wants its share of this growing market. The company has developed prototype green hotels for several of its brands, designing the public space and guest rooms with an eye toward conserving both water and energy. Marriott will build hundreds of these green hotels during the next decade. Thanks to the company's emphasis on saving power, 275 of its hotels already qualify for the US Environmental Protection Agency's Energy Star designation. Marriott is also going green by working with suppliers that operate in environmentally friendly ways. It provides pads made from recycled paper for attendees of business meetings held at its properties and buys key cards made from recycled plastic. Even the pillows in the guest rooms are made from recycled plastic bottles.

Marriott set up a central database to capture details such as how long customers stay and what they purchase and when they stay at any of its hotels or resorts. It also stores demographic data and tracks individual preferences so it can better serve customers. By analysing the information in this huge database, Marriott discovered that many of its customers visit more than one of its brands. Therefore, the company created sophisticated statistical models to target customers for future marketing offers based on their history with Marriott. In one campaign, Marriott sent out three million email messages customised according to each recipient's unique history with the company. Because of its database capabilities, Marriott was able to track whether recipients returned to one of its properties after this campaign – and actual sales results exceeded corporate expectations. This database technology has paid for itself many times over with improved targeting efficiency and higher response rates.

Discussion questions

1 How is Marriott segmenting the market for hotel services?

2 Which of the targeting strategies is Marriott using? Explain your answer.

3 What specific types of data should Marriott have in its customer database for segmentation purposes?

CHAPTER 5

Conglomerate breaks out from India

Unlike multinationals from developed countries that have focused on their core activities where there appeared to be the most attractive global market opportunities and sold off unwanted parts of the business firms from emerging markets have often adopted the conglomerate model, in which hundreds of often disparate businesses are held in an organisation that perhaps resembles a private equity fund.

The activities that have bound these businesses together in the conglomerate model in the past have often been manufacturing or international trading.

Ratan Tata became chairman of Tata Sons, a disorganised family business in 1991. He is a shy and unassuming figure who shuns the trappings of wealth, despite being one of India's richest men. He took over at a time when the Indian government began removing the bureaucratic controls that had previously curtailed the development of Indian firms. He set about rationalising the group's hundreds of businesses with the aim of making them more efficient. The organisation is still diverse, with interests in steel, cars, hotels, mobile telephony, chemicals and tea, and it is one of India's largest software firms. It is also in the top ten of global IT services firms.

A feature of most fast-growing companies from emerging markets is that they have lower costs than their competitors from developed countries. However, Tata's competitive advantage comes not just from the supply of low-cost, well-educated labour necessary for the technology-based activities. It has also built expertise in developing and operating automated, capital-intensive production, typical of steel making. Moreover during India's 1991 reforms Tata learned how to thrive in a highly competitive market place that still had a highly regulated environment and a poor infrastructure, and this serves them well as they pursue a strategy of mergers and acquisitions in different world markets.

Ratan Tata has single-handedly made the company into a respected MNE. In 2007 Tata completed a £6.7 billion takeover of Corus, the British-Dutch steel maker, in the process beating a Brazilian steel-making company CSN. This followed the acquisition of Singapore's Natsteel in 2004 and Thailand's Millennium Steel in 2005.

In 2000 Tata took over Tetley Tea, a British business with a global brand, with the intention of linking India tea production with the overseas tea markets. Tata decided that Tata Motors would make its own car, the Nano, turning away from the possibility of a joint venture with a more established manufacturer, however, Tata did acquire the Jaguar and Land Rover brands. Among many other acquisitions is Citigroup Global Services (US) as part of the group's development in business process outsourcing.

Investment does not only take the form of acquisitions. Tata made Bangladesh's single largest foreign investment of £1.1 billion when it agreed to build a power plant, steel unit and fertiliser factory after the government guaranteed a supply of gas for 20 years from its proven reserves.

Although he has made Tata's businesses more competitive and more global in outlook, the company has a tradition of being public spirited and Ratan Tata has said in interviews that he would prefer his legacy to be 'having caused no damage to others'. The company has a reputation for refusing to accept bribes and treating its workers well. Two-thirds of Tata Sons is owned by charitable trusts that do good works in India. Although the company is competitive, some foreign investors wonder if this approach is right for running the global business.

Discussion question

1 What are the key issues that Tata faces as it progresses to becoming a global company?

Sources: 'Circle the wagons', *The Economist*, 12 October, 2006; 'Steely logic', *The Economist*, 28 October, 2006; 'The shy architect', *The Economist*, 11 January, 2007 and 'Bangladesh wins €1.5bn India deal', *BBC News online*, 19 August, 2004.

CHAPTER 6

Leadership for a new world order

It is hard to imagine the changes that new executives in Middle East companies have faced. Suliaman Al-Muhaidib is chairman of the family owned Al-Muhaidib Group, a conglomerate based in Saudi Arabia that has investments in financial services, real estate, consumer goods, energy and utilities. When he first joined the firm his father told him to learn from the other traders in the same street the business skills he would need in order to manage the firm in the future. His decision-making skills were built around the local culture but Suliaman's son has developed his judgement very differently. He is general manager of a subsidiary, has a staff of 500 and deals with suppliers from around the world.

As the oil rich Middle East nations of Bahrain, Kuwait, Oman, Qatar and Saudi Arabia have invested heavily it has become more open to worldwide business. The managers of the companies created have become leaders of multinationals – a far cry from their humble backgrounds and nomadic family life of 50 years ago when even running water was not widely available. They must bridge the divide between the traditions of the past as well as enthusiastically exploring the global future. The region has new opportunities and can exert new types of influence but they have to manage risk too, typified by the economic crisis in Dubai. In the past the companies relied on expatriates but now many of the new leaders are nationals under 25. Women are also beginning to play a greater role, but not on the scale of their counterparts in other regions of the world. Saddi *et al.* comment that there is a shortage of leaders to manage the rapid growth and highlight three qualities which future leaders need;

- Farsighted vision to build sustainable institutions.
- Pragmatic openness and seek ideas from around the world and customise them for the region.
- Conscious presence in recognising the need to build not only their own organisation but also work together to establish the region as a global player.

Discussion question

1 What are the main differences in leading a national business compared to a global company?

Sources: Saddi, J., Sabbagh, K. and Shediac, R. (2010) 'Measures of Leadership', *Strategy and Business*, Summer: 59, May 25.

CHAPTER 7

BMW recycling the consumer

The creation of the European Recovery and Recycling Association (ERRA) is indicative of growing concern for the environment and consumer awareness of this social issue. With members including Cadbury Schweppes, Coca-Cola, Heineken, Nestlé, L'Oréal, and Tetra Pak, the Brussels-based ERRA has developed a recycling scheme that could lead to the regular collection of discarded packaging – containers and bottles from housing estates, factories, schools, offices and shops – and their sorting and reuse. The scheme in many countries is far from becoming reality, requiring the significant commitment of government, local authorities and, of course, consumers. However, ERRA exists, supported by an extensive array of manufacturers and environmental pressure groups. The public's interest in the environment and in safeguarding the planet and its resources for generations to come has led companies to pay real attention to the Green lobby.

BMW, the German deluxe car maker, has been stressing the 'recyclability' of its vehicles in its television and press advertising for its 3 Series range. These cars are produced using more environmentally friendly production processes, with a greater proportion of components suitable for reworking. BMW's commitment to the future, however, goes further. In Landshut, Germany, it has a recycling factory. Two workers can strip all the reusable parts from a 1970s car in under 45 minutes, including the careful draining of all fluids, at a cost of about £90.

Landshut's role is as a huge scrap merchant, but one that adheres to the strictest code of ethical working practices and the latest understanding of how to dispose of redundant vehicles with the least harm to the environment. BMW executives support the notion of a Europe-wide initiative, requiring an authorised recycler to issue a disposal certificate for every car at the end of its life. Until such a certificate is issued, the last registered owner would continue to be liable to pay road taxes. This initiative would eventually require legislation and the support of governments. Meanwhile, several leading car manufacturers have joined forces, adopting standardised colour coding for all reusable parts.

The investment for BMW is significant, but anticipating eventual EU legislation to enforce recycling, the German manufacturer believes it is thinking strategically and is working towards maintaining its position as a major producer of vehicles. BMW has many partner recycling plants worldwide, with its first UK site in Sussex. Simultaneously, BMW is striving to make more of its cars reclaimable: 50 per cent of the current 3 Series can be stripped down and reused. BMW is clear: 'we feel socially, politically and ecologically responsible for everything we do', leading to the creation of the 'Sustainability. It can be done' forum for addressing manufacturing issues of concern to the wider community.

It is not only companies such as BMW that have responded to increasing social awareness of environmental and Green issues. Bottle banks, which exist in most towns at multiple locations, have been joined by collection containers for waste paper, food and drink cans, and even discarded clothes. The charity Oxfam has provided clothing collection banks in many car parks nationwide. Local councils collect householders' waste paper separately from their refuse for recycling. School children are taught to care for their environment and to encourage their parents to use bottle banks and waste paper collections. Societal pressure has created a new way of thinking that marketers must reflect.

Questions for discussion

1 What has persuaded BMW to launch such initiatives as its recycling plants and the 'Sustainability. It can be done' forum?

2 In what ways are local authorities encouraging recycling?

3 What are the implications of the growing consumer interest in recycling for manufacturers of consumer goods?

Sources: www.bmwgroup.com/e, 2004; 'The can and bottle story: environment', Coca-Cola & Schweppes Beverages Ltd, 1993; 'Helping to solve the waste management puzzle', ERRA, Brussels, 1991; John Eisenhammer, 'Where cars will go when they die', *Independent on Sunday*, 21 February 1993, pp. 24–5; 'Helping the earth begins at home', Central Office of Information, Department of the Environment, HMSO, 1992; BMW 3 Series promotional material, 1995–2004; Warwickshire County Council, 1999; Oxfam, Kenilworth, 1999, 2004; Warwickshire County Council, 2004.

CHAPTER 8

ISS: Cleaning up in the world

ISS is one of the world's largest Facility Services providers with a market presence in 50 countries across Europe, Asia, South America and Australia. Most people think that contract cleaning is done by small local operators, using unskilled, part time, casual, low paid and largely unmotivated staff. Danish company, ISS is proof that it can be done another way as they now employ over 500 000 people.

ISS has grown rapidly on the back of the move by both private and public sector organisations to focus on their core activities and outsource support services and facilities management. ISS offers facilities management services including cleaning, catering, security, office support and property services.

ISS spotted the opportunity to rejuvenate and restructure the cleaning business, which traditionally was characterised by having a negative external image, many small-scale, local and rather unprofessional operations and poor management.

The success of ISS is due to its expertise in contract tendering, project management, its investment in the training of all staff and not just managers to ensure quality and avoid accidents, the use of the appropriate technology, such as the use of the correct cleaning agents and the effective use of time and supplies.

It believes in peer pressure and so even for contracts with SMEs, where normally one person would do the work, ISS provides a two or three person 'hit squad'. This ensures that even a huge multinational has a local 'face'.

ISS's international growth comes partly from winning new contracts and partly from taking over existing cleaning companies that already have a customer base, staff, contacts and a recognised presence in the market.

Every interaction between the cleaner and the customer is vital to the success of the contract and the successful delivery of the services is more important than offering low prices for a service that the customer may not be able to rely on. Relationship management is key, therefore, especially as customers are often reluctant to change a service provider without good reason. Often contracts will be renewed for years. But if there are complaints the contract will be terminated very quickly and the news very rapidly goes through the industry, damaging the firm's reputation.

Good techniques, management systems and human resource processes are essential for dealing with people. Of course, service expectations and service delivery are affected very much by cultural considerations, so this is often a key consideration in maintaining service delivery consistency.

Discussion question

1 Referring to the characteristics of services, how does culture affect delivery of cleaning services?

CHAPTER 9

Virgin Money: Is innovation enough?

Richard Branson's . Virgin brand is known to consumers across a range of products and services, from airlines to entertainment to mobile phones. In 1995, Virgin launched its financial services arm with Virgin Direct. At a time when major retailers such as Marks & Spencer and Tesco were entering many sectors of financial services, from banking to insurance, the entry of Virgin Direct made many of the traditional businesses in the financial services sector very anxious. Branson's reputation among consumers for 'taking on faceless corporations' gave Virgin Direct a head start.

Virgin Direct, replicating the activities of Virgin in other sectors, intended to be seen as an innovator that always strives to offer a value-for-money proposition that strongly benefits the consumer. Virgin launched a tracker fund that tracked shares across the entire stock market rather than across only a limited selection. This innovation was subsequently copied by many rivals. Then Virgin lobbied the government to launch stakeholder pensions. Although successful, it is widely accepted that the eventual appearance of stakeholder pensions has been far from a success story for the industry. Virgin also led the way with off-set mortgages, with the Virgin One account. Virgin found this complex proposition difficult to market to consumers, without face-to-face contact via branches. In 2001, the One Account was handed over to Royal Bank of Scotland, which did have a suitable branch network and has been able to sell this mortgage product to consumers.

Despite such teething problems, Virgin Money – as the company is now known – is profitable and thanks largely to its tie-up with card provider MBNA, has a growing credit card business, too. The business now also offers pensions, insurance, mortgages, savings and investments, in conjunction with partners, such as Santander, Friends Provident and MBNA. The philosophy is simple: Virgin Money intends to introduce more interesting propositions, rather than simply churning out new products. The company has a focus on being customer-led, rather than product-led, explaining that:

We are aiming to make everyone better off

Like all Virgin companies, Virgin Money was launched to give customers a better deal. We aim to offer you a wide range of great value financial products that are easy to understand and sort out. In today's busy world our customers tell us ifs why they choose to deal with Virgin rather than anyone else.

http://uk.virginmoney.com/virgin/about

The Virgin-branded financial services products are always innovative and place an emphasis on addressing consumer needs and consumer concerns about the sprawling global financial services corporations. Value for money, simplicity, ease of setting up and the Virgin brand have proved irresistible propositions for thousands of consumers who perceive Virgin and Branson to represent a desirable alternative to large, faceless corporations. As a result of this approach, Virgin Money has won countless industry awards in recent years, notably for its credit card operation, car insurance, pet insurance and pensions.

Discussion questions

1 Which innovation model does Virgin Money belong to?

2 What marketing strategies should Virgin follow to speed the adoption of Virgin Money around the world?

Sources: Virgin Money; David Benady, 'Virgin Money pushes for its renaissance', *Marketing Week*, 6 May 2004, pp. 20–1; virginmoney.com, January, 2008; http://uk.virginmoney.com, 5 March 2011.

CHAPTER 10

First direct's innovative banking channels

With our 1st Account you'll get £100 for switching and a £250 interest-free overdraft comes as standard. Discover how simple our Easyswitch team make moving your account and just how refreshing it is to talk to real people 24 7 365. We're sure you'll love us.

www1.firstdirect.com, Jun 2011

Most consumers have a bank cheque account from which cash is drawn, bills are paid and cheques written, and into which salaries, pensions or student loan cheques are paid. For many consumers, the bank is a high-street or shopping-centre office – imposing, formal and often intimidating. Whether it's NatWest, Barclays or Lloyds TSB in the UK or ABN AMRO or Rabobank in the Netherlands, each high-street bank is fairly alike, with similar products and services, personnel, branch layouts, locations and opening hours. Differentiation has been difficult to achieve and generally impossible to maintain over any length of time as competitors have copied rivals' moves. Promotional strategy and brand image have been the focus for most banking organisations, supported with more minor tactical changes in, for example, opening hours or service charges. For many bank account holders, however, the branch – with its restricted openings, formal ambience and congested town-centre location – is the only point of contact for the bulk of transactions.

First direct, owned by HSBC but managed separately, broke the mould in 1989. Launched with a then massive £6 million promotional campaign, first direct bypassed the traditional marketing channel. First direct has no branches and no branch overhead and operating costs. It provides free banking, unlike its high-street competitors with their systems of bank charges combined with interest paid on positive balances. First direct is a telephone and online banking service that offers full banking, mortgage, loan, investment/ saving, insurance, foreign currency and credit card services, plus ATM 'hole in the wall' cash cards through HSBC's international service-till network. All normal banking transactions can be completed over the telephone or online.

Initial reactions were positive, with many non-HSBC account holders switching to the innovative new style of banking. The more traditional consumer – who equates the marbled halls of the Victorian branches with heritage, security and traditional values – has been less easily converted. For the targeted, more financially aware and independent income earner, first direct is proving very popular. Research shows that first direct is the most recommended bank with the most satisfied customers.

First direct's services and products are not new, but the chosen marketing channels are innovative: no branches, only telephone call centres, online banking and texting. Customers no longer have to reach inaccessible, parked-up, town-centre branches with queues and restricted opening hours. The company is fast to adopt evolving technologies and opportunities to interact with its customers digitally:

We're always trying to figure out new ways to make our customers' lives easier so as you'd expect, we're at the forefront of new technologies. We offer you Mobile Banking, Text Message Banking, award-winning online Podcasts and Vodcasts and on top of all that we create online spaces for you to communicate with us and other customers, inviting you to become part of our community and give voice to your thoughts. Check out Little Black Book, Talking Point and Social Media Newsroom.

www1.firstdirect.com, Jun 2011

First direct has introduced a service, alien to some more traditional tastes perhaps, that is more readily available and with fewer costs. Hundreds of thousands of consumers have welcomed the launch of this new option, but millions have preferred to bank the traditional way. For HSBC, this is fine: its HSBC proposition caters for those consumers preferring the more traditional banking format, while first direct caters for the new breed of telephone, online and texting customers.

Discussion questions

1 Why is innovation in marketing channels generally difficult to achieve?

2 Why was first direct different from its rivals? What gave it differentiation when it first launched?

3 Why might some potential customers of first direct have reservations about the innovative nature of the service?

Sources: www1.firstdirect.com, Jun 2011; *Marketing: Concepts and Strategies*, 5th edition.

CHAPTER 11

Building Blocks of Change

For the construction industry, the message is clear. While other industries have continuously reduced prices for products and services while maintaining margins, the construction industry has been increasing prices without any corresponding improvement in profitability. At Skanska, transforming and developing supply chains is at the heart of a long-term strategic initiative that reveals huge potential.

With 3000 construction projects per year and a spend volume of about two and half billion euro in Sweden alone, you would expect Skanska to leverage purchasing volumes as a matter of course. This is being done today, but 5 years ago no systematic efforts were made to improve and develop purchasing practices.

The reason for this lack of focus lies in the nature of the industry. A building project, be it a road, a bridge or a building is essentially a local undertaking where the project manager on the spot and his team make all the decisions.

Realising the potential of leveraging volumes, Skanska Sweden launched a major supply chain initiative in 2004. Part of the initiative is a five-step plan to introduce electronic procurement, collaborative commerce with subcontractors, electronic sourcing, logistics and order/invoice matching throughout the company. The plan was first introduced in Sweden.

But any initiative implying change will meet resistance, also in the very traditional construction industry. 'When we started, our first challenge was to convince stakeholders that this initiative really was of strategic importance, that it wasn't just another new scheme from head office,' says the purchasing manager Mikael Sjölund.

His own reaction at being offered a job within purchasing is a typical example. At Skanska I worked first as a production manager then as a construction project manager. In 2001, I was asked if I wanted to work with purchasing. I thought 'No, that is non-core, it is something I might do later in my career. A year later I was asked again and I accepted, because the management team made it clear that purchasing transformation was a strategic necessity. It was such a challenge and had such potential that I really wanted to be part of it,' he says.

His colleague, purchasing development manager Sandra Petersson, also recalls the excitement of discovering the huge potential savings to be made from procurement transformation.

'Wherever we looked we saw possibilities. There were practically no common processes or tools in place, so we had an open field,' she says. For instance, quality issues or delivery issues were difficult to resolve with suppliers because Skanska had no computerised systems in place to measure performance. 'We would get information from a number of construction projects that there were such issues but had no statistics or easily accessible data on earlier supplier performance. That lack of information puts you at a severe disadvantage when it is time to negotiate new service-level agreements or prices,' Sandra Petersson points out.

Changing procurement processes and introducing new tools also means creating a new organisation. The procurement function at Skanska Sweden has gone from 15 to 100 people in 5 years, recruited both from within the company and from the outside.

'In the first wave, we hired 40 people. It was a case of profound belief in the value of transformation. You do not get the go-ahead for this kind of investment from management if they are not 100 per cent committed,' says Petersson.

'Commitment from management is all very well, but you would not come very far if people in the construction projects do not feel concerned by what you are doing,' she warns. 'You absolutely must involve all stakeholders. This takes time, sometimes much more time than you had planned for. That is the struggle: keeping up a long-term effort.'

'You just cannot shove new practices down people's throats, you must involve them in the new practices. That is why any change process will take time,' Petersson reflects.

'For instance, some project managers fear that they might lose touch with market conditions if they rely on the frame agreement suggested by the head office commodity specialists. Therefore, you have to build trust by demonstrating that end-user feedback is taken seriously,' says Sjölund.

Skanska Sweden has a yearly turnover of some €3 billion, of which 70 per cent is cost of purchased goods and services.

'In 4 years we have gone from 15 to 30 per cent of spend under management, defined as a purchase regulated by a frame agreement and processed through our electronic procurement system ... Compared to other industries this might not seem very impressive, but the sums involved are huge and the savings have been considerable,' says Petersson. The next target is to have 50 per cent of spend under management by 2010 ...

Discussion questions

1 Discuss ways in which Skanska Sweden might continue to improve on its savings made through purchasing.

2 Discuss how an approach such as that of Skanska Sweden could be used by other, non construction, B2B companies.

Source: *Efficient Purchasing*, No. 7, 2008, pp. 28–36

CHAPTER 12

Free-product competitors challenge microsoft

Consumers can pay just 20 pence to write with a disposable biro, yet fancy fountain pens have become a common sight in the hands of influential businesspeople.

Such pens have high price tags and are much more difficult to maintain than ballpoints, felt-tip pens or roller-ball pens. However, recent sales figures indicate that the semiobsolete fountain pen is making a comeback as the writing instrument of choice for status-minded individuals. Of the premium-priced fountain pens, those produced by Montblanc are probably the most prestigious. Named after the highest mountain in Europe, these German-made fountain pens cost from about £100 to £5000 (for a solidgold one). The most popular model costs about £300.

Prestige pricing has worked well for Montblanc, placing the pen in the same category as Rolex watches, BMW cars and Gucci luggage.

Discussion questions

1 A company competing in the same sector as Montblanc has asked you to prepare a report explaining the factors that influence the pricing decisions they should make for a new range of pens. What areas should your report include?

2 How does prestige pricing link to value-based pricing?

CHAPTER 13

A web presence: Now routine behaviour

During the 1990s many corporate giants avoided using banners, buttons and other early forms of Internet advertising, believing them to be inefficient and ineffective. Now most large companies embrace Internet advertising and digital communications. McDonald's uses websites, banners and buttons, instant messaging, online games and pop-up windows to engage with consumers through interactivity. *McDonald's on your mobile* and *Wraps on YouTube* are just two examples of McDonald's digital activity. As the company's director for media explains, 'We're not going to sell burgers online, but we can extend the experience of the brand online and bring McDonald's to life online'.

Digital experts believe few consumer or business brands can now avoid harnessing web-based marketing communications, particularly if – as in the case of McDonald's – the target audience is young and made up of consumers who have been brought up as 'digital dream kids' used to twenty-four hour online access anywhere they happen to be, hooked into their online communities.

Nike has many websites, some of which promote specific brands, linking into its sponsorship of entertainers and sports stars. Guerrilla moves, such as mentioning its websites or celebrity tie-ins in chat room messages have been hugely successful for the company in attracting hundreds of thousands of visitors to its websites for specific online promotions and advertising campaigns. Sports-focused video clips, downloadable tracks, musical ePostcards suitable for personalisation, and games have proved a big hit with the youth market targeted by so many Nike products.

As with many brands, a digital presence on Twitter, Facebook and YouTube are now routinised expectations for Pepsi consumers and the company's brand managers. Pepsi online provides entertainment, promotions, news, merchandise offers and access to a digital community of consumers sharing interests and lifestyles in which Pepsi plays a part. With 'Every Pepsi Refreshes the World', the Pepsi refresh project has harnessed the Web to good effect ... consumers are invited to dream it, submit it, get the votes, and then Pepsi will help fund the initiative.

Playgrounds, support programmes for domestic violence victims, aid to disadvantaged groups and entertainment ideas, are just some of the schemes receiving online votes and thereby Pepsi's dollars, all facilitated by Pepsi's online community and digital presence. Pepsi is harnessing the Web to advertise its wares, but also to build its brand.

Discussion questions

1 Outline the importance of an online presence to a B2B company. Are the use of online advertising and social media significant to B2B companies? Why/why not?

2 Imagine you have been employed by a clothing brand attempting to sell through high street shops to women aged 25–34.
   Develop a list of keywords you would use in promoting the clothing through Google's Internet search advertising programme.

CHAPTER 14

Dell plans for a new future

Dell originally made its name selling personal computers directly to customers through its catalogues, phone orders and more recently, websites. Over the years, it has expanded into related product lines while battling aggressive rivals such as Hewlett-Packard and Apple. A few years ago, Dell decided to enter the world of consumer electronics, hoping to drive an ever large portion of revenues and profits from a wider mix of products for use beyond the home office. Flat screen television was one consumer electronics market the company targeted aggressively, seeking to take on Philips, Panasonic and Sony.

With a long history of marketing technology-based products, Dell has become a well-known US brand. Management saw the brand as a strength and set out to exploit it by marketing new flat-screen televisions, tiny digital music players, and other non-computer products. 'We've come out of nowhere to be the number three consumer brand in the United States in less than five years, while Coca-Cola has been doing it for 100 years,' said Dell's general manager of consumer business for the United States, adding, 'We're not in this to be number three. Number one is the only target around here'.

However, despite considerable research and marketing investment, Dell's consumer electronics strategy did not succeed. In fact, it was not long before the company reversed course, pulling back from diversifications to refocus on its core computer expertise. Indeed, many computer sector observers perceived that the diversification had deflected Dell from its core market, enabling computer competitors such as Acer to make inroads.

Unfortunately for Dell, it had launched its consumer electronics items just as major technological developments were changing how consumers bought and used such products. Dell's affordable handheld computers initially sparked a flurry of customer interest, but instigated a price war with Hewlett-Packard as the two fought for market share. However, when Apple, Samsung, Nokia and others began marketing new generation smartphones with built-in computer capabilities and multiple entertainment functions, customers found those offerings more appealing than the kind of stand-alone handhelds that Dell offered.

In addition, Dell was caught in the crossfire of intense competition. At the start of its consumer electronics initiative, the company introduced the *Dell Digital Jukebox,* and the *Dell Music Store,* putting it on a competitive collision course with Apple's popular iPods and iTunes store. Apple had so much momentum that Dell discontinued its own brand of music players and instead resells products made by Samsung and other manufacturers. This allows Dell to satisfy customer demand for certain consumer electronics items but without the expense of researching, developing, manufacturing and marketing the products under the Dell name.

Although Dell is not looking to pioneer revolutionary new lines for early adopters, today the company is expanding into proven markets by introducing products that align with consumer demand. For instance, Dell formed a mobile device division to create products such as mobile phones and other portable devices. After two years of research, Dell entered into an agreement with AT&T to carry its Mini 3 Smart Phone that uses Google's Android software, providing an entry into the growing smartphone market. See www.dell.com/us for an overview of Dell's full range of activities. Meanwhile, by remaining innovative in its product designs, Dell continues to be a major player in the computer industry. Moving away from its traditional policy of only selling directly to customers, Dell began distributing its brand of computers, monitors, printers and accessories through WalMart, PC World, Staples office supply stores and other retailers around the world.

The company is also polishing its brand by improving customer service, an especially important step as PC sales grow more slowly throughout the industry and competitors dig in to defend market share. Dell's relentless cost cutting had damaged its ability to handle technical questions and complaints, which in turn reduces customer satisfaction scores. Dell is rebuilding relationships by increasing its service budget and encouraging customers to have their say.

Dell has been forced to re-think its strategy, re-do its marketing plans and execute a whole new set of marketing programmes. Forecasting and planning have been pivotal to reshaping its strategy, informed by market insights and smarter awareness of customers' expectations and changing requirements.

Discussion questions

1 To what extent should planning have helped Dell to avoid the problems encountered when it first diversified into consumer electronics?

2 In what stage of the product life cycle are personal computers? What are the implications for marketing planning in Dell?

3 Explain how marketing planning might underpin Dell's ongoing selection of opportunities and target markets.

NAME INDEX

SUBJECT INDEX